MISSION COLLEGE
LEARNING RESOURCE SERVICE

16.95

Indexed in Essay &
General Literature

D0400973

Perspectives
on Moral
Responsibility

IE DAT

3 1215 00091 8869

ALSO EDITED BY JOHN MARTIN FISCHER AND MARK RAVIZZA

Ethics: Problems and Principles

Perspectives on Moral Responsibility

EDITED BY

JOHN MARTIN FISCHER
and MARK RAVIZZA

Cornell University Press

ITHACA AND LONDON

Copyright © 1993 by Cornell University

All rights reserved. Except for brief quotations in a review, this book, or parts thereof, must not be reproduced in any form without permission in writing from the publisher. For information, address Cornell University Press, Sage House, 512 East State Street, Ithaca, New York 14850.

First published 1993 by Cornell University Press.

International Standard Book Number 0-8014-2943-9 (cloth)
International Standard Book Number 0-8014-8159-7 (paper)
Library of Congress Catalog Card Number 93-25712

Printed in the United States of America

Librarians: Library of Congress cataloging information appears on the last page of the book.

⊗ The paper in this book meets the minimum requirements of the American National Standard for Information Sciences—Permanence of Paper for Printed Library Materials, ANSI Z39.48-1984.

Contents

Part II   *Hierarchy, Rationality, and the "Real Self"*

Part III   *Moral Responsibility and Alternative Possibilities*

Perspectives
on Moral
Responsibility

Introduction

JOHN MARTIN FISCHER and MARK RAVIZZA

CONSIDER, to begin, the particularly lamentable case of Robert Alton Harris. On July 5, 1978, Robert and his brother Daniel attempted to hotwire a car they intended to use in a bank robbery. Unable to start the car, Robert Harris decided to steal another car in which two youths—John Mayeski and Michael Baker—were eating lunch. Harris approached the car and pointed a Luger at Mayeski's head. Then he climbed into the back seat and instructed the boys to drive east. Daniel followed in the Harrises' car. Both vehicles drove to a secluded canyon area. There Harris told the boys about the upcoming robbery and assured them that they would not be hurt. Indeed, he even offered to leave some of the stolen money in the car to pay for the use of it. The four then agreed that the Harris brothers would leave to rob the bank and that Mayeski and Baker would walk back into town and report the car stolen.

> As the two boys walked away, Harris slowly raised the Luger and shot Mayeski in the back, Daniel said. Mayeski yelled: "Oh, God," and slumped to the ground. Harris chased Baker down a hill into a little valley and shot him four times.
> Mayeski was still alive when Harris climbed back up the hill, Daniel said. Harris walked over to the boy, knelt down, put the Luger to his head and fired.[1]

1. From Miles Corwin, "Icy Killer's Life Steeped in Violence," *Los Angeles Times*, May 16, 1982. Copyright, 1982, *Los Angeles Times*. Reprinted by permission. As cited in Gary Watson, "Responsibility and the Limits of Evil: Variations on a Strawsonian Theme," this volume. Our discussion of this case borrows extensively from Watson's chapter.

Recalling the aftermath of the shooting, Daniel said, "[Robert] was swinging the rifle and pistol in the air and laughing. God, that laugh made blood and bone freeze in me."[2]

After the shooting, Harris drove to a friend's house. There, no more than fifteen minutes after killing two sixteen-year-old boys, Harris took out the remainder of the slain youths' lunch and began eating one of their hamburgers.

> [Robert] offered his brother an apple turnover, and Daniel became nauseated and ran to the bathroom.
>
> "Robert laughed at me," Daniel said. "He said I was weak; he called me a sissy and said I didn't have the stomach for it."
>
> Harris was in an almost lighthearted mood. He smiled and told Daniel that it would be amusing if the two of them were to pose as police officers and inform the parents that their sons had been killed. . . .
>
> . . . [Later, as they prepared to rob the bank,] Harris pulled out the Luger, noticed the blood stains and remnants of flesh on the barrel as a result of the point-blank shot and said, "I really blew that guy's brains out." And then again, he started to laugh.
>
> . . . Harris was given the death penalty. He has refused all requests for interviews since the conviction.
>
> "He just doesn't see the point of talking," said a sister, . . . who has visited him three times since he has been on Death Row. "He told me he had his chance, he took the road to hell and there's nothing more to say."[3]

Given the brutality of his deeds, Harris seems a prime candidate for the moral community's full indignation, resentment, and blame. As State Deputy Attorney General Michael D. Wellington argued during an appeal, "If this isn't the kind of defendant that justifies the death penalty, is there ever going to be one?"[4] Richard (Chic) Mroczko, Harris's Death Row neighbor at San Quentin, summed up his feelings a bit more bluntly: "The guy's a misery, a total scumbag; we're going to party when he goes."[5]

The cold-blooded murder of two innocent youths should clearly inspire moral outrage, but the act alone does not explain the vehemence of these reactions to Harris. Harris's crime is terrible, but the real source of our reactions lies neither exclusively nor even primarily in the crime itself, but in the manner in which the crime was performed. It does not

2. Watson, "Responsibility and the Limits of Evil," 132.
3. Ibid., 133.
4. Ibid., 131.
5. Ibid.

seem merely incidental that Harris snacked on his victims' hamburgers only fifteen minutes after the crime, nor that he lightheartedly joked about blowing Mayeski's brains out. Our full outrage is triggered by Harris's cavalier attitude after the crime, an attitude that seems to drive home his callousness and his utter lack of remorse. Harris appears to be wholeheartedly evil, and this fuels our moral outrage and desire for vengeance.

But now consider the following account of Harris's childhood. It is not a pleasant account. Reflecting on her brother's past in an interview, Harris's sister Barbara "put her palms over her eyes and said softly, 'I saw every grain of sweetness, pity and goodness in him destroyed. It was a long and ugly journey before he reached that point.' "[6]

Here's a description of Robert's day of birth offered by his sister in court declaration. "Mother was bathing [two other children] in the bathtub, and father came in and started kicking her in the abdomen, screaming that it was not his baby, and she fell into the bathtub. He then kicked her in the crotch with his combat boots on, and she began hemorrhaging. He kicked her several more times."

Thus Robert was born, three months premature. Mom was drunk like dad, and the fetal alcohol had taken its toll. Robert had tremors and sleep disorders.

From the start, he was beaten by both parents virtually every day. Mom preferred bamboo sticks. Dad just used his knuckles.

The sister described it this way: "Robert couldn't walk into a room without father kicking or beating him. Sitting at the table, if [Robert] reached out for something without father's permission, he would end up with a fork in the back of his hand." At age 1, Robert's jaw was broken.

The father remains convinced that Robert was sired by another man. When Robert would seek affection by rubbing against his mother's leg, dad would beat both Robert and the mother. In this family everyone got beaten by dad.

Sometimes, for no apparent reason, dad would load his guns and tell his loved ones they had 30 minutes to hide outside the house. He then hunted his family like animals, promising to shoot anyone he found.

Here is a list of drugs, divided by ingestion technique, taken by Robert from age 6 through adolescence. Sniffing: airplane glue, gasoline, oven cleaner, paint, typewriter correction fluid. Injection: cocaine, heroine. Oral: Seconal, methamphetamine, PCP, LSD.

Robert had no friends, did poorly in school, received no help for his problems. Before he was a teen-ager, he revealed the pattern that would dominate his life. He started killing neighborhood pets. The

6. Ibid., 134.

need to hurt and destroy was directed at everything, even himself. Once mom told Robert and a brother to go get switches so she could beat them. The brother brought back a small twig. Robert brought back a club.[7]

The case of Robert Harris raises many of the perplexing issues pertaining to moral responsibility in a salient and striking way. This book addresses such issues through a three-part structure. In the first section, the focus is the "reactive attitudes" allegedly constitutive of moral responsibility: resentment and indignation, love, respect, gratitude, and so forth. Peter Strawson's seminal essay "Freedom and Resentment" serves to organize our discussion. In the second section, various positive accounts of moral responsibility are investigated; that is, various approaches to specifying the conditions of application of the concept of moral responsibility are presented and evaluated. The two general approaches discussed here are the "hierarchical" theory associated with Harry Frankfurt and Gerald Dworkin and the "reasons-responsiveness" theories of Gary Watson, Susan Wolf, and John Martin Fischer and Mark Ravizza.

Finally, the third section focuses on the crucial issue of the relationship between moral responsibility and alternative possibilities. Some philosophers require alternative possibilities for moral responsibility, others do not, while still others require alternatives in some cases but not all. These positions are mapped out and explored. The overall structure of the book (and its Introduction), then, is as follows: first, the concept of moral responsibility; second, its conditions of application; and third, some implications, particularly as regards alternative possibilities.

I. The Concept of Moral Responsibility

An important difference between persons and other creatures is that only persons can be morally responsible for what they do. When we accept that someone is a responsible agent, this acceptance involves more than holding a particular belief about him; it entails a willingness to adopt certain attitudes toward that person and to behave toward him in certain kinds of ways. Imagine, for example, that you return home one evening and find your treasured Waterford vase shattered on the dining room floor. Discovering that the vase has been purposely shattered by a malicious houseguest will give rise to a set of reactions much different from those that would seem appropriate were you to discover that the vase had been accidentally toppled from the shelf by your clumsy kitten.

---

7. Robert A. Jones, "Lessons in the Making of a Demon," *Los Angeles Times*, March 27, 1990. Copyright, 1990, *Los Angeles Times*. Reprinted by permission.

In the latter case, you might feel regret and perhaps even anger at your cat, but you would hardly feel the same sort of resentment and moral indignation that would seem warranted had your guest intentionally broken the vase in order to hurt you. Moreover, it would seem appropriate to blame your guest and to hold her responsible for the misdeed in a way much different from the way you might discipline your kitten and try to train him not to climb on the furniture in the future.

Of course, to make these claims is not to deny that there is one sense in which both the guest and the kitten are responsible for breaking the vase in the respective scenarios. Each is *causally* responsible—each plays a causal role in bringing about the destruction of the vase. But whereas both persons and non-persons can be causally responsible for an event, only persons can be morally responsible. And the suggestion is that this difference accounts for the difference between the sorts of reactions that seem appropriate in the cases of the guest and the kitten.[8]

For many people, questions of moral responsibility are associated primarily with wrongdoing like that described in the above example. According to this view, questions concerning who may legitimately be held responsible stem from more practical questions concerning who should be blamed and punished for their misdeeds. Similarly, a concern to understand the propriety of our responsibility ascriptions is driven mostly by a concern to understand what justifies the punitive measures we take toward those who injure us and violate the norms of society. Such a view helps to give expressions such as "I am going to hold you responsible" or "I promise to find out who is responsible for this" a mostly negative connotation, calling to mind the retributive attitudes and harsh treatment that await wrongdoers.

In contrast to this approach, however, others take a broader view of moral responsibility, associating it not only with negative responses such as resentment and blame but also with more positive responses such as gratitude, respect, and praise. To see the intuition behind this view, imagine once again that you return home after work. This time, instead of finding a shattered vase, you discover that your neighbor's exceedingly ugly tree (which had long blocked the otherwise spectacular view from your living room) has been knocked down. As in the previous examples, your reactions will vary depending on what you subsequently learn about the causes that led to the tree's demise. For instance, you would react quite differently depending on whether the tree's uprooting was the result of a fortuitous gust of wind or the efforts of your consid-

8. It should be noted that the term "responsibility" admits of a variety of uses in addition to causal and moral responsibility. For example, it is used to refer to legal responsibility, corporate responsibility, role-responsibility (i.e., the type of responsibility the captain of a ship assumes for the safety of the vessel), and so forth. In this Introduction, we restrict our attention to the issues surrounding moral responsibility.

erate neighbor, who removed the eyesore as a birthday surprise for you. In the former case, you might feel fortunate or happy, but you would hardly feel the gratitude and desire to praise that would seem appropriate had your thoughtful neighbor torn down the offensive tree just to please you.

The point that the proponent of the broader conception of responsibility stresses is that there is a *spectrum* of reactions that are appropriately applied only to other persons. And, more important, although some of these reactions, such as praise and blame, are quite different from one another, intuitively they stem from the same deep and unique fact about persons, namely that they are morally responsible for what they do. For convenience, we will refer to this spectrum of feelings, attitudes, and practices as "responsibility-reactions."[9]

Of course, not every event brought about by persons merits these sorts of responsibility-reactions. Particular facts about an action may make such responses seem unwarranted even if the action is performed by an agent who ordinarily is considered to be morally responsible. For instance, if the guest in the first example informed you that she inadvertently tipped your vase off the shelf while groping blindly for her lost contact lenses, or that she smashed the vase during an epileptic seizure, then it would seem inappropriate to hold her responsible for the breakage. Similarly, if you learned that your neighbor had knocked down his objectionable tree not out of consideration for your view but by accident while constructing an even more unsightly treehouse, then it would seem natural to suspend the praise and gratitude that you initially were inclined to extend to him.

In light of such considerations, it is useful to distinguish between someone *being* a morally responsible agent and such an agent being responsible *for* particular events such as actions, omissions, and consequences. Following this taxonomy, we may maintain our earlier distinction between the houseguest and the kitten—that the guest is a morally responsible agent, whereas the kitten is not—and at the same time consistently maintain that *in this particular instance* the guest is *not* morally responsible for breaking the vase, since the damage resulted from something—say, a seizure—over which she had no control.

What is required in order for someone to *be* a morally responsible agent? And what conditions must be met in order for someone to be responsible *for* the particular events he brings about? These are the questions that motivate the essays in this volume. Although there is sharp

9. How precisely to characterize and analyze this range of reactions is a matter of considerable controversy, and in this Introduction we canvass some of the various approaches to this question. For the time being, however, we will leave this issue fairly vague and appeal simply to the intuitive sense that there is a set of reactions and practices that apply uniquely to morally responsible agents.

disagreement surrounding the answers to these questions, there are also some common presuppositions that help to structure the debate. One of these presuppositions, often traced back to Aristotle, is that a person's accessibility to praise and blame can be undermined by at least two different types of excusing conditions—ignorance and force.[10]

Consider, for example, the person who backs his car out of his garage unaware that a tiny kitten is snoozing beneath the rear tire. Certainly it would be odd to judge that the driver is morally responsible for the kitten's untimely death, or to insist that he be blamed for the mishap. The reason for this judgment is that he was (through no fault of his own) unaware that he driving over the little cat. This type of ignorance— ignorance of what one is doing—is merely one way in which a person can lack the particular knowledge requisite for being responsible. Aristotle mentions various others.[11] Aristotle's remarks stem from the intuition that in order to be praiseworthy or blameworthy a person must know (or be reasonably expected to know) what he is doing, and he must not be deceived or ignorant about the circumstances and manner in which he is doing it. A person who lacks knowledge in any of these areas is not morally responsible.

A second type of excusing condition is force. As paradigm instances of forced actions, Aristotle offers examples in which a person is carried somewhere by the wind against his will, or taken somewhere by kidnappers who have him in their power. To this pair of cases might be added other stock examples in which responsibility is undermined by force, such as cases involving irresistible psychological impulses, brainwashing, hypnosis, or direct manipulation of the brain.

A theory of moral responsibility ought to accommodate these standard excusing conditions in the sense that the ascriptions of responsibility entailed by the theory ought to match our ordinary intuitions about when agents are and are not morally responsible. Moreover, ideally the theory also should account for these intuitions by explaining why our judgments of responsibility ought to turn on just those conditions that its analysis cites. This explanatory requirement, in effect, makes sure not only that the ascriptions of responsibility entailed by the theory are coextensive with our ordinary judgments, but also that the theory has identified just those conditions that drive our intuitions. Satisfying this explanatory condition is essential if we are to understand in any deep way what responsible agency is all about.

Since a theory of moral responsibility needs to accommodate both of the excusing conditions mentioned above—ignorance and force—it is

10. See *Nicomachean Ethics* 1109b30–1111b5, trans. Terence Irwin (Indianapolis: Hackett, 1985). Aristotle offers these as conditions that undermine the type of voluntariness that is necessary for praise and blame.

11. *Nicomachean Ethics* 1111a3–5.

not surprising that positive analyses of responsibility frequently comprise two conditions, each of which corresponds roughly to one of these negative excusing conditions. The first condition, which may be termed a "cognitive condition," corresponds to the excuse of ignorance. It captures the intuition that an agent is responsible only if she both knows (or can reasonably be expected to know) the particular facts surrounding her action, and also acts with the proper sort of beliefs and intentions. The second condition, which may be termed a "freedom-relevant condition," corresponds to the excuse of force. It captures the sense that an agent is responsible only if his action is unforced, that is, only if he acts freely.

Exactly how to analyze both of these conditions is a topic of considerable debate and controversy. In this collection, many of the essays focus on the issues surrounding the freedom-relevant condition, and we will turn to some of the details broached by these essays in the third part of this Introduction.[12] Here, however, we simply note some traditional characterizations of this freedom-relevant condition in order to bring out a problem that serves as a background for much of the subsequent discussion in this volume.

Many traditional formulations of the freedom-relevant condition share a common theme: an agent has the type of freedom necessary to be morally responsible only if he has "control over his action," the act is "up to him," he was "free to do otherwise," he "could have acted differently," and so forth. However this intuition is expressed, the shared assumption behind these traditional views is that moral responsibility requires the freedom to pursue alternative courses of action. For the purposes of this discussion, let us adopt the following formulation of the "traditional view": an agent is morally responsible only if he has the power freely to bring about one event, and he has the power freely to bring about some alternative event. For two or more events to be alternatives, it must be logically impossible for the agent freely to bring about more than one of them at the same time.

That responsibility is traditionally taken to require the freedom to do otherwise raises a cluster of general problems involving issues as diverse as fatalism, causal determinism, and divine foreknowledge.[13] Representative of these general problems is the worry that the freedom required for moral responsibility is incompatible with causal determinism. One argument—often termed the "Consequence Argument"—in support of this conclusion can be sketched as follows: Causal determinism is the

12. A detailed discussion of issues relevant to the first condition (the cognitive condition) appears in Joel Feinberg, *Harm to Self* (New York: Oxford University Press, 1986), esp. 269–315.

13. For a discussion of how these general worries share a similar structure, see John Martin Fischer, "Introduction: Responsibility and Freedom," in Fischer, ed., *Moral Responsibility* (Ithaca: Cornell University Press, 1986).

claim that a complete statement of the laws of nature and a complete description of the facts about the world at some time t_0 together entail every fact about the world after t_0. If determinism is true, then all of our choices and actions are a *consequence* of the laws of nature and events in the distant past. But no one has, or ever had, any choice about what the laws of nature are; and similarly no one has, or ever had, any choice about what the facts of the world were at some time t_0 in the very remote past. Therefore, if determinism is true, then it follows that no one has, or ever had, any choice about any fact about the world after time t_0— that is, no one has, or ever had, any ability to do, or to choose, otherwise.[14]

There are various ways to fill in the details of the Consequence Argument. A representative example is Peter van Inwagen's modal version of the argument.[15]

Rule Alpha: From $\Box p$ deduce Np ('$\Box$' represents "standard necessity": truth in all possible circumstances. ['Np' stands for "p and no one has, or ever had, any choice about whether p."])

Rule Beta: From Np and $N(p \supset q)$ deduce Nq.

Now let 'P' represent any true proposition whatever. Let 'L' represent the conjunction into a single proposition of all laws of nature. Let 'P_0' represent a proposition that gives a complete and correct description of the whole world at some instant in the remote past—before there were any human beings. If determinism is true, then $\Box (P_0 \ \& \ L \supset P)$. We argue from the consequence of this as follows.

1. $\Box(P_0 \ \& \ L \supset P)$
2. $\Box(P_0 \supset (L \supset P))$ 1; modal and sentential logic
3. $N(P_0 \supset (L \supset P))$ 2; Rule Alpha
4. NP_0 Premise
5. $N(L \supset P)$ 3, 4; Rule Beta
6. $N(L)$ Premise
7. $N(P)$ 5, 6; Rule Beta

If the above argument is sound, then determinism entails that no one has a choice about what he does; hence, causal determinism is incompatible with freedom to do otherwise.

14. In presenting this sketch of the Consequence Argument we follow Peter van Inwagen's discussion in *An Essay on Free Will* (Oxford: Clarendon, 1983).
15. The following formulation of the Consequence Argument is quoted from Peter van Inwagen, "When Is the Will Free?" in *Philosophical Perspectives*, vol. 3, ed. James Tomberlin (Atascadero, Calif.: Ridgeview, 1989), 405. See also van Inwagen, *An Essay on Free Will*, 55–105; Carl Ginet, "In Defense of Incompatibilism," *Philosophical Studies* 44 (1983): 391–400; and Ginet, *On Action* (Cambridge: Cambridge University Press, 1990).

The Consequence Argument gives incompatibilists a powerful way to articulate the reasons that underlie their original intuition that causal determinism would undermine our ability to do otherwise. Of even greater importance (given our present concerns), insofar as the Consequence Argument offers a serious challenge to compatibilistic attempts to reconcile determinism with freedom to do otherwise, this argument also threatens any approach that holds that responsibility requires alternative possibilities (given that it is not evident that causal determinism is false).

There are various ways to respond to such worries about determinism. Let us consider two representative responses: that of the "pessimists" and that of the "optimists."[16] The pessimists accept that causal determinism is incompatible with freedom to do otherwise, and they conclude, therefore, that if the thesis of determinism is true, then our ordinary practices of holding one another responsible are unjustified. One type of pessimist—the libertarian—resists this final conclusion and seeks to preserve and justify our ordinary ascriptions of responsibility. Consequently, the libertarian argues that determinism is false. According to this view, in order to be morally responsible, agents must have a unique type of "metaphysical" or "contra-causal" freedom. The libertarian's intuition is that we could not be morally responsible if our actions were the result of antecedent causes stretching back in time to before our birth, because in such a world we would have no ability to choose or do otherwise. Hence, if we are to be morally responsible, we must be free from the causal nexus that determines other natural events; we must have a type of contra-causal freedom that enables us to initiate causal chains. One way of filling out this picture is to appeal to a notion of agent-causation in which an agent's action is caused by the agent, but there is no antecedent set of causes entailing that the agent will cause this particular action to occur.

If such a libertarian position is ultimately to provide a viable account of moral responsibility, it must defend itself against a variety of standard criticisms. First, as just noted, such theories often involve appeals to agent-causation and are vulnerable to all the charges of obscurity and metaphysical excess that attend such accounts.[17] In part these charges stem from the fact that agent-causation is supposed to be quite unlike ordinary causation. But to explain this notion of agent-causation, either one ends up appealing to analogies with ordinary causation, or one simply leaves the concept a mystery. Second, the denial of determinism has

16. In adopting these labels, we follow Peter Strawson, "Freedom and Resentment," this volume. The following discussion of the optimist and pessimist views and Strawson's response to them owes much to Jonathan Bennett's insightful article "Accountability," in *Philosophical Subjects*, ed. Zak van Straaten (Oxford: Clarendon, 1980), 14–47.

17. For a brief summary of these problems see Gary Watson, "Free Action and Free Will," *Mind* 96 (1987): 145–72.

often been claimed to introduce a randomness that is incompatible with free action and responsibility. The intuition here is that if an action is not completely causally determined, then there is some probability that it will not occur. Hence, such an action is, in some sense, due to chance. Since one cannot be responsible for something that is a matter of chance, one cannot be responsible for an action that is not causally determined.[18]

Fortunately, it is not necessary to resolve these objections in the present context; rather, the point to be stressed is that simply postulating indeterminism does not immediately dispel the deeper worries posed by the Consequence Argument: such a response leaves one with the further challenge of providing a positive libertarian account of free agency.

The difficulties facing the pessimist's response to the problem of determinism are largely avoided by the opposing camp, the optimists. Optimists eschew the metaphysical commitments of the pessimists, and they seek to justify the propriety of our responsibility-reactions without appealing to notions like contra-causal freedom or agent-causation. In contrast to their pessimistic counterparts, optimists hold that determinism *is* compatible with the freedom to do otherwise, and that the concepts and practices associated with responsibility are not, therefore, undermined by causal determinism. One of the most popular optimist strategies— call it the "social-regulation" view[19]—justifies our responsibility-reactions by appeal to the useful consequences that follow from these reactions.[20] Such a consequentialist justification understands our responsibility-reactions primarily as an impersonal, objective means of regulating behavior.[21] According to this view, the point of these reac-

18. For discussion of this kind of argument, see Moritz Schlick, "When Is a Man Responsible?" in *Free Will and Determinism*, ed. Bernard Berofsky (New York: Harper & Row, 1966), 54–63; and R. E. Hobart, "Free Will as Involving Determinism and Inconceivable without It," in *Free Will and Determinism*, ed. Berofsky, 63–95. Philippa Foot rightly criticizes this strict dichotomy between causation and chance in "Free Will as Involving Determinism," in *Virtues and Vices and Other Essays in Moral Philosophy* (Berkeley: University of California Press, 1978), 62–73.

19. This term is Watson's. See his "Responsibility and the Limits of Evil," this volume.

20. For examples of this approach see Hobart, "Free Will as Involving Determinism and Inconceivable without it"; Schlick, "When Is a Man Responsible?"; and J. J. C. Smart, "Free-will, Praise, and Blame," *Mind* 70 (July 1961): 291–306.

21. As is the case with the social-regulation theorists, a consequentialist justification of responsibility frequently leads to a reduced view of the content of responsibility-responses (i.e., it leads to a more detached, objective, and impersonal view that sees our practices primarily in terms of treatment and manipulation, rather than in terms of the personal, reactive attitudes that Strawson's view endorses). This pairing is not analytically necessary, however: a consequentialist justification does not necessarily have to lead to a reduced view of the content of our practices. It is helpful here to distinguish the issue of justification from the issue of content. The former concerns the kind of justification (e.g., consequentialist or deontological) a theory offers for our ascriptions of responsibility; the latter

tions is to educate moral agents and to provide inducements for them to behave in certain ways. Threats of punishment and blame exert pressure on agents to conform their behavior to the laws and norms of society. Similarly, promises of praise and reward offer powerful incentives for agents to strive for the ideals that have currency in a particular moral community.

The social-regulation view appeals to the optimists for a variety of reasons. First, since the legitimacy of our responsibility-reactions is taken to depend only on whether they are indeed efficacious in bringing about the desired behavior, the specter of determinism is not seen to present any threat to our ordinary practices. After all, even if determinism is true, agents still could be properly influenced by the pressures and incentives generated by these practices. Indeed, some optimists argue that one needs to assume the truth of determinism in order to explain the causal role these incentives play in regulating behavior.[22] In short, by construing our responsibility-reactions primarily in terms of social regulation, the optimist is able to justify many of our ordinary practices of praising and blaming without having to invoke the sort of metaphysical commitments he or she finds objectionable in libertarian views.

Of course, the social-regulation view cannot justify *all* of our ordinary responsibility-reactions. In particular, it provides no legitimation for responses that play no role in bringing about better conduct in the future. For example, if in a particular case, retributive attitudes such as resentment or a desire for vengeance will not lead to better future consequences, the social-regulation view must hold that they should be abandoned. For many optimists, however, this "pruning" of our responsibility-reactions is not a disadvantage but a further advantage of their theory, since they see such retributive attitudes as primitive and "barbarous."[23] Such optimists contend that our practices of praise and blame should be forward-looking and that our ascriptions of responsi-

concerns the kind of reactions and practices that are justified (e.g., whether the practices are construed primarily as impersonal, objective means of regulating behavior or as personal, reactive attitudes of the sort Strawson endorses). For a fuller treatment of this sort of distinction, see Richard Double, *The Non-Reality of Free Will* (Oxford: Oxford University Press, 1991), 75–94.

22. For example, Smart writes: "Threats and promises, punishments and rewards, the ascription of responsibility and the non-ascription of responsibility, have therefore a clear pragmatic justification which is quite consistent with a wholehearted belief in determinism. Indeed it implies a belief that our actions are very largely determined: if everything anyone did depended only on pure chance (i.e., if it depended on nothing) then threats and punishments would be quite ineffective." See Smart, "Free-will, Praise, and Blame," 302–3.

23. Representative of this view is Schlick's comment: "The view still often expressed, that [punishment] is a natural *retaliation* for past wrong, ought no longer to be defended in a cultivated society; for the opinion that an increase in sorrow can be 'made good again' by further sorrow is altogether barbarous." See Schlick, "When Is a Man Responsible?" 60.

bility should be driven primarily by a consideration of who will be an appropriate candidate for this type of treatment—that is, who will be sensitive to the type of practices and incentives embodied in our responsibility-reactions. Such an understanding of responsibility leads to a conception of punishment and blame as behavior-modification or therapy rather than as retribution or deserved harsh treatment.

A third and perhaps most significant appeal of the social-regulation view is that it arguably meets the conditions (discussed above) for an adequate theory of responsibility: it entails ascriptions of responsibility that match our intuitive judgments about when agents are and are not morally responsible, and it provides an explanation for why these judgments fall where they do. For the social-regulation optimist, whether an agent is morally responsible depends on whether the moral pressures and incentives created by our responsibility-reactions are efficacious in regulating his behavior. In cases where such inducements lack this causal efficacy, ascriptions of responsibility are not deemed appropriate. For the most part, such an account entails assignments of responsibility that coincide with our normal intuitions. For example, consider a person whose compulsive stealing results from a process that intuitively undermines responsibility, such as brainwashing, irresistible psychological impulses, hypnosis, direct brain manipulation, and the like. Ordinarily, it would not be deemed appropriate to hold such an agent responsible for her thieving, and the social-regulation view offers a plausible explanation for this intuition by noting that this is precisely the type of agent who is not sensitive to the moral pressures exerted by our practices of holding one another responsible.

Although there is something undeniably right about the social-regulation view—we *can* influence, regulate, and perhaps even improve people's behavior by our practices of praise and blame—critics have long complained that something is amiss with this purely consequentialist understanding of moral responsibility. One standard worry (a worry that attends any purely consequentialist justification) concerns the issue of justice. Briefly put, if practices such as blame and punishment are justified only in terms of their instrumental efficacy, then it would seem proper to punish any individual who is such that his punishment will lead to the best consequences, even if this person has done nothing wrong—that is, even if, in some intuitive sense, the person does not *deserve* to be punished.

A second objection involves the suspicion that the social-regulation view has not yet captured what is really driving our ordinary practices of praising, blaming, and holding responsible. According to the social-regulation model, our ascriptions of responsibility are driven mainly by a concern to improve social utility by regulating behavior. At the very least, this understanding of responsibility seems incomplete; at worst,

critics argue, it is simply wrong. Although such regulation may be one
result of the attitudes and practices associated with moral responsibility,
it is far from clear that this is their primary purpose. As Susan Wolf
points out, we do not hold someone responsible first and foremost because we calculate that such an ascription of responsibility will have an
instrumental value in producing some desired results; rather we "find
ourselves reacting to the actions and characters of others, approving of
some, disapproving of others. Unless there is some reason to restrain
ourselves, we simply express what we feel."[24]

According to such critics, even though the judgments entailed by the
social-regulation view may be coextensive with our ordinary practices,
this purely instrumental understanding of responsibility still has failed
to put its finger on the true and proper justification of these practices.
As one critic writes, "Although a distinction based on the utility of a
certain sort of therapy or behavior-control might *coincide* with
accountability/non-accountability, it cannot give the latter's essence, and
the Schlickian [i.e., social-regulation] account of what the line [between
accountability and non-accountability] is *for* does nothing like justice to
the real nature of our praise- and blame-related responses."[25]

Such criticism of the optimist's social-regulation view draws much of
its inspiration from Peter Strawson's landmark essay "Freedom and Resentment." Strawson begins his argument by noting "the very great importance we attach to the attitudes and intentions towards us of other
human beings, and the extent to which our personal feelings and reactions depend upon, or involve, our beliefs about these attitudes and
intentions."[26] When we regard someone as a responsible agent, we do
more than merely form a judgment that the person is susceptible to the
type of moral pressures endorsed by the optimist's social-regulation
view; in addition, we react to the person with a unique set of feelings and
attitudes—for example, gratitude, resentment, love, respect, and forgiveness. Strawson uses the term "reactive attitudes" to refer to this
range of attitudes that "belong to [our] involvement or participation
with others in interpersonal human relationships."[27] In his essay, Strawson is at pains to emphasize how important the participant reactive attitudes and feelings are to us, how deeply we care about them. Such
attitudes characterize our human relationships and point to something
unique about us as persons.

In calling our attention to the importance of the reactive attitudes,
Strawson wants to take issue with both the optimists' and the pessimists'
position. According to Strawson, the social-regulation view adopted by

24. Susan Wolf, "The Importance of Free Will," this volume, 104.
25. Bennett, "Accountability," 20.
26. Peter Strawson, "Freedom and Resentment," this volume, 48.
27. Ibid., 52.

the optimists encourages us to ignore or at least misconstrue the true significance of the reactive attitudes: "The picture painted by the optimists is painted in a style appropriate to a situation envisaged as wholly dominated by objectivity of attitude. The only operative notions invoked in this picture are such as those of policy, treatment, control. But a thorough-going objectivity of attitude, excluding as it does the moral reactive attitudes, excludes at the same time essential elements in the concepts of *moral* condemnation and *moral* responsibility."[28]

The shortcomings of the social-regulation model (and its inevitable distortion of our responsibility-reactions) can be illustrated by imagining a world in which our practices of praise and blame are governed primarily by an objective, instrumental view of responsibility.[29] In such a world, punishment and blame would come to be viewed as little more than manipulative treatment applied to deviant or diseased agents. Gone would be the unique set of attitudes and emotions that traditionally have characterized our interpersonal relations. Blame would no longer be viewed as a deserved expression of resentment and moral indignation. Similarly, praise would no longer convey respect or admiration. Instead, these practices would be understood merely as effective tools for controlling and manipulating behavior. The point here is not that the optimists are wrong to emphasize the efficacious role our responsibility-reactions play in regulating behavior; rather, as Strawson says, "what *is* wrong is to forget that these practices, and their reception, the reactions to them, really *are* expressions of our moral attitudes and not merely devices we calculatingly employ for regulative purposes."[30]

The pessimists rightly point out that by thinking only in terms of social utility the optimists "leave out something vital in our conception of these [responsibility] practices";[31] however, they go too far in thinking that the social-regulation view can be remedied only by introducing a type of metaphysical freedom that is presumed to be necessary in order to justify the reactive attitudes. Strawson hopes to correct each of these excesses, to get each of the two sides to concede something to the other, and in so doing to move both views closer to the proper understanding of responsibility. In brief, Strawson wants the optimists to concede that their social-regulation view leaves out the importance of the reactive attitudes and their central place in our interpersonal lives, and he wants the pessimists to recognize that controversial appeals to metaphysics are not needed to "fill the gap" they correctly perceive in the optimist's account.

28. Ibid., 62.
29. A similar point is made in Herbert Morris, "Persons and Punishment," in *On Guilt and Innocence* (Berkeley: University of California Press, 1976), 31–58.
30. "Freedom and Resentment," 66.
31. Ibid., 63.

According to Strawson, the optimists and the pessimists share a common mistake: they both view our conception of responsibility and its associated practices as resting on a judgment that the agents in question
satisfy some theoretical requirement. (For the optimists this requirement is that the agent is susceptible to the type of treatment that gives
our practices of praising and blaming their social utility; for the libertarian pessimists this requirement is that the agent meet some metaphysical demand such as possessing contra-causal freedom.) Even though
the two sides understand the theoretical grounding of responsibility
quite differently, they both share the same faulty presupposition—"both
seek, in different ways, to overintellectualize the facts."[32]

A central insight of Strawson's position is the suggestion that our
questions about the propriety of the reactive attitudes should be taken
as essentially practical questions, not theoretical ones. In contrast to the
pessimist who thinks that "the gap can be filled only if some general
metaphysical proposition is repeatedly verified,"[33] Strawson holds that it
is these reactive attitudes and practices themselves that are constitutive
of responsibility. Thus, our ascriptions of responsibility do not find their
ground in the truth of some metaphysical proposition (about, say, a creature possessing contra-causal freedom); rather, responsibility is
grounded in nothing more than our adopting these attitudes toward one
another. Jonathan Bennett puts this point well: "My feeling of indignation at what you have done is not a perception of your objective blameworthiness, nor is it demanded of me by such a perception. It expresses
my emotional make-up, rather than reflecting my ability to recognize a
blame-meriting person when I see one. The gap left by the Schlickian
[i.e., social-regulation] account is not to be filled by facts about desert or
about the meriting of blame, facts which are acknowledged by the adoption of reactive attitudes; rather, in Strawson's words, 'it is just these attitudes themselves which fill the gap.' "[34]

The uniqueness of Strawson's theory becomes clear if we compare it
to a slightly different set of theories which might be classified as "ledger
views" of responsibility. On these views, ascriptions of moral responsibility are understood primarily as a form of moral accounting that keeps
track of the worth of agents. Consider the metaphors that Michael J.
Zimmerman uses to express this picture of responsibility:

> Praising someone may be said to constitute judging that there is a
> "credit" in his "ledger of life," or a "positive mark" in his "report-card
> of life," or a "luster" on his "record as a person"; that his "record" has
> been "burnished"; that his "moral standing" has been "enhanced."

32. Ibid., 64.
33. Ibid.
34. Bennett, "Accountability," 24.

Blaming someone may be said to constitute judging that there is a "discredit" or "debit" in his "ledger," or a "negative mark" in his "report card," or a "blemish" or "stain" on his "record"; that his "record" has been "tarnished"; that his "moral standing" has been "diminished." Someone is praiseworthy if he is deserving of such praise; that is, if it is correct, or true to the facts, to judge that there is a "credit" in his "ledger" (etc.). Someone is blameworthy if he is deserving of such blame; that is, if it is correct, or true to the facts, to judge that there is a "debit" in his "ledger" (etc.).[35]

Ledger views construe our ascriptions of responsibility as first and foremost judgments concerning an agent's moral value; the reactive attitudes and the associated practices of praising and blaming take on a secondary role, following from these primary assessments of moral worth like practical consequences. For Strawson, this view of responsibility as involving primarily a theoretical judgment diminishes the vital role that the reactive attitudes play in our conception of responsibility. In contrast to the ledger view, which suggests that assessments of responsibility can be made from an objective, uninvolved, and detached standpoint, Strawson's view maintains that moral responsibility essentially involves reacting to one another with feelings and attitudes that stem necessarily from our concerned involvement as participants in a moral community.

Both Strawson's view and the ledger views associate ascriptions of responsibility with the reactive attitudes and the attendant practices of praise and blame. What is unique about Strawson's view, as we have been presenting it, is that whereas the ledger views understand these attitudes simply to accompany, or to follow from, or to be practical consequences of an independent judgment that someone is responsible, Strawson's theory holds that being morally responsible is nothing other than being a recipient of these attitudes and a participant in the associated practices. As Watson writes "In Strawson's view, there is no such independent notion of responsibility that explains the propriety of the reactive attitudes. The explanatory priority is the other way around: It is not that we hold people responsible because they *are* responsible; rather, the idea (*our* idea) that we are responsible is to be understood by the practice, which itself is not a matter of holding some propositions to be true, but of expressing our concerns and demands about our treatment of one another."[36]

35. Michael J. Zimmerman, *An Essay on Moral Responsibility* (Totowa, N.J.: Rowan & Littlefield, 1988), 38. In this passage Zimmerman is assembling the metaphors found in a variety of authors including Joel Feinberg, *Doing and Deserving* (Princeton: Princeton University Press, 1970); Jonathan Glover, *Responsibility* (London: Routledge & Kegan Paul, 1970); and Morris, *On Guilt and Innocence*.

36. Watson, "Responsibility and the Limits of Evil," 121.

The close connection that Strawson makes between being responsible and actually being the recipient of the reactive attitudes raises questions about the ability of his theory to criticize and revise existing practices. After all, once the actual application of the reactive attitudes is taken to be constitutive of moral responsibility, one wonders what should be said about situations in which communities hold people responsible who intuitively are not. Does the mere fact that certain attitudes are taken toward an agent establish that he is an appropriate candidate for this treatment?

Imagine, for example, a society in which severely retarded or mentally disturbed individuals are resented, blamed, and harshly punished for their failure to adhere to the norms of the community. (Perhaps the society attributes their failure to poor character or an evil nature.) Even though all the members of this community strongly feel moral outrage, resentment, and indignation, should the mere fact of their commitment to these feelings preclude further worry that the adoption of such attitudes toward these agents is not justified? Similarly, imagine a society in which some particular class of citizens (perhaps those of a certain race or sex) are systematically treated only as objects to be used in the interest of social utility, and others have no reactive attitudes toward members of the group. Would this fact alone suffice to warrant that these persons are not morally responsible? The problem here is that Strawson's theory may reasonably be said to give an account of what it is for agents to be held responsible, but there seems to be a difference between being *held* responsible and actually *being* responsible. Surely it seems possible that one can be held responsible even though one in fact is not responsible, and conversely that one can be responsible even though one is actually not treated as a responsible agent. By understanding responsibility primarily in terms of our actual practices of adopting or not adopting certain attitudes toward agents, Strawson's theory risks blurring the difference between these two issues.[37]

To avoid such worries, we can develop the insights behind Strawson's theory in a slightly different manner. This type of theory—call it a "Strawsonian theory"—holds that morally responsible agents are not just those who, as a matter of practice, are recipients of the reactive attitudes; rather, agents are morally responsible if and only if they are *appropriate* recipients—that is, they are rationally accessible to the reactive attitudes.[38] Such an approach moves the theory closer to the ledger ap-

37. In response to this line of questioning, the Strawsonian might insist that our ascriptions of responsibility ought to be relativized to particular societies, and therefore that by giving an account of what it is to be *held* responsible by a given group, the theory is in fact giving the only account that can be given of what it means to *be* responsible *in that society*.

38. This kind of Strawsonian theory is suggested in Fischer, "Introduction: Responsibility and Freedom."

proach in the sense that it views the reactive attitudes as having some grounding in theoretical considerations, and it looks for a rational justification for taking the attitudes toward some agents and not others. However, this version of a Strawsonian theory still differs from ledger views in that it gives the reactive attitudes a primary place in our theorizing about responsibility, and does not see these attitudes merely as follow-on consequences of the primary judgments of moral accounting.

Also, this type of Strawsonian theory (in contrast to the first) allows for a distinction between (1) assessments of moral responsibility and (2) further judgments concerning the application of specific reactive attitudes and the associated practices of praising, blaming, and punishing.[39] The first type of assessment is concerned with whether the agent is indeed an appropriate candidate for some reactive attitude. (To appeal to the ledger metaphor, we might say that an agent is taken to be morally responsible—that is, to *have* a ledger—just in case the agent is rationally accessible to the reactive attitudes. Similarly, an agent is morally responsible for a particular event—that is, the event is appropriate grounds for *placing a mark on the ledger*—just in case the agent is rationally accessible to some reactive attitude based on having brought about that event.) The second judgment is concerned with how the agent should be treated. According to this version of the Strawsonian theory, to judge that an agent is morally responsible is to judge that she is rationally accessible to the reactive attitudes, but in itself this judgment does not tell us which attitudes should be taken and to what degree they should be applied. For example, when a prodigal son returns home after squandering his inheritance on years of dissolute living, the parents might have no doubt that the young man is morally responsible for his wanton ways. Nevertheless, this judgment alone does not suffice to tell them how they should react to the son. Should they resent him? blame him? forgive him? welcome him with open arms? The point that the Strawsonian theory stresses is that judging whether and to what degree to praise or blame someone involves a set of considerations over and above the base assessment that the person is rationally accessible to this sort of reaction.[40]

39. This distinction between assessments of moral responsibility and further judgments concerning the treatment of the agent (i.e., judgments concerning how the reactive attitudes are to be applied) parallels a distinction found in ledger views; for example, see the distinction between appraisability and liability in Zimmerman, *An Essay on Moral Responsibility.*

40. The Strawsonian view under discussion is concerned with the conceptual order in which our reactions to other persons may be justified; it does not purport to capture the actual order in which our interpersonal assessments are typically made. Certainly in the order of experience most of the time we do not sharply distinguish between these two types of judgments. Indeed most of the time we probably just adopt certain reactive

Thus far, we have been focusing primarily on Strawson's criticisms of the optimists' position, and in particular on his argument that the optimists need to remedy the lacuna in their view by taking into consideration the important role the reactive attitudes have over and above their social utility. As we noted above, however, Strawson not only wants the optimists to concede that their position leaves something out; he also wants the pessimists to see that this gap need not be filled by anything other than the reactive attitudes. Let's turn then to his defense of this point.

The pessimists basically make two claims. First, they claim that if the thesis of determinism is true, then we would have a reason to abandon the reactive attitudes. Second, they claim that were we to have a reason to suspend the reactive attitudes, we would be constitutionally able to do so. Strawson weaves together arguments that address each of these claims. In response to the first, he deploys a "rationalistic strategy," arguing that, although determinism may provide some reason to suspend the attitudes, there are stronger reasons for maintaining these attitudes even in light of determinism. In response to the second claim, Strawson adopts a "naturalistic strategy," arguing that, even if we were intellectually persuaded to abandon the reactive attitudes, we would be psychologically unable to do so.[41]

Consider, first, the rationalistic strategy. According to this view, we typically withhold the reactive attitudes for one of two reasons; specific excusing conditions (e.g., accident, ignorance, force) or global exempting conditions (e.g., psychological abnormality, moral underdevelopment). The specific excuses make no claim that the agent is an inappropriate candidate in general for the reactive attitudes; that is, they do not imply that the agent is not a fully responsible agent. Rather, such excuses applied when an otherwise morally responsible agent is not held responsible *for* some particular event. For example, specific excuses are applicable when someone says, "I couldn't help myself," "I didn't know what I was doing," and so forth.

In contrast to specific excusing conditions, the second reason for suspending the reactive attitudes—a global exempting condition—does stem from considerations that the agent is not (either temporarily or permanently) a fully responsible agent, that he or she is not what Strawson calls an appropriate "object of that kind of demand for good will or

---

attitudes toward persons without first explicitly assessing whether they are morally responsible. However, if one asks what justifies these attitudes, it becomes clear that the application of such attitudes implicitly assumes that a person is responsible.

41. The division of Strawson's arguments into a "rationalistic strategy" and a "naturalistic strategy" is found in Paul Russell, "Strawson's Way of Naturalizing Responsibility," *Ethics* 102 (1992): 287–302. The following discussion of these two strategies owes much to Russell's helpful article.

regard which is reflected in our ordinary reactive attitudes."[42] Such exemptions might arise (1) from the fact that the agent is placed in unusual circumstances such as being hypnotized or being under a great strain, or (2) from the notion that the agent is not a normal member of our moral community. This latter group of agents would include the morally underdeveloped (e.g., very small children) and the severely mentally ill. According to Strawson, when we encounter agents in this second group we suspend the reactive attitudes and instead adopt an "objective attitude," seeing the agent as "an object of social policy; as subject for what, in a wide range of sense, might be called treatment; as something certainly to be taken account, perhaps precautionary account, of; to be managed, or handled or cured or trained."[43]

After noting these two groups of excuses and exemptions, the rationalistic strategy goes on to argue that there is nothing about determinism that would require us to abandon the reactive attitudes for either of these reasons. The specific excusing conditions are held not to apply, for surely the truth of determinism does not entail that all our actions are done out of ignorance, by accident, and so forth. Neither are the global exempting conditions deemed applicable, for, as Strawson writes, "the participant attitude, and personal reactive attitudes in general, tend to give place, and, it is judged by the civilized, *should* give place, to objective attitudes, just in so far as the agent is seen as excluded from ordinary adult human relationships by deep-rooted psychological abnormality— or simply by being a child. But it cannot be a consequence of any thesis which is not itself self-contradictory that abnormality is the universal condition."[44]

One charge leveled against this portion of the rationalistic strategy is that it equivocates between abnormality and incapacity.[45] According to this criticism, the pessimists' worry is properly interpreted not as the claim that if determinism is true then everyone would be abnormal, but rather as the claim that if determinism is true, then everyone is incapacitated in some way that undermines responsibility. For instance, the pessimists argue that persons cannot be morally responsible unless they are free to do otherwise, and since determinism is allegedly incompatible with this freedom, all persons would be incapacitated if determinism were true. This distinction between abnormality and incapacity calls into question Strawson's argument. For although it *is* contradictory to say that abnormality is the norm, it is *not* contradictory to say that it is universally true that each person is incapacitated.

42. Strawson, "Freedom and Resentment," 51.
43. Ibid., 52.
44. Ibid., 53–54.
45. See Russell, "Strawson's Way," 298–301.

One response to such criticism may be found by appealing to a second line of argument suggested by the rationalistic strategy. This argument maintains that our practical commitment to the reactive attitudes is so deep, and their role in shaping the quality of our lives so great, that we would have overriding reasons to retain these attitudes no matter what theoretical reasons were advanced. This idea is developed by Bennett, who, after pointing out that a world devoid of all reactive attitudes would be "bleak desolation," concludes that "we cannot be obliged to give up something whose loss would gravely worsen the human condition, and so reactive feelings cannot be made impermissible by any facts, e.g., the fact that men are natural objects."[46] A related point, suggested by Wolf, is that it may be rational to choose to devalue or disregard certain kinds of theoretical considerations, given that the consequences of accepting these facts would greatly undermine the quality of our lives. Thus, just as "it may be rational for a man to choose not to face the fact that he has a terminal illness or for a woman to try to avoid discovering that her husband is having an affair," so, analogously, may it be rational for us to ignore reasons that would force us to abandon the reactive attitudes.[47]

Both Wolf's "Importance of Free Will" and Galen Strawson's "On 'Freedom and Resentment' " discuss the issue of whether the strength of our commitment to the reactive attitudes can provide overriding reasons to dismiss the pessimists' worries. Each recognizes that such an appeal ultimately comes into conflict with another, equally strong commitment, a commitment to truth. We instinctively shun a life built on deception or illusion, for we value the truth and we have a deep and natural desire to live in accord with it. This commitment to truth, combined with what Galen Strawson argues is an equally natural propensity to view determinism as a serious threat to responsibility, gives rise to a sharp conflict between our commitments. Given this conflict between our attachment to the reactive attitudes and our concern to live in accord with the facts, it is far from clear which of these commitments, if any, can provide reasons to trump the other.

Ultimately both Galen Strawson and Wolf concede that the pessimist's worries cannot be entirely defeated by the rationalistic strategy; however, they construe the force and nature of these residual worries quite differently. Whereas Strawson remains unpersuaded that any simple appeal "to the notion of commitment can show the worries of incompatibilist determinists to be wholly misconceived or groundless,"[48] Wolf

---

46. Bennett, "Accountability," 29.
47. Wolf, "The Importance of Free Will," 107.
48. Galen Strawson, "On 'Freedom and Resentment,' " 67. Galen Strawson also calls into question the depth of our commitment to the reactive attitudes, suggesting instead that our deepest commitment is not to regard others as free and responsible but rather to regard ourselves as such. Thus, Peter Strawson's argument "may mislocate the true centre of our commitment in our interpersonal rather than our self-regarding attitudes" (ibid.).

argues that an extension of the rationalistic strategy can show that even if we were not free and responsible beings, we still would have *no* reason to suspend the reactive attitudes and regard ourselves as not responsible. A central theme in her argument is that when we adopt a particular attitude (whether it be reactive or objective) toward ourselves, we assert our freedom and responsibility as attitude-takers. Consequently, even if initially it seems rational to replace the reactive attitudes with the objective attitude in order to live in accord with the facts, in the end we must admit that this choice is not any less irrational than keeping the reactive attitudes, for in adopting the objective stance toward ourselves, we would be asserting the very freedom and responsibility the objective attitude denies.[49] Although this improved version of the rationalistic strategy may seem to silence the pessimists' objections, Wolf concedes that some lingering anxieties remain. After all, the pessimists' deep worry is that if determinism is true, we are little more than marionettes guided by the forces of nature. And even if the rationalistic strategy can show that it is not rational for puppets to abandon the reactive attitudes, still, the pessimist will complain, we do not want to be puppets, and this fear is still with us at the end of the day.

In light of the criticisms facing the rationalistic strategy, defenders of Strawson's view may be tempted to rely even more heavily on the second prong of his response to the pessimists—the naturalistic strategy. This strategy argues that the reactive attitudes would be secure even if the rationalistic strategy fails, because we are constitutionally unable to abandon the reactive attitudes no matter how strong our reasons are to do so. According to this view, the pessimists' suggestion that we should give up these attitudes if determinism is true rests on the faulty assumption that (1) the reactive attitudes stand in need of some external justification and (2) there is some standpoint outside our practices from which these attitudes can be assessed. The trouble with this view, claims the naturalistic strategy, is that it fails to appreciate that the reactive attitudes are an inescapable part of human life, a part we are psychologically unable to abandon.

Critics have charged that in presenting this naturalistic argument Strawson fails to distinguish two distinct versions of the pessimists' position, only one of which is vulnerable to the naturalistic strategy.[50] Interpreted most charitably, the naturalistic strategy defends a view that might be called "type-naturalism." This view holds that our general propensity to adopt the reactive attitudes is a natural part of being human and that these attitudes, therefore, require no justification. This sort of naturalism is appropriately aimed at defeating what Russell calls the

49. Wolf goes on to argue that neither would we have any reason to cease taking attitudes altogether; "The Importance of Free Will," 108ff.

50. This sort of criticism is presented in Russell, "Strawson's Way," from which the terms "type-pessimism," "token-pessimism," and "type-naturalism" are taken.

"type-pessimist"—"one who believes that if determinism is true, then we are not justified in being disposed or prone to reactive attitudes and that we must, therefore (somehow) rid ourselves of this type or species of emotion."[51] It is at least plausible to suppose that type-naturalism can answer the worries voiced by type-pessimism. The problem for Strawson, however, is that this is not the sort of pessimism that best characterizes the real worries of incompatibilists. Such worries are more properly captured by what might be called "token-pessimism." Token-pessimism argues that there are certain circumstances in which the reactive attitudes should be *suspended,* and it then claims that if determinism is true, all of us are in just such a circumstance. Such a view is compatible with type-naturalism, for it does not deny the propriety of our general *disposition* to take reactive attitudes. Rather it merely holds that (given the truth of determinism) it is universally the case that each of us is in a circumstance that makes the *adoption* of these attitudes unjustified. One way to respond would be to claim that it is never appropriate to *suspend* or *fail to adopt* the reactive attitudes toward which we are naturally inclined. But this position is not only implausible, it also is at odds with Strawson's own rationalistic argument, which accepts that there are circumstances in which it is appropriate to excuse or exempt someone and in so doing to suspend the reactive attitudes.

Such are the problems that arise from the general structure of Strawson's replies to the optimists and pessimists. But quite different concerns present themselves once we turn to filling in the details of Strawson's own theory. One issue of this sort concerns the precise nature of Strawson's global exempting conditions. According to one view, these sorts of exempting conditions are best understood as marking the limits of moral address.[52] Thus, someone is exempted from being a morally responsible agent, Strawson says, when the basic "demand for goodwill or regard which is reflected in the ordinary reactive attitudes" is inhibited.[53] Once exempting conditions are interpreted as constraints on moral discourse, however, a particularly difficult problem arises for Strawson's theory in connection with persons who are radically evil. It is reasonable to suppose both that we cannot address someone who cannot understand us, and that (in Watson's words) "understanding requires a shared framework of values."[54] But someone who is radically evil probably will not share our values; thus, the paradox arises that the more evil a person is, the more likely he will fall outside the boundaries of our moral community and be exempted from responsibility.

51. Ibid., 296.
52. See Watson, "Responsibility and the Limits of Evil."
53. Strawson, "Freedom and Resentment," 51.
54. Watson, "Responsibility and the Limits of Evil," 130.

Consider, for example, the case of Robert Harris, which raises a host of questions for a theory such as Strawson's. For example, what role should considerations of Harris's history play in our ascriptions of responsibility? Should our reactive attitudes be influenced once we learn that a person's radical evil, his inability to see the point of moral address or to care about moral incentives, results from a deeply traumatic upbringing? Why do our feelings of resentment diminish once we discover that the victimizer himself was once a victim? (We return to such considerations later in the Introduction.) There is a sense that if we had been in similarly bad circumstances, then we too would have ended up beyond the bounds of the moral community. How should such constitutive "moral luck" factor into our moral assessments? These and similar questions are addressed in Watson's essay, which calls our attention to the kind of challenges that must be met as we work out the details of Strawson's original insights.

II. Accounts of Moral Responsibility

When does the concept of moral responsibility apply? In a series of influential articles, Harry Frankfurt has developed a "hierarchical" model of moral responsibility.[55] By "hierarchical" we mean that the model employs the resources of desires or preferences of various levels in the sense that some of the elements at one level have as their objects elements at other levels. So, in particular, some of the second-order elements have as their objects certain of the first-order elements. This is the sense in which Frankfurt's approach is hierarchical. (On another understanding of "hierarchical," one distinguishes different sources of preferences, or perhaps different contents, and then one claims that there is a hierarchy based on these different sources or contents. Here, the hierarchy is one of "weight" or "hegemony," rather than the object of the desires or preferences.)

In the early work by Frankfurt, the idea is that a certain sort of conformity between one's will (the first-order desire that moves one to action) and a second-order volition (a second-order desire about which first-order desire should be one's will) is a sufficient condition for moral responsibility (given, presumably, that certain epistemic conditions are met). Also, there is the suggestion that what is crucial to moral responsibility is that the agent *identify* with his will. But it is unclear what,

55. Harry G. Frankfurt, "Freedom of the Will and the Concept of a Person," *Journal of Philosophy* 68 (1971): 5–20; "Three Concepts of Free Action II," *Proceedings of the Aristotelian Society* 44 Supp. (1975): 113–25; "Identification and Externality," in *The Identities of Persons*, ed. Amelie Oksenberg Rorty (Berkeley: University of California Press, 1976), 239–51; and "Identification and Wholeheartedness," this volume.

precisely, is the relationship between the two ideas. More specifically, it is unclear whether the conformity between a second-order volition and the will is supposed to be the *analysis* of identification.

In his later work, Frankfurt gives a more explicit account of identification, indicating that the conformity or "mesh" condition is not taken to be an analysis of identification and thus sufficient for moral responsibility. Frankfurt's view is that one identifies with a first-order desire insofar as (1) one has an unopposed second-order volition to act in accordance with it, and (2) one judges that any further deliberation about the matter would issue in the same decision.[56] This view reflects a refinement in the simple mesh theory of Frankfurt's early work. In the later work, the mesh condition is supplemented by a "resonance" condition—in virtue of the judgment that further deliberation would simply issue in the same judgment, one's commitment is alleged to be "decisive" and to "resound" through the various levels of one's motivational states.[57]

It is well known that there are problems with simple versions of the hierarchical model.[58] Eleonore Stump presents some of the problems of such a model in one of her essays in this volume, "Sanctification, Hardening of the Heart, and Frankfurt's Concept of Free Will." Stump identifies three main criticisms of the simple hierarchical account. First, there is the possibility that the relevant higher-order volition is produced directly by someone (or something) else, thus vitiating the claim that the conformity between the higher-order volition and the will is sufficient for moral responsibility.[59] Second, there is the worry about a possible infinite regress of volitions. For an agent to be morally responsible in virtue of the conformity between his will V_1 and a second-order volition V_2, it seems that V_2 must be freely willed. But in order for V_2 to be freely willed, it seems that there must be a third-order volition V_3 with which V_2 is in accord, and V_3 will itself have to be freely willed (and thus will require a fourth-order volition), and so forth. Third, critics have claimed that the hierarchical model rests on an unwarranted notion of what counts as the "real self" and on a false theory of what counts as external or alien to a person. Why should we identify an agent's self (or

56. Frankfurt, "Identification and Wholeheartedness."

57. For critical discussions of Frankfurt's new account, see John Christman, "Autonomy and Personal History," *Canadian Journal of Philosophy* 21 (1991): 1–24; and John Martin Fischer and Mark Ravizza, "Responsibility and History," forthcoming, *Midwest Studies in Philosophy* 19 (1994).

58. For a classic early criticism of the hierarchical approach, see Irving Thalberg, "Hierarchical Analyses of Unfree Action," *Canadian Journal of Philosophy* 8 (1978): 211–26; for a response, see David Zimmerman, "Hierarchical Motivation and Freedom of the Will," *Pacific Philosophical Quarterly* 62 (1981): 354–68. There is a good critical discussion in Wolf, "The Real Self View," this volume.

59. This worry is also articulated forcefully in Michael Slote, "Understanding Free Will," *Journal of Philosophy* 77 (1980): 136–51.

real self) only with his higher-order volitions (or those lower-order elements selected by the relevant higher-order volitions)? Aren't the "darker" sides of our nature, the repudiated or repressed first-order desires, just as much part of our selves as our higher-order desires and the first-order desires of which we approve?[60]

Much recent literature on the hierarchical model consists of an elaboration of these and related worries and various attempts at refining the approach so that it can avoid the putative problems. Indeed, in her two contributions to this volume, Eleonore Stump combines ingredients from Aquinas and Frankfurt to present a sophisticated version of the hierarchical theory that, she claims, circumvents the criticisms presented above. In the spirit of Aquinas's view of intellect's direction of the will, Stump makes the following revision of Frankfurt's account: an agent has a second-order volition V_2 to bring about some first-order volition V_1 only if the agent's intellect at the time of the willing represents V_1, under some description, as the good to be pursued. On this view, a second-order volition is a volition formed as a result of some reasoning (even when the reasoning is neither rational nor conscious) about one's first-order desires.

In contrast to Frankfurt (who has a rather minimalist and formalistic structure), Stump's approach is not silent about the *basis* of the second-order volition. Other hierarchical theorists have presented even more robust accounts that require that the second-order volitions be based on certain considerations, in order for the agent to be morally responsible.[61]

A fascinating discussion of the notion of "identification" (crucial to Frankfurt's theory) is presented in David Velleman's contribution to this volume, "What Happens When Someone Acts?" On Velleman's analysis, the agent plays an indispensable mediating role between reasons and the formation of an intention, and also between the intention and the action. He argues that this role is not sufficiently appreciated by other theorists, including Frankfurt.[62]

60. See, especially, Thalberg, "Hierarchical Analyses." For related criticisms and skepticism about the hegemony of the higher-order motivational states, see Marilyn Friedman, "Autonomy and the Split-level Self," *Southern Journal of Philosophy* 24 (1986): 19–35; there is a response in John Christman, "Autonomy: A Defense of the Split-Level Self," *Southern Journal of Philosophy* 25 (1987): 281–93.

61. See, especially, Charles Taylor, "Responsibility for Self," in *The Identities of Persons,* ed. Rorty, 281–99. Also see Gary Watson, "Free Agency," *Journal of Philosophy* 72 (1975): 205–20. Watson's theory does not employ the apparatus of higher and lower *levels* of motivational states, and thus his theory is "hierarchical" only in the *second* sense identified above.

62. A similar argument appears in Raziel Abelson, *Lawless Mind* (Philadelphia: Temple University Press, 1988). But there are important differences between the approaches of Abelson and Velleman. In particular, whereas Abelson argues that the agent's role in the process leading to action cannot be in any sense analyzed away, Velleman argues that the

Other theories of moral responsibility are more perspicuously treated as essentially non-hierarchical. These theories do not make moral responsibility emerge from a division of different systems of desires or preferences. The most salient non-hierarchical approaches to moral responsibility require not so much that there be a suitable *alignment* or *synchronization* of different motivational states (from different layers or systems of such states), but that there be a suitable *connection* between the agent and certain aspects of external reality. Very roughly put, some such theories require a certain sort of connection between the agent and *values*,[63] and others require a certain connection between the agent and *reasons* given by the world. (Of course, given certain views about the nature of values—and reasons—there will be intimate relationships between these kinds of theory.)

A non-hierarchical theory that is explicitly normative in the sense that it requires an appropriate connection between an agent and values is developed by Susan Wolf.[64] She calls the hierarchical view the "real self view" and says that its problem is that it is too weak; the ability to act in accord with one's real self is not sufficient to justify ascriptions of responsibility, for questions can arise concerning one's responsibility for that real self. But Wolf rejects the impetus to remedy this deficiency by demanding that one's real self be completely undetermined by anything external to the self; in Wolf's view, such a demand for autonomy not only seems impossible to satisfy, it also bestows (or requires) a power to act that no one could have any reason to want. Wolf's "reason view" locates the freedom needed for responsibility in the freedom to pursue the "True and the Good"—to do the right thing for the right reason.

One of the most striking features of the "reason view" is that it takes free will and moral responsibility to be inextricably linked with norma-

---

"functional role" of the agent is played by the motive to act on the best reason. Thus, whereas Abelson's theory embodies a non-reductivist view of the role of the agent, Velleman's theory proposes a reduction.

63. As we have pointed out above, there are various ways of characterizing "hierarchical" theories. On one such view, Watson's theory (presented in "Free Agency") is considered hierarchical insofar as there is a hierarchy of different systems of preferences based on their *source*. Here the system of preferences based on "values" is higher in the hierarchy than the system that is independent of values. Still, Watson's approach is different from the non-hierarchical approaches under consideration in the text here. Whereas Watson's approach identifies different systems of internal states and posits a hierarchy among them, the non-hierarchical approaches posit a certain sort of *connection* between the agent and the external world. It must, however, be conceded that this way of marking a distinction between hierarchical and non-hierarchical theories is rough, and certain particular theories may be difficult to classify neatly.

64. Susan Wolf, "Asymmetrical Freedom," *Journal of Philosophy* 77 (1980): 151–60; "Sanity and the Metaphysics of Responsibility," in *Responsibility, Character, and the Emotions*, ed. Ferdinand Schoeman (Cambridge: Cambridge University Press, 1987), 46–62; and *Freedom within Reason* (New York: Oxford University Press, 1991).

tive considerations—it takes the ascription of these notions to be justified in virtue of the satisfaction not solely of purely metaphysical conditions, but of normative conditions as well. That is, the question of responsibility is no longer simply a question of whether one's actions are completely determined by a real self that in turn is metaphysically independent of any external determining forces, but it involves a distinctive power to exercise right Reason—to appropriately appreciate the good, and to do the right thing for the right reasons. Given this view (together with ancillary ideas), a striking asymmetry thesis emerges. Wolf holds that a person who does the right thing for the right reason need not have been free to do otherwise in order to be held responsible for her action; however, a person who does the wrong thing and acts on bad reasons must have been free to do otherwise in order to be blamed and held responsible for the act.[65]

Another non-hierarchical approach posits a certain sort of connection between an agent and his reasons provided by the world. This class of theories requires (different sorts of) responsiveness to reasons.[66] There are several dimensions of variation among the theories in this class. Some of the theories are "agent-based," whereas others are "mechanism-based." An agent-based theory requires the agent to be responsive to reasons, whereas a mechanism-based theory requires the mechanism on which the agent acts to be responsive to reasons.[67] Also, there is considerable variation in the nature of the reasons involved—moral and non-moral, subjective and objective. Finally, there is a spectrum of variation in the nature and extent of the responsiveness that is required: must the agent (or mechanism) be able to respond to the reason he actually would have, if he did in fact have reason to perform the action in question, to several reasons, to a range of reasons with a certain profile, or simply to one possible reason? When evaluating reasons-responsiveness, one is considering a range of alternative scenarios in which certain reasons are present. Again, there are differences in how the theories conceive of these alternative scenarios: precisely what features of the actual situation are held fixed, and what features are allowed to vary? For example, on some approaches, one holds fixed the agent's preferences and character but allows the reasons (stemming from objective features of the situation) to vary. On other approaches, one

65. For discussion of Wolf's view and the associated asymmetry thesis, see John Martin Fischer and Mark Ravizza, "Responsibility, Freedom, and Reason," *Ethics* 102 (1992): 368–89.

66. There are comprehensive and illuminating surveys of much of this work in David Shatz, "Free Will and the Structure of Motivation," in *Midwest Studies in Philosophy*, vol. 10, ed. Peter A. French, Theodore E. Uehling, Jr., and Howard K. Wettstein (Minneapolis, 1985); and "Compatibilism, Values, and 'Could Have Done Otherwise,'" *Philosophical Topics* 16 (1988): 151–200.

67. It should be pointed out that Wolf's non-hierarchical approach also admits of variation along this dimension.

holds fixed these reasons and allows the agent's preferences and character to vary. Obviously, there are many differences among the theories lumped together under the rubric of reasons-responsiveness.

To fix ideas and focus our discussion, we lay out here a mechanism-based reasons-responsiveness approach to moral responsibility. (Many similar points will apply to agent-based approaches.) We distinguish "strong" and "weak" versions of the theory, then develop some apparent problems with both approaches. Very briefly, the motivation for a mechanism-based theory (rather than an agent-based theory) is the intuitive idea that a different sort of mechanism from the one actually operative might operate in a range of alternative scenarios, and what seems to be relevant to moral responsibility is the responsiveness characteristics of the *actually operative* kind of mechanism. Thus, intuitively, it is appropriate, when ascertaining responsiveness, to hold fixed the kind of mechanism that actually operates.[68]

Let us begin with what might be called "strong reasons-responsiveness." Strong reasons-responsiveness obtains when a certain kind K of mechanism actually issues in an action and if there were sufficient reason to do otherwise and K were to operate, the agent would recognize the sufficient reason and thus choose to do otherwise and do otherwise. To test whether a kind of mechanism is strongly reasons-responsive, one asks what would happen if there were sufficient reason for the agent to do otherwise and the actual-sequence mechanism were to operate. Under such circumstances, three conditions must be satisfied: the agent must take the reason to be sufficient, choose in accordance with the sufficient reason, and act in accordance with the choice. Thus, there can be at least three sorts of "alternative-sequence" failures: failures in the connection between what reasons there are and what reasons the agent recognizes, in the connection between the agent's reason and choice, and in the connection between choice and action.

If the actual kind of mechanism were to operate and none of these failures were to occur, then the actually operative mechanism would be strongly reasons-responsive. There would be a tight fit between the reasons there are and the reasons the agent recognizes, between the agent's reasons and choice, and between the choice and the action. The agent's actions would fit the contours of reasons *closely*.

---

68. Mechanism-based theories are developed in Robert Nozick, *Philosophical Explanations* (Cambridge: Harvard University Press, 1981); and John Martin Fischer, "Responsiveness and Moral Responsibility," in *Responsibility, Character, and the Emotions*, ed. Ferdinand Schoeman (Cambridge: Cambridge University Press, 1987), 81–106. The mechanism-based theory in Nozick is parallel to his mechanism-based epistemology. In Fischer, it is suggested that a mechanism-based approach is a natural way of coming to grips with the "Frankfurt-style" counterexamples to the claim that moral responsibility requires alternative possibilities (discussed below in the text).

Robert Nozick requires this sort of close contouring of action to value for his notion of "tracking value" or "tracking bestness."[69] Nozick claims that an agent who tracks value displays a kind of moral virtue, but it should be pointed out that he does not explicitly claim that tracking value is a necessary condition for moral responsibility. Perhaps Nozick does not endorse this strong reasons-responsiveness approach as necessary for moral responsibility because of the possibility of weakness of will or moral evil. Surely it is too much to require that an agent's actions conform with what is rational or morally prescribed, in order for him to be held morally responsible; we hold weak-willed and morally evil agents responsible.

Moral responsibility requires a "looser fit" between reasons and action. On the other extreme along the spectrum of fit is "weak reasons-responsiveness," which requires only that there be *some* possible scenario in which the actual mechanism operates, the agent has reason to do otherwise, and he does otherwise.[70] But whereas strong reasons-responsiveness seems to be too strong a requirement on moral responsibility, weak reasons-responsiveness may be too weak. Consider, for instance, an example given by Ferdinand Schoeman. Imagine someone who is intuitively genuinely insane. This person commits a barbarous act, such as killing a number of persons on the Staten Island Ferry with a saber. And suppose that the Saber Killer would have killed the persons under all possible circumstances except one: he would have refrained if he had believed that someone on board was eating a Snickers candy bar. Intuitively, the individual is highly irrational and should not be considered morally responsible (on the face of it, at least), and yet he seems to satisfy the condition of acting from a reasons-responsive mechanism. Weak reasons-responsiveness obtains by virtue of the agent's responsiveness to a "bizarre" reason, even though the agent is not responsive to a wide array of "relevant" or good reasons.[71]

Various responses to the problem of bizarreness are possible. One might ask for responsiveness to a greater number of reasons.[72] Or one might require responsiveness to a greater number of reasons constrained by the necessity of certain *patterns* in the reasons. Alternatively, one might place certain constraints on the content of the reasons to which the agent (or the mechanism) is responsive; perhaps the reasons need to be objective or good (in terms of rationality or morality).

69. Nozick, *Philosophical Explanations.*

70. Fischer, "Responsiveness and Moral Responsibility."

71. Schoeman, personal communication. For discussions of this sort of problem, see Shatz, "Compatibilism, Values, and 'Could Have Done Otherwise' "; and Double, *The Non-Reality of Free Will.*

72. See Bernard Gert and Timothy J. Duggan, "Free Will as the Ability to Will," *Nous* 13 (1979): 197–217.

An apparent problem emerges, however, for all the responsiveness theories. This problem is analogous to the first problem for the hierarchical theories presented above. Just as it is possible for the hierarchy to be suitably arranged as a result of direct intervention by some external source, so it also seems that it is possible for some external source simply to "implant" the selected propensity to respond to reasons. This worry is developed in Eleonore Stump's second piece in this volume, "Intellect, Will, and the Principle of Alternate Possibilities." Whether responsiveness theories have the resources to address this objection remains to be seen.

The objection just presented raises the issue of whether one's theory of responsibility is "historical" or "non-historical." A non-historical theory of moral responsibility is purely structural; it focuses solely on the relevant "current time-slice" and its properties. A non-historical theory of moral responsibility claims that an agent's past may be relevant to ascriptions of responsibility, but only *indirectly*—by pointing to and helping us to see underlying properties that are indeed present in the current time-slice and that ground the pertinent responsibility ascriptions. History is relevant here, but only *epistemically*. Harry Frankfurt has defended the thesis that responsibility is a current time-slice notion.[73]

In contrast, a historical theory of moral responsibility claims that the past can be relevant to moral responsibility ascriptions *directly* (and not solely epistemically). On this view, it is possible for two agents to share all the same current time-slice characteristics but differ in their histories and thus in their moral responsibility; moral responsibility attributions do not supervene on current time-slice properties.[74] It seems that the problem of direct external production of the selected structural or responsiveness characteristics points to the advisability of adopting a historical theory (independent of whether one is attracted to a hierarchical or responsiveness model).

Clearly also consideration of the case of Robert Harris should recommend some sort of historical approach to moral responsibility. To explore the relevance of the past to present attributions of responsibility, consider an alternative past that, presumably, Harris might have had. Suppose Robert is a child prodigy born to an extremely wealthy family. From the earliest age he is given every possible advantage. His success in school and obvious superiority to his fellow students breed in him a deep contempt for mediocrity, and he gradually develops a youthful elitism. As a diversion from his studies, Robert voraciously reads detective nov-

---

73. See, especially, Frankfurt, "Three Concepts of Free Action II" and "Identification and Wholeheartedness."

74. For criticisms of non-historical approaches (especially Frankfurt's) and defenses of historical models, see Fischer, "Responsiveness and Moral Responsibility"; Christman, "Autonomy and Personal History"; and Fischer and Ravizza, "Responsibility and History."

els; he spends hours imagining how, unlike the usual blundering criminal, he could commit the perfect crime. During his early teens, extensive reading of Nietzsche and Dostoyevski prompts Robert to adopt a view that morality is a perverse tool that the weak and mediocre use to hold back truly superior individuals—individuals, he proudly notes, not unlike himself. To validate his superiority, Robert decides he must free himself from all the restrictions of conventional morality. He must become a man beyond good and evil, a man for whom everything is permitted. To reach this end, he devises a program to "improve" his character gradually. As a first step, Robert sets out to commit the perfect crime and shoots John Mayeski and Michael Baker.

Given this "Leopold and Loeb" sort of past, perhaps our judgments about Harris's responsibility would be different from those we have in light of his actual past. Learning about Harris's actual past seems to affect our attitudes. But it is not easy to say just how this history affects our judgments. It does not make us revise our original sense of the evil of Harris's crime, nor of the necessity to isolate him from the community at large. As Watson points out, our response to learning of Harris's actual past is not a simple matter of suspending our reactive attitudes but is much more complex. At the very least, our feelings toward Harris take on a new ambivalence. What had been a case in which unqualified resentment and moral indignation were in order now becomes a case in which it is at least debatable how one ought to react. And this is the point that seems to incline one toward a historical approach to moral responsibility. If Harris's peculiarly unfortunate formative circumstances make our reactions more ambivalent, a theory understanding responsible agency in terms of internal harmony alone (or other pure current time-slice features) cannot countenance our altered attitude toward Harris once we learn of his actual past. A snapshot of Harris's motivational state fails to recognize that the very issues about Harris's past that make us ambivalent are independent features not fully captured in the time-slice motivations from which he acts. We do not doubt his wholeheartedness in acting, but the full extent of his culpability becomes ambiguous. It is precisely this element—our altered response to the individual's past—that encourages us to think that the causal origins of his action are relevant to his responsibility.

III. RESPONSIBILITY AND ALTERNATIVE POSSIBILITIES

Traditionally, there has been an association of moral responsibility with alternative possibilities. Indeed, this association has (traditionally, at least) represented a kind of "metaphysical correctness." It has been alleged that moral responsibility requires the existence (at least at *some* appropriate point along the way to an action) of a genuine alternative possibility—freedom to choose, will, do otherwise. Yet recently metaphysical correctness has been called into question in various ways.[75]

Following John Locke, Harry Frankfurt has developed a set of examples that challenge the necessity of alternative possibilities for moral responsibility.[76] To sketch a "Frankfurt-style" example, suppose there is a "counterfactual intervener"—perhaps a mad scientist or nefarious (even nutty) neurologist—who wishes to see you kill Jones.[77] He has rigged up a device that will stimulate your brain to ensure that you will to kill Jones and do so, should you show any inclination not to will to kill Jones. If you voluntarily kill Jones on your own and the scientist's device plays no role in your deliberations or action, it seems that you can be held morally responsible for your action, even though you lack the traditionally required alternative possibilities: you cannot will to do otherwise nor can you do otherwise. Thus, it appears that this (sketchily developed) Frankfurt-style example is a counterexample to the Principle of Alternative Possibilities (which requires alternative possibilities for moral responsibility).

If indeed the Principle of Alternative Possibilities is false and thus moral responsibility does not require alternative possibilities, then compatibilism about causal determinism and moral responsibility becomes considerably more attractive. In this case the possibility will have been opened that causal determinism is compatible with moral responsibility even if causal determinism rules out alternative possibilities. And it seems that the strongest arguments for the incompatibility of causal determinism and alternative possibilities would not translate in any straightforward manner into arguments for the incompatibility of causal determinism and moral responsibility (considered apart from the putative requirement of alternative possibilities).[78] Thus, an "actual-sequence" theory of moral responsibility—one that denies the Principle of Alternative Possibilities—is very attractive.

But various philosophers have resisted the conclusion that moral responsibility does not require alternative possibilities (of any sort). Part of

75. For some skepticism about the importance of alternative possibilities to moral responsibility, see Daniel Dennett, *Elbow Room: The Varieties of Free Will Worth Wanting* (Cambridge: MIT Press, 1984); and "I Could Not Have Done Otherwise—So What?" *Journal of Philosophy* 81 (1984): 553–65.

76. See, especially, Harry Frankfurt, "Alternate Possibilities and Moral Responsibility," *Journal of Philosophy* 45 (1969): 829–39; and "What We Are Morally Responsible For," this volume.

77. For animadversions against such examples, see Dennett, *Elbow Room;* for more measured reflections, see Robert Kane, *Free Will and Values* (Albany: State University of New York Press, 1985).

78. For an argument for the incompatibility of causal determinism and moral responsibility that proceeds independently of considerations of alternative possibilities, see Peter van Inwagen, *An Essay on Free Will,* esp. 182–89.

the strategy of these philosophers is to begin with a careful articulation of the sorts of things for which an agent might be held responsible: traits of character, actions, omissions, and consequences of those actions and omissions (where the consequences might be construed as either consequence-universals or consequence-particulars). The thing for which one is morally responsible, then, is not the thing to which there is no alternative possibility.[79]

To elaborate: Let us suppose again that you kill Jones. More specifically, imagine that you pull the trigger of your gun and shoot Jones, thereby killing him. We might ask (for instance) whether you are morally responsible for a certain *consequence* of what you've done, namely Jones's death. Now one could argue that the answer depends on whether the consequence is construed as a particular or a universal. If it is construed as a particular (as the specific consequence of a certain history), then you may indeed be held morally responsible for it, but it is now unclear that there was no alternative possibility; for if you had refrained from initiating the process leading to the death on your own, the scientist would have initiated the process, and arguably, the resulting consequence-particular would have been different from the actually-occurring particular. That is, arguably the death that would have occurred would have been a different *particular* death from the actual one, insofar as it would have had a crucially different past.

Alternatively, if the consequence is construed as a universal (which itself could have been caused to obtain in various ways), it is evident that you could not have done anything to prevent it. But now it becomes unclear whether you can fairly be held morally responsible for it. Perhaps you can be held responsible for the *particular* death, or the *way the universal is caused to obtain;* but it is unclear that you are responsible for the fact that it obtains (in one way or another). After all, the fact that it obtains in one way or another is something quite out of your control. More careful and detailed discussion of these and other issues pertaining to moral responsibility for consequences can be found in several contributions to this volume: Robert Heinaman's "Incompatibilism without the Principle of Alternative Possibilities," William Rowe's "Causing and Being Responsible for What Is Inevitable," and John Martin Fischer and Mark Ravizza's "Responsibility for Consequences."[80]

The above reflections might tempt one to conclude that on either construal of consequences, there is no *one thing* of which it is true *both* that the agent is morally responsible for it and that there is no alternative possibility to it. That is, in the example above there may be things for

---

79. For this strategy see, especially, Peter van Inwagen, "Ability and Responsibility," *Philosophical Review* 87 (1978): 201–24; and ibid.

80. Also see Bernard Berofsky, *Freedom from Necessity: The Metaphysical Basis of Responsibility* (New York: Routledge and Kegan Paul, 1987); and John Martin Fischer and Mark Ravizza, "The Inevitable," *Australasian Journal of Philosophy* 70 (1992): 388–404.

which an agent is morally responsible, and things to which there is no alternative possibility. But the problem is that these are *different* things.

Similar considerations may apply to the issue of moral responsibility for *omissions*. Suppose, for instance, that Max is strolling along a beach. He sees a child struggling in the water, and he believes that he can rescue the child with minimal effort and inconvenience. But Max decides not to go to the trouble, and he continues walking along the beach. The child drowns. Unbeknownst to Max, a school of sharks is patrolling the water between the beach and the struggling child, and had he jumped into the water, the sharks would have attacked and eaten him.

Is Max morally responsible for failing to rescue the child? We think not. Of course, in his behavior Max manifests something bad about himself, and he *is* morally responsible for *something*. He is, for instance, morally responsible for his failure to *try* to save the child, his failure to jump into the water, and so forth. But he is *not* morally responsible for failing to save the child. If one denied this, one would apparently have to say that Max could be morally responsible for failing to save the child in a variant of the case in which (unbeknownst to Max) the child dies just as (or immediately after) he is contemplating jumping in. But this is very implausible. So again there is a thing to which there is no alternative and various things for which the agent is morally responsible. But the problem is that the things are *different*.[81]

One of the most interesting and powerful responses to the Frankfurt strategy for calling into question the Principle of Alternative Possibilities has been developed in work by William L. Rowe. Rowe presents this sort of response to Frankfurt in one of his chapters in this volume, "Responsibility, Agent-Causation, and Freedom: An Eighteenth-Century View," where he attributes this view—based on the libertarian notion of "agent-causation"—to Thomas Reid.

Rowe concedes that in the Frankfurt-type example presented above, you do not have the traditionally required alternative possibilities: you cannot will to do otherwise nor can you do otherwise. But Rowe insists that this sort of case does not imply that moral responsibility for killing Jones does not require *Reidean freedom*, and he believes this freedom is crucial to moral responsibility. That is to say, he argues that even in this Frankfurt-type case, you have the power *not to cause* the volition to kill Jones. As Rowe puts it in *Thomas Reid on Freedom and Morality*,

> The scientist can cause our agent to will to do A. He does this by causing that act of will in the agent. But if he does so then the agent does

81. For discussion of these issues, especially the relationship between responsibility for actions and responsibility for omissions, see van Inwagen, "Ability and Responsibility" and *An Essay on Free Will*; Frankfurt, "What We Are Morally Responsible For"; and Fischer, "Responsibility and Failure," *Proceedings of the Aristotelian Society* 86 (1985–86): 251–70.

not agent-cause his volition to do A. The real agent-cause is the scientist. So if the agent has the power to cause his volition to do A, he also has the power *not to cause* that volition. If he does not cause the volition and the machine [of the scientist] activates, he nevertheless wills to do A—but *he* is not the cause of that act of will. . . . The agent caused his volition to kill Jones and had it in his power not to cause that volition.[82]

Rowe thus attributes to Reid and also defends a version of a very powerful and attractive sort of response to the Frankfurt-type examples: what we would call the "flicker of freedom" strategy. This strategy, in its general form, suggests that even in the fanciest Frankfurt-type case, one can find at least *some* alternative possibility, even if it is a rather exiguous one. The Reid/Rowe flicker theory embraces the principle that a person is morally accountable for her action A only if she causes the volition to do A and it was in her power not to cause her volition to do A.

This flicker theory is very significant within the context of debates about the relationship between moral responsibility and causal determinism. If moral responsibility requires alternative possibilities and causal determinism rules out such possibilities, then causal determinism rules out moral responsibility. As pointed out above, if moral responsibility does not require alternative possibilities, then there is hope for moral responsibility even if causal determinism obtains and is incompatible with alternative possibilities. But the flicker theory claims that even if the Frankfurt-type examples show that moral responsibility does not require alternative possibilities as traditionally interpreted, it *does* require alternative possibilities: it demands at least a flicker of freedom. Further, the most powerful argument for the conclusion that causal determinism rules out alternative possibilities of the traditional sort (the Consequence Argument sketched above) *also* implies that causal determinism rules out alternative possibilities of the sort envisaged by Reid and Rowe—causal determinism threatens to extinguish even the flicker of freedom. Thus, there is some reason stemming from the analysis of Reid and Rowe to claim that causal determinism is incompatible with moral responsibility, even granting the kernel of truth of Frankfurt's examples.

As above, the flicker theorist will concede that there is something for which the agent is morally responsible and something to which there is no alternative possibility. More specifically, in the example presented above you are morally responsible for causing your volition to shoot and kill Jones, and there was indeed no alternative open to you to shooting and killing Jones. But of course these are *different* things. And it is not

---

82. William L. Rowe, *Thomas Reid on Freedom and Morality* (Ithaca: Cornell University Press, 1991), 85–86.

evident that there is any *one* thing of which it is true both that you are morally responsible for it and that you cannot prevent it.

Thus, there appears to be a *general* strategy of response to Frankfurt's approach to calling into question the requirement of alternative possibilities. The strategy begins with a careful articulation and separation of different things for which one might be held responsible, and it points out that it is difficult to hold that there is any *one* thing of which both crucial claims are true: that one is morally responsible for it and that there is no alternative to it. This strategy might be called "divide and conquer." A proponent of an "actual-sequence" theory of moral responsibility (which does not require alternative possibilities) will need to engage this "divide and conquer" strategy of argumentation.

We do not, however, despair of the possibility of a defense of the actual-sequence approach against the strategy just sketched. Note that the proponent of the flicker theory (and thus the requirement of alternative possibilities for moral responsibility) points out that even the most sophisticated Frankfurt-style examples contain *some* flicker of freedom, some alternative possibility. The actual-sequence theorist might concede this point but go on to argue that nevertheless it is not the flicker that *drives* our intuitions that the relevant agents are morally responsible for what they do. That is, even though there is some alternative possibility in these examples, it does not seem to be *in virtue of* the alternative possibility that the agent is responsible; the alternative possibility does not *ground* our views about responsibility, and indeed the flickers of freedom seem quite irrelevant to our judgments of responsibility.

The dialectic here is rather delicate. The flicker theorist points out that no example has been given in which it is uncontroversially evident that an agent is morally responsible and there is no alternative possibility. The actual-sequence theorist responds that, even if this is so, the alternative possibilities are not what ground the responsibility ascriptions; indeed, they are allegedly irrelevant to such ascriptions. The question then becomes whether there is some *other factor* that grounds our responsibility ascriptions and that also *entails* that there be some alternative possibility. If this were so, then even though it is not the alternative possibility that *grounds* our moral responsibility ascriptions, nevertheless moral responsibility would require alternative possibilities. We suggest that the debate between the flicker theorists and the actual-sequence theorists hinges on this issue.

If the actual-sequence theory can be defended, interesting new light can be shed on Peter Strawson's argument (discussed above). Earlier we pointed out that Strawson holds that the optimists and the pessimists share a common mistake: they both hold that responsibility rests on a judgment that the agent in question satisfies some theoretical requirement. For the optimists, this requirement is that the agent be susceptible to treatment that would alter his behavior in optimal ways. For the libertarian pessimists, this requirement is that the agent meet some metaphysical demand—the possession of contra-causal freedom. Strawson argues that both sides "overintellectualize the facts."

In response, Strawson suggests that *no* theoretical requirement needs to be satisfied for an agent to be morally responsible; rather, the propensity of the community to hold the reactive attitudes toward the agent *constitutes* the agent's moral responsibility. But as pointed out above, this approach is worrisome insofar as it appears to leave little room for criticism of the actual practices of a community. Indeed, Strawson's approach threatens to "underintellectualize the facts."

In contrast, one could maintain that moral responsibility is the *rational accessibility* to the reactive attitudes (as suggested above). Further, one could point out that the pessimist's view of the sort of metaphysical proposition that must ground responsibility ascriptions is unduly narrow. That is, perhaps some sort of freedom is required for moral responsibility, but *not* "contra-causal" freedom. And this is just the point of the actual-sequence theorist. According to the actual-sequence approach, an agent may "act freely" even though she does not have "freedom to do otherwise." That is, the agent may exhibit the liberty of spontaneity, even though she lacks the liberty of indifference. Under such circumstances, one could say that the agent *does* satisfy a theoretical requirement that can ground her rational accessibility to the reactive attitudes: she *does* possess a certain sort of freedom, although not the dark and obscure sort (contra-causal freedom) envisaged by the libertarians.

We might reconstruct the Strawsonian structure as follows. Imagine a putative gap between the Schlickean social-regulation practices and moral responsibility, which apparently involves the reactive attitudes. How can we come to grips with this apparent gap? The optimist argues that *there really is no gap* because the Schlickean practices constitute moral responsibility (and thus moral responsibility does not really involve these attitudes). Strawson rightly rejects this view. The pessimist argues that *the gap can be filled* by a metaphysical ingredient—contra-causal freedom. Strawson also rightly rejects this view. Now Strawson argues that *the gap does not need to be filled;* we should simply recognize that our actual propensities to take the reactive attitudes constitute robust moral responsibility and do not require any further grounding by a theoretical or metaphysical proposition.

Finally, we have suggested another possibility. According to this sort of view, the gap is genuine, cannot be filled by contra-causal freedom, and does indeed need to be filled. It should be filled by an "intellectual"— indeed, in some sense a "metaphysical"—ingredient, although not the one considered by Strawson. This ingredient is a certain sort of freedom, "acting freely" or the freedom of spontaneity. The notion of weak reasons-responsiveness sketched above provides part of an analysis of this sort of freedom, but much more needs to be said about the nature of this sort of freedom, in order to fill in and give more resolution to this kind of response to the Strawsonian dialectic.

Robert Alton Harris was executed on April 21, 1992. Here is an account:

> After an extraordinary bicoastal judicial duel kept his fate in doubt throughout the night, Robert Alton Harris died in San Quentin's gas chamber at sunrise Tuesday, becoming the first person executed in California in 25 years.
>
> Harris, 39, was pronounced dead at 6:21 a.m., just 36 minutes after the U.S. Supreme Court overturned the last of four overnight reprieves that delayed his execution by more than six hours.
>
> Earlier Tuesday, a seemingly jaunty Harris came within seconds of death but was rescued by a federal judge, who halted the execution even as the acid used to form the lethal gas flowed into a vat beneath the prisoner's seat.
>
> That final stay was quickly tossed out by the U.S. Supreme Court, which clearly had had its fill of the Harris case. In an unprecedented ruling that capped a night of coast-to-coast faxes and deliberations, the justices voted 7 to 2 to forbid any federal court from meddling further in the execution.
>
> Moments later, a decidedly more solemn Harris was led a second time through the door of the mint-green gas chamber and strapped without resistance into his metal death chair.
>
> Scanning the faces of 48 witnesses peering through windows just steps away, Harris saw Steve Baker—the father of one of the teen-age murder victims. Harris, his voice inaudible through the thick steel walls, slowly mouthed the words, "I'm sorry." Baker, a San Diego police detective, nodded in return.
>
> Shortly after 6 a.m., a mist of cyanide vapors enveloped the pony-tailed convict. Over the next two minutes, Harris twitched, gave five quick gasps that puffed his flushed cheeks, and slumped forward. Prison doctors said it took him 14 minutes to die.
>
> Harris' relatives and friends—five of whom were witnesses—embraced and turned away as he fell unconscious. Sharon Mankins, the mother of one of his victims, smiled broadly and looked up as if to thank God. Her daughter, Linda Herring, wept in relief.[83]

83. *Los Angeles Times*, April 22, 1992, A1, 10. Copyright, 1992, *Los Angeles Times*. Reprinted by permission. Also, here is a description of the sister of one of Harris's victims:
The first time her brother's killer walked into the gas chamber Tuesday morning, Marilyn Clark saw the same smirking jerk she recalled from old television news footage. That made her indescribably furious.

We claimed above that it is natural to feel a kind of ambivalence toward Harris. Perhaps this final quotation describing the situation the night before Harris's execution in some sense captures the ambivalence.

"The answer, my friend, is blowing in the wind. . ." sang 150 suddenly hopeful opponents of the death penalty as the sun set on San Quentin prison and a surprise legal ruling appeared to temporarily spare Robert Alton Harris.

All this was too much for Claudette Baumgardner, who had come to wait for Harris to die, and to celebrate when he did.

". . . The answer is the gas chamber!" she bellowed over the soft, impassioned singing of the death penalty opponents standing 20 feet away.[84]

The second time, two hours later, Robert Alton Harris was a changed man, Clark said. He walked purposefully into the chamber and sat down, "facing it like a man," she said. Then, surprisingly, he said he was sorry.

She cried in relief and joy. Minutes later, as he was dying, Clark said she felt a tranquil wave of forgiveness wash over her, literally felt it bring her peace, driving away the hatred that had darkened her soul when Harris killed her brother, John Mayeski, and his best friend, Michael Baker.

"It was spiritual," Clark said. "When he leaned over for the last time, everything I went there for just lifted off my shoulders. I felt peace. And I felt for Harris that he was at peace.

"I have justice. . . ." (*Los Angeles Times*, April 22, 1992, A10).

84. *Los Angeles Times*, April 21, 1992, A1. Copyright, 1992, *Los Angeles Times*. Reprinted by permission.

Part I

THE CONCEPT OF
MORAL RESPONSIBILITY

1

Freedom and Resentment

PETER STRAWSON

I

SOME philosophers say they do not know what the thesis of determinism is. Others say, or imply, that they do know what it is. Of these, some—the pessimists perhaps—hold that if the thesis is true, then the concepts of moral obligation and responsibility really have no application, and the practices of punishing and blaming, of expressing moral condemnation and approval, are really unjustified. Others—the optimists perhaps—hold that these concepts and practices in no way lose their *raison d'être* if the thesis of determinism is true. Some hold even that the justification of these concepts and practices requires the truth of the thesis. There is another opinion which is less frequently voiced: the opinion, it might be said, of the genuine moral sceptic. This is that the notions of moral guilt, of blame, of moral responsibility are inherently confused and that we can see this to be so if we consider the consequences either of the truth of determinism or of its falsity. The holders of this opinion agree with the pessimists that these notions lack application if determinism is true, and add simply that they lack it if determinism is false. If I am asked which of these parties I belong to, I must say it is the first of all, the party of those who do not know what the thesis of determinism is. But this does not stop me from having some sympathy with the others, and a wish to reconcile them. Should not ignorance, rationally, inhibit such sympathies? Well, of course, though darkling, one has some inkling—some notion of what sort of thing is being talked about. This lecture is

© The British Academy 1963. Reprinted by permission from *Proceedings of the British Academy* 48 (1962), pp. 1–25.

intended as a move towards reconciliation; so is likely to seem wrong-headed to everyone.

But can there be any possibility of reconciliation between such clearly opposed opinions as those of pessimists and optimists about determinism? Well, there might be a formal withdrawal on one side in return for a substantial concession on the other. Thus, suppose the optimist's position were put like this: (1) the facts as we know them do not show determinism to be false; (2) the facts as we know them supply an adequate basis for the concepts and practices which the pessimist feels to be imperilled by the possibility of determinism's truth. Now it might be that the optimist is right in this, but is apt to give an inadequate account of the facts as we know them, and of how they constitute an adequate basis for the problematic concepts and practices; that the reasons he gives for the adequacy of the basis are themselves inadequate and leave out something vital. It might be that the pessimist is rightly anxious to get this vital thing back and, in the grip of his anxiety, feels he has to go beyond the facts as we know them; feels that the vital thing can be secure only if, beyond the facts as we know them, there is the further fact that determinism is false. Might *he* not be brought to make a formal withdrawal in return for a vital concession?

II

Let me enlarge very briefly on this, by way of preliminary only. Some optimists about determinism point to the efficacy of the practices of punishment, and of moral condemnation and approval, in regulating behaviour in socially desirable ways.[1] In the fact of their efficacy, they suggest, is an adequate basis for these practices; and this fact certainly does not show determinism to be false. To this the pessimists reply, all in a rush, that *just* punishment and *moral* condemnation imply moral guilt and guilt implies moral responsibility and moral responsibility implies freedom and freedom implies the falsity of determinism. And to this the optimists are wont to reply in turn that it is true that these practices require freedom in a sense, and the existence of freedom in this sense is one of the facts as we know them. But what 'freedom' means here is nothing but the absence of certain conditions the presence of which would make moral condemnation or punishment inappropriate. They have in mind conditions like compulsion by another, or innate incapacity, or insanity, or other less extreme forms of psychological disorder, or the existence of circumstances in which the making of any other choice would be morally inadmissible or would be too much to expect of any

1. Cf. P. H. Nowell-Smith, 'Freewill and Moral Responsibility', *Mind*, 1948.

man. To this list they are constrained to add other factors which, without exactly being limitations of freedom, may also make moral condemnation or punishment inappropriate or mitigate their force: as some forms of ignorance, mistake, or accident. And the general reason why moral condemnation or punishment is inappropriate when these factors or conditions are present is held to be that the practices in question will be generally efficacious means of regulating behaviour in desirable ways only in cases where these factors are *not* present. Now the pessimist admits that the facts as we know them include the existence of freedom, the occurrence of cases of free action, in the negative sense which the optimist concedes; and admits, or rather insists, that the existence of freedom in this sense is compatible with the truth of determinism. Then what does the pessimist find missing? When he tries to answer this question, his language is apt to alternate between the very familiar and the very unfamiliar.[2] Thus he may say, familiarly enough, that the man who is the subject of justified punishment, blame or moral condemnation must really *deserve* it; and then add, perhaps, that, in the case at least where he is blamed for a positive act rather than an omission, the condition of his really deserving blame is something that goes beyond the negative freedoms that the optimist concedes. It is, say, a genuinely free identification of the will with the act. And this is the condition that is incompatible with the truth of determinism.

The conventional, but conciliatory, optimist need not give up yet. He may say: Well, people often decide to do things, really intend to do what they do, know just what they're doing in doing it: the reasons they think they have for doing what they do, often really are their reasons and not their rationalizations. These facts, too, are included in the facts as we know them. If this is what you mean by freedom—by the identification of the will with the act—then freedom may again be conceded. But again the concession is compatible with the truth of the determinist thesis. For it would not follow from that thesis that nobody decides to do anything; that nobody ever does anything intentionally; that it is false that people sometimes know perfectly well what they are doing. I tried to define freedom negatively. You want to give it a more positive look. But it comes to the same thing. Nobody denies freedom in this sense, or these senses, and nobody claims that the existence of freedom in these senses shows determinism to be false.

But it is here that the lacuna in the optimistic story can be made to show. For the pessimist may be supposed to ask: But *why* does freedom in this sense justify blame, etc.? You turn towards me first the negative, and then the positive, faces of a freedom which nobody challenges. But the only reason you have given for the practices of moral condemnation

2. As Nowell-Smith pointed out in a later article: 'Determinists and Libertarians', *Mind*, 1954.

and punishment in cases where this freedom is present is the efficacy of these practices in regulating behaviour in socially desirable ways. But this is not a sufficient basis, it is not even the right *sort* of basis, for these practices as we understand them.

Now my optimist, being the sort of man he is, is not likely to invoke an intuition of fittingness at this point. So he really has no more to say. And my pessimist, being the sort of man he is, has only one more thing to say; and that is that the admissibility of these practices, as we understand them, demands another kind of freedom, the kind that in turn demands the falsity of the thesis of determinism. But might we not induce the pessimist to give up saying this by giving the optimist something more to say?

III

I have mentioned punishing and moral condemnation and approval; and it is in connection with these practices or attitudes that the issue between optimists and pessimists—or, if one is a pessimist, the issue between determinists and libertarians—is felt to be particularly important. But it is not of these practices and attitudes that I propose, at first, to speak. These practices or attitudes permit, where they do not imply, a certain detachment from the actions or agents which are their objects. I want to speak, at least at first, of something else: of the non-detached attitudes and reactions of people directly involved in transactions with each other; of the attitudes and reactions of offended parties and beneficiaries: of such things as gratitude, resentment, forgiveness, love, and hurt feelings. Perhaps something like the issue between optimists and pessimists arises in this neighbouring field too; and since this field is less crowded with disputants, the issue might here be easier to settle; and if it is settled here, then it might become easier to settle it in the disputant-crowded field.

What I have to say consists largely of commonplaces. So my language, like that of commonplace generally, will be quite unscientific and imprecise. The central commonplace that I want to insist on is the very great importance that we attach to the attitudes and intentions towards us of other human beings, and the great extent to which our personal feelings and reactions depend upon, or involve, our beliefs about these attitudes and intentions. I can give no simple description of the field of phenomena at the centre of which stands this commonplace truth; for the field is too complex. Much imaginative literature is devoted to exploring its complexities; and we have a large vocabulary for the purpose. There are simplifying styles of handling it in a general way. Thus we may, like La Rochfoucauld, put self-love or self-esteem or vanity at the centre of the picture and point out how it may be caressed by the esteem, or wounded by the indifference or contempt, of others. We might speak, in another jargon, of the need for love, and the loss of security which results from its withdrawal; or, in another, of human self-respect and its connection with the recognition of the individual's dignity. These simplifications are of use to me only if they help to emphasize how much we actually mind, how much it matters to us, whether the actions of other people—and particularly of *some* other people—reflect attitudes towards us of good-will, affection, or esteem on the one hand or contempt, indifference, or malevolence on the other. If someone treads on my hand accidentally, while trying to help me, the pain may be no less acute than if he treads on it in contemptuous disregard of my existence or with a malevolent wish to injure me. But I shall generally feel in the second case a kind and degree of resentment that I shall not feel in the first. If someone's actions help me to some benefit I desire, then I am benefited in any case; but if he intended them so to benefit me because of his general goodwill towards me, I shall reasonably feel a gratitude which I should not feel at all if the benefit was an incidental consequence, unintended or even regretted by him, of some plan of action with a different aim.

These examples are of actions which confer benefits or inflict injuries over and above any conferred or inflicted by the mere manifestation of attitude and intention themselves. We should consider also in how much of our behaviour the benefit or injury resides mainly or entirely in the manifestation of attitude itself. So it is with good manners, and much of what we call kindness, on the one hand; with deliberate rudeness, studied indifference, or insult on the other.

Besides resentment and gratitude, I mentioned just now forgiveness. This is a rather unfashionable subject in moral philosophy at present; but to be forgiven is something we sometimes ask, and forgiving is something we sometimes say we do. To ask to be forgiven is in part to acknowledge that the attitude displayed in our actions was such as might properly be resented and in part to repudiate that attitude for the future (or at least for the immediate future); and to forgive is to accept the repudiation and to forswear the resentment.

We should think of the many different kinds of relationship which we can have with other people—as sharers of a common interest; as members of the same family; as colleagues; as friends; as lovers; as chance parties to an enormous range of transactions and encounters. Then we should think, in each of these connections in turn, and in others, of the kind of importance we attach to the attitudes and intentions towards us of those who stand in these relationships to us, and of the kinds of *reactive* attitudes and feelings to which we ourselves are prone. In general, we demand some degree of goodwill or regard on the part of those who stand in these relationships to us, though the forms we require it to take vary widely in different connections. The range and intensity of our *reactive* attitudes towards goodwill, its absence or its opposite vary no less widely. I have mentioned, specifically, resentment and gratitude; and they are a usefully opposed pair. But, of course, there is a whole continuum of reactive attitude and feeling stretching on both sides of these and—the most comfortable area—in between them.

The object of these commonplaces is to try to keep before our minds something it is easy to forget when we are engaged in philosophy, especially in our cool, contemporary style, viz. what it is actually like to be involved in ordinary inter-personal relationships, ranging from the most intimate to the most casual.

IV

It is one thing to ask about the general causes of these reactive attitudes I have alluded to; it is another to ask about the variations to which they are subject, the particular conditions in which they do or do not seem natural or reasonable or appropriate; and it is a third thing to ask what it would be like, what it *is* like, not to suffer them. I am not much concerned with the first question; but I am with the second; and perhaps even more with the third.

Let us consider, then, occasions for resentment: situations in which one person is offended or injured by the action of another and in which—in the absence of special considerations—the offended person might naturally or normally be expected to feel resentment. Then let us consider what sorts of special considerations might be expected to mod-ify or mollify this feeling or remove it altogether. It needs no saying now how multifarious these considerations are. But, for my purpose, I think they can be roughly divided into two kinds. To the first group belong all those which might give occasion for the employment of such expressions as 'He didn't mean to', 'He hadn't realized', 'He didn't know'; and also all those which might give occasion for the use of the phrase 'He couldn't help it', when this is supported by such phrases as 'He was pushed', 'He had to do it', 'It was the only way', 'They left him no alternative', etc. Obviously these various pleas, and the kinds of situations in which they would be appropriate, differ from each other in striking and important ways. But for my present purpose they have something still more impor-tant in common. None of them invites us to suspend towards the agent, either at the time of his action or in general, our ordinary reactive atti-tudes. They do not invite us to view the *agent* as one in respect of whom these attitudes are in any way inappropriate. They invite us to view the *injury* as one in respect of which a particular one of these attitudes is inappropriate. They do not invite us to see the *agent* as other than a fully responsible agent. They invite us to see the *injury* as one for which he was not fully, or at all, responsible. They do not suggest that the agent is in any way an inappropriate object of that kind of demand for goodwill or regard which is reflected in our ordinary reactive attitudes. They suggest instead that the fact of injury was not in this case incompatible with that demand's being fulfilled, that the fact of injury was quite consistent with the agent's attitude and intentions being just what we demand they should be.[3] The agent was just ignorant of the injury he was causing, or had lost his balance through being pushed or had reluctantly to cause the injury for reasons which acceptably override his reluctance. The offering of such pleas by the agent and their acceptance by the sufferer is something in no way opposed to, or outside the context of, ordinary interpersonal relationships and the manifestation of ordinary reactive attitudes. Since things go wrong and situations are complicated, it is an essential and integral element in the transactions which are the life of these relationships.

The second group of considerations is very different. I shall take them in two subgroups of which the first is far less important than the second. In connection with the first subgroup we may think of such statements as 'He wasn't himself', 'He has been under very great strain recently', 'He was acting under post-hypnotic suggestion'; in connection with the second, we may think of 'He's only a child', 'He's a hopeless schizophrenic', 'His mind has been systematically perverted', 'That's purely compulsive behaviour on his part'. Such pleas as these do, as pleas of my first general group do not, invite us to suspend our ordinary reactive attitudes toward the agent, either at the time of his action or all the time. They do not invite us to see the agent's action in a way consistent with the full retention of ordinary interpersonal attitudes and merely inconsistent with one particular attitude. They invite us to view the agent himself in a different light from the light in which we should normally view one who has acted as he has acted. I shall not linger over the first subgroup of cases. Though they perhaps raise, in the short term, questions akin to those raised, in the long term, by the second subgroup, we may dismiss them without considering those questions by taking that admirably suggestive phrase, 'He wasn't himself', with the seriousness that—for all its being logically comic—it deserves. We shall not feel resentment against the man he is for the action done by the man he is not; or at least we shall feel less. We normally have to deal with him under normal stresses; so we shall not feel towards him, when he acts as he does under abnormal stresses, as we should have felt towards him had he acted as he did under normal stresses.

3. Perhaps not in every case *just* what we demand they should be, but in any case *not* just what we demand they should not be. For my present purpose these differences do not matter.

The second and more important subgroup of cases allows that the circumstances were normal, but presents the agent as psychologically abnormal—or as morally undeveloped. The agent was himself; but he is warped or deranged, neurotic or just a child. When we see someone in such a light as this, all our reactive attitudes tend to be profoundly modified. I must deal here in crude dichotomies and ignore the ever-interesting and ever-illuminating varieties of case. What I want to contrast is the attitude (or range of attitudes) of involvement or participation in a human relationship, on the one hand, and what might be called the objective attitude (or range of attitudes) to another human being, on the other. Even in the same situation, I must add, they are not altogether *exclusive* of each other; but they are, profoundly, *opposed* to each other. To adopt the objective attitude to another human being is to see him, perhaps, as an object of social policy; as a subject for what, in a wide range of sense, might be called treatment; as something certainly to be taken account, perhaps precautionary account, of; to be managed or handled or cured or trained; perhaps simply to be avoided, though *this* gerundive is not peculiar to cases of objectivity of attitude. The objective attitude may be emotionally toned in many ways, but not in all ways: it may include repulsion or fear, it may include pity or even love, though not all kinds of love. But it cannot include the range of reactive feelings and attitudes which belong to involvement or participation with others in inter-personal human relationships; it cannot include resentment, gratitude, forgiveness, anger, or the sort of love which two adults can sometimes be said to feel reciprocally, for each other. If your attitude towards someone is wholly objective, then though you may fight him, you cannot quarrel with him, and though you may talk to him, even negotiate with him, you cannot reason with him. You can at most pretend to quarrel, or to reason, with him.

Seeing someone, then, as warped or deranged or compulsive in behaviour or peculiarly unfortunate in his formative circumstances—seeing someone so tends, at least to some extent, to set him apart from normal participant reactive attitudes on the part of one who sees him, tends to promote, at least in the civilized, objective attitudes. But there is something curious to add to this. The objective attitude is not only something we naturally tend to fall into in cases like these, where participant attitudes are partially or wholly inhibited by abnormalities or by immaturity. It is also something which is available as a resource in other cases too. We look with an objective eye on the compulsive behaviour of the neurotic or the tiresome behaviour of a very young child, thinking in terms of treatment or training. But we *can* sometimes look with something like the same eye on the behaviour of the normal and the mature. We *have* this resource and can sometimes use it: as a refuge, say, from the strains of involvement; or as an aid to policy; or simply out of intellectual curiosity. Being human, we cannot, in the normal case, do this for long, or altogether. If the strains of involvement, say, continue to be too great, then we have to do something else—like severing a relationship. But what is above all interesting is the tension there is, in us, between the participant attitude and the objective attitude. One is tempted to say: between our humanity and our intelligence. But to say this would be to distort both notions.

What I have called the participant reactive attitudes are essentially natural human reactions to the good or ill will or indifference of others towards us, as displayed in *their* attitudes and actions. The question we have to ask is: What effect would, or should, the acceptance of the truth of a general thesis of determinism have upon these reactive attitudes? More specifically, would, or should, the acceptance of the truth of the thesis lead to the decay or the repudiation of all such attitudes? Would, or should, it mean the end of gratitude, resentment, and forgiveness; of all reciprocated adult loves; of all the essentially *personal* antagonisms?

But how can I answer, or even pose, this question without knowing *exactly* what the thesis of determinism is? Well, there is one thing we do know: that if there is a coherent thesis of determinism, then there must be a sense of 'determined' such that, if that thesis is true, then all behaviour whatever is determined in that sense. Remembering this, we can consider at least what possibilities lie formally open; and then perhaps we shall see that the question can be answered *without* knowing exactly what the thesis of determinism is. We can consider what possibilities lie open because we have already before us an account of the ways in which particular reactive attitudes, or reactive attitudes in general, may be, and, sometimes, we judge, should be, inhibited. Thus I considered earlier a group of considerations which tend to inhibit, and, we judge, should inhibit, resentment, in particular cases of an agent causing an injury, without inhibiting reactive attitudes in general towards that agent. Obviously this group of considerations cannot strictly bear upon our question; for that question concerns reactive attitudes in general. But resentment has a particular interest; so it is worth adding that it has never been claimed as a consequence of the truth of determinism that one or another of *these* considerations was operative in every case of an injury being caused by an agent; that it would follow from the truth of determinism that anyone who caused an injury *either* was quite simply ignorant of causing it *or* had acceptably overriding reasons for acquiescing reluctantly in causing it *or . . .*, etc. The prevalence of this happy state of affairs would not be a consequence of the reign of universal determinism, but of the reign of universal goodwill. We cannot, then, find here the possibility of an affirmative answer to our question, even for the particular case of resentment.

Next, I remarked that the participant attitude, and the personal reactive attitudes in general, tend to give place, and, it is judged by the civilized, should give place, to objective attitudes, just in so far as the agent is seen as excluded from ordinary adult human relationships by deep-rooted psychological abnormality—or simply by being a child. But it cannot be a consequence of any thesis which is not itself self-contradictory that abnormality is the universal condition.

Now this dismissal might seem altogether too facile; and so, in a sense, it is. But whatever is too quickly dismissed in this dismissal is allowed for in the only possible form of affirmative answer that remains. We can sometimes, and in part, I have remarked, look on the normal (those we rate as 'normal') in the objective way in which we have learned to look on certain classified cases of abnormality. And our question reduces to this: could, or should the acceptance of the determinist thesis lead us always to look on everyone exclusively in this way? For this is the only condition worth considering under which the acceptance of determinism could lead to the decay or repudiation of participant reactive attitudes.

It does not seem to be self-contradictory to suppose that this might happen. So I suppose we must say that it is not absolutely inconceivable that it should happen. But I am strongly inclined to think that it is, for us as we are, practically inconceivable. The human commitment to participation in ordinary interpersonal relationships is, I think, too thoroughgoing and deeply rooted for us to take seriously the thought that a general theoretical conviction might so change our world that, in it, there were no longer any such things as interpersonal relationships as we normally understand them; and being involved in inter-personal relationships as we normally understand them precisely is being exposed to the range of reactive attitudes and feelings that is in question.

This, then, is a part of the reply to our question. A sustained objectivity of inter-personal attitude, and the human isolation which that would entail, does not seem to be something of which human beings would be capable, even if some general truth were a theoretical ground for it. But this is not all. There is a further point, implicit in the foregoing, which must be made explicit. Exceptionally, I have said, we can have direct dealings with human beings without any degree of personal involvement, treating them simply as creatures to be handled in our own interests, or our side's, or society's—or even theirs. In the extreme case of the mentally deranged, it is easy to see the connection between the possibility of a wholly objective attitude and the impossibility of what we understand by ordinary inter-personal relationships. Given this latter impossibility, no other civilized attitude is available than that of viewing the deranged person simply as something to be understood and controlled in the most desirable fashion. To view him as outside the reach of personal relationships is already, for the civilized, to view him in this way. For reasons of policy or self-protection we may have occasion, perhaps temporary, to adopt a fundamentally similar attitude to a 'normal' human being; to concentrate, that is, on understanding 'how he works', with a view to determining our policy accordingly or to finding in that very understanding a relief from the strains of involvement. Now it is certainly true that in the case of the abnormal, though not in the case of the normal, our adoption of the objective attitude is a consequence of our viewing the agent as *incapacitated* in some or all respects for ordinary inter-personal relationships. He is thus incapacitated, perhaps, by the fact that his picture of reality is pure fantasy, that he does not, in a sense, live in the real world at all; or by the fact that his behaviour is, in part, an unrealistic acting out of unconscious purposes; or by the fact that he is an idiot, or a moral idiot. But there is something else which, *because* this is true, is equally certainly *not* true. And that is that there is a sense of 'determined' such that (1) if determinism is true, all behaviour is determined in this sense, and (2) determinism might be true, i.e., it is not inconsistent with the facts as we know them to suppose that all behaviour might be determined in this sense, and (3) our adoption of the objective attitude towards the abnormal is the result of prior embracing of the belief that the behaviour, or the relevant stretch of behaviour, of the human being in question *is* determined in this sense. Neither in the case of the normal, then, nor in the case of the abnormal is it true that, when we adopt an objective attitude, we do so *because* we hold such a belief. So my answer has two parts. The first is that we cannot, as we are, seriously envisage ourselves adopting a thoroughgoing objectivity of attitude to others as a result of theoretical conviction of the truth of determinism; and the second is that when we do in fact adopt such an attitude in a particular case, our doing so is not the consequence of a theoretical conviction which might be expressed as 'Determinism in this case', but is a consequence of our abandoning, for different reasons in different cases, the ordinary inter-personal attitudes.

It might be said that all this leaves the real question unanswered, and that we cannot hope to answer it without knowing exactly what the thesis of determinism is. For the real question is not a question about what we actually do, or why we do it. It is not even a question about what we would *in fact* do if a certain theoretical conviction gained general acceptance. It is a question about what it would be *rational* to do if determinism were true, a question about the rational justification of ordinary inter-personal attitudes in general. To this I shall reply, first, that such a question could seem real only to one who had utterly failed to grasp the purport of the preceding answer, the fact of our natural human commitment to ordinary inter-personal attitudes. This commitment is part of the general framework of human life, not something that can come up for review as particular cases can come up for review within this general framework. And I shall reply, second, that if we could imagine what we cannot have, viz. a choice in this matter, then we could choose rationally only in the light of an assessment of the gains and losses to human life, its enrichment or impoverishment; and the truth or falsity of a general thesis of determinism would not bear on the rationality of *this* choice.[4]

V

The point of this discussion of the reactive attitudes in their relation—or lack of it—to the thesis of determinism was to bring us, if possible, nearer to a position of compromise in a more usual area of debate. We are not now to discuss reactive attitudes which are essentially those of offended parties or beneficiaries. We are to discuss reactive attitudes which are essentially not those, or only incidentally are those, of offended parties or beneficiaries, but are nevertheless, I shall claim, kindred attitudes to those I have discussed. I put resentment in the centre of the previous discussion. I shall put moral indignation—or, more weakly, moral disapprobation—in the centre of this one.

The reactive attitudes I have so far discussed are essentially reactions to the quality of others' wills towards us, as manifested in their behaviour: to their good or ill will or indifference or lack of concern. Thus resentment, or what I have called resentment, is a reaction to injury or indifference. The reactive attitudes I have now to discuss might be described as the sympathetic or vicarious or impersonal or disinterested or generalized analogues of the reactive attitudes I have already discussed. They are reactions to the qualities of others' wills, not towards ourselves, but towards others. Because of this impersonal or vicarious character, we give them different names. Thus one who experiences the vicarious analogue of resentment is said to be indignant or disapproving, or morally indignant or disapproving. What we have here is, as it were, resentment on behalf of another, where one's own interest and dignity are not involved; and it is this impersonal or vicarious character of the attitude, added to its others, which entitle it to the qualification 'moral'. Both my description of, and my name for, these attitudes are, in one important respect, a little misleading. It is not that these attitudes are essentially vicarious—one can feel indignation on one's own account—but that they are essentially capable of being vicarious. But I shall retain the

4. The question, then, of the connection between rationality and the adoption of the objective attitude to others is misposed when it is made to seem dependent on the issue of determinism. But there is another question which should be raised, if only to distinguish it from the misposed question. Quite apart from the issue of determinism might it not be said that we should be nearer to being purely rational creatures in proportion as our relation to others was in fact dominated by the objective attitude? I think this might be said; only it would have to be added, once more, that if such a choice were possible, it would not necessarily be rational to choose to be more purely rational than we are.

name for the sake of is suggestiveness; and I hope that what is misleading about it will be corrected in what follows.

The personal reactive attitudes rest on, and reflect, an expectation of, and demand for, the manifestation of a certain degree of goodwill or regard on the part of other human beings towards ourselves; or at least on the expectation of, and demand for, an absence of the manifestation of active ill will or indifferent disregard. (What will, in particular cases, *count* as manifestations of good or ill will or disregard will vary in accordance with the particular relationship in which we stand to another human being.) The generalized or vicarious analogues of the personal reactive attitudes rest on, and reflect, exactly the same expectation or demand in a generalized form; they rest on, or reflect, that is, the demand for the manifestation of a reasonable degree of goodwill or regard, on the part of others, not simply towards oneself, but towards all those on whose behalf moral indignation may be felt, i.e. as we now think, towards all men. The generalized and nongeneralized forms of demand, and the vicarious and personal reactive attitudes which rest upon, and reflect, them are connected not merely logically. They are connected humanly; and not merely with each other. They are connected also with yet another set of attitudes which I must mention now in order to complete the picture. I have considered from two points of view the demands we make on others and our reactions to their possibly injurious actions. These were the points of view of one whose interest was directly involved (who suffers, say, the injury) and of others whose interest was not directly involved (who do not themselves suffer the injury). Thus I have spoken of personal reactive attitudes in the first connection and of their vicarious analogues in the second. But the picture is not complete unless we consider also the correlates of these attitudes on the part of those on whom the demands are made, on the part of the agents. Just as there are personal and vicarious reactive attitudes associated with demands on others for oneself and demands on others for others, so there are self-reactive attitudes associated with demands on oneself for others. And here we have to mention such phenomena as feeling bound or obliged (the 'sense of obligation'); feeling compunction; feeling guilty or remorseful or at least responsible; and the more complicated phenomenon of shame.

All these three types of attitude are humanly connected. One who manifested the personal reactive attitudes in a high degree but showed no inclination at all to their vicarious analogues would appear as an abnormal case of moral egocentricity, as a kind of moral solipsist. Let him be supposed fully to acknowledge the claims to regard that others had on him, to be susceptible of the whole range of self-reactive attitudes. He would then see himself as unique both as one (*the* one) who had a general claim on human regard and as one (*the* one) on whom human beings in general had such a claim. This would be a kind of moral solipsism. But it is barely more than a conceptual possibility; if it is that. In general, though within varying limits, we demand of others for others, as well as of ourselves for others, something of the regard which we demand of others for ourselves. Can we imagine, besides that of the moral solipsist, any other case of one or two of these three types of attitude being fully developed, but quite unaccompanied by any trace, however slight, of the remaining two or one? If we can, then we imagine something far below or far above the level of our common humanity—a moral idiot or a saint. For all these types of attitude alike have common roots in our human nature and our membership of human communities.

Now, as of the personal reactive attitudes, so of their vicarious analogues, we must ask in what ways, and by what considerations, they tend to be inhibited. Both types of attitude involve, or express, a certain sort of demand for inter-personal regard. The fact of injury constitutes a prima-facie appearance of this demand's being flouted or unfulfilled. We saw, in the case of resentment, how one class of considerations may show this appearance to be mere appearance, and hence inhibit resentment, *without* inhibiting, or displacing, the sort of demand of which resentment can be an expression, without in any way tending to make us suspend our ordinary inter-personal attitudes to the agent. Considerations of this class operate in just the same way, for just the same reasons, in connection with moral disapprobation or indignation; they inhibit indignation without in any way inhibiting the sort of demand on the agent of which indignation can be an expression, the range of attitudes towards him to which it belongs. But in this connection we may express the facts with a new emphasis. We may say, stressing the moral, the generalized aspect of the demand, considerations of this group have no tendency to make us see the agent as other than a morally responsible agent; they simply make us see the injury as one for which he was not morally responsible. The offering and acceptance of such exculpatory pleas as are here in question in no way detract in our eyes from the agent's status as a term of moral relationships. On the contrary, since things go wrong and situations are complicated, it is an essential part of the life of such relationships.

But suppose we see the agent in a different light: as one whose picture of the world is an insane delusion; or as one whose behaviour, or a part of whose behaviour, is unintelligible to us, perhaps even to him, in terms of conscious purposes, and intelligible only in terms of unconscious purposes; or even, perhaps, as one wholly impervious to the self-reactive attitudes I spoke of, wholly lacking, as we say, in moral sense. Seeing an agent in such a light as this tends, I said, to inhibit resentment in a wholly different way. It tends to inhibit resentment because it tends to inhibit ordinary inter-personal attitudes in general, and the kind of demand and expectation which those attitudes involve; and tends to promote instead the purely objective view of the agent as one posing problems simply of intellectual understanding, management, treatment, and control. Again the parallel holds for those generalized or moral attitudes towards the agent which we are now concerned with. The same abnormal light which shows the agent to us as one in respect of whom the personal attitudes, the personal demand, are to be suspended, shows him to us also as one in respect of whom the impersonal attitudes, the generalized demand, are to be suspended. Only, abstracting now from direct personal interest, we may express the facts with a new emphasis. We may say: to the extent to which the agent is seen in this light, he is not seen as one on whom demands and expectations lie in that particular way in which we think of them as lying when we speak of moral obligation; he is not, to that extent, seen as a morally responsible agent, as a term of moral relationships, as a member of the moral community.

I remarked also that the suspension of ordinary inter-personal attitudes and the cultivation of a purely objective view is sometimes possible even when we have no such reasons for it as I have just mentioned. Is this possible also in the case of the moral reactive attitudes? I think so; and perhaps it is easier. But the motives for a total suspension of moral reactive attitudes are fewer, and perhaps weaker; fewer, because only where there is antecedent personal involvement can there be the motive of seeking refuge from the strains of such involvement; perhaps weaker, because the tension between objectivity of view and the moral reactive attitudes is perhaps less than the tension between objectivity of view and the personal reactive attitudes, so that we can in the case of the moral reactive attitudes more easily secure the speculative or political gains of objectivity of view by a kind of setting on one side, rather than a total suspension, of those attitudes.

These last remarks are uncertain; but also, for the present purpose, unimportant. What concerns us now is to inquire, as previously in connection with the personal reactive attitudes, what relevance any general thesis of determinism might have to their vicarious analogues. The answers once more are parallel; though I shall take them in a slightly different order. First, we must note, as before, that when the suspension of such an attitude or such attitudes occurs in a particular case, it is *never* the consequence of the belief that the piece of behaviour in question was determined in a sense such that all behaviour *might be,* and, if determinism is true, all behaviour *is,* determined in that sense. For it is not a consequence of any general thesis of determinism which might be true that nobody knows what he's doing or that everybody's behaviour is unintelligible in terms of conscious purposes or that everybody lives in a world of delusion or that nobody has a moral sense, i.e. is susceptible of self-reactive attitudes, etc. In fact no such sense of 'determined' as would be required for a general thesis of determinism is ever relevant to our actual suspensions of moral reactive attitudes. Second, suppose it granted, as I have already argued, that we cannot take seriously the thought that theoretical conviction of such a general thesis would lead to the total decay of the personal reactive attitudes. Can we then take seriously the thought that such a conviction—a conviction, after all, that many have held or said they held—would nevertheless lead to the total decay or repudiation of the vicarious analogues of these attitudes? I think that the change in our social world which would leave us exposed to the personal reactive attitudes but not to all their vicarious analogues, the generalization of abnormal egocentricity which this would entail, is perhaps even harder for us to envisage as a real possibility than the decay of both kinds of attitude together. Though there are some necessary and some contingent differences between the ways and cases in which these two kinds of attitudes operate or are inhibited in their operation, yet, as general human capacities or pronenesses, they stand or lapse together. Finally, to the further question whether it would not be *rational,* given a general theoretical conviction of the truth of determinism, so to change our world that in it all these attitudes were wholly suspended, I must answer, as before, that one who presses this question has wholly failed to grasp the import of the preceding answer, the nature of the human commitment that is here involved: it is *useless* to ask whether it would not be rational for us to do what it is not in our nature to (be able to) do. To this I must add, as before, that if there were, say, for a moment open to us the possibility of such a godlike choice, the rationality of making or refusing it would be determined by quite other considerations than the truth or falsity of the general theoretical doctrine in question. The latter would be simply irrelevant; and this becomes ironically clear when we remember that for those convinced that the truth of determinism nevertheless really would make the one choice rational, there has always been the insuperable difficulty of explaining in intelligible terms how its falsity would make the opposite choice rational.

I am aware that in presenting the arguments as I have done, neglecting the ever-interesting varieties of case, I have presented nothing more than a schema, using sometimes a crude opposition of phrase where we have a great intricacy of phenomena. In particular the simple opposition of objective attitudes on the one hand and the various contrasted attitudes which I have opposed to them must seem as grossly crude as it is central. Let me pause to mitigate this crudity a little, and also to strengthen one of my central contentions, by mentioning some things which straddle these contrasted kinds of attitude. Thus parents and others concerned with the care and upbringing of young children cannot have to their charges either kind of attitude in a pure or unqualified form. They are dealing with creatures who are potentially and increasingly capable both of holding, and being objects of, the full range of human and moral attitudes, but are not yet truly capable of either. The treatment of such creatures must therefore represent a kind of compromise, constantly shifting in one direction, between objectivity of attitude and developed human attitudes. Rehearsals insensibly modulate towards true performances. The punishment of a child is both like and unlike the punishment of an adult. Suppose we try to relate this progressive emergence of the child as a responsible being, as an object of non-objective attitudes, to that sense of 'determined' in which, if determinism is a possibly true thesis, all behaviour *may* be determined, and in which, if it is a true thesis, all behaviour *is* determined. What bearing *could* such a sense of 'determined' have upon the progressive modification of attitudes towards the child? Would it not be grotesque to think of the development of the child as a progressive or patchy emergence from an area in which its behaviour is in this sense determined into an area in which it isn't? Whatever sense of 'determined' is required for stating the thesis of determinism, it can scarcely be such as to allow of compromise, borderline-style answers to the question, 'Is this bit of behaviour determined or isn't it?' But in this matter of young children, it is essentially a borderline, penumbral area that we move in. Again, consider—a very different matter—the strain in the attitude of a psychoanalyst to his patient. *His* objectivity of attitude, *his* suspension of ordinary moral reactive attitudes, is profoundly modified by the fact that the aim of the enterprise is to make such suspension unnecessary or less necessary. Here we may and do naturally speak of restoring the agent's freedom. But here the restoring of freedom means bringing it about that the agent's behaviour shall be intelligible in terms of conscious purposes rather than in terms only of unconscious purposes. *This* is the object of the enterprise; and it is in so far as *this* object is attained that the suspension, or half-suspension, of ordinary moral attitudes is deemed no longer necessary or appropriate. And in this we see once again the *irrelevance* of that concept of 'being determined' which must be the central concept of determinism. For we cannot both agree that this object is attainable and that its attainment has this consequence and yet hold (1) that neurotic behaviour is determined in a sense in which, it may be, all behaviour is determined, and (2) that it is because neurotic behaviour is determined in this sense that objective attitudes are deemed appropriate to neurotic behaviour. Not, at least, without accusing ourselves of incoherence in our attitude to psychoanalytic treatment.

VI

And now we can try to fill in the lacuna which the pessimist finds in the optimist's account of the concept of moral responsibility, and of the bases of moral condemnation and punishment; and to fill it in from the facts as we know them. For, as I have already remarked, when the pessimist himself seeks to fill it in, he rushes beyond the facts as we know them and proclaims that it cannot be filled in at all unless determinism is false.

Yet a partial sense of the facts as we know them is certainly present to the pessimist's mind. When his opponent, the optimist, undertakes to show that the truth of determinism would not shake the foundations of the concept of moral responsibility and of the practices of moral condemnation and punishment, he typically refers, in a more or less elaborated way, to the efficacy of these practices in regulating behaviour in socially desirable ways. These practices are represented solely as instruments of policy, as methods of individual treatment and social control. The pessimist recoils from this picture; and in his recoil there is, typically, an element of emotional shock. He is apt to say, among much else, that the humanity of the offender himself is offended by *this* picture of his condemnation and punishment.

The reasons for this recoil—the explanation of the sense of an emotional, as well as a conceptual, shock—we have already before us. The picture painted by the optimists is painted in a style appropriate to a situation envisaged as wholly dominated by objectivity of attitude. The only operative notions invoked in this picture are such as those of policy, treatment, control. But a thoroughgoing objectivity of attitude, excluding as it does the moral reactive attitudes, excludes at the same time essential elements in the concepts of *moral* condemnation and *moral* responsibility. This is the reason for the conceptual shock. The deeper emotional shock is a reaction, not simply to an inadequate conceptual analysis, but to the suggestion of a change in our world. I have remarked that it is possible to cultivate an exclusive objectivity of attitude in some cases, and for some reasons, where the object of the attitude is not set aside from developed inter-personal and moral attitudes by immaturity or abnormality. And the suggestion which seems to be contained in the optimist's account is that such an attitude should be universally adopted to all offenders. This is shocking enough in the pessimist's eyes. But, sharpened by shock, his eyes see further. It would be hard to make *this* division in our natures. If to all offenders, then to all mankind. Moreover, to whom could this recommendation be, in any real sense, addressed? Only to the powerful, the authorities. So abysses seem to open.[5]

But we will confine our attention to the case of the offenders. The concepts we are concerned with are those of responsibility and guilt, qualified as 'moral', on the one hand—together with that of membership of a moral community; of demand, indignation, disapprobation and condemnation, qualified as 'moral', on the other hand—together with that of punishment. Indignation, disapprobation, like resentment,

5. See J. D. Mabbott's 'Freewill and Punishment', in *Contemporary British Philosophy*, 3rd ser. (London: Allen & Unwin, 1956).

tend to inhibit or at least to limit our goodwill towards the object of these attitudes, tend to promote an at least partial and temporary withdrawal of goodwill; they do so in proportion as they are strong; and their strength is in general proportioned to what is felt to be the magnitude of the injury and to the degree to which the agent's will is identified with, or indifferent to, it. (These, of course, are not contingent connections.) But these attitudes of disapprobation and indignation are precisely the correlates of the moral demand in the case where the demand is felt to be disregarded. The making of the demand *is* the proneness to such attitudes. The holding of them does not, as the holding of objective attitudes does, involve as a part of itself viewing their object other than as a member of the moral community. The partial withdrawal of goodwill which *these* attitudes entail, the modification *they* entail of the general demand that another should, if possible, be spared suffering, is, rather, the consequence of *continuing* to view him as a member of the moral community; only as one who has offended against its demands. So the preparedness to acquiesce in that infliction of suffering on the offender which is an essential part of punishment is all of a piece with this whole range of attitudes of which I have been speaking. It is not only moral reactive attitudes towards the offender which are in question here. We must mention also the self-reactive attitudes of offenders themselves. Just as the other-reactive attitudes are associated with a readiness to acquiesce in the infliction of suffering on an offender, within the 'institution' of punishment, so the self-reactive attitudes are associated with a readiness on the part of the offender to acquiesce in such infliction *without* developing the reactions (e.g. of resentment) which he would normally develop to the infliction of injury upon him; i.e. with a readiness, as we say, to accept punishment[6] as 'his due' or as 'just'.

I am not in the least suggesting that these readinesses to acquiesce, either on the part of the offender himself or on the part of others, are always or commonly accompanied or preceded by indignant boilings or remorseful pangs; only that we have here a continuum of attitudes and feelings to which these readinesses to acquiesce themselves belong. Nor am I in the least suggesting that it belongs to this continuum of attitudes that we should be ready to acquiesce in the infliction of injury on offenders in a fashion which we saw to be quite indiscriminate or in accordance with procedures which we know to be wholly useless. On the contrary, savage or civilized, we have some belief in the utility of practices of condemnation and punishment. But the social utility of these practices, on which the optimist lays such exclusive stress, is not what is now in question. What is in question is the pessimist's justified sense that to speak in terms of social utility alone is to leave out something vital in our conception of these practices. The vital thing can be restored by

6. Of course not *any* punishment for *anything* deemed an offence.

attending to that complicated web of attitudes and feelings which form an essential part of the moral life as we know it, and which are quite opposed to objectivity of attitude. Only by attending to this range of attitudes can we recover from the facts as we know them a sense of what we mean, i.e. of *all* we mean, when, speaking the language of morals, we speak of desert, responsibility, guilt, condemnation, and justice. But we *do* recover it from the facts as we know them. We do not have to go beyond them. Because the optimist neglects or misconstrues these attitudes, the pessimist rightly claims to find a lacuna in his account. We can fill the lacuna for him. But in return we must demand of the pessimist a surrender of his metaphysics.

Optimist and pessimist misconstrue the facts in very different styles. But in a profound sense there is something in common to their misunderstandings. Both seek, in different ways, to overintellectualize the facts. Inside the general structure or web of human attitudes and feelings of which I have been speaking, there is endless room for modification, redirection, criticism, and justification. But questions of justification are internal to the structure or relate to modifications internal to it. The existence of the general framework of attitudes itself is something we are given with the fact of human society. As a whole, it neither calls for, nor permits, an external 'rational' justification. Pessimist and optimist alike show themselves, in different ways, unable to accept this.[7] The optimist's style of overintellectualizing the facts is that of a characteristically incomplete empiricism, a one-eyed utilitarianism. He seeks to find an adequate basis for certain social practices in calculated consequences, and loses sight (perhaps wishes to lose sight) of the human attitudes of which these practices are, in part, the expression. The pessimist does not lose sight of these attitudes, but is unable to accept the fact that it is just these attitudes themselves which fill the gap in the optimist's account. Because of this, he thinks the gap can be filled only if some general metaphysical proposition is repeatedly verified, verified in all cases where it is appropriate to attribute moral responsibility. This proposition he finds it as difficult to state coherently and with intelligible relevance as its determinist contradictory. Even when a formula has been found ('contracausal freedom' or something of the kind) there still seems to remain a gap between its applicability in particular cases and its supposed moral consequences. Sometimes he plugs this gap with an intuition of fittingness—a pitiful intellectualist trinket for a philosopher to wear as a charm against the recognition of his own humanity.

---

7. Compare the question of the justification of induction. The human commitment to inductive belief-formation is original, natural, non-rational (not *irrational*), in no way something we choose or could give up. Yet rational criticism and reflection can refine standards and their application, supply 'rules for judging of cause and effect'. Ever since the facts were made clear by Hume, people have been resisting acceptance of them.

Even the moral sceptic is not immune from his own form of the wish to overintellectualize such notions as those of moral responsibility, guilt, and blame. He sees that the optimist's account is inadequate and the pessimist's libertarian alternative inane; and finds no resource except to declare that the notions in question are inherently confused, that 'blame is metaphysical'. But the metaphysics was in the eye of the metaphysician. It is a pity that talk of the moral sentiments has fallen out of favour. The phrase would be quite a good name for that network of human attitudes in acknowledging the character and place of which we find, I suggest, the only possibility of reconciling these disputants to each other and the facts.

There are, at present, factors which add, in a slightly paradoxical way, to the difficulty of making this acknowledgment. These human attitudes themselves, in their development and in the variety of their manifestations, have to an increasing extent become objects of study in the social and psychological sciences; and this growth of human self-consciousness, which we might expect to reduce the difficulty of acceptance, in fact increases it in several ways. One factor of comparatively minor importance is an increased historical and anthropological awareness of the great variety of forms which these human attitudes may take at different times and in different cultures. This makes one rightly chary of claiming as essential features of the concept of morality in general, forms of these attitudes which may have a local and temporary prominence. No doubt to some extent my own descriptions of human attitudes have reflected local and temporary features of our own culture. But an awareness of variety of forms should not prevent us from acknowledging also that in the absence of *any* forms of these attitudes it is doubtful whether we should have anything that *we* could find intelligible as a system of human relationships, as human society. A quite different factor of greater importance is that psychological studies have made us rightly mistrustful of many particular manifestations of the attitudes I have spoken of. They are a prime realm of self-deception, of the ambiguous and the shady, of guilt-transference, unconscious sadism and the rest. But it is an exaggerated horror, itself suspect, which would make us unable to acknowledge the facts because of the seamy side of the facts. Finally, perhaps the most important factor of all is the prestige of these theoretical studies themselves. That prestige is great, and is apt to make us forget that in philosophy, though it also is a theoretical study, we have to take account of the facts in *all* their bearings; we are not to suppose that we are required, or permitted, as philosophers, to regard ourselves, as human beings, as detached from the attitudes which, as scientists, we study with detachment. This is in no way to deny the possibility and desirability of redirection and modification of our human attitudes in the light of these studies. But we may reasonably think it unlikely that our progressively greater understanding of certain aspects of ourselves will lead to the total disappearance of those aspects. Perhaps it is not inconceivable that it should; and perhaps, then, the dreams of some philosophers will be realized.

If we sufficiently, that is *radically*, modify the view of the optimist, his view is the right one. It is far from wrong to emphasize the efficacy of all those practices which express or manifest our moral attitudes, in regulating behaviour in ways considered desirable; or to add that when certain of our beliefs about the efficacy of some of these practices turns out to be false, then we may have good reason for dropping or modifying those practices. What *is* wrong is to forget that these practices, and their reception, the reactions to them, really *are* expressions of our moral attitudes and not merely devices we calculatingly employ for regulative purposes. Our practices do not merely exploit our natures, they express them. Indeed the very understanding of the kind of efficacy these expressions of our attitudes have turns on our remembering this. When we do remember this, and modify the optimist's position accordingly, we simultaneously correct its conceptual deficiencies and ward off the dangers it seems to entail, without recourse to the obscure and panicky metaphysics of libertarianism.

2

On "Freedom and Resentment"

GALEN STRAWSON

I. Feelings, Attitudes, Practices, Concepts, and Beliefs

I wish to consider P. F. Strawson's commitment theory of freedom, which stresses our commitment to certain *attitudes* and *practices* which appear to presuppose belief in true responsibility, rather than directly stressing our commitment to belief in true responsibility.[1] I will first suggest that it cannot by appealing to the notion of commitment show the worries of incompatibilist or 'hard' determinists to be wholly misconceived or groundless. Then I will suggest that it may mislocate the true centre of our commitment in our interpersonal rather than in our self-regarding attitudes.

In so far as it holds the truth or falsity of determinism to be irrelevant to the question of whether or not we can correctly be said to be free, Strawson's view counts as a variety of compatibilism, and one may therefore avail oneself of the assumption that determinism is true in putting it to the test. There is, however, a determinism-independent argument for the impossibility of self-determination, or for 'non-self-determinability', which poses exactly the same problem for freedom as determinism does.[2] And so although I will speak in a traditional fashion of determinism and the problems that it poses, I could equally well (if more laboriously) speak of the problems posed for freedom by the

© Galen Strawson 1986. Reprinted from *Freedom and Belief* by Galen Strawson (1986) by permission of Oxford University Press.

1. 'Freedom and Resentment', this volume.
2. Cf. my *Freedom and Belief* (Oxford: Oxford University Press, 1986), ch. 2, esp. 2.1.

impossibility of self-determination or by non-self-determinability. The basic question is this: can a commitment theory of freedom really avoid the problems that seem to be posed by determinism (or non-self-determinability)?

Consider a man who becomes a determinist. He is often pictured as being faced first and foremost with the problem of what he is to make of other people, given his new belief. But of course his judgement of determinedness extends also, and far more immediately, to himself. He cannot see himself as an ordinary (and ordinarily responsible) man in an otherwise determined world. Or if he does—as he may, if the self-regarding aspects of commitment to belief in freedom are indeed less easy to renounce than the interpersonal ones—he should not. His first problem is himself.

But still, what should he make of other people? It seems that most people would find abandonment of the ordinary, strong notion of responsibility intolerable, not to say practically speaking impossible, from a social point of view. It would undermine the foundations of their conception of what human life is. For it is not as if one can excise one's inclination to praise and blame people while leaving all one's other attitudes to them untouched. If determinism is called upon to justify any such excision, one whole central range of what Strawson calls 'personal-reactive' or 'reactive' feelings and attitudes is thereby put at risk: attitudes and feelings, both moral and non-moral, to and about oneself and others; feelings, more or less considered and complicated, of condemnation and approbation, of gratitude and resentment, of despite and scorn; certain feelings of admiration for people's achievements and creations; certain aspects of feelings of hatred, anger, love, affection, and so on; feelings of guilt and remorse, pride and shame with regard to oneself and one's doings.

Such feelings and attitudes, and associated practices like praising and blaming, are all similarly threatened to the extent that their propriety depends in some way on our supposing that people are truly responsible for what they do. The connection of dependence seems very clear in the majority of cases even if, irrational and anthropomorphistic, some of our feelings for and attitudes to non-human and even inanimate entities go by the same name. It is also clear that we are deeply committed to the belief that people can be truly responsible for what they do. Just as it is clear that determinism (or non-self-determinability) raises a major prima-facie doubt about the validity of this belief.

Can appeal to the undeniable fact of our commitment to these personal-reactive attitudes and practices show this doubt to be unwarranted? One argument that it can might go as follows: there is indeed a clear connection between (*a*) the personal-reactive attitudes and practices and (*b*) belief in true responsibility. Indeed one can argue *from* the fact of our practically speaking unrenounceable commitment to these (at least partly) non-epistemic things, these feelings, attitudes, and practices, *to* the conclusion that no claim that the belief in true responsibility is false needs to be taken seriously. For if the truth of the belief in true responsibility is indeed *in some sense* a necessary condition of the justifiability of these attitudes and practices, the justifiability of these attitudes and practices is by the same token a sufficient condition of the truth of the belief. So if these attitudes and practices are independently justifiable, in some sense of 'justifiable'—if they are justifiable without appeal to the belief in responsibility (perhaps just by appeal to the fact that it is an absolutely fundamental natural fact about us that we are deeply and perhaps unrenounceably committed to them)—then they can plausibly be taken to uphold the belief in responsibility, when pressure is put upon it. Instead of being supported by it, they can support it, being supported in turn by the ground-floor fact of our unrenounceable commitment.

Strawson does not offer precisely this argument. But he does claim, in a comparable way, that we are *non-rationally* committed to the personal-reactive attitudes and practices—and, hence, presumably, to belief in the applicability of the concepts of responsibility and freedom— in such a way that it cannot be right to suppose that to give them up would be the correct or rational thing to do if determinism were shown to be true. In fact, he suggests, we are in any case incapable of giving them up, practically speaking. We could not at will adopt a completely 'objective' attitude to people (including ourselves), never praising or blaming them, never, in short, treating them as if they were properly responsible agents.

FEELINGS, attitudes, practices, concepts, and beliefs are all different things, and Strawson is mainly concerned with certain of the personal-reactive *feelings, attitudes,* and *practices*—those which have in common that they involve reacting to people as if they were genuinely self-determining and truly responsible agents. He has less to say about the more problematic-seeming questions that arise about the applicability of the related *concepts* of responsibility and freedom, and about the truth or falsity of *beliefs* in responsibility and freedom. But, considering the concept of moral responsibility in § 6, he does link attitudes and practices to concepts and beliefs. He suggests that the "pessimist" (or incompatibilist) about freedom is wrong to think that one cannot by appealing to the personal-reactive attitudes and practices "fill the gap" in the "optimist's" (or conventional compatibilist's) account of the concept of responsibility.

I take this suggestion to involve the claim (*a*) that the concepts of, and belief in, moral responsibility and freedom are *in some sense* shown to have application, and to be justified, respectively, by the mere fact of the existence of our commitment to the personal-reactive attitudes and practices; and (*b*) that the concepts of responsibility and freedom that are in this way shown to have application are in *some* way essentially stronger or richer concepts than those that can be admitted by conventional compatibilists. For they 'fill the gap' in the conventional compatibilist account.

It may be, though, that Strawson's argument is best understood simply as an attempt to draw attention to, and connect up, the two following things: the viability of (1) the conventional compatibilist account as far as it goes, and (2) the natural fact of our commitment to personal-reactive attitudes, emotions, and practices. They connect up in that reference to the latter fills the gap that the pessimists discern in the former. But, on this view, reference to (2) does not fill the gap in (1) in the sense that it supports and straightforwardly justifies belief in the proper applicability of a notion of responsibility that is essentially stronger than that allowed for in (1). It fills the gap in (1) only in the sense that it suplements (1) with an account of the primordially important role in human thought and action of a belief in a kind of responsibility that (1) can never show to be justified: it fits this belief into, and illuminates it in its proper place in, the general human 'form of life'. And, once placed in its true (and, essentially, partly non-rational) context, the belief can be seen to be immune, in some vital respect, to attack by any argument from determinism (or non-self-determinability). One could put this in a Humean way: belief in responsibility is "more properly an act of the sensitive, than of the cogitative part of our natures".[3] So the products of the pessimists' excogitations, although properly called beliefs, simply fail to connect with our *non*-cogitatively natural belief in responsibility in such a way that they and it can be assessed (with negative result) for mutual consistency.

This is an attractive reconciliation. One thing that someone who adopts such a position may simply underestimate, however, is the equal naturalness of the pessimists' position, when they insist that determinism is incompatible with freedom. Secure in theoretical indefeasibility, the reconciler may tend to mistake for a failure of subtlety in his opponent what is in fact a proper sensitivity to the power of the basic incompatibilist intuition that determinism is incompatible with freedom. The fact that the incompatibilist intuition has such power for us is as much a natural fact about cognitive beings like ourselves as is the fact of our quite unreflective commitment to the reactive attitudes. What is more, the roots of the incompatibilist intuition lie deep in the very reactive attitudes that are invoked in order to undercut it. The reactive attitudes

3. Hume, D. *A Treatise of Human Nature*, ed. L. A. Selby-Bigge, 2d ed. (Oxford: Clarendon Press, 1978).

enshrine the incompatibilist intuition. The notion of true responsibility comes easily to the non-philosophizing mind, and is not found only in (or behind) what Strawson calls the 'panicky metaphysics' of philosopher libertarians.[4]

On balance, then, it is not clear that Strawson's appeal to commitment can undercut the pessimists' demand for an account, incompatible with determinism, of what it is that actually makes us truly responsible. Nor can it clearly assuage the pessimism of those who think that no such account can possibly be given.

II. COMMITMENT AND RATIONALITY

Strawson suggests that a question (1) "about what it would be *rational* to do if determinism were true, a question about the rational justification of ordinary inter-personal attitudes in general", could (2) seem "real only to one who had failed to grasp the purport" of the point about "our natural human commitment to ordinary inter-personal attitudes. This commitment is part of the general framework of human life, not something that can come up for review . . . within this general framework."[5] It is (3), "*useless* to ask whether it would not be rational for us to do what it is not in our nature to (be able to) do".[6] If (4) "we could imagine what we cannot have, viz. a choice in this matter [a choice in the matter of our commitment to the ordinary interpersonal attitudes], then we could choose rationally only in the light of the gains and losses to human life, its enrichment or impoverishment; and the truth or falsity of a general thesis of determinism could not bear on the rationality of *this* choice."[7]

He concludes, (5), that "the question . . . of the connection between rationality and the adoption of the objective attitude to others is misposed when it is made to seem dependent on the issue of determinism"; and, (6), that "it would not necessarily be rational to choose to be more purely rational than we are . . . if such a choice were possible".[8]

With regard to the first three quotations: one might again object, that while we have a deep and perhaps ineracinable commitment to the reactive attitudes and practices, it is also in our nature to take determinism to pose a serious problem for our notions of responsibility and freedom. (This is so even if we grant that indeterminism cannot help.) Our commitments are complex, and conflict. Although our thoughts about de-

---

4. By 'libertarian' I mean someone who believes that we are free, and that freedom is incompatible with determinism, and that determinism is therefore false.

5. 'Freedom and Resentment', p. 55.

6. Ibid., p. 60.

7. Ibid., p. 55–56.

8. Ibid., p. 56 n. 4. For a more recent statement of his position, see *Skepticism and Naturalism: Some Varieties* (New York: Columbia University Press, 1985), pp. 31–8.

terminism appear in actual fact quite impotent to disturb our natural and unconsidered reactive attitudes and feelings (this reveals one commitment), it also seems very difficult for us not to acknowledge that the truth of determinism or of non-self-determinability brings the propriety of the reactive attitudes seriously into doubt (this reveals the other commitment). Defenders of the reactive attitudes may be unwise to seek to strengthen their position by appealing to the fact that commitment to the reactive attitudes is, unlike the opposed commitment, *practically* basic. For the incompatibilist 'pessimists' may then reply that, while the commitment they are concerned to stress is of an essentially more theoretical character, it appears to represent the simple *truth*. There is a very real conflict of commitment.

At one point in his characterization of the nature of our commitment to the reactive feelings and attitudes, Strawson compares it to our commitment to belief in the validity of inductive procedures. This commitment to inductive belief-formation is "original, natural, non-rational (not *ir*rational), in no way something we choose or could give up".[9] It cannot be supposed to be purely rational, as Hume showed. Yet it can plausibly be said to be a commitment we are not wrong to have—it is quite implausible to say that it is simply irrational. It is very hard, furthermore, to see how we could give it up. And it seems absurd to suppose that it might be rational to do so, or more rational to do so than not to do so.

The claim implicit in the comparison appears to be this: that our commitment to the reactive attitudes and, derivatively, to belief in responsibility, is similarly non-rational in such a way that it is something that we are not wrong to have in the face of determinism (or non-self-determinability). But there appears to be an important difference. The correct sceptical objection to commitment to the validity of inductive belief-formation is not that it involves a demonstrably false belief, but only that it involves a belief that cannot be shown to be true, and in that sense cannot be justified, although it may in fact be true (it may in fact be true that there is a real material world governed by certain fundamental forces that are intrinsic to the very constitution of matter, a world in which everything takes place in accordance with what one may perfectly well call 'natural necessity'). The sceptical objection to belief in true responsibility, however, is that it is a belief that is apparently demonstrably false. This objection is then extended into a criticism of the reactive attitudes as demonstrably inappropriate given their essential dependence on a belief that is demonstrably false.

9. 'Freedom and Resentment', p. 64 n. 7.

Even if the two commitments are of the same depth and strength just *qua* commitments, then, there is a respect in which they are different in nature. But are they in fact of the same depth and strength? They may resemble each other in this, that it would no more be right or rational to (try to) give up the reactive attitudes than it would be to (try to) give up reliance on inductive belief-formation. But merely placing them side by side does not show that this is so; and it does not seem so inconceivable that we should weaken in our commitment to the reactive attitudes as it does that we should weaken in our commitment to inductive belief-formation. (One possibility not allowed for by this all-or-nothing view of our commitment to the reactive attitudes is that of local erosions, within the general framework of human life, of certain facets of this commitment.)

On balance, it does not seem that the question about what it would be rational to do if determinism were true can yet be rejected as an unreal one. It is in our nature to be deeply committed to the reactive attitudes. But it is also in our nature to take determinism (non-self-determinability) to pose a serious problem for the notions of freedom and responsibility.

QUOTATIONS (4)–(6) have roughly the same import, but they merit separate comment. Consider a man who is an incompatibilist, and who comes to believe that determinism is true. He has a great love of truth, or, rather, a great desire to be correct in all things, to have justified attitudes. Surely he can act rationally in choosing to (try to) adopt the objective attitude to people, in the light of this desire and belief in determinism? The quotations suggest that the truth or falsity of determinism is never relevant to such a choice, and that the nature of human commitment to the reactive attitudes is such that one can legislate quite generally about what constitute gains and losses to human life, without considering the widely differing aims and preferences of individuals. But even if most people agree that the truth of determinism does not give them good reason to try to adopt the objective attitude, given other considerations about gains and losses to human life, the egregious lover of truth just mentioned, who now believes in determinism and so feels that his reactive attitudes are not justified, can reasonably claim that it is rational for him to try to adopt more objective attitudes. It is true that belief in determinism cannot *by itself* make it rational to adopt the objective attitude. But this is merely because no non-evaluative belief of this kind can ever provide a reason for action by itself.

In general, it simply is not clear that the fact of commitment makes it a mistake to suppose that the truth of determinism renders one's personal-reactive attitudes unjustified in some way.[10] Nor is it clear that the fact of commitment makes it impossible for us as we are to adopt universally objective attitudes to people.[11] And it surely cannot make it impossible for us to *try* to adopt the objective attitude (though in section V I will suggest that newly fledged incompatibilist determinists may find themselves unable to adopt any rational plan of action at all, given their belief in determinism).

In the other case imagined by Strawson, that of choosing between our actual world and a world in which everyone adopts the objective attitude, we would, certainly, make our choice "in the light of the gains and losses to human life". But again this is not to say that there is a single rational choice. For it depends on what the chooser wants or thinks best, and there is a crucial sense in which desires and values are simply not comparable in respect of rationality.[12] Most would opt for the actual world. But a utilitarian who believed that personal-reactive-attitude-involving human relations cause more suffering than happiness overall would think it right or rational for us to choose to be more purely rational than we are, given the choice, in order to cancel the balance of suffering.[13]

In conclusion: it does not follow, from the fact that the truth of determinism cannot by itself make it rational to try to adopt the objective attitude, or from the fact that there is no single rational choice to be made in this case, that the correctness of the objective attitude does not in some sense follow from the truth of determinism. It does seem to be true that praising, blaming or resenting what other people do is in some sense completely inappropriate, given the truth of determinism, even if

10. This may be so even if assuming the falsity of determinism is of no help in an attempt to demonstrate their appropriateness. (Those who agree that indeterminism is no better than determinism, so far as the prospects for freedom are concerned, can replace '(the truth of) determinism' by 'the way things are' throughout sections I–II.)

11. It is conceivable that one could have a choice in the matter—it could be a simple matter of wiring up one's brain and pushing a button.

12. If I desire something impossible—to grow parsley on the moon—I am not *in any way* irrational, only unlucky; and I am not irrational, only subject to conflict of desire, if I desire to achieve something achievement of which is incompatible with achievement of my other desires. One's fear of (English) spiders may be said to be irrational because it is only rational to fear what one believes to be harmful; and such irrationality may be supposed to infect one's corresponding desire not to come into contact with spiders. But even if one's desire is wholly derived from a fear that can properly be called irrational, it is not in itself irrational; one can have the same desire without the fear. (Derek Parfit has argued convincingly that certain patterns of preference may be intrinsically irrational; see *Reasons and Persons* [Oxford: Oxford University Press, 1984], § 46. But his unusual cases do not affect the present point.)

13. A man might rate more highly than anything else a diminution in the rate of *crimes passionnels;* he might find this kind of killing far more terrible than any other kind. Confident that this would diminish drastically upon universal adoption of the objective attitude, he might regard all the other effects of its adoption as a price well worth paying.

it is odd to talk of 'correct' attitudes. (For if determinism is true, then to pass moral judgements on people, and to say that they acted morally rightly or wrongly, is, in a crucial respect, exactly like saying they are beautiful, or ugly—something for which they are not responsible.) And it seems that this is so whatever one's desires are, and whatever one thinks one should do. Finally, while there may indeed be no single right answer to the question of what it would be rational to do if determinism were shown to be true, the question has not been shown to be unreal. I will now consider it further, in conjunction with some more strictly phenomenological themes.

III. FEELINGS AND THE CAUSALITY OF REASON; DOINGS AND HAPPENINGS

Many of our ordinary 'personal-reactive' attitudes and feelings seem to be somehow inappropriate or incorrect, given the truth of determinism (or of non-self-determinability). It is true that feelings and attitudes are correct or incorrect, if at all, only in some derivative sense—only in so far as they are tied to beliefs. Nevertheless, it seems reasonable to say that if determinism is true (or since true self-determination is impossible), the attitudes and feelings currently in question can be shown to be appropriate only by appeal to beliefs which are in fact incorrect; it seems that they stand in a sufficiently close relation to certain beliefs to depend for their correctness or appropriateness on the correctness of those beliefs. Accordingly, there appears to be room for the exercise of reason in thinking through the consequences of one's beliefs for one's attitudes and feelings. It does not seem that the bare fact of one's commitment to these attitudes and feelings renders any such exercise of reason simply pointless.

How might such reasoning go? Well, just as believing 'if p then q' and coming to believe 'p' is likely to *cause* one to come to believe that q, according to what one could call the 'natural causality of reason', so, similarly, if one genuinely believes that the propriety of certain of one's feelings presupposes the correctness of certain beliefs, and if one then comes to think that these beliefs are false, then this may understandably cause one to cease to have these feelings; it may cause them to change or weaken, at least. On the other hand, if the feelings are linked to inherently non-rational emotions and desires, the natural 'causality of reason' will be impeded. Clearly it will vary in its operation with the individual case.

But does this have any consequences for the question of what one should *do*? If a change in one's feelings and attitudes were produced in this way by one's coming to believe in determinism, this would be some-

thing that happened to one, not something one did.[14] And the difficulties that attend Strawson's question about what it might be rational to do
if one came to believe, say, that both incompatibilism and determinism
were true are not diminished by the fact that there is a real and unproblematic question about what might *happen* to one in such a case.

So: what should one do—if anything? What might one do, in any
case?

One can hardly decide to take no notice of what one now believes—
that people, including oneself, are, in some unequivocal sense, in no way
responsible for their actions. But if one's reaching this theoretical conclusion (many have) has not in fact caused one's reactive attitudes to
change in any way (this has often been the case), is one then bound to *try*
to stop treating people as proper objects of gratitude and resentment,
praise and blame, and to undertake some course of action to that end?
Say one doesn't want to. Isn't that a sufficient reason not to?

It is not clear that it is; or rather, it is not clear that these questions
really arise. For it is of course true that if one believes that there are
okapi in San Diego zoo, but has not been to check, there is no reason
why one should check if one doesn't want to. But the present case is different. One has formed a belief, and there is in a clear sense nothing
hidden from view that remains to be actively checked. To claim that one
need not try to take into account the apparent fact that people are not
proper objects of reactive attitudes if one doesn't want to seems rather
like claiming that one need not believe something one believes if one
doesn't want to. But one doesn't have such a choice; belief is not subject
to the will in this way.[15]

All this may be true; and yet it is also true that the theoretical incompatibilist determinists' reactive attitudes are very unlikely to have
been much perturbed by their theoretical views. But can they reasonably
tolerate this? Shouldn't they do something about it? It seems that we
have to ask once again whether the fact of non-rational commitment
can somehow justify, as well as explain, their imperturbability; or
whether, alternatively, it can somehow pre-empt the need for any such
justification.

The problem is important, because it is not just a problem for incompatibilist determinists. The fact of the impossibility of true self-
determination threatens to propel us all into this difficulty—whatever
we believe about determinism. People do not make themselves to be the

14. This is part of a general point about reasoning. One does not really act at all, in
reasoning. Rather one 'sees'—one realizes—that this follows from that. Reasoning is more
like sensation (or perception) than action: the action in reasoning is at most the getting of
the premises together, and the bringing of the mind to bear on them, if it is anything. It
is not the reasoning as such; that is what happens when you do these other things. The
same goes for thinking in general.

15. Although one could hire a hypnotist to wipe out one's belief.

way they are. And this gives rise to a vital sense in which they are not ultimately responsible for what they do. But they go on thinking of themselves as if they were thus responsible.

It is no good saying 'I am determined to go on having these feelings and attitudes'. To suppose that this dissolves the problem is to make the mistake of fatalism (the mistake of thinking that nothing one can do can change what will happen). It may be true that one is so determined that one does make this mistake. But it is also true—even if everyone is determined to believe everything that he, or she, believes— that it is a mistake, and that people who think clearly will not make it.[16] And if such people are not convinced that appeal to the fact of non-rational commitment can justify as well as explain our reactive feelings and attitudes, or decisively pre-empt the demand for justification, then they cannot really avoid the problem of what now to think, what now to do.[17]

IV. Determinism, Action, and the Self; a Thought-Experiment

Reflections such as these can start up odd intellectual fatigues, veering sleights of mind, or a deep and almost contemptuous rejection of the apparently manifest demands of reason. One's commitment to the reactive attitudes is instrumental in this; largely, I suggest, because one's deepest commitment is not to belief in the appropriateness of the interpersonal reactive attitudes, but to belief in the appropriateness of certain self-concerned reactive attitudes. One's deepest commitment is to the view of oneself as truly responsible, both in general and in particular cases of action. The sleights of mind begin because the biggest problems raised by the apparent demands of reason concern oneself. Trying to think through the consequences of these demands, it seems that one risks thinking oneself out of existence, as a *mental someone*. ('A mental someone' is a good description of one absolutely central way in which we think of ourselves. Here as elsewhere I am concerned only with this fact of 'cognitive phenomenology', and not at all with the question of what if anything a 'mental someone' could possibly be, factually or metaphysically speaking.)

16. Here I am assuming the invalidity of the argument that one cannot believe in determinism because this belief undercuts one's right to appeal to the notions of truth and falsity altogether (cf. J. R. Lucas, *The Freedom of the Will*, § 21; cf. also *Freedom & Belief*, and D. Wiggins, 'Freedom, Knowledge, Belief and Causality' in G. Vesey ed., *Knowledge and Necessity* [London: Macmillan, 1970].

17. "Carelessness and in-attention alone can afford us any remedy. For this reason", Hume says, "I rely entirely upon them" (*Treatise*, I. iv. 2, p. 218).

Why does one risk thinking oneself out of existence as a mental someone? Because what one naturally takes oneself to be, *qua* mental someone, is a truly self-determining agent of the impossible kind.[18] One takes
it (however unreflectively) that this is an *essential* aspect of what one is,
mentally considered: given the way I am, mentally considered, I could
not continue to exist and lack this property. So the risk is not merely that
a process of tenacious concentration on the thought of determinism (or
non-self-determinability) might force me to cease to believe that I had a
certain property—true responsibility—whose possession meant a lot to
me. It is rather that there might remain nothing that was recognizable
as me at all; nothing recognizable as me, the 'agent-self', but only a bare
consciousness-function, a zombie.

Perhaps the best way to see the force of this suggestion is by means of
the following thought-experiment; for it may seem rather vague and far-
fetched. It is not particularly vague, in fact. What may be true, though,
is that one really does have to stop and think about it for oneself with
concentration and imagination.

The thought-experiment consists simply in the rigorous application of
the belief in determinism to the present course of one's life: one does
one's best to think rapidly of every smallest action one performs or
movement one makes—or indeed everything whatsoever that happens,
so far as one is oneself concerned—as determined; as not, ultimately,
determined by oneself; this for a minute or two, say.

THIS should have the effect of erasing any sense of the presence of a
freely deciding and acting 'I' in one's thoughts; for—so it seems—there
is simply no role for such an 'I' to play. It may even be strangely, faintly
depressing; or it may give rise to a curious, floating feeling of detached
acquiescence in the passing show of one's own psychophysical being; a
feeling, not of impotence, but of radical uninvolvement. Or alternatively
the feeling may be: I am not really a person; there isn't really anyone
there at all.[19]

I take this effect to indicate that one's sense of self is of a profoundly
libertarian cast; and to indicate that one naturally and unreflectively
conceives of oneself, *qua* the mental planner of action, as standing in
some special impossible relation of true-responsibility-creating origina-
tion to one's choices and actions. One disappears in the thought-
experiment because it reveals that one is not possible, so conceived.

18. The fact that one also takes oneself to be an embodied agent capable of physical
action is not presently relevant.

19. The thought-experiment might make a good meditation exercise for certain schools
of Buddhists—see further section VIII below.

At the same time, of course, one does not—cannot—disappear just like that. One's thought naturally and inevitably occurs for one in terms of 'I',[20] and one's conception of this 'I' remains a conception of a truly responsible self-determining someone. So while one's attempts to grasp the consequences of determinism fully may succeed in bursts, they will in the longer term always break up on one's rock-hard commitment to a self-conception which is wholly incompatible with fully fledged, continually applied belief in determinism.[21]

When this happens, one may continue to have, and to try to apply, the thought that everything about one is determined; but it will not be striking with its full force. And when it is striking with less than its full force the thought of one's total determinedness will probably not make it seem that one does not really exist at all (as a mental someone), but, rather, that although one does somehow or other exist (as a mental someone), and although one does continue to act in various ways, still one cannot truly be said to do anything oneself, because determinism gobbles up everything, revealing everything one does to be not really *one's own doing.* (Remember that this is a claim about how things will appear to someone who takes the problem of free will seriously and pursues the thought-experiment; as such it is not a rejection of theoretical compatibilism.)

I suggest, therefore, that there are two principal poles around which one's thought is likely to oscillate when one is trying to apply the thought that one is totally determined. At one pole, the freely deciding and acting 'mental someone' somehow goes out of existence altogether. At the other pole, the mental someone continues to exist, but one can no longer see oneself as a freely deciding and acting being in any way. One's thought is likely to oscillate around this second pole when the thought-experiment has not been engaged with full force, and is not having its full effect of strangely dissolving the (sense of) self.[22]

This is not likely to convince anyone who does not seriously attempt the thought-experiment; and such an appeal to thought-experiment is

20. This is why Lichtenberg's famous objection to Descartes—that he should not have affirmed the certainty of 'I think' but only of 'It thinks' or 'It's thinking' (on the analogy of 'It's raining')—is wrongly put. The correct point is simply that when one makes Descartes's move one should not suppose that any conclusion about one's substantial nature follows from the certainty of 'I think'.

21. Hardened conventional compatibilists are likely to have the most trouble with the thought-experiment, for they are not likely to confuse their theoretical opinions (or prejudices) with their real everyday attitudes to themselves and their actions—in a way that makes it difficult to see the problem.

22. It is at the second pole that we may most vividly encounter what Thomas Nagel calls "the . . . erosion of what we do by the subtraction of what happens". See his 'Moral Luck', in *Mortal Questions* (Cambridge: Cambridge University Press, 1979), esp. pp. 37–8. Cf. also Bernard Williams's paper on 'Moral Luck', in *Moral Luck* (Cambridge: Cambridge University Press, 1981), to which Nagel's paper was a response.

likely to encounter scepticism. But I do not think that the point can be made adequately in words.

It may be claimed that the thought-experiment is not practicable: the 'I' as it occurs in thought[23] can never fully attain the thought that it is itself just part of the determined world, because it can never quite catch up with itself: any judgement of determinedness on its part necessarily involves its taking an eternal view of the object of the judgement, which it cannot have of itself *qua* the thinking subject presently making the judgement. But this is no real problem. Even if one were to become aware of this point,[24] it would not check the *general* effect that would be produced in one by thinking of everything one is and does as totally determined—the effect of seeming to erase the 'I' as ordinarily conceived. Suppose one did think about one's thinking in particular as a completely determined phenomenon. Then whatever thought one had, one would, pursuing the thought-experiment, think of that thought too as determined. And, this being so, no thought would ever be able to emerge as the true product of the familiar 'I', the putative true originator of thoughts, decisions, and actions that is not a merely determined phenomenon: this 'I' would perpetually evanesce, however far one pursued the possible regress of thoughts about thoughts about thoughts. (This is just one way among others in which the thought-experiment could develop.)

In fact the idea that one cannot be supposed to be a truly responsible originator of one's thoughts or ideas can acquire experiential (as opposed to merely theoretical) impact without recourse to the tricky rigours of this thought-experiment. The point is a familiar one (already touched on in note 14). Thoughts simply 'occur' to one; one just 'has' ideas, they simply 'come to one'—whether they are philosophical, mathematical, or scientific (in which case the occurrence of one's thoughts and ideas is somehow controlled by one's wish to arrive at the truth) or whether they are musical, fictional, or poetical (in which case their occurrence may be controlled by many things). There is a commonly felt sense in which one has no real responsibility for any of them.[25] I think

23. Here again I am concerned only with the *character* of our thought, not with the idea that there could be some special mental entity called the 'I' or the 'self'.

24. Discussed by Ryle in 'The Systematic Elusiveness of "I" ', *The Concept of Mind* (Harmondsworth: Penguin, 1969), ch. 6, § 7.

25. It is worth quoting Rimbaud's well-known remarks in full: "C'est faux de dire: Je pense: on devrait dire on me pense. . . . JE est un autre. Tant pis pour le bois qui se trouve violon" (letter to Georges Izambard, 13 May 1871); and again "Les romantiques . . . prouvent si bien que la chanson est si peu souvent l'oeuvre, c'est à dire la pensée . . . *comprise* du chanteur. . . . Car Je est un autre. Si le cuivre s'éveille clairon, il n'y a rien de sa faute. Cela m'est évident: J'assiste à l'éclosion de ma pensée [I am a spectator at the unfolding of my thought]: je la regarde, je l'écoute. . . ." (Letter to Paul Demeny, 15 May 1871; *Oeuvres Complètes* [Paris: Gallimard, 1972]).

it is helpful to dwell on this (it is part of doing philosophy). And it is worth reflecting on Hume's famous observation, that when one earnestly inspects one's own mind for the 'I', the self, one never finds anything there.[26]

SERIOUS incompatibilist determinists (or non-self-determinationists, i.e. those who believe that true self-determination is necessary for freedom and that it is impossible) should try the thought-experiment; for them, after all, undertaking it involves nothing more than dwelling with special concentration on something they already believe to be true. Those who learn to maintain the state of mind induced by the thought-experiment will be well on the way to a truly thoroughgoing, truly lived, or as I shall say *genuine* belief in determinism or non-self-determinability. (They may be on the way to nirvana.) But it is important to be clear what this involves. A person may *theoretically* fully accept that he, or she, is wholly a product of his or her heredity and environment—many of us do—and yet, in everyday life, have *nothing like* the kind of self-conception that is here required of the genuine incompatibilist determinist (non-self-determinationist). In fact such a self-conception seems scarcely possible for human beings. It seems to require the dissolution of any recognizable human sense of self. Certainly one cannot adopt such a radically 'objective' attitude to oneself at will.

Perhaps this is not very clearly expressed. But I think the general idea will become clear to most of those who concentrate on the problem, or undertake the thought-experiment. Those who disdain the thought-experiment, or claim that it does not work, may fail to grasp the general idea. It does work; and this is a very important fact about us.

V. WHAT MIGHT HAPPEN

These considerations suggest that there may after all be a sense in which the question (considered in section II) about what it would be rational to do if determinism were true is an 'unreal' question. For it may be an unreal question for anyone who has become a *genuine* incompatibilist determinist (non-self-determinationist) in the present sense—for anyone who has gone beyond merely theoretical acceptance of determinism (or non-self-determinability).

Consider a man who is an incompatibilist and who has just come to believe that determinism is true, and who is struggling to attain a true perspective on his situation. How is he to think of himself as he sits back, rubs his eye, looks for a book in the bookshelves, debates whether to give

26. D. Hume, *Treatise*, I, iv. 6, p. 252.

more money to famine relief, thinking perhaps, of each of his thoughts and movements that it is determined, and thinking that his thinking this is determined in turn, and so on?

We may suppose that he does not make the fatalist mistake—the mistake (for example) of ceasing to try to get what he wants because he thinks it is already determined whether he will get it or not, in such a way that he can do nothing about it. He knows perfectly well that his own planning and action are real and effective parts of the continuing deterministic process. It is rather that when he does something intentionally which he feels to be reprehensible (say), he may then think to himself: that was determined to happen, and yet if I had not done it that too would have been determined to happen. This is a very ordinary thought in philosophy. But what is it like to take it seriously in life, trying to apprehend every detail of one's life as determined?

He may find that he feels that *he* (i.e. he the truly responsible agent, he as he automatically conceives of himself in his natural, unreconstructed thought about himself) can do nothing at all. Here he is at the second of the two main poles of serious self-applied determinism: he feels he exists, but that he cannot really *act* at all. This is how he puts it, at least. Or rather, this is how he would put it, were it not for the fact that, relaxing his application of the thought of determinism to himself, and being an as yet unreconstructed incompatibilist determinist, he still feels completely responsible for what he has done. He feels he simply knows that he knew at the time of action that he could have done otherwise. He is unable to accept that he is exempt from responsibility or blame, or indeed from praise, because it was determined to happen as it did. (Perhaps he followed his desires and neglected his duty.) Yet he also now believes that the way he is, and his decision, are things for which he is ultimately in no way responsible. And when, see-sawing back, he concentrates again on this thought, he finds, again, that he can no longer make sense of the idea of his performing an action that is truly *his* action. For the sense of self he naturally has (and which is expressed here by the italicization of 'he' and 'his') is irremediably incompatible with any deep acceptance of the idea that all he is and does is determined.[27]

HE may think as follows: that to choose to (try to) abandon his personal-reactive attitudes is not really possible, because only a free agent, which he does not now consider himself to be, can really have a reason for action which is really its own reason. There may be a train of practical deliberation going on in his head, but he feels that it is not really *his* thought at all (although it feels just like it, as soon as he stops concentrating on his determinedness), but (because) a determined process. He

27. With suitable minor adjustments, the same story can be told of a non-self-determinationist.

thinks that he cannot reason or deliberate in a way that culminates in a decision which is truly his, and which is such that the ensuing action is something for which he is truly responsible; or indeed something that *he* really did. For he knows that what he thinks of as his choice is determined, however much he may hesitate or contrasuggestibly change his mind. And so, stuck with his unreconstructed sense of self, he cannot think of it as really *his* choice. To talk of freedom here, as compatibilists do, is, he thinks, to talk of the freedom of the turnspit, or of the self-sealing tank.[28] It is the "wretched subterfuge" of compatibilism, a "petty word-jugglery".[29] It is "so much gobbledegook".[30] It is not really to talk of freedom at all.

So the whole picture of the thoughtful incompatibilist determinist coming to believe in determinism, and then raising the question of what to do about it, may be ill-conceived. The question may be completely unreal for him, so long as he concentratedly applies the thought of determinism to himself. For he may then feel that he cannot really choose to do, or do, anything, in the way he thought. This rejection of the possibility of real choice or action is, certainly, a piece of reasoning on his part. But it too cannot be thought to have any practical consequences, or to rationalize any decision—such as a decision not to choose or decide anything on the grounds that it is strictly speaking impossible to do so. One cannot decide not to decide anything on the grounds that one cannot decide anything.

But nor can he decide to abandon himself to his determinedness, for that too would be something determined, hence not something he really did, in the vital sense. He cannot think 'I find that these reasons to do X occur to me, and *since* X now appears to me (determinedly, I know) to be the best thing to do, I will do X', as if he thus had access to a further reason to do X—the knowledge that reasons to do X have determinedly outweighed reasons to do anything else (or, worse, as if ability to take account of what was determinedly the case, so far as his reason-state was concerned, somehow gave him access to a secret, undetermined fulcrum point of free decision). These would be simple mistakes. Correcting himself, and foreseeing the paralytic regresses that threaten, he may tell himself not to think about the nature of his practical reasoning any more than he used to. But this too will involve a decision—a decision to try to think nothing. So it will not really be his decision, in his view.

28. Cf. Kant in the *Critique of Practical Reason*, trans. L. W. Beck (Indianapolis: Bobbs-Merrill, 1956; trans. T. K. Abbott [London: Longmans, 1898]), p. 191 (*Ak. V.* 97); and D. Davidson in 'Freedom to Act', in *Essays on Freedom on Action*, ed. T. Honderich (London: Routledge & Kegan Paul, 1973), p. 141.

29. Kant, *Critique of Practical Reason*, pp. 189–90 (*Ak. V.* 96).

30. G. E. M. Anscombe, 'Causality and Determination', *Metaphysics and the Philosophy of Mind* (Oxford: Blackwell, 1981), p. 146.

This is a strange drama, an enactment of the deep problem of free will. In the end only the exigencies of everyday life will carry him forward. The continual tendency of his unreconstructed thought will be to reinsert him, conceived as a truly self-determining mental someone, into his thought and deliberation. And continually he will correct this tendency. For nothing, he realizes, can be done by him, so conceived. Nothing can be done by him in the sense that matters to him; things can only happen. Whatever he starts to plan and do, it is whipped away from him, only to appear as not really his own, by the thought that it is entirely determined.

It seems, then, that a genuine belief in determinism or non-self-determinationism, uneasily coupled with an unreconstructed conception of self, may produce a *total paralysis* of all purposive thought as it is ordinarily conceived and experienced. To experience things in this way is not to make the mistake of fatalism. It is simply to experience the clash between determinism (non-self-determinationism) and our ordinary conception of freedom in a particularly vivid manner. (It is useful to think of morally weighted choices here.)

There are certainly other more compatibilistic ways of thinking and theorizing about deliberation and action, some of which will be discussed in the next section, and which are of such a kind that when we employ them, we may find that we are quite untroubled by the thought of determinism. But it does not follow that the present story is not accurate as a story of what might happen to a newly fledged, thoughtful incompatibilist determinist (non-self-determinationist). What may follow is that we are deeply inconsistent in our characteristically very vague thought about freedom, action, deliberation, and ourselves. (Seasoned philosophical compatibilists are likely to find it much harder than most to appreciate the force of these points. Perhaps they should imagine facing the following choice: if you agree to submit to twenty years of torture—torture of a kind that leaves no time for moral self-congratulation—you will save ten others from the same fate. [Perhaps they should agree to be hypnotized into believing that they really are facing such a choice—hypnotized in such a way that, afterwards, they remember exactly what it felt like.])

THIS story is not just a curiosity, for although determinism is unverifiable even if it is true, the non-self-determinationist position—according to which true self-determination is (a) necessary for true responsibility and (b) probably impossible—appears to be correct.[31] It is therefore worth considering some other suggestions about what might happen to a new incompatibilist determinist or non-self-determinationist.

31. Cf. *Freedom and Belief,* 2.1.

One possibility is this. One might simply cease to believe that the specifically moral reactive attitudes and practices of praise and blame were justified or appropriate, and losing this belief might cause one to cease to be moved to praise and blame. Generally, believing determinism to be true and just being generally speaking very rational*istic* might cause a man to come to have more objective attitudes, without his trying to *do* anything. And this might occur despite the fact that he felt that the quality of his life suffered greatly as a result. On the other hand, his moral and non-moral reactive attitudes might be quite unaffected by his new theoretical belief, given the strength of his commitment to them. (This is what usually happens.) We are all effortlessly capable of the magnificent inconsistency of beliefs and attitudes that this appears to involve. And this, of course, is something that gives extremely powerful support to the commitment theorists' claim about the unrenounceability of the commitment.

Perhaps one may picture the reactive feelings and attitudes as composing a spectrum. At one end—this is very rough—there are the most basic feelings and sentiments of pleasure and 'unpleasure', aggression, animal attraction, fear, anger, and so on—the 'true' passions, those most clearly undergone or suffered. At the other end there are the most purely moral sentiments and feelings of approval and disapproval, praise and blame. Resentment and gratitude may be seen as lying somewhere near the centre of the spectrum, distanced from the basic passions by their appearing to involve a considerable degree of mental sophistication, but distanced also from the most purely moral feelings and sentiments—for resentment and gratitude could survive recognition of inappropriateness where tendencies to praise and blame succumbed: 'I realize it's absurd to blame him (the lunatic), but I can't help feeling resentful'; 'I know it's only an android robot, but I can't help feeling grateful.'

There are different ways of categorizing emotions and feelings, but this ranking according to basicness seems to match closely the ordering which may be derived by comparing their dependence for appropriateness upon certain beliefs, such as belief in true responsibility, and the relative likelihood of their alteration given change in these beliefs. Dependence upon beliefs varies inversely with basicness. For example: a tendency to get angry with people is less likely to diminish in response to belief in determinism than a tendency to blame them (inanimate objects can make one angry, and it does not seem that this is irrational, whereas blaming them is.)

Any individual's case will be far more complicated than this schema suggests, however. In a particular case there will doubtless be special non-rational dependencies, formed as a result of traumatic experiences, for example, or a religious upbringing. And then, some people are naturally far more quick to anger—and to forgive—than others. One man's anger at people might turn to anger at the whole creation by his acquiring a belief in determinism—this would be a case of a 'basic' feeling responding to a change in belief. Alternatively, he might hold that a natural and ultimate feature of creation was a rigid code of punishment, and thus retain his practice of moral judgement even after coming to believe in determinism: 'It is perhaps a terrible fault in creation, but you have done wrong and are to blame.' This would be a case of a more purely moral sentiment failing to respond to change in belief. Calvinists do not hold (earthly) punishment to have a purely pragmatic justification.

What would happen generally is unpredictable. But it does seem conceivable that a highly rationalistic and generally un-neurotic man, low on non-rational dependencies, might lose (not actively abandon) only those attitudes which were in his view justifiable only by his discarded belief in true responsibility; being one in whom, as one might say, the causality of reason was strong, and non-rational commitment to belief in true responsibility weak. But he could not simply lose them by choice. Nor does calling him 'rationalistic' carry any implication that others would be rational to set about trying to abandon these attitudes. Nor do I think that we can fully imagine what it would be like to be him, if he did lose all the attitudes in question.[32]

VI. NATURAL COMPATIBILISM

Our sense of self and of freedom is in many respects profoundly libertarian in character. But it is also naturally and unhesitatingly compatibilistic in many other respects. And since this *natural compatibilism* is part of what underlies our commitment to belief in freedom, it deserves some consideration at this point. (A full treatment of it would be a lengthy matter; but Hume made some of the relevant points in the *Enquiry*, and many others have been made by compatibilists since.)[33]

32. The quite remarkable readiness with which human beings slip into adopting apparently true-responsibility-presupposing attitudes (like blame, resentment, and gratitude) to many classes of objects—animals, stones, cars, aeroplanes, computers, the world in general—that they would not in their cooler moments dream of classifying as free agents can be interpreted in more than one way. It can be seen simply as further evidence of how profoundly we are committed to true-responsibility-presupposing feelings and attitudes. Or (less usefully) it can be seen as casting doubt on the extent to which these attitudes are essentially true-responsibility-presupposing. The truth is that they are true-responsibility-presupposing; it is just that we are even more irrational than we think.

33. D. Dennett's *Elbow Room: The Varieties of Free Will Worth Wanting* (Oxford: Clarendon Press, 1985) is among other things a contribution to the description of the extent of our natural compatibilism.

The principal idea is this: so far as many aspects of our general sense of ourselves as free agents are concerned, we are not inclined to think that they are put in question *in any way* by the truth of determinism or non-self-determinability. Sometimes this is a reasonable attitude on our part, sometimes it is not. It depends on what aspect of our sense of freedom is in question. But in either case it is a natural compatibilist attitude, in the present sense of the phrase.

1. Thus—for example—many people are naturally (pre-philosophically) inclined to accept accounts of how they came to be as they are that simply rule out any kind of true self-determination; and they can in addition easily be brought to see that true self-determination is not really possible. (To say this may seem inconsistent with the account of our natural sense of self given above; but the inconsistency is in our view of ourselves, not in the account given of our view of ourselves.) Many people accept that they are, ultimately, entirely determined in all aspects of their character by their heredity and environment. But it follows from this that, whether the heredity-and-enviroment process that has shaped them is deterministic or not, they cannot themselves be truly or ultimately self-determining in any way. And yet they do not feel that their freedom is put in question by this—even though they naturally conceive of themselves as free in the ordinary, strong, true-responsibility-involving sense. To this extent they are natural compatibilists. This is a very common position.

Those who occupy this position cannot have thought about the matter very hard, you may say. That may be so. But very many thoughtful and intelligent people occupy exactly this position. Even those who are, as philosophers, revisionary compatibilists who hold that our ordinary strong notion of freedom is indefensible, reveal unmistakably, in the everyday conduct of their lives, that they too occupy it.

2. To this one may add the fact that we are neither inclined to suppose that we can be self-determining with respect to (the particular content of) our beliefs (for we simply desire that what we believe should be determined in a reliable, truth-inducing manner by the way things are), nor inclined to suppose that we can be radically self-determined with respect to our desires—or, generally, with respect to all those things other than beliefs that motivate our actions. It is true, as remarked, that we can cultivate tastes and traits; but we readily recognize that, if we do so, we do so because we are motivated to do so by certain desires and attitudes that we already have; or by certain beliefs about what is true or right that we already have, beliefs with respect to which we have our normal attitude: that of supposing that they are true, and, briefly, that we have in coming to hold them been determined to do so simply by the way things are. That is, in our ordinary thought we recognize, more or less explicitly, that true self-determination is impossible—even indepen-

dently of acknowledging the truth of physical determinism or heredity-and-environment determinism. But we also feel that the fact that it is impossible poses no threat at all to our freedom. And in this we are again natural compatibilists.

It is true that one reason why we feel that this impossibility poses no threat to freedom is that we naturally credit ourselves with an *in*compatibilistically conceived power of free decision that we see as rendering us somehow independent of our ultimately non-self-determined beliefs, desires, and so on (cf. *Freedom a Belief*, 2.9, 3.4). But we also naturally accept that explanations in terms of ultimately non-self-determined beliefs and desires can be *full* explanations of our actions, without our freedom being threatened; and it is this that makes it reasonable to see the present point about beliefs and desires as illustrating part of our natural compatibilism.

3. The above description of natural compatibilism involves reference to determinism, and in particular to heredity-and-environment determinism, and it may be questioned to what extent it can be said to articulate a *natural* (unreflective, pre-philosophical) compatibilistic outlook. The claim that it is natural can be defended by appeal to the idea that even if people do not ordinarily think at all about heredity and environment, or about how or why they are free, still there are certain things that they—we—would naturally be led to say if asked certain questions about freedom. Presented with objections to their initial responses (questioned further in a genially aporetic manner) there are certain further moves that they would also be naturally inclined to make. All these can be supposed to form part of natural compatibilism as currently understood.

As remarked, a full discussion of natural compatibilism would be a lengthy business. Here, by way of example, I propose to consider just one natural compatibilist aspect of the general phenomenology of freedom: a point about our attitude to our desires or non-epistemic motives generally considered. (Note that the phenomenology of freedom is not restricted to description—to saying what our sense of freedom is like. It can also offer explanations—explanations of why we have the sort of sense of freedom we do have.)

4. For any desire with which we are concerned at some particular time, we are not usually in the least concerned to be able to say that we are, somehow, the originators of the desire—whatever sense can be made of this. Our unreflective attitude to it is that it is simply there, in the way that a chair, a feature of the world, is simply there. I don't and I can't choose my desires. And I don't have to choose them for them to be mine (or to be free when they move me to act). They are just a part of me. This is how I am. One's desires are not of course publicly observable in the way that chairs are. The point of the analogy is rather one's desires are or can be as much a fact about the world that one confronts

as the fact of a chair's being there. I like loganberries, the chair is there in front of me. A desire can be importunate, I can bump into a chair. There are of course important differences in the 'being-there' of desire and chair—in the experience one has, with respect to both desire and chair, of being passive with respect to the fact of their existence or presence. But there are also important similarities.[34]

One might say that some desires are more like the fact of having a body of a particular sort than they are like chairs in particular places, in that they are part of oneself, and are more permanently 'just there', and are unthinkingly taken into account in one's thought and action (as is one's body both by proprioceptive and kinasesthetic sense, and by one's less immediate sensory and cognitive awareness of it). This point does not displace the point about chair-like objectivity of some desires, however, it only complicates it. For it remains true that many desires are in an important sense apprehended by us as just being there; as being in a sense external to the mental self that confronts them. And it remains true that their just-thereness is not seen as posing any sort of threat to freedom. And this fact forms part of the explanation of part of our natural compatibilism. It forms part of the explanation of why we may be naturally quite unworried when confronted by philosophers with the thought that our desires can be said to be determined in us in the sense of not having been freely adopted during some process of self-determination: we never really thought they were the result of self-determination anyway, or that they had to be if we were to be free.[35]

But it also forms part of the explanation of our natural *in*compatibilism. (This is a typical complication in the phenomenology of freedom.) For it also forms part of the explanations of the strength of our tendency to conceive of ourselves as possessed of a self separate from, and somehow irreducibly over and above, all its particular desires, pro-attitudes, and so on. And in this respect it turns out to be central to the naturally occurring libertarian notion of the truly self-determining 'agent-self' that is in its choice of action potentially completely independent of any of its particular (determined or not self-determined) desires, pro-attitudes, and so on. This is just one more instance in which naturally compatibilist and naturally incompatibilist (and indeed libertarian) elements in our thought about freedom share common roots.

5. The principal idea behind the suggestion that there is a sense in which we are naturally compatibilist in our thought about freedom is, as remarked, simply this: there are a great many aspects of our experience

34. Moral beliefs also characteristically have this sort of just-thereness; one confronts the chair, one confronts one's belief that one ought to do X.

35. It is *also* arguable, however, that there is a (rather slippery) sense in which we conceive our relation to our desires, pro-attitudes and so on as if they were things we were somehow or in some degree responsible for. See the next section. Both arguments may be correct.

of ourselves as free agents which, *either for good or for bad reasons,* we do not feel to be threatened in any way by the truth of determinism or non-self-determinability. Most presentations of natural compatibilism have been undertaken by philosophers who are themselves compatibilists, and who wish to show that compatibilism is true. They are therefore only interested in the good reasons. But uncommitted phenomenology of freedom takes the bad reasons with the good, and finds them of equal interest in giving an account of the ways in which we are naturally compatibilist.

In conclusion, let me mention something which has intentionally been ignored until now, and which not only provides one of the strongest arguments in favour of compatibilism considered as a philosophical theory, but is also one of the principal features of natural compatibilism. It is this. Behind the whole compatibilist enterprise lies the valid and important insight that, from one centrally important point of view, freedom is nothing more than a matter of being able to do what one wants or chooses or decides or thinks right or best to do, *given* one's character, desires, values beliefs (moral or otherwise), circumstances, and so on. Generally speaking, we have this freedom. For determinism does not affect it at all, and it has nothing whatever to do with any supposed sort of ultimate self-determination, or any particular power to determine what one's character, desires, and so on will be. It is true that the fact that we generally have this freedom provides no support for the idea that we are or can be 'truly' self-determining in the way that still appears to be necessary for true responsibility. But we can indeed be self-determining in the compatibilist sense of being able by our own action, and in the light of our necessarily non-self-determined characters and desires, to determine to a very considerable extent what happens to us.

Compatibilists who stress this point have a powerful question to ask: "What else could one possibly suppose, or reflectively require, that freedom could or should be, other than this?' But the old incompatibilist answer remains. This account of freedom does nothing to establish that we are truly responsible for our actions, nor, in particular, to establish that we are or can be truly *morally* responsible for our actions, in the ordinary, strong, desert-entailing sense. Nor, correspondingly, does it provide any reason for thinking that people either are or can be free or truly responsible in a way that could render the 'personal-reactive' attitudes truly appropriate. It seems that nothing can do this. But this still seems to be what we want.

So much for natural compatibilism; it can be developed much further. I wish now to say something more about our natural incompatibilism, and in so doing to return to the question of the nature of our commitment to belief in freedom.

VII. THE TRUE CENTRE OF COMMITMENT

If our commitment to belief in freedom and responsibility were entirely (or even only primarily) grounded in our experience of other people, then I think we would lack a truly satisfactory explanation of its strength. Such an explanation is swiftly forthcoming when it is realized that it is grounded primarily in our experience of our own agency, and only secondarily in our experience of other people as proper objects of the reactive attitudes. The true centre of one's commitment to the notion of human freedom lies in one's attitude to and experience of oneself. The notion is integral to one's deepest sense of oneself as a self-determining planner and performer of action, someone who can create things, make a sacrifice, do a misdeed.

To say that the true centre of one's commitment lies in one's attitude to and experience of oneself is not to deny that one's attitude to and experience of oneself is deeply determined by one's interaction with others, and, in particular, by the kind of interaction necessary for acquisition of language (though it will be argued later that a solitary being could have an ordinarily strong sense of self as truly responsible). So far as human beings are concerned, it is simply to consider two things that develop in us in the course of our necessarily social development—our sense of ourselves as truly responsible and our sense of others as truly responsible; to claim that the nature and causes of these two things can profitably be distinguished, in certain respects at least; and to claim that the former is more important than the latter, so far as our general commitment to belief in true-responsibility-creating self-determination is concerned.

A naturalistic explanation of this sense of self-determination would connect it tightly with our sense, massively and incessantly confirmed since earliest infancy, of our ability to do what we want to do in order to (try to) get what we want, by performing a vast variety of actions, great and small, walking where we want, making ourselves understood, picking up this and putting down that. We pass our days in more or less continual and almost entirely successful self-directing intentional activity, and we know it.[36] Even if we don't always achieve our aims, when we act, we almost always perform a movement of the kind we intended to perform, and in that vital sense (vital for the sense of self-determining self-control) we are almost entirely successful in our action.

This gives rise to a sense of freedom to act, of complete self-control, of responsibility in self-directedness, that is in itself compatibilistically unexceptionable, and is quite untouched by arguments against true re-

36. Most of these actions are routine or trivial, more or less thoughtlessly performed. But this in no way diminishes the importance of the experience of their performance as a source of the sense of self-determinability that we ordinarily have.

sponsibility based on the impossibility of self-determination. But it is precisely this compatibilistically speaking unexceptionable sense of freedom and efficacy that is one of the fundamental bases of the growth in us of the compatibilistically speaking *im*permissible sense of true responsibility. To observe a child of two fully in control of its limbs, doing what it wants to do with them, and to this extent fully free to act in the compatibilist sense of the phrase, and to realize that it is precisely such unremitting experience of self-control that is the deepest foundation of our naturally *in*compatibilistic sense of true-responsibility-entailing self-determination, is to understand one of the most important facts about the genesis and power of our ordinary strong sense of freedom.

One reason why we advance from the permissible to the impermissible sense of freedom is perhaps a merely negative one, remarked on by Spinoza: ignorant of the causes of our desires, we do not normally experience our character, desires, or pro-attitudes as determined in us in any way at all; let alone in any objectionable way. We don't think back behind ourselves as we now find ourselves. It can happen that we do so, of course. But even if it does happen—even if some particular desire is experienced, in its importunacy, as somehow foreign, imposing itself from outside the self, as it were—this probably only serves, by providing a contrast, to strengthen our general sense that our desires and pro-attitudes are not determined in us. For if a desire is experienced as importunate, as imposing itself on one, as unwanted, then there must be present some other desire or pro-attitude in the light of which the first one is experienced as unwanted or as imposing itself. And the second desire or pro-attitude will presumably not also be experienced as an imposition, as alien. It will presumably be a pro-attitude which one 'identifies' with, and apprehends as part of oneself, and acquiesces in.

A great deal is locked up in this acquiescence. (It is here that our naturally incompatibilist thought appears to run directly counter to our naturally compatibilist acceptance of the 'just-thereness' of desires discussed in the last section.) For although it is unlikely to involve any explicit sense that one has been in any way actively self-determining as to character, it does nevertheless seem to involve an implicit sense that one is, generally, somehow in control of and answerable for how one is; even, perhaps, for those aspects of one's character that one doesn't particularly like.[37] As for those pro-attitudes and aspects of one's character that are welcome to one, it is as if the following ghostly subjunctive conditional lurks in one's attitude to them: if *per impossibile* I were to be (had

37. Consider the sense of sin. People who see themselves as sinners do not only feel guilty about giving in to bad aspects of their character; they also feel guilty about (responsible for having) these bad features in the first place.

been) able to choose my character, then these are the features I would choose (would have chosen).[38] This, I suggest, contributes importantly to the impermissible sense of true responsibility for themselves that most people have, more or less obscurely, more or less constantly.[39]

But it is not the principal reason for which we have the impermissible sense of true responsibility. The principal reason, I think, concerns the nature of our experience of choice. It is simply that we are, in the most ordinary situations of choice, unable not to think that we will be truly or absolutely responsible for our choice, whatever we choose. Our natural thought may be expressed as follows: even if my character is indeed just something given (a product of heredity and environment, or whatever), I am still able to choose (and hence act) completely freely and truly responsibly, given how I now am and what I now know; this is so whatever else is the case—determinism or no determinism.

This thought is reinforced by the point just considered: according to which something that is in itself negative—the absence of any general sense that our desires, pro-attitudes, character, and so on are *not* ultimately self-determined—is implicitly taken as equivalent to some sort of positive self-determination. Certainly we do not ordinarily suppose that we have gone through some sort of active process of self-determination at some particular past time; but it seems accurate to say that we do unreflectively experience ourselves rather as we would experience ourselves if we did believe that we had engaged in some such activity of self-determination.

There are many complexities here. But the main causes of the development of our sense of true responsibility out of our unremitting and compatibilistically speaking unexceptionable sense of complete self-control may perhaps be summarized as follows.

1. We tend to think that we have a will (a power of decision) distinct from all our particular motives.
2. In all ordinary situations of choice, we think that we are absolutely free to choose *whatever* else is the case (even if determinism is true, for example), and are so just because of the fact of our full appreciation of our situation. (Our experience of freedom is of course particularly vivid in cases of morally significant decisions.)

38. It is hardly surprising that the subjunctive conditional as it were confirms the central, acceptable *status quo;* for the 'I' that features in the conditional is in a sense actually constituted, as something with pro-attitudes that imagines choosing its pro-attitudes, by the very pro-attitudes that it imagines choosing.

39. To say this is not to say that people cannot occasionally—or even chronically—be disgusted by themselves. There are many complications here. Some of them are illustrated by H. Frankfurt in *The Importance of What We Care About* (Cambridge: Cambridge University Press, 1988), ch. 2, 4, 5.

3. In some vague and unexamined fashion, we tend to think of ourselves as in some manner responsible for—answerable for—how
   we are.[40]

All these aspects of the sense of true responsibility directly concern only
one's experience of oneself and one's own agency.[41]

Various other ways of bringing out the independence of the sense of
oneself as truly responsible from the sense of other people as so responsible suggest themselves. For example: surely one could come to be a
sceptic about other minds and still continue to believe as strongly as ever
in one's own freedom?

To this it may be objected that belief in the existence of other minds is
at least a genetic condition of acquisition of commitment to belief in
freedom. But the objection can be met as follows: (*a*), belief in other
minds, may perhaps be a genetic condition of—or at least an invariable
concomitant of—(*b*), the acquisition of a sense of self, and of (*c*),
language-acquisition (and indeed of (*d*), acquisition of the intellectual
complexity necessary for conceiving explicitly of, and then doubting the
existence of, other minds). And (*b*) and even perhaps (*c*) may be conditions of the possibility of (*e*), the acquisition of a sense of oneself as truly
responsible. But a genetic-condition claim of this sort is simply not a
claim of the right kind to provide grounds for an objection to the view
that one could come to doubt the existence of other minds without this
affecting one's conviction as to one's own freedom in any way; and there

40. For these points, see my *Freedom and Belief*, 2.8, 3.4, 36. E. H. Carr asserts that "normal adult beings are morally responsible for their own personality" (*What Is History?*,
p. 89); Kant wrote of "man's character, which he himself creates" (*Critique of Practical
Reason*, trans. L. W. Beck, p. 101); Sartre talked of "le choix que tout homme fait de sa
personnalité".

41. There are a number of other familiar things that prevent us from experiencing
ourselves and the world as determined in a way that might undermine our sense of freedom. For example: there is the fact that a person's own future choices and decisions are
'unpredictable in principle' for that person (cf. e.g. D. M. MacKay, 'On the Logical Inde-
terminacy of a Free Choice', *Mind* 69 [1960], and D. F. Pears, 'Predicting and Deciding',
in *Questions in the Philosophy of Mind* [London: Duckworth, 1975]). There is the experiential
quality of uncertainty and dithering indecision: it seems that things could so easily go
either way (cf. Hume, *Treatise*, p. 408): it seems absurd to say that it is entirely determined
which way they do go. There is the fact that even if determinism is true, what happens in
the world in general does not produce any sense in us that it is deterministic in character
(though we may be convinced materialists and believe firmly in the existence of deterministic laws of nature). For there are so many things that 'could so easily have happened'
that did not happen in fact (or vice versa). One might so easily not have met one's lover,
husband, or wife. Glancing at a newspaper left on the underground train, one may pick
it up and read an announcement that changes one's life. Most lives contain many events
of this sort. What happens seems to us to have an essentially fluid and open character.
Perhaps we are not sufficiently reflective, but it is hard for us, in such circumstances, to
be very *impressed* by the thought that our choices and actions may be entirely determined
phenomena.

does not seem to be any special, independent connection between (*a*) and (*e*), such as might be shown to hold if it could be shown that possession of other-reactive attitudes were actually essential for possession of the notion of true responsibility.[42]

More simply: it seems possible that a being might develop a strong sense of freedom (a sense of freedom that was in all essentials the same as ours) in a world in which there were no other creatures like itself, and no creatures which were such as to cause it to come to suppose that they were free—although there were, we may suppose, creatures which were such as to cause it to form the belief that they had experiences and pursued goals. The solitary being's sense of freedom might derive from its having to make difficult choices, life-determining choices, perhaps, about which of several equally attractive but very different and not co-attainable ends to pursue. It would not have to have any sense of moral good and bad. It might simply have a powerful sense that it was entirely up to it what it did. (This said, it must be granted that a sense of moral right and wrong acts powerfully in fostering a sense of true responsibility, as Kant saw.)[43]

It may be objected that the solitary being would have to be linguistically endowed, and self-conscious, in order to be free—that these may be necessary conditions of free agenthood. If so, it might be said, it would need company, in order to acquire a language. However, logical possibility provides for the idea that it may just be created self-conscious and

42. Furthermore: although unreflective belief in the existence of other minds is doubtless an invariable concomitant of language-learning here on earth, and as things are, it seems quite possible that a child might learn a language from other people (or even from actually experienceless robots) a constant theme of whose everyday conversation (or 'conversation') was that there was nothing it was like to be them. Although this might not at first make much sense to the child, and although it might at first suppose them to be like itself, it could presumably grow up into the firm (and possibly true) belief that there was nothing it was like to be any of its interlocutors. Growing up in this way, it could acquire a normally powerful sense of its actions being up to it in some absolute fashion.

43. Here there is a complication worth noting. It is true that the general experience of difficult choice contributes vitally to the 'impermissible' sense of true responsibility, in the ordinary case. But the phenomenology of making a difficult (and let us say non-moral) choice in which one believes that there is a *right* and a *wrong* decision, if only one could work out which was which, need involve nothing at all that conflicts with a wholly compatibilistic view of things. In this case one considers and reconsiders the pros and the cons, and what one wants is simply that it should become clear which is the right choice. One wants to come to see which is best; and there is nothing in this experience that either involves or gives rise to any sense of true responsibility—any more than there is in considering which of a number of melons is ripest, or in wanting to be able to read the words on a sign that is just too far away. In cases like this the phenomenology of difficult choice is essentially that of wanting to form a true belief, and, so far at least, need involve nothing of the sense of radical freedom that may be produced by facing a dramatic conflict of duty and desire, or an important, life-determining choice between two very different morally neutral options which are in one's opinion equally attractive all things considered (between which there is 'nothing to choose').

already possessed of a language, or at least of the capacity for language-like thought.[44] Alternatively, it may be brought up by other members of its own species to a point at which it is fully possessed of language, and then left to fend for itself after all memory of the existence of other sentient beings has been wiped from its mind. Surviving and flourishing, making difficult choices, it may develop or retain a strong sense of freedom of choice without any thought of others at all.

Suppose that this solitary being is persistently but by no means always hindered by constraining circumstances in the execution of its intentions. This being so, it may acquire a sense of freedom of *action*—that which it feels when unhindered—which is importantly different from the sense of freedom of *choice* just mentioned. Neither of these senses of freedom depends essentially on interaction with other people, or upon preparedness to attribute freedom to others, but only on the private experience of deliberation and action. One's belief that others are free has the power it has because it is, first and foremost, a belief that they are like one finds oneself to be. We attribute to others the same sort of consciousness of responsibility for, and hence freedom of, choice and action that we cannot but attribute to ourselves. It is not as if adversion either to the circumstances of our learning the word 'free', as members of a linguistic community, or to the dubiety of the 'argument from analogy', can undercut this point. On the contrary: the availability of this point, and others like it, illustrates the risk of exaggerating both the consequences of Wittgenstein's 'private language' argument and the error allegedly involved in putting forward the argument from analogy in answer to certain sceptical puzzles.

Certainly our acquisition of an understanding of the words 'free' and 'truly responsible' proceeds in such a way that we are, ordinarily, *as* prepared to apply these words to others as we are to ourselves. And certainly we are in being committed to the reactive attitudes to other people committed to the belief that they are truly responsible agents. This is not denied. The claim is merely that the deepest point of attachment of one's commitment to belief in true responsibility lies in the experience one comes to have, *as* a social, linguistic being, of one's own agency. Even if it were true that a being could not develop in such a way as to come to attribute true responsibility to itself without having been participant in a social and linguistic community, this fact would provide no basis for an objection to the above claim, which is merely a claim about the deepest

44. Possessed, that is, of at least the following: a disposition to have just the same sorts of experience, qualitatively speaking, that a solitary Robinson Crusoe who had forgotten that other people existed might have, so far as those of his experiences that he himself would be inclined to classify as experiences of thinking or speaking in language were concerned.

foundation of our present commitment to belief in true responsibility, not about the conditions of our past acquisition of such a belief.

IT is not the 'general framework' of social life, then, that is currently in question. It is the agent's private experience of agency. It is one's commitment to belief in one's own efficacy, control, self-determination, and total responsibility (in normally unconstrained circumstances), rather than one's commitment to holding others responsible and treating them as proper objects of reactive attitudes, that is primarily unrenounceable.

IT only remains to say that, to the extent that it is primarily in one's attitudes to and conception of oneself that the roots of one's commitment to belief in true (moral) responsibility lie, the problems which determinism (and non-self-determinability) raises for that belief are particularly acute in one's own case. What on earth is one to think that one is, or is doing, if one thinks that one cannot really be responsible at all for what one does? Those who have fully understood what the application of the thought of determinism to themselves involves should be bewildered by this question (recall the thought-experiment in section V).

But it is likely to leave them undisturbed. And it is this equanimity in the face of the problem, this equanimity with which we continue to discuss the problem of freedom and determinism, that is perhaps the best indication of the strength of our commitment to belief in freedom.

VIII. SATKĀYADṚṢṬI

The suggestion that one's commitment to belief in freedom and the reactive attitudes may be of such a kind that its abandonment is practically speaking impossible has not so far been challenged. But it has been suggested that one might be able to engineer (or might simply undergo) partial but not total erosions of this commitment; and that it is perhaps not equally unrenounceable in all areas. For example: one's commitment to belief in one's own responsibility for action seems to be more deeply founded than one's commitment to belief in the responsibility of others, even if this difference is not revealed in a difference of surface strength in everyday life; and so it seems correspondingly more likely that one might cease to be moved to blame others, on account of belief in determinism or non-self-determinability, than that one might cease to feel guilty about what one took to be one's own miscreance.

But perhaps one can raise a more general doubt about arguments for unrenounceable commitments to attitudes or beliefs that appear to be false from some natural point of view. Consider certain Buddhist philosophers who argue, on a variety of metaphysical grounds, that our natural notion of the persisting individual self is a delusion. Having reached this conclusion, they set themselves a task: that of overcoming the delusion.

There are several routes to the doctrine of *satkāyadṛṣṭi, the 'false view of individuality'*.[45] Which one is taken is of no present importance. The Buddhists presently in question hold that (*a*), the false sense or conception of self, leads to (*b*), suffering because it is essentially bound in with, as a necessary condition of, (*c*), the having of desires and aversions, which is itself a condition of the possibility of suffering.[46] To realize that there is no such thing as the individual self, to undermine the false view of individuality in oneself, is to cease to be bound by desires, cravings, and aversions, and hence to achieve liberation from suffering. It is, ultimately, to achieve the 'blowing out' of self in nirvana, and thereby to cease to suffer and to fear old age, sickness, and death.

These Buddhists not only have theoretical reasons for believing that their natural sense or conception of self is delusory; they also have powerful practical reasons for trying to improve their grasp on the fact of its delusoriness. They recognize, however, that one cannot simply abolish one's sense of individuality, by some sort of effortless, rationally motivated, self-directed intellectual fiat. Delusions delude, after all; and the ordinary, strong sense of self (and hence of self-determination) is a particularly powerful delusion. They therefore recommend the adoption of a certain practice—that of meditation—the eventual effect of which, they claim, is to cause the delusion to dislimn.[47]

Now a decision to adopt such a practice of meditation is presumably motivated by some desire. It can be simply a desire for an undeluded view of things—a love of truth or of correct attitude. In the Buddha's case, the originally predominant motive was his desire to overcome his horror of old age, sickness, and death: suffering, decrepitude and death are fearful only to a man who has desires and aversions of such a kind that he confronts himself as an object to worry about, and who has a sense of himself as a continuing entity, a person.[48]

45. *An-ātman,* or 'no-soul', denotes the corresponding positive doctrine that there is no soul or self; and the experiential or phenomenological correlate of the factual or metaphysical error involved in *satkāyadṛṣṭi* is called *asmimāna,* or the " 'I am' idea". See *Selfless Persons,* by S. Collins (Cambridge: Cambridge University Press, 1982), pp. 94, 100.

46. (*b*) requires (*c*) and (*c*) requires (*a*). So to eliminate (*a*) is to eliminate (*b*). Obviously the unselfconscious—dogs, bats, and so on—can also suffer. The point is made in this particular way because it is the basis of a practical recommendation for human beings.

47. Perhaps we may suppose that their goal is to achieve some kind of affectively speaking selfless but cognitively speaking fully self-conscious state of mind. See however *Freedom and Belief,* Appendix E, § III.

48. If there is, in a sense, no 'I', then there is nothing to fear in death and dissolution, and there is no one there to feel fear in any case. For it is precisely the 'I' 's dissolution that is feared, and it is precisely the 'I' that does the fearing.

What is curious about this general project is that if one attains nirvana, or at least a state of desirelessness, then one's desire for truth or correctness of attitude, or one's wish to escape from one's fear of mortal ills, lapses with all other desires, so that it is no longer there to be finally fulfilled by the course of action that it set in motion. Thus a man who attains nirvana, or a state of desirelessness, can never give any current reason—if this involves adducing a present desire presently satisfied—for being the way he is. Nevertheless, given his love of truth or of correctness of attitude, or his fear of old age and death, his adoption of the practice of meditation *was* rational, even if he is now (practically speaking) non-rational, and is so as a result of that practice.

THE foregoing enables one kind of person, at least, to answer the question of what it would be rational to do given belief in determinism and incompatibilism (or in non-self-determinability): someone who had such a belief, and wished to lose any sense of self as free or truly self-determining in any way, in order to achieve a more correct attitude to the world, would do well to adopt the allegedly self-dissolving practice of meditation. A sense of self is not only a necessary condition of fear for one's future; it is also, obviously, a necessary condition of possession of the allegedly illegitimate sense of oneself as a truly self-determining planner and performer of action.

A more general point is this. There appear to be powerful lines of reasoning available, within what Strawson calls our 'general framework' of attitudes and ideas, which question the correctness of the framework—or of paramount aspects of it—from within. There are, to say the least, some major tensions in it. No doubt a decision to adopt the 'objective' attitude to oneself and others cannot be implemented overnight, given the nature and strength of the framework and our commitment to it. But there is no such difficulty with a decision to initiate some practice which may more gradually undermine or alter the supposedly inflexible constraints of the framework. And, if we admit the possibility of partial alterations in attitudes or habits of thought to which we are as things are deeply committed, then this points to the possibility of a progressive abandonment of these attitudes or habits of thought which, gradually achieved, amounts to a total abandonment relative to the original position. It is not implausible to suppose that Buddhist monks and other mystics have succeeded in altering quite profoundly their experience of themselves (and others) as acting, thinking, and feeling beings.

And—finally—it is not implausible to say that they have in so doing achieved what is in certain respects a more correct view of the world, precisely to the extent that they have ceased to regard themselves and others as truly self-determining sources of actions, and have thereby

3

The Importance of Free Will

SUSAN WOLF

THE assumption that we have free will is generally thought to lurk behind the justifications of many of our current practices. That is, it is generally thought that only if we have free will can it be appropriate for us
to engage in these practices, and that, if we should conclude that we
don't have free will, we would have reason to give these practices up.
The importance of the problem of free will in philosophy is often
thought to depend on its relation to the justification of these practices.
Thus, if an adequate justification of these practices were to be found, it
may be thought that either the free will problem would thereby be
solved or that, at least, it would thereby cease to be of interest.

In this paper, I shall argue that the justification of these practices
need not rest on the assumption that we do have free will, and that the
conclusion that we don't have free will gives us no reason at all to abandon these practices. My argument, however, seems to me to leave both
the problem and its importance intact. The thought that our wills may
not be free is no less disturbing even when all ties to the justification of
our practices are completely and irrevocably severed.

Of course, there are some for whom the problem of free will was
never disturbing in the first place. This paper is not likely to provide
them with any new reason to be disturbed. Moreover, to those who have
been and continue to be disturbed by the problem, this paper is not
likely to offer much solace. Still, my paper is primarily addressed to this

Reprinted from *Mind* 90 (1981): 386–405 by permission of Oxford University Press.

More people have benefited me by their comments and criticism of drafts of this paper
than I am able to acknowledge here. Of the many to whom I am grateful, special thanks
are due to Jonathan Bennett and to Martha Nussbaum.

latter group, for, if it cannot provide solace, it may still provide insight into why—and why not—such solace is needed.

I shall begin by outlining a naive attempt at expressing the fears of those who find the problem of free will upsetting, and a naive response by those who think that the problem of free will gives us nothing to worry about. This expression of fear and the response to it constitute a first stage of debate, which focuses on the justification of our practices of overt reward and punishment. The inadequacies at this stage of the argument suggest a way of advancing to a deeper stage, which focuses not on the overt practices themselves, but on the attitudes these practices typically express. Proceeding by way of two analogical cases, I shall argue that these attitudes, too, are safe from the threat of being undermined by reason and metaphysics. Nonetheless, I think that feelings of dissatisfaction may reasonably remain. I shall finally attempt to express what I take to be the appropriate focus of these feelings.

THE JUSTIFICATION OF REWARD AND PUNISHMENT

I shall hereafter refer to the group who find the problem of free will upsetting as 'the pessimists'. In this, I follow P. F. Strawson in his article 'Freedom and Resentment'.[1] The pessimists include all those who believe, first, that whether or not we have free will depends on which metaphysical hypotheses are true, and, second, that it is not unlikely that the wrong metaphysical hypotheses are true. Perhaps the most common pessimists are those who believe that the thesis of determinism is both incompatible with free will and very likely true. However, they are also pessimists who believe that indeterminism is both incompatible with free will and, at least, very possibly true. And there are some, who may be said to be more pessimistic still, who believe that both determinism and indeterminism are incompatible with free will. For the remainder of this paper, I shall address myself to the first sort of pessimist, but it should be obvious how what I have to say to him can, with minimal adjustments, be addressed as significantly to the concerns of the other sorts of pessimist as well.

The opposing group, the optimists, are likely to doubt that the question of whether or not we have free will can profitably be said to depend on the truth of 'hypotheses', metaphysical or otherwise, at all. But, in any case, they believe that in so far as free will does depend on the truth of hypotheses, the facts already known to us are sufficient to guarantee that the appropriate hypotheses are true.

Of course, in calling the group who believes that we probably lack free will pessimistic, I adopt their accompanying view that the absence of free

1. P. F. Strawson, 'Freedom and Resentment', this volume. I am indebted to this brilliant article for many of the ideas in this paper.

will would be a very bad thing. Unfortunately, when it comes to explaining why it would be a very bad thing, the pessimists tend to be distressingly obscure. Of the practices they feel to be potentially undermined by the absence of free will, those associated with attributions of moral responsibility are most often cited. That is, they seem to think that the practices of praising and blaming people, punishing and rewarding them on the basis of the moral quality of their actions would be irrational, inappropriate, and unjustifiable if the thesis of determinism were true.

If this is all that the pessimists are worried about, however, the optimists have a ready reply. For they can provide a justification of the allegedly threatened practices that is in no way invalidated by the truth of determinism. They can argue, in particular, that the way in which we justify—or at least, the way in which we ought to justify—the application of these practices is one that depends on the consequences of engaging in them. We should praise or blame an individual, they may argue, if and only if by doing so we shall improve the moral quality of actions in the future. Or they may argue that we should praise or blame an individual if and only if by doing so we shall be obeying rules the institution of which will improve the moral quality of actions in the future. The hypotheses on which both these justifications of moral praise and blame rest are guaranteed to be true by the facts we already possess. We already know that we can improve the moral quality of actions by maintaining institutions of punishment that serve functions of rehabilitation and deterrence. We already know that we can improve the moral quality of actions by maintaining institutions of reward that provide incentives. Thus, we know that our practices of reward and punishment are justified whether or not the thesis of determinism is true.

I take it that this forward-looking, consequentialist type of justification of the practices of overt moral praise and blame is a good one, and therefore I take it that the intelligent pessimist will think it a good one as well. But in conceding this, the pessimist is likely to withdraw not his fear of determinism, but only his account of it. For the pessimist is likely to feel that the optimist's response somehow misses the pessimist's point. There is a striking difference between the type of justification of moral praise and blame that the optimist offers and a type of justification on which we ordinarily rely. It is in this difference that the pessimist's point, on a revised account, may be said to lie.

The justification of praise and blame the optimist suggests is one that emphasizes the fact that we can view praising and blaming as kinds of action, which, like any other actions, may or may not be sensible conclusions of practical reasoning. Whether or not to engage in these practices is on this view to be decided, like many other practical questions, according to whether engaging in these practices is a good way of achieving other desired ends. But we do not ordinarily praise and blame other persons because, as a result of engaging in practical deliberation, we have reached the conclusion that it would be in our interests to do so. Rather, we praise and blame persons as natural expressions of natural responses to what we see people do. We do not ordinarily *decide* whether a word of praise or a public scolding would be a useful directive to future behaviour. Rather, we find ourselves *reacting* to the actions and characters of others, approving of some, disapproving of others. Unless there is reason to restrain ourselves, we simply express what we feel.

In other words, although moral praising and blaming *can* be considered as kinds of actions, our ordinary experience of these phenomena encourages us to consider them as expressions of a kind of judgment. Accordingly, although one *can* justify these practices in a way that is analogous to justifications of other kinds of action, one can also try to justify these practices in a way that is analogous to justifications of other kinds of judgment. In particular, one can try to justify them by showing how the relevant judgments are fitting for, appropriate to, or, most aptly, *deserved by* the relevant objects of these judgments—in this case, human agents.

To justify praise and blame in the way the optimist suggests is to leave out of account such judgments of individual desert. It is to leave out of account any question of whether it is an individual's fault that he has done something wrong or whether it is to the individual's credit that he has done something right. In short, to justify the praise and blame of persons in the way the optimist suggests is to justify these practices in the same way that we justify the praise and blame of lower animals—in the same way, that is, that we justify the reward and punishment of pets, of pigeons in the laboratory, of monkeys in the circus. It is to justify these practices only as a means of manipulation or training.

The pessimist's fear may now be expressed as the fear that if determinism is true, this consequentialist justification of praise and blame is the only kind of justification that would be available to us. If determinism is true, the pessimist fears, the type of justification of praise and blame that rests on judgments of individual desert can never be appropriate or valid. He fears that if we discover that determinism is true, we will be rationally obliged to give up making and relying on such judgments—and, more important perhaps, we will be rationally obliged to give up the attitudes which are essentially tied to these judgments.

It is notoriously difficult to give any precise characterization of these attitudes, to do more than be merely suggestive about their range and significance. The attitudes I have in mind include admiration and indignation, pride and shame, respect and contempt, gratitude and resentment. P. F. Strawson, in the article I mentioned earlier, has called this set of attitudes 'the reactive attitudes.' They are attitudes one has toward individuals only in so far as one views these individuals as persons. In contrast to the reactive attitudes, we may take what Strawson calls 'the objective attitude' toward the individuals with whom we interact. This is the attitude we do take—or at least, the attitude we rationally ought to take—toward most animals, present-day machines, and very young children.

THE JUSTIFICATION OF THE REACTIVE ATTITUDES

What the pessimist really fears, then, is that if determinism is true, we must give up not the practices of praise and blame themselves, but the attitudes and judgments these practices typically express. We must give up all reactive attitudes, and adopt the objective attitude toward ourselves and each other, as we do toward everything else. It may be thought that in restating the pessimist's concerns, the scope and importance of his fears have considerably shrunk. The changing of attitudes seems to be such a private and insubstantial affair that it might be thought to make very little difference in the world. On second glance, however, we can see that the abandonment of all the reactive attitudes would make a very great difference indeed. To replace our reactive attitudes with the objective attitude completely is to change drastically—or, as most would say, reduce—the quality of our involvement or participation in all our human relationships.

Imagine for a moment what a world would be like in which we all regarded each other solely with the objective attitude. We would still imprison murderers and thieves, presumably, and we would still sing praises for acts of courage and charity. We would applaud and criticize, say 'thank you' and 'for shame' according to whether our neighbors' behaviour was or was not to our liking. But these actions and words would have a different, shallower meaning than they have for us now. Our praises would not be expressions of admiration or esteem; our criticisms would not be expressions of indignation or resentment. Rather, they would be bits of positive and negative reinforcement meted out in the hopes of altering the character of others in ways best suited to our needs.

An act of heroism or of saintly virtue would not inspire us to aim for higher and nobler ideals, nor would it evoke in us a reverence or even admiration for its agent. At best we would think it a piece of good fortune that people occasionally do perform acts like this. We would consider how nice it must be for the beneficiaries and decide to encourage this kind of behavior. We would not recoil from acts of injustice or cruelty as insults to human dignity, nor be moved by such acts to reflect with sorrow or puzzlement on the tide of events that can bring persons to stoop so low. Rather, we would recognize that the human tendency to perform acts like this is undesirable, a problem to be dealt with, like any other, as scientifically and efficiently as possible.

The most gruesome difference between this world and ours would be reflected in our closest human relationships—in the relations between siblings, parents and children, and especially spouses and companions. We would still be able to form some sorts of association that could be described as relationships of friendship and love. One person could find another amusing or useful. One could notice that the presence of a certain person was, like the sound of a favourite song, particularly soothing or invigorating. We could choose friends as we now choose clothing or home furnishings or hobbies, according to whether they offer, to a sufficient degree, the proper combination of pleasure and practicality. Attachments of considerable strength can develop on such limited bases. People do, after all, form strong attachments to their cars, their pianos, not to mention their pets. Nonetheless, I hope it is obvious why the words 'friendship' and 'love' applied to relationships in which admiration, respect, and gratitude have no part, might be said to take on a hollow ring. A world in which human relationships are restricted to those that can be formed and supported in the absence of the reactive attitudes is a world of human isolation so cold and dreary that any but the most cynical must shudder at the idea of it.

It is such a world in which the pessimist fears we would be rationally obliged to live if we came, once and for all, to the conclusion that the thesis of determinism was true. It is such a world, so much bleaker and more barren than our present world, to which the pessimist fears the truth of determinism would rationally force us. Once the optimist recognizes just what it is that the pessimist fears is at stake, however, the optimist once again has a ready reply. One thing he can point out is that even if the truth of determinism would give us some *reason* to regard ourselves differently, we would be psychologically incapable of changing our attitudes in the appropriate way. Another is that even if the truth of determinism would give us *some* reason to regard ourselves differently, we would have an overriding reason to keep the attitudes we currently hold. The overriding reason, of course, is that were we to give up our reactive attitudes, we would drastically reduce our sense of the meaning and value of our lives.

In light of the magnitude of this potential loss, it seems to me not irrational for the pessimist once again to concede the optimist's point. Once again, however, in conceding this, the pessimist is likely to withdraw not his fear of determinism but only his account of it. In other words, the pessimist might accept the optimist's argument—but he will accept it with despair. For with the first of his arguments, the optimist does not even attempt to allay the pessimist's fear that we will be forced to the conclusion that our attitudes toward ourselves are unjustified. Rather, he only seeks to show the pessimist how impotent this conclusion, if reached, would be. With the second of his arguments, the optimist suggests a way to avoid the feared conclusion. However, in so far as the optimist's justification takes the form of providing reasons that *override* other reasons, the justification can be only as satisfying as the acceptance of the lesser of two evils can be. How satisfying that is depends, in turn, on how evil is the evil we are forced to accept. Thus, it is worthwhile to get clear about the evil with which the pessimist now thinks we are left—the reason, in other words, for giving up the reactive attitudes which the optimist's argument must override.

Recall, then, that for the pessimist, whether or not we have free will is a matter of metaphysical fact. If determinism is true, then we do not have free will—that is, we are not free and responsible beings. In so far as we take reactive attitudes towards ourselves and each other, however, we regard ourselves as free and responsible beings. If determinism is true, then by continuing to take these attitudes, we live in a way that is discordant with the facts.[2]

The reason for giving up our reactive attitudes, then, is that by doing so we will be living in accordance with the facts. We will be accepting our status as creatures who are no more responsible for their lives and characters than are animals and machines. We will be accepting our status as agents to whom notions of personal credit, discredit, and desert fail to apply. If, despite the knowledge that this is our status, we choose to retain our reactive attitudes, we choose to live as if we were a kind of being that we know we are not. In doing this, we choose something akin to self-deception.[3]

As I said earlier, I believe such a choice may be rational. With Strawson, I think that it may be rational to choose *not* 'to be more purely rational than we are.'[4] It may be rational for a man to choose not to face the fact that he has a terminal illness or for a woman to try to avoid discovering that her husband is having an affair. If the costs would be high enough, it may be rational to override the reason for a course of action that is given by the acknowledgment that only that course of action would constitute living in accordance with the facts. To override this reason, however, is not just to choose to leave a desire unsatisfied. It is to choose to leave a value unrealized, a value, moreover, which is arguably

2. Discordance with the facts is weaker than logical inconsistency. It is logically consistent to take attitudes that are essentially subject to certain standards of justification while at the same time believing that no such justifications are possible.

3. On this I part company with Strawson. For an excellent alternative account of these matters more faithful to Strawson's own views, see Jonathan Bennett, 'Accountability', in Zak Van Straaten (ed.), *Philosophical Subjects: Essays Presented to P. F. Strawson* (the Clarendon Press, 1980).

4. Strawson, p. 56 n. 4.

one of considerable depth and importance.[5] To choose to act against, or contradict, a value as deep as this one, is inevitably to suffer a significant loss. It should not be surprising if the conviction that such a choice may be rational fails to bring the pessimist peace of mind.

Even to this last account of the pessimist's fear, I believe that the optimist has a reply which should make the pessimist withdraw his attempt to express and explain the threat of determinism yet another time. For I believe that even if determinism is true, and even if this implies that as a matter of metaphysical fact we are not free and responsible beings, this gives us *no reason at all* to regard ourselves as unfree, unresponsible beings. That is, we have no reason at all to abandon our reactive attitudes and to adopt the objective attitude in their place. If we have no reason at all to abandon these attitudes, then we have nothing we need to override, no value we need to contradict in choosing to keep these attitudes. Our retention of the reactive attitudes need not be viewed as a choice between the lesser of two evils.

At first glance, it may appear that *this* conclusion must finally put the pessimist's mind at ease. We shall return to this claim later. First we must understand why this conclusion is warranted.

The case of the addict. Let us consider a hypothetical but not unrealistic situation: the situation of a drug addict who cannot help but take the drug to which he is addicted regardless of the attitude or value or second-order desire he has concerning his addiction. Let us further assume that in other respects our addict is a normally functioning, intelligent human being. Then the degree to which we hold this individual responsible for his drug-taking actions will vary in proportion to the degree to which we think he approves of—or, at least, doesn't disapprove of—the fact that he takes these actions. If the addict, with apparent sincerity, says and shows that he is relatively content to be an addict, that he sees no sufficient reason for trying to resist his addiction, then he is, in effect, accepting responsibility for taking the drug. He is affirming the fact that his efforts to obtain and to take the drug are *his actions,* that they effect and contribute to his character and his life in a way that may fairly enter into an assessment of what kind of person he is. It is therefore rational for us to regard him as responsible for taking the drug. If, on the other hand, the addict says and shows that he repudiates his addiction, that he makes all possible efforts to resist taking the drug, then he effectively removes himself from responsibility for taking the drug. He shows that he takes the drug only because he is addicted and that he would not take the drug if he could help it. It is therefore rational for us to regard him as not responsible for taking the drug. In other words, the addict's own attitude toward taking the drug gives us a reason (perhaps

5. For a good account of the distinction between values and other desires, see Gary Watson, 'Free Agency', *The Journal of Philosophy,* lxxii (24 April 1975), pp. 205–220.

the reason) by which to establish ours—that is, it gives us the means by which to decide whether we ought to regard him as responsible for taking the drug.

The addict's actions are not free because whether or not he chooses to take the drug, he will take the drug because he is compelled to do so. However, the addict's responsibility for his actions turns on the truth or falsity of an independent claim: namely, that whether or not the addict is compelled to take the drug, he will take the drug because he chooses to do so.[6] The addict, then, in taking an attitude toward his unfree actions, can thereby claim or disclaim responsibility for them. But whichever attitude the addict does take, the addict, in taking *an* attitude, asserts himself as a free and responsible being. By this I mean that if the addict accepts responsibility for taking the drug, he claims in effect that as a free and responsible being he chooses to take it, and if the addict rejects responsibility for taking the drug, he claims in effect that as a free and responsible being he does not choose to take it. The fact that we take the addict's own attitudes to his drug-taking actions seriously—that is, the fact that his attitudes count as a reason for us to hold him more or less responsible for these actions—rests on our belief that the addict, qua attitude-taker, *is* a free and responsible being. If we believed that the addict's approval or disapproval of his actions were itself determined by influence of the drug, we would not regard his attitude as giving us a reason by which to establish ours.

The case of the robot. Let us turn now to a second case which takes us into the realm of science fiction. Let us imagine an individual who has been and continues to be very completely and elaborately programmed. He is programmed not only to make various choices and perform various actions, but also to engage in various thought processes, to form various second-order volitions and so forth, in coming to perform these actions. Indeed, this individual is programmed in such a way as to appear to be an ordinary human being in every respect. If no one were informed that this individual was programmed, he would appear both to us and to himself to be 'one of us'. I shall hereafter refer to this individual as a robot, but I believe that whether he is a member of the human species or not is irrelevant to the case.

Let us further assume that the robot's programming is not of any normal or familiar kind. In particular, let us assume it is not the case that any complete program is installed in the robot before he is, as it were, released into the world. Rather, let us assume that the robot is pro-

6. I take it that I am agreeing here with Harry Frankfurt in 'Freedom of the Will and the Concept of a Person', *The Journal of Philosophy*, lxviii (14 January 1971), pp. 5–20. My description of the addict was suggested by his discussion of three kinds of addict—the willing addict, the unwilling addict, and the wanton, who has no attitude or second-order desire concerning his addiction. I am concerned only with the first two kinds.

grammed on a day-to-day or moment-to-moment basis: the programmer implants the robot's responses to situations as these very situations arise. One might imagine the relation between robot and programmer to be very much like a possible relation between author and character; or, perhaps even better, one might imagine the relation to be like the relation between a magician and a human being over whose thoughts and bodily movements the magician has complete control.

In light of the nature of the robot's programming, I believe that the only way of living in accordance with the facts would be by regarding the robot solely with the objective attitude.[7] That is, I believe that the robot is not a free and responsible being in whatever sense of 'free and responsible' the objects of our reactive attitudes are ordinarily assumed to be. Were we to be purely rational, we would allow ourselves to feel some emotions toward the robot, but we would not feel those emotions or sentiments constitutive of our reactive attitudes. For though the robot might choose to perform the actions he performs, he chooses to perform them only because he is programmed to so choose. Though his decisions and judgments may be preceded by thoughts which look or sound like reasons, he cannot be said to reason to these conclusions in the way we do. He is not in ultimate control of his value, his personality, or his actions. He is, properly speaking, only a vehicle for carrying out the plans (if plans there be) of his programmer.

Were such a robot to live within our society, it may well be that we would not ultimately regard him in the way that I have suggested it would be purely rational for us to regard him. The sheer difficulty of keeping in mind the fact that the robot is programmed (along with all its implications) may make it psychologically impossible for us to take the objective attitude towards him consistently. Moreover, we might decide that, though there is some reason for us to treat the robot objectively, there are overriding reasons to treat him as a normal member of the community. Or perhaps we would take some sort of middle ground. (For example, we might treat him as if he had some of the rights of a normal person, but we would shrink from allowing one of our daughters to marry him.)[8] All that is important for my purposes is that we take it to be purely rational to regard the robot objectively. For this should carry at least some weight in determining how we ought ultimately to regard him.

7. Some philosophers will resist this conclusion, and the few remarks I add (directly below) by way of support may be insufficient to convince them. However, I believe the pessimist would think that this conclusion is correct, and it is with the pessimist's position that I am primarily concerned.

8. This recalls a scene from a play by Woody Allen: Two characters in the play appeal for help in their dialogue from the members of the audience. An attractive woman comes to their aid, with whom one of the characters begins to fall in love. The other character, trying to discourage the romance, asks his friend, 'What kind of children would you have? She's Jewish, you're fictional!'

Let us now assume that, after years of thinking himself to be like other human beings, the robot comes to believe that he is completely programmed. If at this point we were to adopt the robot's interests as our own, would it be rational for us to urge (to the programmer, presumably) that the robot take the objective attitude toward himself?

By this question I mean to approach the question 'Would it be rational for the robot to adopt the objective attitude toward himself?' as closely as my standards of conceptual coherence allow. I am not sure that we can make sense of the question 'What would it be rational for the robot to do?', because the attempt to answer it seems to require that we imaginatively endow the robot with the powers of a free and responsible being while, at the same time, remaining convinced that the robot lacks these same powers. However, I see nothing to prevent us from reasoning *on the robot's behalf*. Thus, to repeat my question, I ask, if we were to adopt the robot's interests as our own, would it be rational for us to urge that the robot take the objective attitude toward himself?

Well, I can imagine some situations in which it might be. If, for example, the robot were an individual unusually tormented by an awareness of his limitations, the belief that he was not responsible for the meagreness of his abilities might be a source of some comfort to him. Or, if the members of the robot's community did take the purely rational attitude toward the robot, the robot's own adoption of the objective attitude toward himself might allow him to take this treatment less personally. (Of course, here as always, it will ultimately be up to the programmer whether the robot's adoption of the objective attitude would serve the purposes that I have suggested they might serve. But let us assume at this point that the programmer is cooperative.)

In so far as we argue that the robot should adopt, or try to adopt, the objective attitude toward himself for reasons such as these, however, we are not arguing for the adoption of this attitude simply on the grounds that the attitude is appropriate. That is, we are not arguing that the robot should take this attitude simply because of his (and our) value in living in accordance with the facts. Our reasons for urging that the robot should take the objective attitude are, rather, utilitarian ones: his life will be less painful if he takes the objective attitude toward himself.

Furthermore, if the robot were programmed to take this attitude, he would not really be taking an attitude that would be in accordance with the facts. In believing that reactive attitudes toward himself are inappropriate, he would not be accepting all the implications of the fact that he is programmed; he would not be denying his freedom and responsibility completely. For the robot, in taking an objective view of himself, necessarily leaves a part of himself out of this view—specifically, he leaves out that part of himself which is taking the objective attitude. The robot perhaps takes comfort in the fact that *he*—as it were, 'his self'—is not responsible for his meagre abilities; or, the robot takes comfort in thinking that he is not responsible for the fact that he is merely a robot. But the robot's alienation from his abilities on the one hand, or from his robot-ness on the other, presupposes a self from whom these things are alien-ated, a self whose fault these things are not. And of course, in this example, the robot's self is itself the result of his programming. To the extent that being programmed justifies a denial of responsibility for *any* feature of the robot's existence, it justifies—indeed, demands—a denial of responsibility for *every* feature of his existence—including, in partic-ular, his denial of responsibility for every other feature.

We can bring this out by comparing the case of the robot to that of the addict. For, recall that the addict, in taking any attitude toward his ad-diction, asserts himself as a free and responsible being. If he accepts re-sponsibility for taking the drug, he claims that as a free and responsible being he chooses to take it. If he rejects responsibility for taking the drug, he claims that as a free and responsible being he does not choose to take it. Similarly, the robot in taking an attitude toward himself, as-serts himself as a free and responsible being. But unlike the addict, the robot is not a free and responsible being in any respect whatsoever. He is in a position analogous to that of the addict whose attitude toward his addiction is itself determined by the influence of the drug. Thus, the robot's own attitude toward himself cannot have any weight for us. If the robot, as a matter of metaphysical fact, is an unfree, unresponsible be-ing, then *his* acceptance of this fact gives us no extra reason to regard him as such.

The case of our (determined) selves. We may finally turn to the question of what it would be purely rational for us to do if we came to believe that the thesis of determinism was true and that this implied that, as a matter of metaphysical fact, we were not free and responsible beings. Perhaps the pessimist thinks that if determinism is true, then the whole world is in a position analogous to that of the robot—that, in other words, the thesis of determinism is not different in any relevant respect from the thesis that the whole world is, like the robot, completely programmed. In this case, would it be rational for us to take the objective attitude to-ward ourselves? Again, we might answer, as we did when reasoning on behalf of the robot, that we can imagine some situations in which it might be. In particular, it would be rational for us to take this attitude if by doing so we would become, on the whole, better off. But consider-ations of the sort I suggested earlier make this possibility seem very un-likely. It is hard to believe that more of our desires (all orders inclusive)[9] would be satisfied if we ceased to take the reactive attitudes and adopted the objective attitude in their place. Still, among our desires, we must include the often very strong desire to live in accordance with the facts.

9. The idea of higher-order desires is taken from Harry Frankfurt, ibid.

Indeed, as I said earlier, this is not just a desire, but a value of considerable depth and importance. If, by taking the objective attitude toward ourselves, we would better realize this value, then, regardless of our ultimate decision, we would have at least some reason to adopt the objective attitude.

It should now be clear, however, that we would *not* be realizing this value by adopting the objective attitude. If we were to view ourselves objectively, we would, like the robot, necessarily leave a part of ourselves out of this view. In taking any attitude toward ourselves, including the attitude that we are not free or responsible beings, we would be asserting ourselves *as* free and responsible beings.[10] Any attitude we take, then, would involve a false step—any attitude would be unjustified. Thus, it seems that the only way we could live in accordance with the facts would be by ceasing to have any attitudes at all—by ceasing, that is, to make or rely on any judgments about an individual's responsibility or lack of it at all.

The truth of determinism, then, gives us no reason at all to replace our present reactive attitudes with the objective attitude. Some might think, however, that it gives us reason to do something even more drastic—namely, to give up the taking of attitudes altogether. For I have said that we place a considerable value in living in accordance with the facts. And I have also said that if determinism were true, and if this implied that, as a matter of metaphysical fact, we were not free and responsible beings, then the only way in which we would be living in accordance with the facts would be by giving up the taking of attitudes altogether.

Of course, in answer to the question 'Would it be rational for us to give up all our attitudes?', pragmatic replies of the sort I suggested earlier will be all the more poignant. That is, even if determinism gave us some *reason* to give up all our attitudes, we would be psychologically incapable of meeting this demand. And even if determinism gave us *some* reason to give up our attitudes, we would have overriding reason to retain them.

If our sense of the value and meaning of our lives would be sharply reduced in a world without reactive attitudes, it would be altogether eliminated in a world in which no attitudes were taken at all. For the only way we could give up taking either the attitudes that regard others as responsible for their actions or the attitude that regards others as not responsible for their actions would be by giving up thinking in terms of the notions of responsibility and desert at all. Giving this up, I believe, would require in turn that we give up a great deal more. We would have to stop thinking in terms of what ought and ought not to be. We would have to stop thinking in terms that would allow the possibility that

10. Perhaps this claim can be taken as a reformulation of the liar paradox: 'Do not take me seriously.'

some lives and projects are better than others.[11] Were we to make ourselves into the kind of creatures that ceased to think in these terms, we would lose the distinction between desires and values and, therefore, our distinction as valuing creatures. We would lose our ideals, our sense of self, and, I think, our status as persons. A world without reactive attitudes would be a tragic world of human isolation; a world without reactive attitudes or the objective attitude would be a bleak, blank world of human brutes.

Thus, as I said, in answer to the question 'Would it be rational for us to give up all our attitudes?', pragmatic replies will be all the more poignant. If the optimist's arguments stopped here, however, the pessimist could still sigh and point out once again that pragmatic replies are merely pragmatic. As such, they can be only as satisfying as the acceptance of the lesser of two evils can be. However, I believe that the optimist's arguments need not stop here, with the merely pragmatic. If we *had* some reason to give up all our attitudes, we would have overriding reason to retain them. But, in fact, I believe, we have no reason at all to take this very drastic step. We have no reason at all to fulfil our desire to live in accordance with the facts, when the facts in question are facts such as these. In other words, the desire is itself irrational in relation to facts such as these. If the facts are that we are, in all relevant respects, like the robot, there is no point to living in accordance with them.

Unfortunately, it is not at all clear what the point of this desire normally is. The desire to live in accordance with the facts is more easily felt than explained. It is this desire, I take it, that people sometimes express when they say that they want to live in the Real World. It is this desire that makes people shudder at the thought of passing their days hooked up to a pleasure machine. This desire shows up in more realistic situations when we consider how important it is to us that we not only feel ourselves to be loved, but that we truly be loved, or when we see how important it is to us that we not only believe that our efforts to achieve something in the world have succeeded, but that they really have succeeded.

Why is it so important to us that our conception of our lives correspond to some more objective fact? Why does it matter so much that the world we live in is the Real World? I can think of two possible answers.

First, I think it plausible that we place a primitive, unanalysable value on 'getting things right'. Perhaps, that is, we value being right for its own sake. From this value, the value of living in accordance with the facts would follow as a direct corollary. If so, it should at least give us pause to

11. Here I assume that 'ought' and 'better' have the force of objective reason. Once the thought that some things ought to be is allowed, so is the thought that some things ought to be done (by oneself, for instance). And this, I think, leads inevitably to the thought that one is, *ceteris paribus*, responsible for doing them.

notice that living in accordance with the fact that we are not free and responsible beings would require us to give up our value in being right. For living in accordance with the fact that we are not free and responsible beings would require us to give up all our values. More important, if we were to live in accordance with the fact that we are not free and responsible beings by giving up the taking of attitudes altogether, we would not even realize our (past) value in getting things right. We would admittedly cease to be getting some things wrong, for we would cease to regard ourselves as free and responsible beings. But we would do this at the cost of ceasing to regard ourselves as anything at all.

On the other hand, our desire to live in accordance with the facts— our desire, that is, to live in the Real World—may rest essentially on the belief that it is the Real World, and the beings within it, that matter. In other words, we may want to live in accordance with the facts because we want ourselves to matter in the right sort of way, to make the right sort of difference to the world and the beings who do matter and to whom we might matter. But all the beings that could possibly be encompassed by these concerns must themselves be within the grasp of the same determinism as ourselves.[12] If the point of living in accordance with the facts is to make the right kind of difference to the right kind of beings, then it cannot possibly be an achievement to eliminate the right kind of beings *en masse*.

It might be rational for the robot to commit a kind of suicide of self as a result of the realization that he is, unlike the rest of us, a robot. For it seems plausible that the realization that you cannot, and/or rationally ought not, matter to the people or to the world that matters to you— indeed, to the people or to the world that matter independently of you—might give you a reason to commit suicide.[13] But the realization that you are determined because your whole world is determined cannot generate such a reason. For us, either this world matters or none at all. If this world matters, then it would be irrational to destroy it. And if this world does not matter, then it certainly doesn't matter that we do or do not choose to destroy it.

Thus, we reach the conclusion that the truth of determinism gives us no reason at all to give up our reactive attitudes. Let me briefly review the argument.

We first considered the suggestion that the recognition that, as a matter of metaphysical fact, we were not free or responsible beings would

12. As perhaps all the people a person in a dream can concern himself with are themselves dream-people. Perhaps, one might think, we can also concern ourselves with the programmer (or God), if there is one, and this individual would not be in the grasp of the same determinism as ourselves. Even if this were correct, however, we could in no way improve our status with such a being by living in accordance with the facts.

13. Douglas MacLean once suggested to me that Kafka's *Metamorphosis* might be interpreted as an illustration of just this point.

give us a reason to regard ourselves as unfree, unresponsible beings—it would give us a reason, that is, to replace our present reactive attitudes with the objective attitude toward ourselves and each other. But we saw that this change would fail to achieve its purpose; it would not satisfy the desire to live in accordance with the facts. For it is only rational to take some particular attitude toward ourselves as attitude-takers, free and responsible beings. Therefore, we would be no less irrational if we chose to take the objective attitude than if we chose to take the other alternative.

Second, we considered the suggestion that the desire to live in accordance with the facts might give us a reason to cease to take attitudes altogether. But we saw that if living in accordance with the facts required *this* change, we would have no reason to live in accordance with them. For there seemed to be two possible sources of our desire to live in accordance with the facts. According to the first, this desire rests on the belief that by living in accordance with the facts we will promote our ability to get things right. According to the second, this desire rests on the belief that living in accordance with the facts would put us in the world that is most worth living in—the world, that is, with valuable and valuing selves. But if determinism is true, and if this implies that we are not free and responsible beings, then neither of these beliefs is justified. On neither of these accounts would it be rational to live in accordance with the fact that determinism is true.

Thus, the truth of determinism gives us no reason at all to choose to take one attitude rather than another. And the truth of determinism gives us no reason at all to choose to take no attitude rather than some.

Since the truth of determinism gives us no reason at all, we must look elsewhere for reasons by which to decide which attitudes, if any, it would be best for us to take. Presumably, we would have to look at the consequences of these various decisions—and, looking at these, we would, presumably, choose to keep our present reactive attitudes. This brings us to the apparently optimistic conclusion that, even if determinism were true, and even if this implied that, as a matter of metaphysical fact, we were not free or responsible beings, it would still be rational—and without impurification—to retain our present reactive attitudes.

THE IMPORTANCE OF FREE WILL

Some might think that this conclusion must finally silence the pessimist. For it should convince him that no answer to the problem of free will can have any practical, pessimistic consequences whatsoever. But here again, I believe the pessimist might withdraw not his fear of determinism, but only his account of it. If the argument I have presented as the justification of our attitudes is the only justification we can have, the pessimist again, might accept this justification—but he will accept it with despair. For the position I have outlined might be said to reduce, in effect, to something like this: 'Even if we are puppets on the strings of the hands of God, there is nothing at all we can do about it. It would therefore not be rational to try to do anything about it, nor would it be rational, because of *this*, to commit suicide. Since there are no rational options by which to respond to this possibility, the option we do take cannot be irrational. So we are rationally permitted—perhaps, even obliged—to go on living our (possibly puppet—) lives.'

This argument, unfortunately, takes nothing away from the fact that we don't *want* to be puppets. We don't want to be, or be no better than, objects of someone else's manipulation. Of course, it is nice to know that, whatever the facts, the rationality of our practices is not open to criticism. It is nice to know that, whatever the facts, we are not making fools of ourselves. It is also nice to know that, as new facts come to light, nothing can happen that will generate, or that even ought to generate, a practical crisis. We will not have to choose between the lesser of two evils; we will not have to choose self-deception. But the guarantee that we are not behaving irrationally or serving as the unwitting agents of our own humiliation and error—the guarantee, in other words, that *we* cannot be faulted for taking an inappropriate attitude towards ourselves and our place in the world—is not the only guarantee that one can reasonably wish for. And the onset of a practical crisis, of the recognition of the need to confront an inconsistency in ourselves and to change our personalities and practices in undesirable ways, is not the only state of affairs that one can reasonably fear.

The pessimist fears that if determinism is true, then we are no better off than puppets. And the lives of puppets, the pessimist thinks, are meaningless and absurd. No one would dream of faulting the puppets for this—the thought that puppets are blameworthy for not recognizing their puppethood and integrating their recognition into the way they live their lives is at worst incoherent and at best simply false. Nonetheless, the puppets' lives are meaningless, and, from the puppets' point of view, that would be too bad. The pessimist fears that if determinism is true, then we are no better off than puppets. Naturally, from the pessimist's point of view, if determinism were true, that would be too bad. The fact that we don't have to *change* our values is of little solace if it may be the case that we are, now and forever, incapable of *realizing* our values. The fact that we don't have to think that our lives are meaningless is of little comfort if, for all that, our lives may actually *be* meaningless.

Thus, the apparently optimistic conclusion that it is completely rational for us to regard ourselves as free and responsible beings must, in order to silence the pessimist, be reached in a more optimistic way. No

4

Responsibility and the Limits of Evil: Variations on a Strawsonian Theme

GARY WATSON

> Responsibility is . . . one aspect of the identity of character and conduct. We are responsible for our conduct because that conduct is ourselves objectified in actions.
> —John Dewey, "Outlines of a Critical Theory of Ethics"

> There is nothing regrettable about finding oneself, in the last analysis, left with something which one cannot choose to accept or reject. What one is left with is probably just oneself, a core without which there could be no choice belonging to the person at all. Some unchosen restrictions on choice are among the conditions of its possibility.
> —Thomas Nagel, *The Possibility of Altruism*

> Our practices do not merely exploit our natures, they express them.
> —Peter Strawson, "Freedom and Resentment"

INTRODUCTION

REGARDING people as responsible agents is evidently not just a matter of belief. So regarding them means something in practice. It is shown in an embrace or a thank you, in an act of reprisal or obscene gesture, in a

Reprinted by permission of Cambridge University Press from Ferdinand David Schoeman, ed., *Responsibility, Character and the Emotions* (1987), pp. 256–286.

To Sally Haslanger and Brian Skyrms, I am grateful for discussing bits and pieces of this material with me; to Ferdinand Schoeman, for comments on an earlier draft.

feeling of resentment or sense of obligation, in an apology or demand for an apology. To regard people as responsible agents is to be ready to treat them in certain ways.

In "Freedom and Resentment,"[1] Peter Strawson is concerned to describe these forms of treatment and their presuppositions. As his title suggests, Strawson's focus is on such attitudes and responses as gratitude and resentment, indignation, approbation, guilt, shame, (some kinds of) pride, hurt feeling, (asking and giving) forgiveness, and (some kinds of) love. All traditional theories of moral responsibility acknowledge connections between these attitudes and holding one another responsible. What is original to Strawson is the way in which they are linked. Whereas traditional views have taken these attitudes to be secondary to seeing others as responsible, to be practical corollaries or emotional side effects of some independently comprehensible belief in responsibility, Strawson's radical claim is that these "reactive attitudes" (as he calls them) are *constitutive* of moral responsibility; to regard oneself or another as responsible just is the proneness to react to them in these kinds of ways under certain conditions. There is no more basic belief which provides the justification or rationale for these reactions. The practice does not rest on a theory at all, but rather on certain needs and aversions that are basic to our conception of being human. The idea that there is or needs to be such an independent basis is where traditional views, in Strawson's opinion, have gone badly astray.

For a long time, I have found Strawson's approach salutary and appealing. Here my aim is not to defend it as superior to its alternatives, but to do something more preliminary. A comparative assessment is not possible without a better grasp of what Strawson's theory (or a Strawsonian theory)[2] *is*. As Strawson presents it, the theory is incomplete in important respects. I will investigate whether and how the incompleteness can be remedied in Strawsonian ways. In the end, I find that certain features of our practice of holding responsible are rather resistant to such remedies, and that the practice is less philosophically innocent than Strawson supposes. I hope that the issues uncovered by this investigation will be of sufficient importance to interest even those who are not as initially sympathetic to Strawson's approach as I am.[3]

---

1. This volume. Hereafter, page references are given in the text.
2. My interpretation of Strawson's essay will be in many places very conjectural; and I will sometimes signal this fact by speaking of a "Strawsonian" theory.
3. I have learned much from the penetrating exploration of Strawson's essay by Jonathan Bennett: "Accountability," in *Philosophical Subjects*, edited by Zak van Straaten, Oxford: Clarendon Press, 1980, pp. 14–47.

Strawson's Theory

Strawson presents the rivals to his view as responses to a prima facie problem posed by determinism. One rival—consequentialism—holds that blaming and praising judgments and acts are to be understood, and justified, as forms of social regulation. Apart from the question of its extensional adequacy, consequentialism seems to many to leave out something vital to our practice. By emphasizing their instrumental efficacy, it distorts the fact that our responses are typically personal reactions to the individuals in question that we sometimes think of as eminently appropriate reactions quite aside from concern for effects. Rightly "recoiling" from the consequentialist picture, some philosophers have supposed that responsibility requires a libertarian foundation, that to bring the "vital thing" back in, we must embrace a certain metaphysics of human agency. This is the other rival.

What these otherwise very different views share is the assumption that our reactive attitudes commit us to the truth of some independently apprehensible proposition which gives the content of the belief in responsibility; and so either the search is on for the formulation of this proposition, or we must rest content with an intuition of its content. For the social-regulation theorist, this is a proposition about the standard effects of having and expressing reactive attitudes. For the libertarian, it is a proposition concerning metaphysical freedom. Since the truth of the former is consistent with the thesis of determinism, the consequentialist is a compatibilist; since the truth of the latter is shown or seen not to be, the libertarian is an incompatibilist.

In Strawson's view, there is no such independent notion of responsibility that explains the propriety of the reactive attitudes. The explanatory priority is the other way around: It is not that we hold people responsible because they *are* responsible; rather, the idea (*our* idea) that we are responsible is to be understood by the practice, which itself is not a matter of holding some propositions to be true, but of expressing our concerns and demands about our treatment of one another. These stances and responses are expressions of certain rudimentary needs and aversions: "It matters to us whether the actions of other people . . . reflect attitudes toward us of good will, affection, or esteem on the one hand or contempt, indifference, or malevolence on the other." Accordingly, the reactive attitudes are "natural human reactions to the good or ill will or indifference of others toward us [or toward those we care about] as displayed in *their* attitudes and actions" (p. 53). Taken together, they express "the demand for the manifestation of a reasonable degree of good will or regard, on the part of others, not simply towards oneself, but towards all those on whose behalf moral indignation may be felt. . ." (p. 57).

Hence, Strawson accuses rival conceptions of "overintellectualizing" our practices. In their emphasis on social regulation, consequentialists lose sight of sentiments these practices directly express, without which the notion of moral responsibility cannot be understood. Libertarians see the gaping hole in the consequentialist account, but rather than acknowledging that "it is just these attitudes themselves which fill the gap" (p. 64), they seek to ground these attitudes in a metaphysical intuition— "a pitiful intellectualist trinket for a philosopher to wear as a charm against the recognition of his own humanity" (p. 64). Holding responsible is as natural and primitive in human life as friendship and animosity, sympathy and antipathy. It rests on needs and concerns that are not so much to be justified as acknowledged.

Excusing and Exempting

To say that holding responsible is to be explained by the range of reactive attitudes, rather than by a commitment to some independently comprehensible proposition about responsibility, is not to deny that these reactions depend on a context of belief and perceptions in particular contexts. They are not mere effusions of feeling, unaffected by facts. In one way, Strawson is anxious to insist that these attitudes have no "rationale," that they neither require nor permit a "rational justification" of some general sort. Nevertheless, Strawson has a good deal to say about the particular perceptions that elicit and inhibit them. Reactive attitudes do have internal criteria, since they are reactions to the moral qualities exemplified by an individual's attitudes and conduct.[4]

Thus, reactive attitudes depend upon an interpretation of conduct. If you are resentful when jostled in a crowd, you will see the other's behavior as rude, contemptuous, disrespectful, self-preoccupied, or heedless: in short, as manifesting attitudes contrary to the basic demand for reasonable regard. Your resentment might be inhibited if you are too tired, or busy, or fearful, or simply inured to life in the big city. These are causal inhibitors. In contrast, you might think the other was pushed, didn't realize, didn't mean to. . . . These thoughts would provide reasons

4. Reactive attitudes thus permit a threefold classification. Personal reactive attitudes regarding others' treatment of one (resentment, gratitude, etc.); vicarious analogues of these, regarding others' treatment of others (indignation and approbation); self-reactive attitudes regarding one's own treatment of others (and oneself?) (guilt, shame, moral self-esteem, feeling obligated). Many of the reactive attitudes reflect the basic demand (on oneself and others, for oneself and others), whereas others (for example, gratitude) directly express the basic concern.

Contrary to some of Strawson's discussion, responsibility does not concern only other-regarding attitudes. You can hold yourself responsible for failing to live up to an ideal that has no particular bearing on the interests or feelings of others. It may be said that others cannot *blame* you for this failure; but that would be a moral claim.

for the inhibition of resentment. What makes them reasons is, roughly, that they cancel or qualify the appearance of noncompliance with the basic demand.[5]

In this way, Strawson offers a plausible account of many of the "pleas" that in practice inhibit or modify negative reactive attitudes. One type of plea is exemplified by the aforementioned reasons for inhibited sentiments. This type of plea corresponds to standardly acknowledged *excusing* conditions. It works by denying the appearance that the other failed to fulfill the basic demand; when a valid excuse obtains, the internal criteria of the negative reactive attitudes are not satisfied. Of course, justification does this as well, but in a different way. "He realized what he was doing, but it was an emergency." In general, an excuse shows that *one* was not to blame, whereas a justification shows that one was not to *blame*.

Strawson distinguishes a second type of plea. These correspond roughly to standard *exempting* conditions. They show that the agent, temporarily or permanently, globally or locally, is appropriately exempted from the basic demand in the first place. Strawson's examples are being psychotic, being a child, being under great strain, being hypnotized, being a sociopath ("moral idiot"), and being "unfortunate in formative circumstances." His general characterization of pleas of type 2 is that they present the other either as acting uncharacteristically due to extraordinary circumstances, or as psychologically abnormal or morally undeveloped in such a way as to be incapacitated in some or all respects for "ordinary adult interpersonal relationships."

In sum, type-2 pleas bear upon the question of whether the agent is an appropriate "object of that kind of demand for goodwill or regard which is reflected in ordinary reactive attitudes" (p. 51). If so, he or she is seen as a responsible agent, as a potential term in moral relationships, as a member (albeit, perhaps, in less than good standing) of the moral community. Assuming the absence of such exemptions, type-1 pleas bear upon the question of whether the basic demand has been met. These inhibit negative reactive attitudes because they give evidence that their internal criteria are not satisfied. In contrast, type-2 pleas inhibit reactive attitudes because they inhibit the demand those attitudes express (p. 52).

When reactive attitudes are suspended on type-2 grounds, we tend to take what Strawson calls an "objective view." We see individuals not as ones to be resented or esteemed but as ones to be controlled, managed, manipulated, trained. . . . The objective view does not preclude all emotions: "It may include repulsion and fear, it may include pity or even love," though not reciprocal adult love. We have the capacity to adopt an objective view toward capable agents as well; for certain kinds of thera-

5. Below, this remark is qualified significantly.

peutic relationship, or simply to relieve the "strains of involvement," we sometimes call upon this resource.

As we have seen, one of Strawson's concerns is to deny the relevance of any theoretical issue about determinism to moral responsibility. In effect, incompatibilists insist that the truth of determinism would require us to take the objective attitude universally. But in Strawson's view, when we adopt the objective attitude, it is never a result of a theoretical conviction in determinism, but either because one of the exempting pleas is accepted, or for external reasons—fatigue, for example, or relief from the strain of involvement. No coherent thesis of determinism entails that one or more of the pleas is always valid, that disrespect is never meant, or that we are all abnormal or undeveloped in the relevant ways. Holding responsible is an expression of the basic concern and the basic demand, whose "legitimacy" requires neither metaphysical freedom nor efficacy. The practice does not involve a commitment to anything with which determinism could conflict, or which considerations of utility could challenge.

Blaming and Finding Fault

This is the basic view as Strawson presents it. For convenience, we may call it the expressive theory of responsibility. With certain caveats,[6] the expressive theory may be called a nonconsequentialist form of compatibilism; but it is not the only such form. It can be clarified by contrasting it with another.

Consider the following common view of blame and praise: To blame someone morally for something is to attribute it to a moral fault, or "shortcoming," or defect of character, or vice,[7] and similarly for praise. Responsibility could be constructed in terms of the propriety conditions of such judgments: that is, judgments to the effect that an action or attitude manifests a virtue or vice.[8]

As I understand the Strawsonian theory, such judgments are only part of the story. They indicate what reactive attitudes are reactions *to*

6. The term "compatibilism" denotes the view that determinism is compatible with responsibility. Hence it may presuppose that determinism is an intelligible thesis. Since Strawson seems skeptical about this presupposition, he might refuse this appellation.

7. See Robert Nozick, *Philosophical Explanations* (Harvard University Press, 1981, p. 224).

8. Such a view is hinted at by James Wallace: "Answers to [the question of when an action is fully characteristic of an excellence or a vice] are fundamental for an account of the conditions for the appropriateness of praise, blame, reward and punishment and for an account of the derivative notion of responsibility" (*Virtues and Vices*, Cornell University Press, p. 43). This also seems to be R. Milo's view in *Immorality* (Princeton University Press, 1984). I don't say that such a view is necessarily incompatibilist—it could be insisted that conduct fully exemplifies a virtue or a vice only if determinism is false (this is clearly the Abélardian view, discussed below)—but it is clear how a compatibilist version would go.

(namely, to the quality of the other's moral self as exemplified in action and attitude), but they are not themselves such reactions. Merely to cite such judgments is to leave out something integral to the practice of holding responsible and to the concept of moral responsibility (of being one to whom it is appropriate to respond in certain ways). It is as though in blaming we were mainly moral clerks, recording moral faults, for whatever purposes (the Last Assizes?).[9] In a Strawsonian view, blaming is not merely a fault-finding appraisal—which could be made from a detached and austerely "objective" standpoint—but a range of responses to the agent on the basis of such appraisals.[10] These nonpropositional responses are constitutive of the practice of holding responsible.

I will have something to say later about the nature of these responses. Clearly they make up a wide spectrum. Negative reactive attitudes range from bombing Tripoli to thinking poorly of a person. But even those at the more covert and less retributive end of the spectrum involve more than attributions of defects or shortcomings of moral character. Thinking poorly (less well) of a person is a way of regarding him or her in view of those faults. It has subtle implications for one's way of treating and interacting with the other. (Where the other is dead or otherwise out of reach, these implications will be only hypothetical or potential.) It is the sort of attitude that is forsworn by forgiveness, which itself presupposes the attribution of (former) fault.

Some Critical Questions

I turn now to certain hard questions for the expressive theory. It accounts nicely for "excusing conditions," pleas of type 1; but exactly—or even roughly—what is its account of type-2 pleas? The "participant" reactive attitudes are said to be "natural human reactions to the good or ill-will or indifference of others as displayed in their attitudes and actions" (p. 53); but this characterization must be incomplete, for some agents who display such attitudes are nevertheless exempted. A child can be malicious, a psychotic can be hostile, a sociopath indifferent, a person under great strain can be rude, a woman or man "unfortunate in formative circumstances" can be cruel. Evidently reactive attitudes are

9. Consider Jonathan Glover's remark: "Involved in our present practice of blame is a kind of moral accounting, where a person's actions are recorded in an informal balance sheet, with the object of assessing his moral worth." (*Responsiblity*, Routledge and Kegan Paul, 1970, p. 44.)

10. "Blaming is a type of response to faults in oneself or in others," Robert Adams, "Involuntary Sin," *Philosophical Review*, January 1985, p. 21. Adams does not tell us what kind of response it is. Since he thinks that thinking poorly of someone *is* a form of unspoken blame (ibid.), he must think that thinking poorly of is more than noting a moral fault. I think this is correct.

sensitive not only to the quality of others' wills, but depend as well upon a background of beliefs about the objects of those attitudes. What are those beliefs, and can they be accommodated without appealing to the rival accounts of responsibility that Strawson sets out to avoid?

Strawson says that type-2 pleas inhibit reactive attitudes not by providing an interpretation which shows that the other does not display the pertinent attitudes, but by "inhibiting" the basic demand. It would seem that many of the exemption conditions involve *explanations* of why the individuals display qualities to which the reactive attitudes are otherwise sensitive. So on the face of it, the reactive attitudes are also affected by these explanations. Strawson's essay does not provide an account of how this works or what kinds of explanations exempt.

The problem is not just that the theory is incomplete, but that what might be necessary to complete it will undermine the theory. Strawsonian rivals will rush to fill the gap with their own notions. So it will be said that what makes some of these explanations exempting is that they are deterministic; or it will be said that these conditions are exempting because they indicate conditions in which making the basic demand is inefficacious. To the extent that some such account seems necessary, our enterprise is doomed.

In the following sections, I investigate a Strawsonian alternative. Following Strawson's idea that type-2 pleas inhibit reactive attitudes *by* inhibiting the basic demand, I propose to construe the exempting conditions as indications of the constraints on intelligible moral demand or, put another way, of the constraints on moral address.

I shall not attempt anything like a comprehensive treatment of the type-2 pleas mentioned by Strawson. I discuss, first and rather briefly, the cases of being a child and being under great strain. I then turn to a more extended discussion of "being unfortunate in formative circumstances," for this looks to be entirely beyond the resources of the expressive theory.

Demanding and Understanding

As Strawson is fully aware, being a child is not simply exempting. Children "are potentially and increasingly capable both of holding, and being objects of, the full range of human and moral attitudes, but are not yet fully capable of either" (pp. 60–61). Children are gradually becoming responsible agents; but in virtue of what are they potentially and increasingly these things? A plausible partial answer to this question is "moral understanding." They do not yet (fully) grasp the moral concepts in such a way that they can (fully) engage in moral communication, and so be unqualified members of the moral community.

The relevance of moral understanding to the expressive theory is this: The negative reactive attitudes express a *moral* demand, a demand for reasonable regard. Now a very young child does not even have a clear sense of the reality of others; but even with this cognitive capacity, children may lack an understanding of the effects of their behavior on others. Even when they understand what it is to hurt another physically, they may lack a sense of what it is to hurt another's feelings, or of the various subtle ways in which that may be done; and even when these things are more or less mastered, they may lack the notion of *reasonable* regard, or of justification. The basic demand is, once more, a moral demand, a demand for reasonable regard, a demand addressed to a moral agent, to one who is capable of understanding the demand. Since the negative reactive attitudes involve this demand, they are not (as fully) appropriately directed to those who do not fully grasp the terms of the demand.

To be intelligible, demanding requires understanding on the part of the object of the demand. The reactive attitudes are incipiently forms of communication, which make sense only on the assumption that the other can comprehend the message.

No doubt common views about the moral capacities of children are open to challenge, and the appeal to the notion of understanding itself raises important issues.[11] However, what is important here is whether these views can be understood by the Strawsonian theory, and it seems the ordinary view that reactive attitudes make less sense in the case of children is intelligible in Strawsonian terms; this exemption condition reflects constraints arising from the notion of moral demand.

In a certain sense, blaming and praising those with diminished moral understanding loses its "point." This way of putting it smacks of consequentialism, but our discussion suggests a different construction. The reactive attitudes are incipient forms of communication, not in the sense that resentment et al. are usually communicated; very often, in fact, they are not. Rather, the most appropriate and direct expression of resentment is to address the other with a complaint and a demand. Being a child exempts, when it does, not because expressing resentment has no

11. Do *we adults* fully comprehend the notions of justification and reasonable regard? Does understanding presuppose a disputable cognitive view of morality? Certainly conceptions of children are subject to cultural variation. William Blackstone discusses the case of an 8-year old boy who was tried for setting fire to some barns. Because he was found to exhibit "malice, revenge, and cunning, he was found guilty, condemned and hanged accordingly." (In *Commentaries on the Laws of England (1765-7)*, as quoted by Jennifer Radden. *Madness and Reason*, George Allen and Unwin, 1985, p. 136.)

It is doubtful that diminished moral understanding is the only relevant factor here. Surely various capacities of concentration and "volitional" control are relevant as well. I do not know how the expressive theory could take these into account.

desirable effects; in fact, it often does. Rather the reactive attitudes lose their point as forms of moral address.[12]

Not Being Oneself

Let's consider whether this kind of explanation can be extended to another of Strawson's type-2 pleas: "being under great strain." Strawson includes this plea in a subgroup of exemptions that include "he wasn't himself" and "he was acting under posthypnotic suggestion." His statement of the rationale in the case of stress is somewhat cryptic:

> We shall not feel resentment against the man he is for the action done by the man he is not; or at least we shall feel less. We normally have to deal with him under normal stresses; so we shall not feel towards him, when he acts under abnormal stresses, as we should have felt towards him had he acted as he did under normal stresses. (p. 51)

I take it that what leads Strawson to group these cases together is that in each case the agent, due to special circumstances, acts *uncharacteristically.*

When you learn that someone who has treated you extremely rudely has been under great strain lately, has lost a job, say, or is going through a divorce, you may reinterpret the behavior in such a way that your erstwhile resentment or hurt feelings are inhibited and now seem inappropriate. How does this reinterpretation work? Notice, again, that unlike type-1 pleas, the new interpretation does not contradict the *judgment* that the person treated you rudely; rather, it provides an explanation of the rudeness.

What Strawson says about this case seems plausible. What seems to affect your reactive attitudes is the thought that she's not herself, that the behavior does not reflect or fully reflect the person's moral "personality." The following remark indicates the same phenomena: "He was drunk when he said that; I wouldn't hold it against him." (There is room here for disagreement about the bounds of the moral self. Some parts of folk wisdom have it that one's "true self" is revealed when drunk. To my

---

12. Reactive attitudes are even more clearly pointless in the case of a radically disintegrated personality, one that has no coherent moral self to be addressed. The case of the sociopath is much more complicated, but arguably something similar may be said here. Those who deal with sociopaths often lose the sense that such characters have a moral self at all; despite appearances, there is "no one home."

For case studies and psychiatric commentary, see Hervey Cleckley, *The Mask of Sanity,* C. V. Mosby, 1941. For philosophical discussion, see Herbert Fingarette, *On Responsibility,* Chap. 2; Vinit Haksar, "The Responsibility of Psychopaths," *The Philosophical Quarterly,* Vol. 15 (1965); M. S. Pritchard, "Responsibility, Understanding, and Psychopathology," *The Monist,* Vol. 58 (1974); Antony Duff, "Psychopathy and Moral Understanding," *American Philosophical Quarterly,* Vol. 14 (1977); and Jeffrie Murphy, "Moral Death: A Kantian Essay on Psychopathy," *Ethics,* Vol. 82 (1972).

knowledge, this has never been claimed about stress.) Again, what is the Strawsonian rationale?

Perhaps this type of case can also be understood in terms of the conditions of intelligible moral address. Insofar as resentment is a form of reproach addressed to an agent, such an attitude loses much of its point here—not, as before, because the other does not fully understand the reproach, but because *he* or *she* (the true self) repudiates such conduct as well. Unlike the case in which the agent acts rudely in the absence of "strain," here the target of your resentment is not one who "really" endorses the behavior you are opposing. You see the behavior as not issuing from that person's moral self, and yet it is the person, qua moral self, that your resentment would address.

The point can be put more generally in this way: Insofar as the negative reactive attitudes express demands (or in some cases appeals) addressed to another moral self, they are conceptually conditioned in various ways. One condition is that, to be fully a moral self, the other must possess sufficient (for what?) moral understanding; another is that the conduct in question be seen as reflecting the moral self. Insofar as the person is subject to great stress, his or her conduct and attitudes fail to meet this latter condition.

I am unsure to what extent these remarks accord with Strawson's own views. They are in any case exceedingly sketchy, and raise problems I am unable to take up here. For one thing, the notion of moral address seems essentially interpersonal, and so would be unavailing in the self-reflexive case. We have negative reactive attitudes toward and make moral demands upon ourselves. To determine whether this is a fatal asymmetry, we would have to investigate the reflexive cases in detail. For another thing, the notion of moral self is certainly not altogether transparent. Why are our responses under stress not reflections of our moral selves—namely, reflections of the moral self under stress? Clearly then, the explanation requires development.

It will be recalled, however, that I am not trying to determine whether a Strawsonian account of the exemption conditions is the *best* account, but to indicate what such an account might be. It will be enough for my purposes here if we can be satisfied that a Strawsonian theory has the resources to provide *some* explanation.

To recapitulate, then, the thesis is this: First, type-2 pleas indicate in different ways limiting conditions on moral address. These are relevant to reactive attitudes because those attitudes are incipiently forms of moral address. This thesis makes sense of Strawson's remark that pleas of this type inhibit reactive attitudes by inhibiting moral demand. Second, given that those conditions are satisfied, type-1 pleas indicate that the basic demand has not been flouted, contrary to appearances (though here again, we must distinguish excuse from justification).

On this account, the practice of holding responsible does indeed seem metaphysically modest, in that it involves no commitments to which issues about determinism are relevant. In a subsequent section I will consider some more bothersome features of our practice; but first I want to call attention to some general issues raised by the account given so far.

Evil and the Limits of Moral Community

To understand certain exempting and extenuating considerations, I have appealed to the notion of the conditions in which it makes sense morally to address another. I suggested that in different ways these conditions are not (fully) satisfied by the child and the person under severe stress. In the case of children, it seemed plausible to speak of a lack of understanding. What is involved in such understanding is a complex question. Obviously we do not want to make *compliance* with the basic demand a condition of moral understanding. (After all, for the most part, children *do* "comply," but without full understanding.) For the negative reactive attitudes come into play only when the basic demand has been flouted or rejected; and flouting and rejecting, strictly speaking, require understanding.

These remarks raise a very general issue about the limits of responsibility and the limits of evil. It is tempting to think that understanding requires a shared framework of values. At any rate, some of Strawson's remarks hint at such a requirement on moral address. He writes that the reactive attitudes essentially involve regarding the other as "a morally responsible agent, as a term of moral relationships, as a member of the moral community" (p. 59). This last phrase suggests shared ends, at some level, or a shared framework for practical reasoning. Thus, comembers of the moral community are potential interlocutors. In his discussion of Strawson's essay, Lawrence Stern suggests this point:

> . . . when one morally disapproves of another person, it is normal to believe that he is susceptible to the appeal of the principles from the standpoint of which one disapproves. He either shares these principles or can come to share them.[13]

Does morally addressing another make sense unless we suppose that the other can see some reason to take us seriously, to acknowledge our claims? Can we be in a moral community with those who reject the basic terms of moral community? Are the enemies of moral community themselves members? If we suppose that moral address requires moral

13. "Freedom, Blame, and Moral Community," *Journal of Philosophy*, February 14, 1974.

community, then some forms of evil will be exempting conditions. If holding responsible requires the intelligibility of moral address, and if a condition of such address is that the other be seen as a potential moral interlocutor, then the paradox results that extreme evil disqualifies one for blame.

Consider the case of Robert Harris.

On the south tier of Death Row, in a section called "Peckerwood Flats" where the white inmates are housed, there will be a small celebration the day Robert Alton Harris dies.

A group of inmates on the row have pledged several dollars for candy, cookies and soda. At the moment they estimate that Harris has been executed, they will eat, drink and toast to his passing.

"The guy's a misery, a total scumbag; we're going to party when he goes," said Richard (Chic) Mroczko, who lived in the cell next to Harris on San Quentin Prison's Death Row for more than a year. "He doesn't care about life, he doesn't care about others, he doesn't care about himself.

We're not a bunch of Boy Scouts around here, and you might think we're pretty cold-blooded about the whole thing. But then, you just don't know that dude."

San Diego County Assistant Dis. Atty. Richard Huffman, who prosecuted Harris, said, "If a person like Harris can't be executed under California law and federal procedure, then we should be honest and say we're incapable of handling capital punishment."

State Deputy Atty. Gen. Michael D. Wellington asked the court during an appeal hearing for Harris, "If this isn't the kind of defendant that justifies the death penalty, is there ever going to be one?"

What crime did Robert Harris commit to be considered the archetypal candidate for the death penalty? And what kind of man provokes such enmity that even those on Death Row . . . call for his execution?

On July 5, 1978, John Mayeski and Michael Baker had just driven through [a] fast-food restaurant and were sitting in the parking lot eating lunch. Mayeski and Baker . . . lived on the same street and were best friends. They were on their way to a nearby lake for a day of fishing.

At the other end of the parking lot, Robert Harris, 25, and his brother Daniel, 18, were trying to hotwire a [car] when they spotted the two boys. The Harris brothers were planning to rob a bank that afternoon and did not want to use their own car. When Robert Harris could not start the car, he pointed to the [car] where the 16-year-olds were eating and said to Daniel, "We'll take this one."

He pointed a . . . Luger at Mayeski, crawled into the back seat, and told him to drive east . . .

Daniel Harris followed in the Harrises' car. When they reached a canyon area . . . , Robert Harris told the youths he was going to use their car in a bank robbery and assured them that they would not be hurt. Robert Harris yelled to Daniel to get the .22 caliber rifle out of the back seat of their car.

"When I caught up," Daniel said in a recent interview, Robert was telling them about the bank robbery we were going to do. He was telling them that he would leave them some money in the car and all, for us using it. Both of them said that they would wait on top of this little hill until we were gone, and then walk into town and report the car stolen. Robert Harris agreed.

"Michael turned and went through some bushes. John said,'Good luck,' and turned to leave."

As the two boys walked away, Harris slowly raised the Luger and shot Mayeski in the back, Daniel said. Mayeski yelled: "Oh, God," and slumped to the ground. Harris chased Baker down a hill into a little valley and shot him four times.

Mayeski was still alive when Harris climbed back up the hill, Daniel said. Harris walked over to the boy, knelt down, put the Luger to his head and fired.

"God, everything started to spin," Daniel said. "It was like slow motion. I saw the gun, and then his head exploded like a balloon, . . . I just started running and running. . . . But I heard Robert and turned around.

"He was swinging the rifle and pistol in the air and laughing. God, that laugh made blood and bone freeze in me."

Harris drove [the] car to a friend's house where he and Daniel were staying. Harris walked into the house, carrying the weapons and the bag [containing] the remainder of the slain youths' lunch. Then, about 15 minutes after he had killed the two 16-year-old boys, Harris took the food out of the bag . . . began eating a hamburger. He offered his brother an apple turnover, and Daniel became nauseated and ran to the bathroom.

"Robert laughed at me," Daniel said. "He said I was weak; he called me a sissy and said I didn't have the stomach for it."

Harris was in an almost lighthearted mood. He smiled and told Daniel that it would be amusing if the two of them were to pose as police officers and inform the parents that their sons were killed. Then, for the first time, he turned serious. He thought that somebody might have heard the shots and that police could be searching for the bodies. He told Daniel that they should begin cruising the street near the bodies, and possibly kill some police in the area.

[Later, as they prepared to rob the bank,] Harris pulled out the Luger, noticed blood stains and remnants of flesh on the barrel as a result of the point-blank shot, and said, "I really blew that guy's brains out." And then, again, he started laughing.

. . . Harris was given the death penalty. He has refused all requests for interviews since the conviction.

He just doesn't see the point of talking," said a sister, . . . who has visited him three times since he has been on Death Row. "He told me that he had his chance, he took the road to hell and there's nothing more to say."

. . . Few of Harris' friends or family were surprised that he ended up on Death row. He had spent seven of the previous 10 years behind bars. Harris, who has an eighth-grade education, was convicted of car theft at 15 and was sentenced to a federal youth center. After being released, he was arrested twice for torturing animals and was convicted of manslaughter for beating a neighbor to death after a dispute.

Barbara Harris, another sister, talked to her brother at a family picnic on July 4, 1978. He had been out of prison less than six months, and his sister had not seen him in several years.

. . . Barbara Harris noticed his eyes, and she began to shudder. . . . "I thought, 'My God, what have they done to him?' He smiled, but his eyes were so cold, totally flat. It was like looking at a rattlesnake or a cobra ready to strike. They were hooded eyes, with nothing but meanness in them.

"He had the eyes of a killer. I told a friend that I knew someone else would die by his hand."

The next day, Robert Harris killed the two youths. Those familiar with the case were as mystified as they were outraged by Harris' actions. Most found it incomprehensible that a man could be so devoid of compassion and conscience that he could kill two youths, laugh about their deaths and then casually eat their hamburgers. . . .

. . . Harris is a dangerous man on the streets and a dangerous man behind bars, said Mroczko, who spent more than a year in the cell next to Harris'. . . .

"You don't want to deal with him out there," said Mroczko, . . . "We don't want to deal with him in here."

During his first year on the row, Mroczko said, Harris was involved in several fights on the yard and was caught trying to supply a prisoner in an adjacent yard with a knife. During one fight, Harris was stabbed and the other prisoner was shot by a guard. He grated on people's nerves and one night he kept the whole cell block awake by banging his shoe on a steel water basin and laughing hysterically.

An encounter with Harris always resulted in a confrontation. If an inmate had cigarettes, or something else Harris wanted, and he did not think "you could hold your mud," Mroczko said, he would try to take them.

Harris was a man who just did not know "when to be cool," he said. He was an obnoxious presence in the yard and in his cell, and his behavior precipitated unwanted attention from the guards. . . .

He acted like a man who did not care about anything. His cell was filthy, Mroczko said, and clothes, trash, tobacco and magazines were scattered on the floor. He wore the same clothes every day and had little interest in showers. Harris spent his days watching television in his cell, occasionally reading a Western novel.[14]

On the face of it, Harris is an "archetypal candidate" for blame. We respond to his heartlessness and viciousness with moral outrage and loathing. Yet if reactive attitudes were implicitly "invitations to dialogue" (as Stern puts it), then Harris would be an inappropriate object of such attitudes. For he is hardly a potential moral interlocutor, "susceptible to the appeal of the principles from the standpoint of which one disapproves." In this instance, an invitation to dialogue would be met with icy silence (he has "nothing more to say") or murderous contempt.

However, not all communication is dialogue. Harris refuses dialogue, and this refusal is meant to make a point. It is in effect a repudiation of the moral community; he thereby declares himself a moral outlaw. Unlike the small child, or in a different way the psychopath, he exhibits an inversion of moral concern, not a lack of understanding. His ears are not deaf, but his heart is frozen. This characteristic, which makes him utterly unsuitable as a moral interlocutor, intensifies rather than inhibits the reactive attitudes. Harris's form of evil *consists* in part in being beyond the boundaries of moral community. Hence, if we are to appeal to the constraints on moral address to explain certain type-2 pleas, we must not include among these constraints comembership in the moral community or the significant possibility of dialogue—unless, that is, evil is to be its own exemption. At these outer limits, our reactive attitudes can be nothing more (or less) than a denunciation forlorn of the hope of an adequate reply.

The Roots of Evil

I said that Harris is an archetypal candidate for blame—so, at least, we react to him. Does it matter to our reactions how he came to be so? Strawson thinks so, for, among type-2 pleas, he includes "being unfortunate in formative circumstances." We must now investigate the relevance of such historical considerations to the reactive attitudes. As it happens, the case of Robert Harris is again a vivid illustration.

[During the interview] Barbara Harris put her palms over her eyes and said softly, "I saw every grain of sweetness, pity and goodness in him destroyed. . . . It was a long and ugly journey before he reached that point."

14. From Miles Corwin, "Icy Killer's Life Steeped in Violence," *Los Angeles Times,* May 16, 1982. Copyright, 1982, *Los Angeles Times.* Reprinted by permission. For the length of this and the next quotation, I ask for the reader's patience. It is very important here to work with realistic and detailed examples.

Robert Harris' 29 years . . . have been dominated by incessant cruelty and profound suffering that he has both experienced and provoked. Violence presaged his birth, and a violent act is expected to end his life.

Harris was born Jan. 15, 1953, several hours after his mother was kicked in the stomach. She was 6½ months pregnant and her husband, an insanely jealous man, . . . came home drunk and accused her of infidelity. He claimed that the child was not his, threw her down and kicked her. She began hemorrhaging, and he took her to the hospital.

Robert was born that night. His heartbeat stopped at one point . . . but labor was induced and he was saved. Because of the premature birth, he was a tiny baby; he was kept alive in an incubator and spent months at the hospital.

His father was an alcoholic who was twice convicted of sexually molesting his daughters. He frequently beat his children . . . and often caused serious injury. Their mother also became an alcoholic and was arrested several times, once for bank robbery.

All of the children had monstrous childhoods. But even in the Harris family, . . . the abuse Robert was subjected to was unusual.

Before their mother died last year, Barbara Harris said, she talked incessantly about Robert's early years. She felt guilty that she was never able to love him; she felt partly responsible that he ended up on Death Row.

When Robert's father visited his wife in the hospital and saw his son for the first time, . . . the first thing he said was, "Who is the father of that bastard?" When his mother picked him up from the hospital . . . she said it was like taking a stranger's baby home.

The pain and permanent injury Robert's mother suffered as a result of the birth, . . . and the constant abuse she was subjected to by her husband, turned her against her son. Money was tight, she was overworked and he was her fifth child in just a few years. She began to blame all of her problems on Robert, and she grew to hate the child.

"I remember one time we were in the car and Mother was in the back seat with Robbie in her arms. He was crying and my father threw a glass bottle at him, but it hit my mother in the face. The glass shattered and Robbie started screaming. I'll never forget it," she said. . . .

"Her face was all pink, from the mixture of blood and milk. She ended up blaming Robbie for all the hurt, all the things like that. She felt helpless and he was someone to vent her anger on."

. . . Harris had a learning disability and a speech problem, but there was no money for therapy. When he was at school he felt stupid and classmates teased him, his sister said, and when he was at home he was abused.

"He was the most beautiful of all my mother's children; he was an angel," she said. "He would just break your heart. He wanted love so bad he would beg for any kind of physical contact.

"He'd come up to my mother and just try to rub his little hands on her leg or her arm. He just never got touched at all. She'd just push him away or kick him. One time she bloodied his nose when he was trying to get close to her."

Barbara Harris put her head in her hands and cried softly. "One killer out of nine kids. . . . The sad thing is he was the most sensitive of all of us. When he was 10 and we all saw 'Bambi,' he cried and cried when Bambi's mother was shot. Everything was pretty to him as a child; he loved animals. But all that changed; it all changed so much."

. . . All nine children are psychologically crippled as a result of their father, she said, but most have been able to lead useful lives. But Robert was too young, and the abuse lasted too long, she said, for him ever to have had a chance to recover.

[At age 14] Harris was sentenced to a federal youth detention center [for car theft]. He was one of the youngest inmates there, Barbara Harris said, and he grew up "hard and fast."

. . . Harris was raped several times, his sister said, and he slashed his wrists twice in suicide attempts. He spent more than four years behind bars as a result of an escape, an attempted escape and a parole violation.

The centers were "gladiator schools," Barbara Harris said, and Harris learned to fight and to be mean. By the time he was released from federal prison at 19, all his problems were accentuated. Everyone in the family knew that he needed psychiatric help.

The child who had cried at the movies when Bambi's mother dies had evolved into a man who was arrested several times for abusing animals. He killed cats and dogs, Daniel said, and laughed while torturing them with mop handles, darts and pellet guns. Once he stabbed a prize pig more than 1,000 times.

"The only way he could vent his feelings was to break or kill something," Barbara Harris said. "He took out all the frustrations of his life on animals. He had no feeling for life, no sense of remorse. He reached the point where there wasn't that much left of him."

. . . Harris' family is ambivalent about his death sentence. [Another sister said that] if she did not know her brother's past so intimately, she would support his execution without hesitation. Barbara has a 16-year-old son; she often imagines the horror of the slain boy's parents.

"If anyone killed my son, I'd try my damnedest, no matter what it took, to have my child revenged," Barbara Harris said. "I know how those parents must suffer every day.

"But Robbie in the gas chamber. . . ." She broke off in mid-sentence and stared out a window. "Well, I still remember the little boy who used to beg for love, for just one pat or word of kindness. . . . No I can't say I want my brother to die."

. . . Since Harris has been on Death Row, he has made no demands of time or money on his family. Harris has made only one request; he wants a dignified and serene ceremony after he dies—a ceremony in marked contrast to his life.

He has asked his oldest brother to take his ashes, to drive to the Sierra, hike to a secluded spot and scatter his remains in the trees.[15]

No doubt this history gives pause to the reactive attitudes. Why does it do so? "No wonder Harris is as he is!" we think. What is the relevance of this thought?

Note, to begin with, that the story in no way undermines the judgments that he is brutal, vicious, heartless, mean.[16] Rather, it provides a kind of explanation for his being so. Can the expressive theory explain why the reactive attitudes should be sensitive to such an explanation?

Strawson's general rubric for type-2 pleas (or the subgroup in which this plea is classified) is "being incapacitated for ordinary interpersonal relationships." Does Harris have some independently identifiable incapacity for which his biography provides evidence? Apparently, he *is* incapacitated for such relationships—for example, for friendship, for sympathy, for being affected by moral considerations. To be homicidally hateful and callous in Harris's way is to lack moral concern, and to lack moral concern is to be incapacitated for moral community. However, to exempt Harris on these grounds is problematic. For then everyone who is evil in Harris's way will be exempt, independently of facts about their background. But we had ample evidence about *this* incapacity before we learned of his childhood misfortunes, and that did not affect the reactive attitudes. Those misfortunes affect our responses in a special and nonevidential way. The question is why this should be so.

This would seem to be a hard question for compatibilist views generally. What matters is whether, in one version, the practice of holding responsible can be efficacious as a means of social regulation, or whether, using the expressive theory, the conditions of moral address are met. These questions would seem to be settled by how individuals *are*, not by how they came to be. Facts about background would be, at most, evidence that some other plea is satisfied. In themselves, they would not seem to matter.

A plea of this kind is, on the other hand, grist for the incompatibilists' mill. For they will insist on an essential historical dimension to the concept of responsibility. Harris's history reveals him to be an inevitable product of his formative circumstances. And seeing him as a product is inconsistent with seeing him as a responsible agent. If his cruel atti-

---

15. Miles Corwin, op. cit. Copyright, 1982, *Los Angeles Times*. Reprinted by permission.

16. Although significantly, when his past is in focus, we are less inclined to use certain *reactive* epithets, such as "scumbag." This term is used to express an attitude about the appropriate treatment of the individual (that he is to be thrown in the garbage, flushed down the toilet, etc.). Some other reactive terms are "jerk," "creep," "son of a bitch."

tudes and conduct are the inevitable result of his circumstances, then he is not responsible for them, unless he was responsible for those circumstances. It is this principle that gives the historical dimension of responsibility and of course entails the incompatibility of determinism and responsibility.

In this instance, however, an incompatibilist diagnosis seems doubtful. In the first place, our response to the case is not the simple suspension of reactive attitudes that this diagnosis would lead one to expect, but ambivalence. In the second place, the force of the example does not depend on a belief in the *inevitability* of the upshot. Nothing in the story supports such a belief. The thought is not "It had to be!" but, again, "No wonder!"

SYMPATHY AND ANTIPATHY

How and why, then, does this larger view of Harris's life in fact affect us? It is too simple to say that it leads us to suspend our reactive attitudes. Our response is too complicated and conflicted for that. What appears to happen is that we are unable to command an overall view of his life that permits the reactive attitudes to be sustained without ambivalence. That is because the biography forces us to see him as a *victim*, and so seeing him does not sit well with the reactive attitudes that are so strongly elicited by Harris's character and conduct. Seeing him as a victim does not totally dispel those attitudes. Rather, in light of the "whole" story, conflicting responses are evoked. The sympathy toward the boy he was is at odds with outrage toward the man he is. These responses conflict not in the way that fear dispels anger, but in the way that sympathy is opposed to antipathy. In fact, each of these responses is appropriate, but taken together they do not enable us to respond overall in a coherent way.

Harris both satisfies and violates the criteria of victimhood. His childhood abuse was a misfortune inflicted upon him against his will. But at the same time (and this is part of his very misfortune) he unambivalently endorses suffering, death, and destruction, and that is what (one form of) evil is. With this in focus, we see him as a victimizer and respond to him accordingly. The ambivalence results from the fact that an overall view simultaneously demands and precludes regarding him as a victim.

What we have here is not exactly a clash between what Thomas Nagel has called the objective and subjective standpoints.[17] It is not that from the more comprehensive viewpoint that reveals Harris as a victim, his responsibility is indiscernible. Rather, the clash occurs within a single point of view that reveals Harris as evil (and hence calling for enmity and moral opposition) and as one who is a victim (calling for sympathy

17. In *The View from Nowhere*, Oxford University Press, 1985.

and understanding). Harris's misfortune is such that scarcely a vestige remains of his earlier sensibilities. Hence, unless one knew Harris as a child or keeps his earlier self vividly in mind, sympathy can scarcely find a purchase.

Moral Luck and Moral Equality

However, what is arresting about the Harris case is not just the clash between sympathy and antipathy. The case is troubling in a more personal way. The fact that Harris's cruelty is an intelligible response to his circumstances gives a foothold not only for sympathy, but for the thought that if *I* had been subjected to such circumstances, I might well have become as vile. What is unsettling is the thought that one's moral self is such a fragile thing. One tends to think of one's moral sensibilities as going deeper than that (though it is not clear what this means). This thought induces not only an ontological shudder, but a sense of equality with the other: I too am a potential sinner.[18]

This point is merely the obverse of the point about sympathy. Whereas the point about sympathy focuses on our empathetic response to the other, the thought about moral luck turns one's gaze inward. It makes one feel less in a position to cast blame. The fact that my potential for evil has not been nearly so fully actualized is, for all I know, something for which I cannot take credit. The awareness that, in this respect, the others are or may be like oneself clashes with the distancing effect of enmity.

Admittedly, it is hard to know what to do with this conclusion. Equality of moral potential does not, of course, mean that Harris is not actually a vile man; on the contrary, it means that in similar circumstances I would have become vile as well. Since he is an evil man, we cannot and should not treat him as we would a rabid dog. The awareness of moral luck, however, taints one's own view of one's moral self as an achievement, and infuses one's reactive attitudes with a sense of irony. Only those who have survived circumstances such as those that ravaged Harris are in a good position to know what they would have done. We lucky ones can only wonder. As a product of reflection, this attitude is, of course, easily lost when the knife is at one's own throat.

DETERMINISM AND IGNORANCE

Nothing in the foregoing reflections is necessarily inconsistent with the expressive theory. The ways in which reactive attitudes are affected by

18. In "Determinism and Moral Perspectives," *Philosophy and Phenomenological Research*, September 1960, Elizabeth Beardsley calls attention to the perspective evoked by such cases as Harris, though she links this perspective too closely, in my opinion, to the notion of determinism.

sympathy and moral luck are intelligible without appealing to any of the conceptions of responsibility that Strawson eschews. Nevertheless, our attitudes remain puzzling in a number of respects.

Earlier we questioned an incompatibilist diagnosis of our example on the grounds that the historical explanation need not be construed as deterministic. Horrid backgrounds do not inevitably give rise to horrid people. Some manage somehow to survive a similar magnitude of misfortune, if not unscathed, at least as minimally decent human beings. Conversely, people are sometimes malicious despite a benign upbringing. What do we suppose makes the difference?

Strictly speaking, no one who is vicious in *just* the way we have interpreted Harris to be could fail to have had an abusive childhood. For our interpretation of who Harris is depends upon his biography, upon our interpretation of his life. Harris's cruelty is a response to the shattering abuse he suffered during the process of socialization. The objects of his hatred were not just the boys he so exultantly murdered, but the "moral order" that mauled and rejected him. (It is significant that Harris wanted to go out and kill some cops after the murder; he wanted not just to reject authority, but to confront it.) He defies the demand for human consideration because he had been denied this consideration himself. The mistreatment he received becomes a ground as well as a cause of the mistreatment he gives. It becomes part of the content of his "project."

Thus, someone who had a supportive and loving environment as a child, but who was devoted to dominating others, who killed for enjoyment, would not be vicious in the way Harris is, since he or she could not be seen as striking back at "society"; but such a person could be just *as* vicious. In common parlance, we sometimes call such people "bad apples," a phrase that marks a blank in our understanding. In contrast to Harris, whose malice is motivated, the conduct of "bad apples" seems inexplicable. So far, we cannot see them as victims, and there is no application for thoughts about sympathy and moral luck.

However, do we not suppose that *something* must have gone wrong in the developmental histories of these individuals, if not in their socialization, then "in them"—in their genes or brains? (Suppose a certain kind of tumor is such that its onset at an early age is known to be strongly correlated with the development of a malicious character. This supposition is no doubt bad science fiction; that a complex and articulated psychological structure could be caused by gross brain defect seems antecedently implausible.) Whatever "nonenvironmental" factors make the difference, will they not play the same role as Harris's bad upbringing—that is, will they not have victimized these individuals so that thoughts about sympathy and moral luck come into play? Or can evil be the object of unequivocal reactive attitudes only when it is inexplicable?

If determinism is true, then evil is a joint product of nature and nurture. If so, the difference between any evil person and oneself would seem to be a matter of moral luck. For determinism seems to entail that if one had been subjected to the internal and external conditions of some evil person, then one would have been evil as well. If that is so, then the reflections about moral luck seem to entail that the acceptance of determinism should affect our reactive attitudes in the same way as they are affected in Harris's case. In the account we have suggested, then, determinism seems to be relevant to reactive attitudes after all.

Actually, this conclusion does not follow without special metaphysical assumptions. For the counterfactuals that underlie thoughts about moral luck must be constrained by the conditions of personal identity. It may be that no one who had been exposed to just the internal and external conditions of some given individual could have been me. To make sense of a counterfactual of the form, "If *i* had been in *C*, then *i* would have become a person of type *t*," *C* must be supposed to be compatible with *i*'s existence as an individual (*i* must exist in the possible world in which *C* obtains). For example, it is widely held that genetic origin is essential to an individual's identity. In that case, the counterfactual, "If I had had Harris's genetic origin and his upbringing, then I would have been as evil as he," will not make sense. Now it might be that Harris's genetic origins are among the determinants of his moral development. Thus, even if this is a deterministic world, there may be no true counterfactual that would support the thought that the difference between Harris and me is a matter of moral luck. There is room for the thought that there is something "in me" by virtue of which I would not have become a vicious person in Harris's circumstances. And if that factor were among my essential properties, so to speak, then that difference between Harris and me would not be a matter of moral luck on my part, but a matter of who we essentially were. That would not, of course, mean that I was essentially good or Harris essentially evil, but that I would not have been corrupted by the same circumstances as those that defeated Harris. To be sure, to suppose that this difference is in itself to my moral credit would be odd. To congratulate me on these grounds would be to congratulate me on being myself. Nevertheless, this difference still might explain what is to my credit, such moral virtues as I may possess. This will seem paradoxical only if we suppose that whatever is a ground of my moral credit must itself be to my credit. But I see no compelling reason to suppose this.

Historical Responsibility

Libertarians believe that evil is the product neither of nature nor of nurture, but of free will. Do we understand what this might mean?

It is noteworthy that libertarians will be able to agree with much of what we have said about moral luck. Harris's history affects us because it makes us wonder how *we* would have responded, and thus shakes our confidence that we would have avoided a pernicious path in those circumstances. But this effect is perfectly compatible with Harris's responsibility for how he did respond, just as we would have been responsible for how we would have responded. The biography affects us not because it is deterministic, libertarians can say, but because it shakes our confidence that we would have exercised that freedom rightly in more dire straits. We are not, of course, responsible for our formative circumstances—and in this respect we are morally lucky and Harris is unlucky—but those circumstances do not determine our responses to them. It is the individual's own response that distinguishes those who become evil from those who do not.

This idea is nicely captured by Peter Abélard: "Nothing mars the soul except what is of its own nature, namely consent."[19] The idea is that one cannot simply be caused to be morally bad by the environment. So either Harris's soul is not (morally) marred, or he has been a willing accomplice to the malformation of the self. His evil means that he has consented to what he has become—namely, one who consents to cruelty. Thus, Abélardians try to fill the statistical cracks with the will. The development of the moral self, they will say, is mediated by consent.

We should be struck here by the a priori character of libertarian convictions. How is Harris's consent to be construed, and why *must* it have occurred? What evidence is there that it occurred? Why couldn't Harris just have become that way? What is the difference between his having acquiesced to what he became and his simply having become that way? The libertarian faces the following difficulty: If there is no such difference, then the view is vacuous, for consent was supposed to explain his becoming that way. If there is a difference, what evidence is there that it obtains in a particular case? Isn't there room for considerable doubt about this, and shouldn't libertarians, or we, insofar as we are libertarians, be very doubtful about Harris's responsibility—and indeed, on the Abélardian thesis, even about whether Harris is an evil man, whether his soul is morally marred? (Notice that the tumor case is a priori impossible on that thesis, unless we think of the tumor somehow as merely presenting an occasion for consent—as inclining without necessitating.) One suspects that the libertarian confidence in their attributions of historical responsibility is rooted in a picture according to which the fact that Harris became that way *proves* that he consented. Then, of course, the appeal to consent is explanatorily vacuous.

Epistemology apart, the attempt to trace the evil self to consent at an earlier stage is faced with familiar difficulties. If we suppose (fancifully)

19. From "Intention and Sin," reprinted in Herbert Morris (ed.), *Freedom and Responsibility* (Stanford University Press), p. 169.

that Harris, earlier on, with full knowledge and deliberation, launched himself on his iniquitous career,[20] we would be merely postponing the inquiry, for the will which could fully and deliberately consent to such a career would have to have its roots in a self which is already morally marred—a self, therefore, which cannot itself be seen simply as a product of consent. Are we instead to suppose that at some earlier stage Harris slipped heedlessly or recklessly into patterns of thought and action which he ought to have known would eventuate in an evil character? (This seems to have been Aristotle's view in *Nicomachean Ethics*, Book III.5.) In that case, we would be tracing his present ways to the much less egregious faults of negligence.[21]

RESPONSIBILITY FOR THE SELF

Strawson and others often charge libertarians with a metaphysically dubious conception of the self. The foregoing reflections indicate a basis for this charge. Libertarianism combines the Abélardian view about consent (or something like it) with the principle (or something like it) that to be responsible for anything, one must be responsible for (some of) what produces it. If we think of agents as consenting to this or that *because* they are (or have?) selves of a certain character, then it looks as though they are responsible for so consenting only if they are responsible for the self in which that consent is rooted. To establish this in each case, we have to trace the character of the self to earlier acts of consent. This enterprise seems hopeless, since the trace continues interminably or leads to a self to which the individual did not consent. The libertarian seems committed, then, to bearing the unbearable burden of showing how we can be responsible for ourselves. This burden can seem bearable only in a view of the self as an entity that mysteriously both transcends and intervenes in the "causal nexus," because it is both product and author of its actions and attitudes.

Must libertarians try to bear this burden? Perhaps the idea that they must rests upon a view of the self to which libertarians need not be committed. Perhaps the trouble arises in the first place from viewing the self as a thing standing in causal relation to acts of consent. The libertarian might say that to talk about the (moral) self is not to talk about an entity which necessitates specific acts of consent, but to talk about the sorts of things to which an individual tends to consent. To speak of Harris's moral self is not to explain his conduct, but to indicate the way he is morally. What we are responsible for are the particular things we consent to. We need not consider whether we are responsible for the genesis of the

20. If such a thing ever occurred, it must have occurred at a stage when Harris clearly would have fallen under the exemption condition of "being a child."
21. Adams makes this point; op. cit.

entity whose characteristics necessitate those acts of consent, for there is no such entity. In a way, of course, one is derivatively responsible for one's self, since one's moral self is constituted by the character of what one consents to, and one is responsible for what one consents to.[22]

The historical dimension of the concept of responsibility results from the principle that one is not responsible for one's conduct if that is necessitated by causes for which one is not responsible. This leads to a problematic requirement that one be responsible for one's self only if one thinks of the self as an entity that causes one's (its) actions and willings. Libertarians can reject this view. What they must affirm is that we are responsible for what we consent to, that consent is not necessitated by causes internal or external to the agent, and that if it were, we could not properly hold the individual responsible for what he or she consents to. These claims are far from self-evident. But they hardly amount to a "panicky metaphysics." (p. 66).[23]

In the end, however, I do not think that libertarianism can be so readily domesticated. The idea that one is responsible for and only for what one consents to is not of course distinctive of libertarianism; that idea has no historical implications. What is distinctive is the further requirement that consent be undetermined. I do not think the idea that consent is undetermined is in itself particularly problematic. The trouble begins only when we ask why this is *required*. The ground of this requirement is the intuition that unless consent were undetermined, we would not truly be *originators* of our deeds. We would be merely products, and not, as it were, producers. It is this intuition to which the libertarian finds it so difficult to give content. "Being an originator" does not mean just "consenting to," for that is already covered by the first thesis. Nor is this notion captured simply by adding the requirement of indeterminism; that is a merely negative condition. Attempts to specify the condition in positive terms either cite something that could obtain in a deterministic world, or something obscurely transcendent.

I suspect, then, that any metaphysically innocuous version of libertarianism must leave its incompatibilist component unmotivated.

IGNORANCE AND SKEPTICISM

I have been exploring some ways in which the expressive theory might explain the relevance of certain historical considerations. Whatever the

22. It is noteworthy that Harris himself seems to accept responsibility for his life: "He told me he had his chance, he took the road to hell and there's nothing more to say." (From the end of the first extract from the Corwin article.)

23. For an attempt at libertarianism without metaphysics, see David Wiggins, "Towards a Credible Form of Libertarianism," in T. Honderich (ed.), *Essays on Freedom of Action*, Routledge and Kegan Paul, 1973.

best explanation may be, the remarkable fact is that we are, for the most part, quite ignorant of these considerations. Why does our ignorance not give us more pause? If, for whatever reason, reactive attitudes are sensitive to historical considerations, as Strawson acknowledges, and we are largely ignorant of these matters, then it would seem that most of our reactive attitudes are hasty, perhaps even benighted, as skeptics have long maintained. In this respect, our ordinary practices are not as unproblematic as Strawson supposes.

It might be thought that these suspicions about reactive attitudes have no bearing on responsibility, but with the expressive theory, that cannot be easily maintained. As we normally think of the matter, not all considerations that affect reactive attitudes are strictly relevant to responsibility. For example, if one shares a moral fault with another, one may feel it inappropriate to blame the other. Here the point is not that the other is not responsible or blameworthy, but that it is not *one's* business to blame. One should tend to one's own faults first.[24] Thoughts about moral luck seem to be continuous with this ordinary phenomenon. The thought is not that the other is not blameworthy, but that one may be no better, and that indignation on one's part would be self-righteous and indulgent. By calling our attention to our general ignorance of historical considerations, the skepticism we have just been considering is merely an extension of these reflections.

With an expressive theory, however, it is not clear that a general skepticism about the propriety of the reactive attitudes can be separated from skepticism about responsibility. For the latter concept *is* the concept of the conditions in which it is appropriate to respond to one another in reactive ways. In a Strawsonian view, there is no reason for a wedge between the practices that evince the reactive attitudes and the belief in responsibility. In a particular case, one may believe another to be responsible without actually responding to him or her in reactive ways (due to strains of commitment and so on), because one may regard the other as blameworthy, as an appropriate object of the reactive attitudes by others in the moral community. But if one thinks that *none* of us mortals is in a position to blame, then it is doubtful that any sense can be given to the belief that the other is nonetheless blameworthy. One can still attribute cowardice, thoughtlessness, cruelty, and so on, to others; but as we have seen, these judgments are not sufficient in a Strawsonian view to characterize the practice of holding responsible. We might try to appeal to the reactive attitudes of a select group of actual or hypothetical judges (here is another job

24. Montaigne would not agree: "To censure my own faults in some other person seems to me no more incongruous than to censure, as I often do, another's in myself. They must be denounced everywhere, and be allowed no place of sanctuary." ("On the Education of Children," in *Essays*, Penguin Classics, 1971, p. 51.)

for God to do),[25] but then the connection to reactive attitudes becomes so tenuous or hypothetical that the attitudes lose the central role they are given in "Freedom and Resentment," and the expressive theory loses its distinctive character. It then collapses into the view discussed in the section called "Blaming and Finding Fault."

OBJECTIVITY AND ISOLATION

It remains unclear to what extent our ordinary practices involve dubious beliefs about ourselves and our histories. To acknowledge the relevance of historical considerations is, on any account, to acknowledge a potential source of skepticism about those practices; moreover, in a Strawsonian account (though not in a libertarian account), such skepticism cannot be readily separated from skepticism about responsibility itself. In this respect, Strawson is inordinately optimistic about our common ways.

However, these practices are vulnerable to a different kind of suspicion. This suspicion is related to Strawson's conception of the place of "retributive" sentiments in those practices, and to his claim that that practice, so conceived, is not something that is optional and open to radical criticism, but rather is part of the "framework" of our conception of human society. One could agree that the expressive theory best gives the basis and content of the practice of holding responsible and still maintain that abandoning this practice is not only conceivable but desirable, for what it expresses is itself destructive of human community. I conclude with some comments on this further issue.

Consider some remarks by Albert Einstein:

> I do not at all believe in human freedom in the philosophical sense. Everybody acts not only under external compulsion but also in accordance with inner necessity. Schopenhauer's saying, "A man can do what he wants, but not want what he wants," has been a very real inspiration to me since my youth; it has been a continual consolation in the face of life's hardships, my own and others', and an unfailing wellspring of tolerance. This realization mercifully mitigates the easily paralysing sense of responsibility and prevents us from taking ourselves and other people all too seriously; it is conducive to a view of life which, in particular, gives humor its due.[26]

Significantly, in the same place Einstein speaks of himself as a "lone traveler," with a "pronounced lack of need for direct contact with other human beings and human communities," who has

25. Just as Berkeley tried to save the thesis that material objects consist in ideas.
26. Albert Einstein, *Ideas and Opinions*, Crown Publishers, 1982, pp. 8–9.

never belonged to my country, my home, my friends, or even my immediate family, with my whole heart; in the face of all these ties, I have never lost a sense of distance and a need for solitude—feelings which increase with the years.

The point that interests me here is not that these remarks confute Strawson's claim that reactive attitudes are never in practice affected by an acceptance of determinism, but that they corroborate his central claim about the alternative to the reactive, participant stance. The "distance" of which Einstein speaks is just an aspect of the "detachment" Strawson thinks characterizes the objective stance. At its extremes, it takes the form of human isolation. What is absent from Einstein's outlook is something that, I suspect, Strawson cherishes: the attachment or commitment to the personal, as it might be called.[27]

Whatever its grounds, Einstein's outlook is not without its appeal. Perhaps part of its appeal can be attributed to a fear of the personal, but it is also appealing precisely on account of its repudiation of the retributive sentiments. In another place, Einstein salutes the person "to whom aggressiveness and resentment are alien."[28] Can such an ideal of the person be pursued only at the cost of the attachment to the personal? Must we choose between isolation and animosity?

Some of Strawson's remarks imply that we must:

> Indignation, disapprobation, like resentment, tend to inhibit or at least to limit our goodwill towards the object of these attitudes, tend to promote at least partial and temporary withdrawal of goodwill . . . (These, of course, are not contingent connections.) But these attitudes . . . are precisely the correlates of the moral demand in the case where the demand is felt to be disregarded. The making of the demand *is* the proneness to such attitudes. The holding of them does not . . . involve . . . viewing their object other than as a member of the moral community. The partial withdrawal of goodwill which these attitudes entail, the modification *they* entail of the general demand that another should if possible be spared suffering, is . . . the consequence of *continuing* to view him as a member of the moral community; only as one who has offended against its demands. So the preparedness to acquiesce in that infliction of suffering on the offender which is an es-

27. To what extent Einstein lived up to this outlook, I am not prepared to say. Some other writings suggest a different view: "External compulsion can . . . reduce but never cancel the responsibility of the individual. In the Nuremberg trials, this idea was considered to be self-evident. . . . Institutions are in a moral sense impotent unless they are supported by the sense of responsibility of living individuals. An effort to arouse and strengthen this sense of responsibility of the individual is an important service to mankind" (op. cit., p. 27). Is Einstein taking a consequentialist stance here?
28. Ibid.

sential part of punishment is all of a piece with this whole range of attitudes. . . . (pp. 62–63)

This passage is troubling. Some have aspired to rid themselves of the readiness to limit goodwill and to acquiesce in the suffering of others not in order to relieve the strains of involvement, nor out of a conviction in determinism, but out of a certain ideal of human relationships, which they see as poisoned by the retributive sentiments. It is an ideal of human fellowship or love which embodies values that are arguably as historically important to our civilization as the notion of moral responsibility itself. The question here is not whether this aspiration is finally commendable, but whether it is compatible with holding one another morally responsible. The passage implies that it is not.

If holding one another responsible involves making the moral demand, and if the making of the demand *is* the proneness to such attitudes, and if such attitudes involve retributive sentiments and hence[29] a limitation of goodwill, then skepticism about retribution is skepticism about responsibility, and holding one another responsible is at odds with one historically important ideal of love.

Many who have this idea, such as Gandhi or King,[30] do not seem to adopt an objective attitude in Strawson's sense. Unlike Einstein's, their lives do not seem characterized by human isolation: They are often intensely involved in the "fray" of interpersonal relations. Nor does it seem plausible to suppose that they do not hold themselves and others morally responsible: They *stand up* for themselves and others against their oppressors; they *confront* their oppressors with the fact of their misconduct, *urging* and even *demanding* consideration for themselves and others; but they manage, or come much closer than others to managing, to do such things without vindictiveness or malice.

Hence, Strawson's claims about the interpenetration of responsibility and the retributive sentiments must not be confused with the expressive theory itself. As these lives suggest, the retributive sentiments can in principle be stripped away from holding responsible and the demands and appeals in which this consists. What is left are various forms of reaction and appeal to others as moral agents. The boundaries of moral responsibility are the boundaries of intelligible moral address. To regard another as morally responsible is to react to him or her as a moral self.[31]

29. Rather than attempting to separate retribution from responsibility, one might try to harmonize retribution and goodwill. This possibility seems to me worth exploring.

30. For these examples, and the discussion in this section, I am indebted to Stern (op. cit.).

31. We have, of course, seen reasons why these boundaries require further delineation.

Part II

HIERARCHY, RATIONALITY, AND THE "REAL SELF"

5

The Real Self View (In Which a Nonautonomous Conception of Free Will and Responsibility Is Examined and Criticized)

SUSAN WOLF

I HAVE before presented the related problems of responsibility and free will as problems the forcefulness and structure of which could be understood by reference to the dilemma of autonomy. Through the recognition that autonomy appears at once necessary for responsibility and impossible to realize or achieve, I have suggested, the concepts of responsibility and free will can be seen to be deeply problematic or obscure. For if autonomy is necessary for responsibility, there is reason to think that responsibility and free will are impossible. And if autonomy is not necessary for responsibility, then there is reason to think that we are fundamentally confused about what responsibility and free will are. In this context, the question "What kinds of beings must we be if we are ever to be responsible for the results of our wills?" takes the shape of a demand to know whether or not we must, in particular, be autonomous beings. And the alternative answers to this question give structure in turn to the related question of how, if at all, responsibility is possible. For if responsibility requires autonomy, we need to know how, if at all, *autonomy* is possible. And if responsibility does not require autonomy, we need to know what features of presumptively nonautonomous beings could give sense and justification to attributions of responsibility to *them*.

Readers who are familiar with discussions of the metaphysical problems of responsibility and free will may be used to thinking about these problems in somewhat different terms. For the "free will debate" that is carried on in philosophical journals tends to focus, not on the connection between free will and autonomy, but rather on the connection be-

From *Freedom within Reason* by Susan Wolf. Copyright © 1990 by Oxford University Press, Inc. Reprinted by permission.

tween free will and various forms of determinism. To most such readers, the connections between these discussions and the discussion to follow will be obvious. Still, it is worthwhile to make some of these connections explicit, both to better orient the reader and clarify the ways in which these other discussions address and are addressed by this one.

RELATING THE PROBLEMS OF FREE WILL AND RESPONSIBILITY TO DETERMINISM

That there is a philosophical problem about free will and determinism can be explained as a result of the following two facts: On the one hand, the claim that we are free and responsible beings seems incompatible with the claim that determinism is true. On the other hand, determinism, or some form of it that seems incompatible with free will and responsibility, seems likely, or at any rate not unlikely, to *be* true. This poses a dilemma that is formally similar to the dilemma of autonomy. If free will and responsibility are incompatible with determinism, then there is reason to think that we may not be free and responsible beings. But if free will and responsibility are compatible with determinism, then we need to know more about what free will and responsibility are that will explain why the appearance of incompatibility is so persistent.

Once this dilemma is posed, however, we can see that we need to know more about what free will and responsibility are in any case. For we cannot discover whether free will and responsibility are compatible with determinism without a better understanding of these concepts. That is, before we can answer the question of whether free will is compatible with determinism, we need a conceptual analysis, or elaboration, of the concepts of free will and responsibility that will make the essence of these concepts, so to speak, more apparent in terms that will allow the question more readily to be grasped. Indeed, insofar as the debate about free will and determinism is a coherent and unified one, some such analyses or elaborations must be already implicitly at work. That is, the incompatibilists, as they are called, must share a common conception of free will and responsibility, in virtue of which they take the application of these concepts to be incompatible with determinism, and the compatibilists, insofar as they form a unified group, must share some general beliefs about why the incompatibilists' conceptions of free will and responsibility are mistaken.

The suggestion that the problems of free will and responsibility can be structured by reference to the dilemma of autonomy implicitly offers an interpretation of what contrasting conceptual analyses underlie the debate about free will and determinism. According to this interpretation, incompatibilism (or the predominant form of it) is grounded in the belief that autonomy is required for responsibility and that autonomy is incompatible with determinism. Compatibilism, by contrast, issues from a view according to which autonomy is not required for responsibility and according to which what is required is clearly compatible with determinism's being true. In other words, the suggestion is that most incompatibilists are incompatibilists because they have autonomous conceptions of free will and responsibility, and most compatibilists are compatibilists because they have nonautonomous conceptions of these notions of a kind that raise no *prima facie* problems with respect to their compatibility with determinism.

The plausibility of this suggestion can best be evaluated only after the autonomous and nonautonomous conceptions of free will and responsibility are more fully laid out. I hope and expect that compatibilists will be able to identify their positions in the nonautonomous conceptions of free will and responsibility I will explore in this chapter. But it should be acknowledged at the outset that proponents of autonomous and nonautonomous conceptions of free will and responsibility are not logically committed respectively to advocating incompatibilism and compatibilism. It is possible to believe that autonomy, though necessary for free will and responsibility, is compatible with the determinism. In fact, Kant and Sartre, two of the most compelling defenders of autonomous conceptions, both seem to have views of this sort. And it is possible to believe that although autonomy is not required for responsibility, what is required is also incompatible with determinism. Though at this point this view may seem to have little to recommend it, reasons for taking it seriously will emerge as the discussion proceeds.

AVOIDING AUTONOMY: DEVELOPING THE IDEA OF AN AGENT'S REAL SELF

We may now return to the problems of responsibility and free will as they are structured by reference to the dilemma of autonomy. Since the condition of autonomy seems at once necessary for responsibility and impossible to realize or achieve, a defense of the possibility of responsibility must take one of two possible paths: Either it must provide a nonautonomous conception of responsibility or it must provide a coherent and realizable conception of autonomy. Recalling the way in which we were led initially to accept the condition of autonomy gives us reason to attempt to construct a defense along the former path first. For we were led to accept the condition of autonomy in an effort to explain the intuitive appropriateness of exempting agents in certain exceptional situations from responsibility. Accepting this condition, however, seems to lead to the counterintuitive (and highly undesirable) conclusion that all agents are always exempt from responsibility, or perhaps that the very concept of responsibility makes no sense. Thus the condition of autonomy, which was attractive because it seemed to offer an explanation of some of our intuitions, turns out (apparently) to explain too much. It seems natural to doubt our purported explanation before we doubt the deeply entrenched belief that an acceptance of this explanation seems rationally to require.

Reexamining our purported explanation, we can see why it explains too much. It is because the features of the agents and their situations on which we focused in the attempt to explain why in these exceptional cases the agents were not responsible for their actions turned out, on examination, to be features that were common to exceptional and non-exceptional cases alike. But while victims of hypnosis, coercion, and mental illness are, in some respects, just like our normal selves, it is also clear that in some respects they are quite different. If we can find an alternative explanation for our intuitions regarding these exceptional cases that focuses on features that distinguish these examples from ones more typical of adult human life, then we may be able to formulate a more lenient condition of responsibility that, in accordance with our intuitions, excludes the agents in the problematic examples without threatening our claim to be, by and large, and in most situations, responsible beings ourselves.

To this very purpose, David Hume suggested an alternative explanation which other philosophers of mind have subsequently elaborated and refined. Hume acknowledged, as we did, that cases of the sort illustrated by the three cases described earlier are problematic because the agents in these cases had to perform the actions they did—because, in other words, these actions were necessitated by forces in some sense external to the agents themselves. But, Hume points out, there are two senses of "necessity," which our previous response to these problematic cases failed to distinguish. On the one hand, there is a sense of "necessity" that seems "to imply something of force, and violence, and constraint," to which "the liberty of spontaneity" may be said to be opposed; on the other hand, there is a sense of "necessity" that is inextricably connected to the idea of causation, to which "the liberty of indifference," but not the liberty of spontaneity, is opposed. According to Hume, it is the former kind of necessity that makes the problematic cases problematic, and this should suggest that the kind of liberty opposed to it—the liberty of spontaneity—is a condition of responsibility. Failing to notice the difference between this sense of necessity and the sense connected to the idea of causation, however, we misidentified the problematic elements in the cases above and thus mistakenly formulated the condition of autonomy that requires the responsible agent to have not the liberty of spontaneity but the liberty of indifference.[1]

Of course, the ideas of "force, and violence, and constraint" are themselves in need of clarification if Hume's claim that only these sorts of causes are incompatible with responsibility is to seem plausible. If this claim is to provide a basis for explaining the case of hypnosis, "force" must not be restricted to *physical* force; and if it is to provide a basis for explaining the case of kleptomania, "constraint" must not be restricted to observable, *external* constraint. Nonetheless, it seems true that all these cases contain features that deprive the agents in them of a kind of liberty that we normally have—features, in other words, that interfere with or inhibit the agents' normal abilities to control their behavior in accordance with the values and choices of their deepest selves. Perhaps the best way to clarify the notion of "constraint" that is relevant to a defense of Hume's view is by offering a characterization of these normal abilities and a model of action that involves the free exercise of them. Then constraint may be defined as anything that prevents the agent from conforming to this positive model.

In a sense, I have already suggested a very simplistic positive model of this sort: Under normal conditions of freedom, an agent is able to govern her behavior on the basis of her will, which in turn can be governed by the set of the agent's desires.[2] But recalling the cases of hypnosis and kleptomania yet again, we can see that this model is too simplistic to separate the normally free actions from the ones that are intuitively unfree. For these cases remind us that there are occasions when an agent may be constrained by her own desires, and situations in which an agent may feel forced to act from a will that, in one sense but not in another, is not her own. An agent, in other words, may be alienated from her own desires or from her own will. In some cases—for example, the kleptomaniac case—the agent might say that she would not have the desire in question if she could choose. In others—the hypnosis case might serve as an example—the answer to whether the agent would have the desire if she could choose may be indeterminate. The agent's alienation from her desire arises rather from the recognition that her choice is irrelevant—that, in other words, her having the desire in question is independent of her choosing to have it. In still other cases, the agent may not feel alienated from her desires at all, but may feel alienated from her

1. David Hume, *A Treatise Concerning Human Nature* (1888), ed. L. A. Selby-Bigge (Oxford: Oxford University Press, 1967), p. 407.

2. Some philosophers of mind might object that this characterization is redundant, for there is at least one very broad sense of "desire" according to which it is tautological that if an agent willed, or intended, to do something, she must have wanted, or desired, to do it. But because, as we shall see, the question of which desires shape the content of the agent's will is important to a more satisfactory model of normally free action, it is useful to distinguish the will from the set of desires from the start.

will, because she would not have chosen to act on her desires in the way she did. A dieter, for example, might identify with her sweet tooth and yet prefer to refrain from indulging it. When she accepts the offer of dessert anyway, she does so "despite herself," feeling, perhaps, compelled by (what is admittedly) her own desire for sweets.

An agent does not have absolute authority over the question of what desires and actions are to be identified with or deeply attributed to her. An agent who claims to be moved by a desire that is not her own may be in bad faith; an agent who regards herself as a victim of internal compulsion may be merely a victim of self-deception. Conversely, an agent may regard herself as a fully responsible agent acting from desires that are wholly her own, and yet be compelled or constrained by forces of whose power or existence she is unaware. (The influence of alcohol or drugs provides ready examples of this.) Although these facts point to the considerable difficulties involved in establishing the claim that an agent is acting under constraint, they are irrelevant to our present task of analyzing the meaning of such a claim.

Whether or not the agent who claims to be acting from an inner compulsion is right, we may ask what it would mean for her to be right, for by doing so we may refine our positive model of unconstrained human action, which, prior to the intrusion of philosophical thinking, seemed intuitively free enough for the agent to be justifiably held responsible for it. We have already agreed that this agent is at liberty to perform whatever action she wills to perform—what she thinks she lacks, and what she may truly lack, is the liberty to will whatever action she wants to will.[3] She is alienated from her will, because her will is not, in an important sense, the result of her choice.

We might try to characterize the positive model from which the actions of this agent diverge as one according to which the agent acts according to her will, and the agent wills according to her choice. But there are reasons for finding this characterization unsatisfactory. For if an agent can be alienated from her will, one might think, she can also be alienated from her choice. Indeed, one might think that if an agent performs an action intentionally—that is, as a result of her willing it—there must be some sense in which she chooses to perform it. So if she is alienated from her will, then she *must* be alienated, in that sense, from her choice. Of course, one might say that the unfree agent does not choose to make *that* choice, thus locating the distinction between the unfree and the free at one level further down, as it were. But this begins to make our positive model look implausible. For we do not naturally think of our ordinary actions as resulting from a *series* of choices: we do not ordinarily choose to choose to will to act. And even if there are some excep-

3. This analysis derives from Harry Frankfurt, "Freedom of the Will and the Concept of a Person," *Journal of Philosophy* 68 (January 1971): 5–20.

tional situations in which it makes sense to characterize an agent in this way, this characterization will not distinguish the free agents from the unfree. For an agent who is alienated from her first-order choice may be alienated from her higher-order choices as well.

It would be better, then, to characterize our positive model, from the beginning, in terms not of the quantity of choices underlying the action the agent ultimately performs, but rather in terms of the quality of the choices, however many there are. The crucial feature distinguishing unalienated from alienated action is that the will (or the choice, or the multitude of choices) of the unalienated agent arises from the agent's unalienated self—from her real self, if you will, the self with which the agent is to be properly identified. Our positive model of action, from which the apparently unfree actions discussed above can be seen to diverge, must be a model according to which the agent's actions are governed by her will and her will is governed by her unalienated, real self. Obviously, our positive model must include some characterization of an agent's real self, a characterization that avoids the temptation to distinguish what is from what is not a part of that self by reference to whether the aspect of the agent in question is one the agent has chosen to have.

Gary Watson[4] has suggested that we can provide the characterization we are after if we recognize the difference between what he calls the agent's values, on the one hand, and the agent's desires, on the other. Or rather, since the agent's values are themselves desires of a certain kind, the distinction of importance is that between the agent's values and the rest of the agent's desires. According to Watson, an agent values something (whether an object, a state of affairs, a disposition, or whatever) if she thinks it good, or if she thinks there is some reason to want it. By contrast, an agent may want something that she does not think it is good to have or want; indeed, she may be motivated to attain some object while at the same time believing that it would be wholly bad or wrong to attain it. Watson points out that such unvalued desires may be impulsive and transient, as, for example, the desire to drown one's baby in the bathwater, or the desire to smash the face of one's squash competitor with one's racket. Others may be long-standing, dispositional desires, such as the desire to smoke cigarettes, or the desire to sleep with one's best friend's spouse. Desires that are not values are desires we may be indifferent or even uncomfortable about having—the prospect of satisfying such desires may not be preferable to the prospect of eliminating these desires in other ways. Our values mean more to us than that—it will be important that they be satisfied rather than otherwise eliminated, and, if they cannot be satisfied, we may even prefer the prospect of living with the discomfort of unsatisfied desires to the prospect of

4. Gary Watson, "Free Agency," *Journal of Philosophy* 72 (April 1975): 205–20.

ceasing to have these desires at all. (Consider, for example, our attitudes toward the desires for justice and love.)

If the distinction between values and desires is to serve as a basis for understanding what a person's real self is, Watson's own characterization of this distinction must be slightly modified. For the identification of a person's values with what that person thinks good or supported by reason unconditionally puts a person's reason, or her faculties of judgment, broadly construed, at the core of the person's real self. Indeed, Watson acknowledges his debt to Plato's division of the soul into Reason and Appetite and suggests that values correspond roughly to those desires which have the support of or their origin in the agent's Reason. Admittedly, many people, and particularly many philosophers, are likely to identify their deepest selves with their faculties of reason. But there are some who trust their hearts more than their minds, and it is not incoherent for a person to care deeply about something and yet be uncertain as to whether she thinks the thing she cares about is good. It is possible for a person to embrace a commitment to a principle, person, or group, and yet lack the ability and even the inclination to justify that commitment. We can, however, construe the notion of values somewhat more broadly, as comprising those things which a person cares about, or alternatively, as including all and only those things which *matter* to a person in some positive way, without losing the distinction between what a person values and what she merely wants, or desires, or likes.

In light of this, it seems plausible to distinguish those desires which are part of the agent's real self from those which are not according to whether the desires in question are also values for the agent. But our primary concern is to understand not which desires but which actions may be attributed to the agent's real self, and, although there is promise to the suggestion that the right class of actions is made up of those actions which arise out of the agent's values, this suggestion must be elaborated and made more precise if it is adequately to capture the class we have in mind.

An agent who has values will almost certainly value some things more highly than others, and, when values compete, the relative weights she assigns them will inform her judgment about what, all things considered, is the thing for her to do. Just as there can be a disparity between what an agent values and what she desires (and is therefore to some extent motivated to do), there can be a disparity between how highly an agent values something and how strongly she is motivated to pursue it. In accordance with the distinction between values and desires, Watson distinguishes between valuational and motivational systems. An agent's judgments of the form that, all things considered, X is the thing for her to do, arise out of the agent's valuational system. An agent's will, however, depends on what the agent is most strongly motivated to do, and this may or may not accord with the agent's valuational judgment. Thus, the dieter mentioned earlier might not only desire but truly value the appreciation of a fine chocolate mousse, in addition to valuing the attainment of a lower body weight. Then it would be true in a sense that whether the agent takes the mousse or not, her action could be said to arise out of her values. But if the judgment that issues from the agent's valuational system would have her refrain from eating dessert, it is understandable that the agent who takes the dessert anyway might think herself constrained by her own values.

This suggests that we can more accurately characterize the class of actions that are attributable to an agent's real self as the class of actions that arise, not simply out of the agent's values, but out of her valuational system. But if we are to identify the class of actions that are attributable to the agent's real self with the class of actions for which we ordinarily consider ourselves responsible, this characterization still needs to be amended. For the suggestion that all the actions that are truly mine arise out of my valuational system seems to endow my actions generally with a more profound significance than they typically have. When I pour myself a second cup of coffee, or put on a sweater, or walk to the subway, I am not ordinarily expressing deeply held values or judging at all whether, all things considered, my action is a worthwhile or good one to perform. Although, in the absence of a special context, it would be strange for someone actively to claim responsibility for actions of this sort, it would be stranger still to deny responsibility for them. Moreover, an action that is not in accord with my valuational system may seem at least somewhat significant precisely because that action is attributable to me. I may, for instance, hold myself responsible for the weakness of my will or for my lack of self-discipline.

These facts are easily explained if we recall that the positive model we have been trying to characterize is a model of acting with the full range of *liberties* that we ordinarily think ourselves to have. For what seems crucial to our sense of responsibility for the kinds of actions just described is that, whether or not our actions *are* governed by our valuational systems, there seems to be nothing that *prevents* our actions from being so governed. In other words we are, or think we are, at liberty to exercise valuational judgment, and to make such judgment effective in governing our behavior; the full resources of our valuational systems are, as it were, *available* to us as agents, use them as we may.

Thus, we may say that an agent's behavior is attributable to the agent's real self—and therefore that the agent behaves as she does in the absence of undue constraint—if she is at liberty (or able) both to govern her behavior on the basis of her will and to govern her will on the basis of her valuational system. On the other hand, an agent may be said to be unduly constrained if something inhibits, interferes with, or otherwise prevents the effective exercise of these abilities.

Using this definition of constraint, we can explain the cases that earlier troubled us along the lines that Hume suggested. For the victims of hypnosis, coercion, and kleptomania all do seem constrained. These agents do seem unable to govern their actions on the basis of their respective valuational systems. The kleptomaniac's will and the will of the person who is under hypnosis are governed by desires that are presumably not among the agents' values at all. And even if the desires that move the victim of coercion are also values of hers, it is not the importance of the values but the strength of the desires that determines the content of her will. Of course, for these agents to be truly constrained, it must be the case not only that their actions *are* not determined by their valuational systems but that they *cannot* be. But it is plausible to think this is true of the agents in the cases at hand. For it is plausible to think that the agents in these cases are either in situations that inhibit their ability to make valuational judgments at all or are in the grip of desires so strong as to compel them to act as they do, whether they value these actions or not.[5]

Because the agents in these cases are unduly constrained, their actions are not attributable to their real selves. And the fact that their actions are not attributable to their selves seems to justify our intuition that they are not responsible for their actions. Moreover, the notion of a real self may be used to throw further light on our intuition that lower animals and young children are not responsible for their actions. For lower animals and young children do not seem to have real selves—they do not, or not yet, have valuational systems, as distinguished from a mere set of desires, and so there is no possibility that their actions can be in accordance with them.

Thus the suggestion that an agent is responsible only for those actions which are attributable to her real self, understanding an action to be attributable to one's real self only if in performing it one is at liberty to govern one's actions on the basis of one's valuational system, seems at once to unify and to comprehend all our intuitive responses to cases we have considered thus far. Every agent we have considered who does not seem to be responsible for her actions either lacks a real self entirely or

---

5. This should be qualified, since the coercion example, as I have so sketchily described it, might plausibly be interpreted in either of two ways. On the one hand, we may interpret it in the way I have above as a case in which, given the strength of the agent's desire, his circumstances compel him to act as the coercer demands, independently of whether he judges it permissible or right. In that case, the agent is not responsible for what he does. On the other hand, it may be interpreted as a case in which the agent's behavior is not literally compelled, but is rather dependent on his judgment that, given his circumstances, obeying the coercer's wishes is reasonable. In that case, the agent is responsible for what he does, though not—at least if we agree with his judgment—blameworthy for it.

lacks the freedom to express it. By contrast, most fully developed human beings seem to have real selves which, in ordinary circumstances, they are at liberty to express and, more generally, to use in governing their behavior. Thus, unlike the requirement of autonomy, the requirement that an agent's behavior be attributable to the agent's real self is a condition of responsibility that can explain and justify our tendency to think that some agents are not responsible for their behavior without throwing doubt on the possibility that any agents are.

The view that the attributability of an agent's behavior to her real self constitutes a necessary and sufficient condition of responsibility offers us an alternative to the view that responsibility requires autonomy. For this view does not require an agent to be endlessly accountable to herself—that is, it does not require that her self be governable by her self *ad infinitum*. It is required that an agent *have* a real self, and that she be able to govern her behavior in accordance with it. But it does not matter where her real self comes from, whether it comes from somewhere else or from nowhere at all. Let us call this the Real Self View.

If Hume is right, then our earlier inclination to accept the condition of autonomy was just a mistake, based on a confusion between the idea of causation and the idea of constraint. In light of our analysis of constraint, we may relate this confusion to a different one—namely, the confusion between the idea of a person's real self and the idea, so to speak, of her undifferentiated self. In any case, it may appear that the reasoning that led us to accept the condition of autonomy was persuasive only because we failed to recognize the psychological complexity of the human agent. Failing to recognize relevant differences among the ways in which an agent might be caused to will to act, or to recognize relevant differences among the types of control that an agent might have, we misidentified the source of our thought that the agents in the three problematic cases discussed were not responsible for their actions. Attending to these complexities, we should be able to see that the problems lay not in *whether* but in *how* the actions in these cases were caused. That is, the problems had to do not with the ultimacy but with the type of the agents' control of their behavior.

PROBLEMS WITH THE REAL SELF VIEW

Despite the attractiveness of this view, the doubts that earlier beset us might reasonably remain. For even if the three problematic cases that originally led us to formulate the condition of autonomy can be explained without appeal to this troubling condition after all, other problematic cases cannot be so comfortably disposed of. Moreover, once the idea of autonomy was introduced, it seemed to make an intuitive kind of sense that it should be a requirement of responsibility, and the intuitive fittingness of this requirement does not vanish when we attend, as Hume suggested, to the distinction between causation and constraint, or when we attend to the distinction between a person's real self and the rest of her psychology. If the tendency to think that autonomy is necessary for responsibility is based on a confusion, the confusion must be deeper than the ones that have been suggested, and it is hard to see how the alternative view that an agent is responsible if and only if her behavior is attributable to her real self can provide a basis for unmasking this confusion, if it is one.

It will help us to understand these objections more fully, if we call attention to the central place the Real Self View gives to the point of view of the agent in determining whether the agent is responsible for her actions. For if the condition that the agent's actions be attributable to the agent's real self is to serve not just as a necessary but also as a sufficient condition of responsibility, then it follows that any agent who has a real self is responsible at least for any action that is actually governed by her valuational system. Thus any agent who has a real self is responsible for any wholly unalienated actions, for any actions that the agent would, on reflection and in light of relevant information, unqualifiedly regard as actions that are truly hers.

It does not follow that an agent will be an absolute authority as to whether she is responsible for her actions. For, if weakness of the will is possible, then an agent may be responsible for an action from which she feels (and, depending on how one defines one's terms, from which she may truly be) alienated. For she may be at liberty to act in accordance with her valuational system and yet act in a way that does not so accord. Conversely, an agent may think she is responsible for an action for which she is not, for an agent may be unaware of factors that alienate her from her actions. While under hypnosis, for example, an agent may not be able to recognize a discrepancy between her values and the motives she is hypnotized to have. And she may never recognize this, if she never learns that she was hypnotized or if she never comes out of her hypnotized state.

Still, an agent will generally be able to tell whether she is alienated from her actions or not, and, with the exception of certain cases of weakness of the will, an agent's own disposition to regard an action as an expression of her real self will, on this view, conform to an objective assessment of the agent's responsibility for it. In light of this, we can see why this view can account for the three problematic cases above. These are all cases of agents whose actions are in potential conflict with their judgments of their real, unalienated selves. Moreover, we can see why this view can account for the majority of problematic cases that are apt to come to mind. For we are rarely disposed to question the responsibility of an agent who does not question it herself.

Nonetheless, we sometimes do question the responsibility of a fully developed agent even when she acts in a way that is clearly attributable to her real self. For we sometimes have reason to question an agent's responsibility *for* her real self. That is, we may think it is not the agent's fault that she is the person she is—in other words, we may think it is not her fault that she has, not just the desires, but also the values she does. There may be forms of insanity that give rise to these thoughts. For although many mental disorders may, like kleptomania, leave a large part of a person's independently identifiable real self intact, and others may undermine a person's capacity to have any unified real self at all, there is no reason to think it impossible for mental illness to take the form of infecting someone's values in such a way that the self with which the victim completely and reflectively identifies is a self that other persons reasonably regard as being drastically mentally ill. (The Son of Sam murderer who made headlines some years ago might be an example of this sort.) Similarly, whether or not hypnosis is necessarily limited to transient effects on a mere portion of an agent's psyche, we can easily envision other forms of psychological conditioning (consider, for example, Orwell's *1984*) that could make more permanent and pervasive changes in the most central features of a person's self. Finally, and perhaps most disturbingly, there are persons whose values we are apt to explain as resulting from deprived or otherwise traumatic childhoods—persons who have fully developed intelligences and a complete, complex range of psychological structures, levels, and capacities for judgment, but who nonetheless do not seem responsible for what they are or what they do.

The claim that the sorts of people just described are not at all responsible for some of the actions that arise out of their real, unalienated selves is admittedly controversial. Some people think that such persons are somewhat responsible for the actions in question, but less responsible than they would be if they had not been afflicted with the deprivations or diseases or otherwise traumatic experiences of the kind I have mentioned. It should be noted that this weaker claim is enough to cast doubt on the claim that an agent is responsible for all and only those actions which are attributable to the agent's real self. For the agents in question seem fully to have real selves, with which their actions are wholly in accord. That is, they have fully developed psyches, with valuational systems, as distinct from motivational systems, that are as well-defined in their cases as in others, and with the same abilities to make valuational judgments, to use reason and argument, and so on. In this respect, they are different from children. And the actions in question are actions that, by hypothesis, they wholly want and choose to perform. If they had conflicting thoughts before performing these actions, these conflicts were resolved *in favor of* performing them, and if they later have regrets, these regrets are like the regrets we have when, as wholly unconstrained, unalienated agents, we do something that we later wish we had not done. Since these actions, then, are wholly attributable to these agents' fully developed real selves, on the view we are now considering one would expect these agents to be wholly responsible. If these agents are less than wholly responsible, this view must be leaving something out.

There are some, however, who do think such people are wholly responsible for their actions. They believe that no answer to the question of how someone's character or real self was formed could possibly lessen that person's responsibility for the actions that are "truly his." To the suggestion that such considerations might be mitigating factors, at least one philosopher has replied:

> He did not make his character; no, but he made his acts. Nobody blames him for making such a character, but only for making such acts. And to blame him for that is simply to say that he is a bad act-maker.[6]

I must confess that I feel an unbridgeable gulf between this point of view and my own. This breakdown of shared intuitions seems to indicate a difference in outlook so basic as to leave little hope of finding a more basic common ground to which both parties can appeal. Of course, it is easy to say that philosophers like Hobart (the author of the passage quoted above) have forced their intuitions into conformity with an otherwise attractive philosophical picture—that, in other words, they are in the grip of a philosophical picture that subverts their ability to evaluate objectively the sorts of cases that should serve as tests for that view. But such claims can be made from either side of the dispute.

Because the case of the victim of the deprived childhood, and other cases that are relevantly similar in form, are typically controversial, it would be wrong to place too much weight on one's intuitions about these cases. The character of the controversy, however, is revealing in a way that is independent of its settlement, and attention to it may help us express more general reasons for being dissatisfied with the Real Self View. For the fact that some people are reluctant to regard the agents in these cases as responsible beings is enough to motivate the question of why these agents are responsible beings, if in fact they are. The reply that these agents are acting in accordance with their real selves only begs the question at this point, restating the condition that, if offered as a sufficient condition of responsibility, is itself in need of support.

Nonetheless, defenders of this position often admit that they have nothing else to say, and express puzzlement over the fact that others still

6. R. E. Hobart, "Free Will as Involving Determination and Inconceivable without It," in Bernard Berofsky, ed., *Free Will and Determinism* (New York: Harper & Row 1966), p. 83.

feel something is missing. This seems to indicate that defenders of this position think they have reached rock bottom in our potential for understanding the nature of responsibility. For them, the attributability of an agent's behavior to an agent's real self is not just a necessary and sufficient condition of responsibility, it is more like a definition, which captures the meaning of "responsibility."

If we read the passage quoted above with a particular emphasis, the view seems attributable to Hobart:

> He did not make his character; no, but he made his acts. Nobody blames him for making such a character, but only for making such acts. And to blame him for that *is* simply to say that he is a bad act-maker.

We can understand this remark as an indication of a more general view: To be a responsible agent is simply to be, as it were, a fully formed act-maker. A bad act-maker deserves to be blamed; a good one deserves to be praised. And a maker of acts that are neutral in value may simply be acknowledged as such.

If this is the view to which proponents of the Real Self View are, or ought to be, committed—if, in other words, this is the view that provides the most coherent and plausible defense of that position—then we have reason to reject it. For it is just not true that to blame someone for an action is simply to say that he is a bad act-maker. At least it is not true of the particular kind of blame that is associated with the philosophical question of responsibility.

Earthquakes, defective tires, and broken machines are, at least sometimes, bad act-makers, as are dogs and children and adults with various physical and mental handicaps. But we do not blame them, at least not in the way in which we sometimes blame normal adult human beings. More generally, inanimate objects, natural phenomena, lower animals, and normal adults in a wide range of contexts exhibit all sorts of behavior that can be seen to have all sorts of positive, negative, or neutral value. We can recognize that these individuals behave in these ways, and recognize that their behaviors have the values they do, and yet find it completely inappropriate to blame or praise or otherwise attribute responsibility to these individuals for the behaviors in question.

The ability to express this point clearly is complicated by the fact that we sometimes use the word "responsibility" simply to identify what we may call the primary causal agent(s) of an event or state of affairs. For example, "the bent axle is responsible for the noise the car is making," "the muddy track is responsible for the horse's poor performance," "the beautiful weather is responsible for the picnic's success." We may even "blame" the car's noise "on" the axle, or say that we have the good weather "to thank." But this use of "responsibility" and related words and phrases seems different in kind from the uses that are understood when we are considering questions of moral responsibility; and it is easy to construct examples in which an individual is responsible for an event in the former sense but not responsible for it in the latter.

We may refer to the former sense of "responsibility" as superficial responsibility, and, in connection with this, we may speak of superficial praise and blame. When we say that an individual is responsible for an event in the superficial sense, we identify the individual as playing a causal role that, relative to the interests and expectations provided by the context, is of special importance to the explanation of that event. And when we praise or blame an individual in the superficial sense, we acknowledge that the individual has good or bad qualities, or has performed good or bad acts. But when we hold an individual morally responsible for some event, we are doing more than identifying her particularly crucial role in the causal series that brings about the event in question. We are regarding her as a fit subject for credit or discredit on the basis of the role she plays. When, in this context, we consider an individual worthy of blame or of praise, we are not merely judging the moral quality of the event with which the individual is so intimately associated; we are judging the moral quality of the individual herself in some more focused, noninstrumental, and seemingly more serious way. We may refer to the latter sense of responsibility as deep responsibility, and we may speak in connection with this of deep praise and blame.

While moral responsibility is probably the least controversial and best-examined species of deep responsibility, there may be other species of deep responsibility, or other contexts in which we attribute deep responsibility to agents as well. At least some of the judgments we make when we evaluate an individual's intellectual, physical, and artistic accomplishments seem to involve attributions of credit or discredit that are not reducible to an acknowledgment of these individuals' causal roles. (Recall, for example, the contrast between the child's fingerpainting and the more mature artist's watercolor.) And qualities like courage, patience, arrogance, closed-mindedness, which are not moral qualities in the narrow sense of that term that connects morality to benevolence or impartiality, may yet serve as the basis for deep compliments and criticism that are of, as opposed to merely about, the person in question.

There may be no clear or sharp line separating the deep instances of praise and blame or other attributions of responsibility from the superficial ones, and there may be no clear or sharp line separating the instances when deep, as opposed to merely superficial, praise, blame, and the like would be appropriate. Nonetheless, the difference in character between these two kinds of responsibility cannot be denied. For it is intelligible to wonder whether a person is deeply responsible for an action even after we have removed all doubt that she really did perform that action. We can coherently acknowledge that a person really did play a relevantly crucial role in bringing a very good or very bad event about, and yet be uncertain about whether the person deserves to be praised or blamed for it. In other words, we can understand that a person is superficially responsible for the effects of her behavior and yet wonder whether and why that person should be considered deeply responsible for them. So that with respect to deep praise and blame, it cannot be the case that to blame (praise) someone *is* simply to say that she is a bad (good) act-maker.

A defender of the view under consideration might try to invoke a distinction between act-makers and Act-makers. Full-blown Act-makers, or Agents, are not just identifiable individuals who somehow or other produce effects—they are individuals with selves, indeed, with real selves, and the effects they produce can properly be called their Acts only if these effects are related to their real selves in specifiable ways. But the suggestion that we can understand the difference between superficial and deep responsibility simply by attending to the distinctively interesting and complex relation that agents with real selves may have to some of their acts will not do. For the difference between superficial and deep responsibility is not simply a difference between a general relation and a more specific and particularly interesting and complex species of that relation. It is rather a more dramatic difference in kind—a difference, as the labels suggest, in depth.

The set of instances of deep praise and blame is not simply a subset of instances of praise and blame more generally that take a particular class of agents as their objects under conditions in which these agents perform their acts in a particular way. If it were, then the difference between deep and superficial praise or blame would be merely a difference in the precision with which we identify the cases of recognizably desirable or undesirable events, and expressions of deep praise or blame would differ from expressions of superficial praise or blame only in offering different amounts of information about what objects and what processes involving those objects played particularly crucial roles in bringing about those events. It would be the same kind of difference, then, as the difference between our blaming an accident on a car, as opposed to its driver or the weather, and our blaming it more precisely on the left front tire, and, more precisely still, on a defective tire, rather than an old one or one that has been improperly attached to the wheel. But the characters of deep and superficial attributions of praise, blame, and responsibility differ in a more fundamental way: Deep attributions seem to be more serious than superficial ones; they seem to have a different and special significance.

When we subject a person to deep praise and blame, we regard that person in a different light from that in which we regard other objects whose qualities and effects we can evaluatively assess. When we hold a person deeply responsible for things, we understand her to be accountable for them in a different way from that in which other objects can be accountable. It is only in the context of this distinctive kind of accountability that the question of whether an individual *deserves* praise or blame, or of whether she should be given credit or discredit *for* her recognizably good or bad features or actions, makes sense. It may be that the class of deeply responsible agents coincides exactly with the class of agents who have real selves, and that the class of actions and qualities for which these agents are deeply responsible coincides exactly with the class of actions and qualities that proceed from the agents' real selves in the sense already described. But, even if this were so, we would need an explanation of why these classes coincide. Why should the distinctive kind of complexity that is constituted by the possession of a real self make a person subject to a different kind of accountability from that to which other creatures and objects are subject? Why should the fact that a person's real self is superficially responsible for an event imply that, in addition, the person is deeply responsible for that event?

Attention to the psychological complexities that are distinctive to persons does not yield an answer to these questions. Such attention may help us explain why, if any individuals are deeply responsible, they will be individuals with real selves and with the ability to govern their actions and characters on the basis of them. But it will not explain why we think that any individuals are deeply responsible at all, and it will not provide us with a means of discovering whether this thought is coherent or justifiable.

The view that deep responsibility is equivalent to attributability to an agent's real self is incomplete without an explanation of why this equivalence holds. It cannot offer a solution to the problems of free will and responsibility without such an explanation—without, as it were, an explanation of why real selves should also be deep selves.

The controversial examples of victims of comprehensive insanity, psychological conditioning, and dramatically deprived childhoods suggest that, in fact, real selves may not always be deep selves. In other words, they suggest that some individuals with fully developed real selves may not deserve praise and blame for what they do and what they are.[7] If they do deserve praise and blame—or if they do not but there are others who do—we need to know why they deserve these things. But to do this, we must go beyond an examination of the internal complexities of a particular class of agents and consider the relation these agents, by contrast to other agents, have to the world in which they act.

7. This and related suggestions are discussed further in Susan Wolf, "Sanity and the Metaphysics of Responsibility," in Ferdinand Schoeman, ed., *Responsibility, Character, and the Emotions* (Cambridge: Cambridge University Press, 1987), pp. 46–62.

Enlarging the scope of our vision in this way, searching for a difference in the relations between an agent and her world that could account for the difference in depth, seems to draw us irresistibly to a reconsideration of the condition of autonomy. For the inclination to regard the victim of a deprived childhood as an individual who is not responsible for her behavior arises from the thought that, though she acts from a fully developed real self, she is not responsible *for* that real self. That is, she is not in control of who she ultimately is, and thus when she acts in accordance with her real self, her actions are the mere unfolding of the inevitable role she is fated to play in the blind, ceaseless flow of the world's events. Clearly, the kind of control of who the agent ultimately is that we feel to be lacking cannot be supplied by the addition of another loop to the internal structure of the agent. But if the difference between agents who have and agents who lack this kind of control is not a difference in the complexity of the kind of control an agent has over her character and her acts, one might think that it must be a difference in the ultimacy of the agent's control. And this is precisely what distinguishes autonomous agents from all others.

Autonomous agents, unlike other agents, are neither inevitable products of the inevitable interactions among things in the world that exist prior to themselves, nor brute existents whose natures are arbitrarily and unalterably given to them. Autonomous agents choose what role they will play in the world, so to speak; they act not only *in* the world but *on* the world, from a position that allows them a point of view that is, at least in part, independent of the world. Autonomous agents, then, have a kind of control over their behavior that is different in kind from the control that other agents have, and it is plausible to regard this difference in kind as, in some sense, a difference in depth.

A satisfactory theory of (deep) responsibility must not only be able to identify which agents are responsible, and for what—it must be able to explain why they are responsible, and, ultimately, why the idea of responsibility makes any sense at all. In the absence of such an explanation, the view that responsibility is equivalent to attributability to an agent's real self cannot even be regarded as a candidate for a satisfactory theory of responsibility. The idea of autonomy seems to offer a possible basis for such an explanation, which defenders of the view under consideration might try to make use of to fill the gap that must be filled. But in that case, the view under consideration would be not an alternative to the view that connects responsibility to autonomy but rather an elaboration of a particular form of that view.

6

Identification and Wholeheartedness

HARRY FRANKFURT

I

THE phrase "the mind–body problem" is so crisp, and its role in philosophical discourse is so well established, that to oppose its use would simply be foolish. Nonetheless, the usage *is* rather anachronistic. The familiar problem to which the phrase refers concerns the relationship between a creature's body and the fact that the creature is conscious. A more appropriate name would be, accordingly, "the consciousness–body problem." For it is no longer plausible to equate the realm of conscious phenomena—as Descartes did—with the realm of mind. This is not only because psychoanalysis has made the notion of unconscious feelings and thoughts compelling. Other leading psychological theories have also found it useful to construe the distinction between the mental and the nonmental as being far broader than that between situations in which consciousness is present and those in which it is not.

For example, both William James and Jean Piaget are inclined to regard mentality as a feature of all living things. James takes the presence of mentality to be essentially a matter of intelligent or goal-directed behavior, which he opposes to behavior that is only mechanical:

> *The pursuance of future ends and the choice of means for their attainment are the mark and criterion of the presence of mentality* in a phenomenon.

Reprinted by permission of Cambridge University Press from Ferdinand David Schoeman, ed., *Responsibility, Character and the Emotions* (1987), pp. 27–45.

We all use this test to discriminate between an intelligent and a mechanical performance.[1]

Piaget similarly, but with even greater emphasis, construes the difference between the mental and the nonmental in terms of purposefulness:

> There is no sort of boundary between the living and the mental or between the biological and the psychological. . . . [Psychology] is not the science of consciousness only but of behavior in general . . . of conduct. . . . [Psychology begins] when the organism behaves with regard to external situations and solves problems.[2]

Powerful currents of thought, then, lead away from the supposition that being conscious is essential to mentality. The psychoanalytic expansion of the mind to include unconscious phenomena does not itself actually require, of course, that mentality be attributed to creatures who are entirely *incapable* of consciousness. On the other hand, the conceptions of James and Piaget do entail that mentality characterizes the lives of vast numbers of creatures—not only animals but plants as well—which enjoy no conscious experience at all.[3]

Now what is this *consciousness*, which is distinct from mentality and which we generally suppose to be peculiar to human beings and to the members of certain relatively advanced animal species? Anthony Kenny offers the following view:

> I think that consciousness . . . is a matter of having certain sorts of ability. To be conscious is, for instance, to see and hear. Whether somebody can see or hear is a matter of whether he can discriminate between certain things, and whether he can discriminate between certain things is something that we can test both in simple everyday ways and in complicated experimental ways.[4]

Kenny's suggestion is that to be conscious is to be able to discriminate. But what is it to discriminate? It would seem that discriminating between two things is in the most fundamental sense a matter of being affected differently by the one than by the other. If my state remains exactly the same regardless of whether a certain feature is present in my environment or absent from it, then I am not discriminating between the presence and the absence of that feature. If my state does differ according to

1. William James, *The Principles of Psychology I* (Cambridge, MA: Harvard University Press, 1983), p. 21.
2. J.-C. Bringuier, *Conversations with Piaget* (Chicago: University of Chicago Press, 1980), pp. 3, 4.
3. Piaget himself cites the behavior of sunflowers as indicative of mentality.
4. Anthony Kenny et al., *The Nature of Mind* (Edinburgh: University Press, 1972), p. 43.

the presence or absence of the feature, then that is a mode of discriminating between its presence and its absence. To discriminate sounds, colors, levels of temperature, and the like just means—in its most general sense—to respond differentially to them.

It does seem indisputable that discrimination is central to consciousness: Seeing necessarily involves responding to differences in color, hearing to differences in sound, and so on. By no means, however, does this effectively grasp what we ordinarily think of as consciousness. The usual way of identifying the state of being conscious is by contrasting it to unconsciousness; and one way of being unconscious is to be asleep. But even while they are asleep, animals respond to visual, auditory, tactile, and other stimuli. Otherwise it would be difficult to wake them up. To be sure, the range of responses when they are sleeping is narrower than when they are awake. But they do not while asleep entirely lack the ability to discriminate, and Kenny cannot therefore regard them as being at that time altogether unconscious.

Now it might well be acceptable to consider sleep as consistent with a certain level of consciousness—lower than that of wakefulness, but above zero. In the view Kenny proposes, however, it is not only sleeping animals that are conscious—so is everything else in the world. After all, there is no entity that is not susceptible to being differentially affected by something. If the notion of consciousness is understood as having merely the very general and primitive sense allotted to it by Kenny's account, then a piece of metal is conscious of the ambient temperature to the extent that it becomes hotter and colder, or expands and contracts, as that temperature changes. Consciousness so construed is a state to which the contrasting state is clearly not unconsciousness, understanding unconsciousness to be what we ordinarily attribute to those who are deeply asleep or anesthetized or in a coma. Rather, the state to which consciousness in this sense contrasts is causal isolation.

Consciousness in the everyday sense cannot be exclusively a matter of discrimination, then, since all sorts of discriminating responses may occur (so to speak) in the dark. One might perhaps avoid this difficulty by saying that consciousness is the ability to discriminate *consciously*, but that would not be helpful. In any event, I wish to consider another feature, distinct from discrimination, which is essential to ordinary consciousness: *reflexivity*. Being conscious necessarily involves not merely differentiating responses to stimuli, but an awareness of those responses. When I am awake on a hot day, the heat raises the temperature of my skin; it also raises the surface temperature of a piece of metal. Both the metal and I respond to the heat, and in this sense each of us is aware of it. But I am also aware of my response, while the metal is not. The increase in the temperature of my skin is itself something which I discriminate, and this is essential to the mode of being conscious that consists in feeling warm.

Of course the fact that a creature responds to its own responses does not entail that it is conscious. It goes without saying that the second response may be no more conscious than the first. Thus, adding reflexivity to discrimination does not provide an explanation of how consciousness arises, nor of how it and unconsciousness differ. Nonetheless, being conscious in the everyday sense does (unlike unconsciousness) entail reflexivity: It necessarily involves a secondary awareness of a primary response. An instance of exclusively primary and unreflexive consciousness would not be an instance of what we ordinarily think of as consciousness at all. For what would it be like to be conscious of something without being aware of this consciousness? It would mean having an experience with no awareness whatever of its occurrence. This would be, precisely, a case of unconscious experience. It appears, then, that being conscious is identical with being self-conscious. Consciousness *is* self-consciousness.[5]

The claim that waking consciousness is self-consciousness does not mean that consciousness is invariably dual in the sense that every instance of it involves both a primary awareness and another instance of consciousness which is somehow distinct and separable from the first and which has the first as its object. That would threaten an intolerably infinite proliferation of instances of consciousness. Rather, the self-consciousness in question is a sort of *immanent reflexivity* by virtue of which every instance of being conscious grasps not only that of which it is an awareness, but also the awareness of it. It is like a source of light which, in addition to illuminating whatever other things fall within its scope, renders itself visible as well.

II

There is a baffling problem about what consciousness is *for*. It is equally baffling, moreover, that the function of consciousness should remain so baffling. It seems extraordinary that, despite the pervasiveness and familiarity of consciousness in our lives, we are uncertain in what way (if at all) it is actually indispensable to us.[6] Be this as it may, the importance

5. What I am here referring to as "self-consciousness" is neither consciousness of a self—a subject or ego—nor consciousness that there is awareness. Both require rational capacities beyond what would seem to be necessary for consciousness itself to occur. The reflexivity in question is merely consciousness's awareness of itself. To hear a sound consciously, rather than to respond to it unconsciously, involves being aware of hearing it or being aware of the sound as heard.

6. Thus the Nobel laureate physiologist John Eccles says: "I would like to . . . [ask] as a neurophysiologist, why do we have to be conscious at all? We can, in principle, explain all our input-output performances in terms of activity of neuronal circuits; and, consequently, consciousness seems to be absolutely unnecessary. I don't believe this story, of course; but

of *reflexivity* to those in whose lives it occurs is readily apparent. A creature's sensitivity to its own condition—whether it is by way of the inwardness or immanent reflexivity of waking consciousness, or by way of a less dazzling variety of secondary responsiveness—is essential for purposeful behavior.

The metal does not change in any purposeful way when it becomes hot; on the other hand, under certain conditions a sunflower turns toward the light. Both the metal and the sunflower respond to what goes on around them. Each is affected by, and hence discriminates, environmental stimuli. But the sunflower, unlike the metal, makes second-order as well as primary discriminations. This contributes essentially to its capacity for purposeful change. The metal lacks this capacity, since it is insensitive to its own responses—which is to say that it is altogether unresponsive or indifferent to what happens to it. A creature engaged in secondary responsiveness is monitoring its own condition; to that extent the creature is in a position, or at least is closer to being in a position, to do something about its condition.

Thus reflexivity has a point, just as action itself does, in virtue of the riskiness of existence. It enables a creature, among other things, to respond to the circumstance that its interests are being adversely affected. This makes reflexivity an indispensable condition for behavior that is directed purposefully to avoiding or to ameliorating circumstances of this kind, in which there is a conflict between the interests of a creature and forces that are endangering or undermining them.

There is also another sort of reflexivity or self-consciousness, which appears similarly to be intelligible as being fundamentally a response to conflict and risk. It is a salient characteristic of human beings, one which affects our lives in deep and innumerable ways, that we care about what we are. This is closely connected both as cause and as effect to our enormous preoccupation with what other people think of us. We are ceaselessly alert to the danger that there may be discrepancies between what we wish to be (or what we wish to seem to be) and how we actually appear to others and to ourselves.

We are particularly concerned with our own motives. It matters greatly to us whether the desires by which we are moved to act as we do motivate us because we want them to be effective in moving us, or whether they move us regardless of ourselves or even despite ourselves.

at the same time I do not know the logical answer to it. In attempting to answer the question, why do we have to be conscious? it surely cannot be claimed as self-evident that consciousness is a necessary requisite for such performances as logical argument or reasoning, or even for initiative and creative activities." In J. Eccles, ed., *Brain and Conscious Experience* (New York, 1966). Perhaps, despite Eccles's reluctance to admit it, the inwardness of human life is an ontological absurdity—something that takes itself enormously seriously, but that actually has no important role to play at all.

In the latter cases we are moved to act as we do without it being the case that we want wholeheartedly to be motivated as we are. Our hearts are at best divided, and they may even not be in what we are doing at all.

This means, moreover, that we are to some degree passive with respect to the action we perform. For in virtue of the fact that we do not unequivocally endorse or support our own motive, it can appropriately be said that what we want—namely, the object of our motivating desire, and that desire itself—is in a certain ordinary sense not something which we *really* want. So while it may be that we perform our action on account of the motivating force of our own desire, it is nonetheless also true that we are being moved to act by something other than what we really want. In that case we are in a way passive with respect to what moves us, as we always are when we are moved by a force that is not fully our own.

It is possible for a human being to be at times, and perhaps even always, indifferent to his own motives—to take no evaluative attitude toward the desires that incline him to act. If there is a conflict between those desires, he does not care which of them proves to be the more effective. In other words, the individual does not participate in the conflict. Therefore, the outcome of the conflict can be neither a victory for him nor a defeat. Since he exercises no authority, by the endorsement or concurrence of which certain of his desires might acquire particular legitimacy, or might come to be specially constitutive of himself, the actions engendered by the flow and clash of his feelings and desires are quite wanton.

III

Now what conceptualization of this range of phenomena fits its contours in the most authentic and perspicuous way? My own preference has been for a model that involves levels of reflexivity or self-consciousness. According to this schema, there are at the lowest level first-order desires to perform one or another action. Whichever of these first-order desires actually leads to action is, by virtue of that effectiveness, designated the will of the individual whose desire it is. In addition, people characteristically have second-order desires concerning what first-order desires they want; and they have second-order volitions concerning which first-order desire they want to be their will. There may also be desires and volitions of higher orders.

This makes it rather natural to distinguish two ways in which the volitional aspects of a person's life may be radically divided or incoherent. In the first place, there may be a conflict between how someone wants to be motivated and the desire by which he is in fact most powerfully moved. An example of this sort of inner conflict is provided by the situation of a person who wants to refrain from smoking—that is, who wants the desire to refrain from smoking to be what effectively motivates his behavior—but whose desire for a cigarette proves to be so strong that it becomes his will despite the fact that he prefers not to act upon it and even struggles against it. Here there is a lack of coherence or harmony between the person's higher-order volition or preference concerning which of his desires he wants to be most effective and the first-order desire that actually is the most effective in moving him when he acts. Since the desire that prevails is one upon which he would prefer not to act, the outcome of the division within him is that he is unable to do what he really wants to do. His will is not under his own control. It is not the will he wants, but one that is imposed upon him by a force with which he does not identify and which is in that sense external to him.

Another sort of inner division occurs when there is a lack of coherence within the realm of the person's higher-order volitions themselves. This does not concern the relation between volitions and will. It is not a matter of volitional strength, but of whether the highest-order preferences concerning some volitional issue are *wholehearted*. It has to do with the possibility that there is no unequivocal answer to the question of what the person really wants, even though his desires do form a complex and extensive hierarchical structure. There might be no unequivocal answer because the person is *ambivalent* with respect to the object he comes closest to really wanting: In other words, because, with respect to that object, he is drawn not only toward it, but away from it too. Or there might be no unequivocal answer because the person's preferences concerning what he wants are not fully integrated, so that there is some *inconsistency* or *conflict* (perhaps not yet manifest) among them.

Incoherence of the first kind (the kind that afflicts the smoker) might be characterized as being *between* what the person really wants and other desires—like the rejected but nonetheless inescapably preemptive desire to smoke—that are *external* to the volitional complex with which the person identifies and by which he wants his behavior to be determined. The second kind of incoherence is *within* this volitional complex. In the absence of wholeheartedness, the person is not merely in conflict with forces "outside" him; rather, he himself is divided.

One advantage of this model is that it provides a convenient way of explaining how, as in the case of the reluctant smoker, passivity or impaired autonomy may be due to the force of what are in some basically literal sense the individual's own desires. The model also lends itself in fairly obvious ways to the articulation and explication of a variety of useful concepts pertaining to structural features of the mind (e.g., weakness of the will, ego-ideal, and so on). However, the model's central notion of a hierarchy of desires seems not to be entirely adequate to its purpose.

For it appears to be impossible to explain, using the resources of this notion alone, in what way an individual with second-order desires or volitions may be less wanton with respect to *them* than a wholly unreflective creature is with respect to its first-order desires.[7]

Someone does what he *really wants* to do only when he acts in accordance with a pertinent higher-order volition. But this condition could not be sufficient unless the higher-order volition were *itself* one by which the person *really wanted* to be determined. Now it is pretty clear that this requirement cannot be satisfied simply by introducing *another* desire or volition at the next higher level. That would lead to a regress which it would be quite arbitrary to terminate at any particular point. The difficulty bears on both types of volitional incoherence I have distinguished above. A characterization of either type of incoherence requires construing some of a person's desires as integral to him in a way in which others are not. Yet it is not obvious what account to give of the distinction between volitional elements that are integrated into a person and those that remain in some relevant sense external to him.

The mere fact that one desire occupies a higher level than another in the hierarchy seems plainly insufficient to endow it with greater authority or with any constitutive legitimacy. In other words, the assignment of desires to different hierarchical levels does not by itself provide an explanation of what it is for someone to be *identified* with one of his own desires rather than with another. It does not make clear why it should be appropriate to construe a person as *participating* in conflicts within himself between second-order volitions and first-order desires, and hence as vulnerable to being defeated by his own desires, when a *wanton* is not to be construed as a genuine participant in (or as having any interest in the outcomes of) conflicts within himself between desires all of which are of the first order. Gary Watson has formulated the issue succinctly:

> Since second-order volitions are themselves simply desires, to add them to the context of conflict is just to increase the number of contenders; it is not to give a special place to any of those in contention.[8]

It appears that the hierarchical model cannot as such cope with this difficulty. It merely enables us to describe an inner conflict as being between desires of different orders. But this alone is hardly adequate to

7. The notion of reflexivity seems to me much more fundamental and indispensable, in dealing with the phenomena at hand, than that of a hierarchy. On the other hand, it is not clear to me that adequate provision can be made for reflexivity without resorting to the notion of a hierarchical ordering. While articulating volitional life in terms of a hierarchy of desires does seem a bit contrived, the alternatives—such as the one proposed by Gary Watson in "Free Agency" (*Journal of Philosophy*, 1975)—strike me as worse: more obscure, no less fanciful, and (I suspect) requiring a resort to hierarchy in the end themselves.

8. Watson, op. cit., p. 218.

determine—with respect to that conflict—where (if anywhere) the person himself stands.[9]

I tried some time ago to deal with this problem, in the following passage:

> When a person identifies himself *decisively* with one of his first-order desires, this commitment "resounds" throughout the potentially endless array of higher orders. . . . The fact that his second-order volition to be moved by this desire is a decisive one means that there is no room for questions concerning the pertinence of volitions of higher orders. . . . The decisiveness of the commitment he has made means that he has decided that no further questions about his second-order volition, at any higher order, remain to be asked.[10]

The trouble with what I wrote in this passage is that the notions I invoked—namely, "identification," "decisive commitment," "resounding"—are terribly obscure. Therefore, the passage left it quite unclear just how the maneuver of avoiding an interminable regress by making a decisive commitment can escape being unacceptably arbitrary. Thus, Watson says:

> We wanted to know what prevents wantonness with regard to one's higher-order volitions. What gives these volitions any special relation to "oneself"? It is unhelpful to answer that one makes a "decisive commitment", where this just means that an interminable ascent to higher orders is not going to be permitted. This *is* arbitrary.[11]

Now in fact Watson is in error here. As I shall attempt to explain, making a decisive commitment does not consist merely in an arbitrary *refusal* to permit an interminable ascent to higher orders.

IV

Consider a situation somewhat analogous to that of a person who is uncertain whether to identify himself with one or with another of his own desires, but which is rather more straightforward: the situation of someone attempting to solve a problem in arithmetic. Having performed a calculation, this person may perform another in order to check his an-

9. The problem of explaining identification is not, of course, peculiar to the hierarchical model. It must be dealt with by any account of the structure of volition. Accordingly, it is not a fault of the hierarchical model that it requires an explanation of identification.

10. "Freedom of the Will and the Concept of a Person," *Journal of Philosophy*, 1971, p. 16.

11. Watson, op. cit., p. 218.

swer. The second calculation may be just the same as the first, or it may be equivalent to it in the sense that it follows a procedure which is different from the first but which must yield the same result. In any case, suppose the first calculation is confirmed by the second. It is possible that both calculations are faulty, so the person may check again. This sequence of calculations can be extended indefinitely. Moreover, there is nothing about the position of any particular item in the sequence that gives it definitive authority. A mistake can be made at any point, and the same mistake may be repeated any number of times. So what is to distinguish a calculation with which the person can reasonably terminate the sequence? How does the person avoid being irresponsible or arbitrary when he ends at some particular point a sequence of calculations that he might extend further?

One way in which a sequence of calculations might end is that the person conducting it simply quits, negligently permitting the result of his last calculation to serve as his answer. Perhaps he just loses interest in the problem, or perhaps he is diverted from further inquiry by some compelling distraction. In cases like these, his behavior resembles that of a wonton: He allows a certain result to stand without evaluating its suitability or considering the desirability of allowing it to be his answer. He does not *choose* a result, nor does he *endorse* one. He acts as though it is a matter of complete indifference to him whether there is in fact adequate support for the acceptability of his answer.

On the other hand, a sequence of calculations might end because the person conducting it *decides for some reason* to adopt a certain result. It may be that he is unequivocally confident that this result is correct, and therefore believes that there is no use for further inquiry. Or perhaps he believes that even though there is some likelihood that the result is not correct, the cost to him of further inquiry—in time or in effort or in lost opportunities—is greater than the value to him of reducing the likelihood of error. In either event there may be a "decisive" identification on his part. In a sense that I shall endeavor to explain, such an identification resounds through an unlimited sequence of possible further reconsiderations of his decision.

Suppose the person is confident that he knows the correct answer. He then expects to get that answer each time he accurately performs a suitable calculation. In this respect, the future is transparent to him, and his decision that a certain answer is correct resounds endlessly in just this sense: It enables him to anticipate the outcomes of an indefinite number of possible further calculations. Now suppose he is not entirely confident which answer is correct, but is convinced that it would nonetheless be most reasonable for him to adopt a certain answer as his own. Then he cannot with full confidence expect this answer to be confirmed by further inquiry; he acknowledges that accurate calculation might produce a different result. But if he has made a genuinely unreserved commitment to the view that adopting the answer is his most reasonable alternative, he can anticipate that *this* view will be endlessly confirmed by accurate reviews of it.

The fact that a commitment resounds endlessly *is* simply the fact that the commitment is *decisive.* For a commitment is decisive if and only if it is made without reservation. And making a commitment without reservation means that the person who makes it does so in the belief that no further accurate inquiry would require him to change his mind. It is therefore pointless to pursue the inquiry any further. This is, precisely, the resonance effect.[12]

Now what leads people to form desires of higher orders is similar to what leads them to go over their arithmetic. Someone checks his calculations because he thinks he may have done them wrong. It may be that there is a conflict between the answer he has obtained and a different answer which, for one reason or another, he believes may be correct; or perhaps he has merely a more generalized suspicion, to the effect that he may have made some kind of error. Similarly, a person may be led to reflect upon his own desires either because they conflict with each other, or because a more general lack of confidence moves him to consider whether to be satisfied with his motives as they are.

Both in the case of desires and in the case of arithmetic a person can without arbitrariness terminate a potentially endless sequence of evaluations when he finds that there is no disturbing conflict, either between results already obtained or between a result already obtained and one he might reasonably expect to obtain if the sequence were to continue. Terminating the sequence at that point—the point at which there is no conflict or doubt—is not arbitrary. For the only reason to continue the sequence would be to cope with an actual conflict or with the possibility that a conflict might occur. And given that the person does not have this reason to continue, it is hardly arbitrary for him to stop.

Perhaps it will be suggested that there remains an element of arbitrariness here, in the judgment that no pertinent conflict can be found: This judgment is also subject to error, after all, and it would be possible to reassess it endlessly without any of the reassessments being inherently definitive or final. Whatever the merit of this point, however, it does not imply a deficiency specific to the principle that a person is justified in terminating a sequence of calculations or reflections when he sees no conflict to be avoided or resolved. For the point is quite general. It is

12. I am here agreeing with the suggestion concerning the relation between resonance and decisive commitment made by Jon Elster, in his *Ulysses and the Sirens: Studies in Rationality and Irrationality* (Cambridge: Cambridge University Press, 1979), p. 111, n. 135. My own treatment of these matters owes much to Descartes's discussion of clear and distinct perception.

always possible, in the deployment of any principle whatever, to make a mistaken or an unwarranted judgment that the conditions for applying the principle correctly have been satisfied. It should go without saying that no criterion or standard can guarantee that it will be wielded accurately and without arbitrariness.

V

The etymological meaning of the verb "to decide" is "to cut off." This is apt, since it is characteristically by a decision (though, of course, not necessarily or even most frequently in that way) that a sequence of desires or preferences of increasingly higher orders is terminated. When the decision is made without reservation, the commitment it entails is a decisive one. Then the person no longer holds himself at all apart from the desire to which he has committed himself. It is no longer unsettled or uncertain whether the object of that desire—that is, what he wants—is what he really wants: The decision determines what the person really wants by making the desire upon which he decided fully his own. To this extent the person, in making a decision by which he identifies with a desire, *constitutes himself*. The pertinent desire is no longer in any way external to him. It is not a desire that he "has" merely as a subject in whose history it happens to occur, as a person may "have" an involuntary spasm that happens to occur in the history of his body. It comes to be a desire that is incorporated into himself by virtue of the fact that he has it *by his own will*.

This does not mean that it is through the exercise of the will that the desire originates; the desire may well preexist the decision made concerning it. But even if the person is not responsible for the fact that the desire *occurs,* there is an important sense in which he takes responsibility for the fact of having the desire—the fact that the desire is in the fullest sense his, that it constitutes what he really wants—when he identifies himself with it. Through his action in deciding, he is responsible for the fact that the desire has become his own in a way in which it was not unequivocally his own before.

There are two quite different sorts of conflicts between desires. In conflicts of the one sort, desires compete for priority or position in a preferential order; the issue is which desire to satisfy *first*. In conflicts of the other sort, the issue is whether a desire should be given *any* place in the order of preference at all—that is, whether it is to be endorsed as a legitimate candidate for satisfaction or whether it is to be rejected as entitled to no priority whatsoever. When a conflict of the first kind is resolved, the competing desires are *integrated* into a single ordering, within which each occupies a specific position. Resolving a conflict of the second kind involves a radical *separation* of the competing desires, one of which is not merely assigned a relatively less favored position, but extruded entirely as an outlaw. It is these acts of ordering and of rejection—integration and separation—that create a self out of the raw materials of inner life. They define the intrapsychic constraints and boundaries with respect to which a person's autonomy may be threatened even by his own desires.[13]

Aristotle maintained that behavior is voluntary only when its moving principle is inside the agent. This cannot be correct if "inside" is construed in its literal sense: The movements of an epileptic seizure are not voluntary, but their moving principle or cause is spatially internal to the agent. The location of a moving principle with respect to the agent's body is plainly less relevant than its "location" with respect to the agent's volition. What counts, even with respect to a moving principle that operates as an element of his psychic life, is whether or not the agent has constituted himself to include it. On the one hand, the principle may be internal, in the sense pertinent to whether the behavior to which it leads is voluntary, by virtue of the fact that the person has joined himself to what moves him by commitment through which he takes responsibility for it. On the other hand, the moving principle of his behavior may remain external to the person in the pertinent sense because he has not made it part of himself.

This suggests another respect in which Aristotle's theory is unsatisfactory. He maintains that a person may be responsible for his own character on account of having taken (or having failed to take) measures that affect what his habitual dispositions are. In other words, a person acquires responsibility for his own character, according to Aristotle, by acting in ways that are causally instrumental in bringing it about that he has the particular set of dispositions of which his character is comprised. I think that Aristotle's treatment of this subject is significantly out of focus because of his preoccupation with causal origins and causal responsibility. The fundamental responsibility of an agent with respect to his own character is not a matter of whether it is as the effect of his own actions that the agent *has* certain dispositions to feel and to behave in various ways. That bears only on the question of whether the person is responsible for having these *characteristics*. The question of whether the person is responsible for his own *character* has to do with whether he has *taken responsibility for* his characteristics. It concerns whether the dispositions at issue, regardless of whether their *existence* is due to the person's own initiative and causal agency or not, are characteristics with which he

13. The determining conditions that are pertinent here are exclusively *structural* arrangements. I mention this, although I do not pursue the point, since it bears on the familiar issue of whether *historical* considerations—especially causal stories—have any essential relevance to questions concerning whether a person's actions are autonomous.

identifies and which he thus by his own will incorporates into himself as constitutive of what he is.

When someone identifies himself with one rather than with another of his own desires, the result is not necessarily to eliminate the conflict between those desires, or even to reduce its severity, but to alter its nature. Suppose that a person with two conflicting desires identifies with one rather than with the other. This *might* cause the other—the desire with which the person does not identify—to become substantially weaker than it was, or to disappear altogether. But it need not. Quite possibly, the conflict between the two desires will remain as virulent as before. What the person's commitment to the one eliminates is not the conflict between it and the other. It eliminates the conflict *within the person* as to which of these desires he prefers to be his motive. The conflict between the *desires* is in this way transformed into a conflict between *one* of them and the *person* who has identified himself with its rival. That person is no longer uncertain which side he is on, in the conflict between the two desires, and the persistence of this conflict need not subvert or diminish the wholeheartedness of his commitment to the desire with which he identifies.

VI

Since it is most conspicuously by making a decision that a person identifies with some element of his psychic life, deciding plays an important role in the formation and maintenance of the self. It is very difficult to articulate what the act of deciding consists in—to make fully clear just what we do when we perform it. But while the nature of deciding is aggravatingly elusive, at least it is apparent that making a decision is something that we do *to ourselves*. In this respect it differs fundamentally from making a choice, the immediate object of which is not the chooser, but whatever it is that he chooses. This difference between deciding and choosing accounts for the fact that deciding to make a certain choice is not the same as actually making it (after all, the time or occasion for doing that may not yet have arrived), while deciding to make a particular decision (that is, deciding to decide things a certain way) cannot be distinguished from making the decision himself.

In some languages, the reflexivity of deciding—the fact that it is an action done to oneself—is indicated in the form of the pertinent verb. Thus, the French verb is *se décider*. The closest parallel among English synonyms for "to decide" is the phrase "to make up one's mind," in which there is an explicit representation of the reflexive character of deciding. Now what are we to make of the rather protean metaphor this phrase invokes? Is making up one's mind like "making up a story," or is it like "making up a bed"? Is it like "making up one's face," or is it rather like "making up a list of things to do"? Or is it, perhaps, more like "making up after a quarrel"? What is the difference, in these various instances, between what is made up and what is not? And which of these differences corresponds most closely to the difference between a mind that is made up and one that is undecided?

The use of cosmetics pertains to a contrast between what a person looks like naturally and how the person may contrive to appear. A similar contrast is implicit in the idea of making up a story, which resembles making up a face in that the outcome is in both cases something artificial or fictitious; it does not simply exhibit the way things really are. One difference between using makeup and making up a story is, of course, that there is a face before it is made up—something to which being made up happens. This has no ready analogue in the case of a story, which is not transformed by being made up, but which comes into existence only as it is contrived. In this respect, making up a face more closely resembles making up a bed. As for making up a list, it plainly has nothing to do with the fictitious or the contrived; it is more a matter of establishing certain relationships among the items listed, or of recording relationships among them that already exist.

What appears to be fundamentally common in all occurrences of the notion of making something up is not the contrast between fiction and reality or between the natural and the artificial, but the theme of creating an orderly arrangement. It seems to me that in this light the closest analogue to a situation in which someone makes up his mind is, rather surprisingly perhaps, a situation in which two people make up their differences. People who do that after a quarrel pass from a condition of conflict and hostility to a more harmonious and well-ordered relationship. Of course people do not always make up when their quarrel ends; sometimes their hostility continues even after the conflict that was its original cause has been resolved. Moreover, people who have been quarreling may restore harmony between themselves even though their disagreement continues. Making up concerns healing a relationship disrupted by conflict, and it has nothing directly or necessarily to do with whether or not the conflict has ended.

Construed on this analogy, the making of a decision appears to differ from the self-reparative activities of the body, which in some other ways it resembles. When the body heals itself, it *eliminates* conflicts in which one physical process (say, infection) interferes with others and undermines the homeostasis or equilibrium in which health consists. A person who makes up his mind also seeks thereby to overcome or to supersede a condition of inner division and to make himself into an integrated whole. But he may accomplish this without actually eliminating the desires that conflict with those upon which he has decided, as long as he dissociates himself from them.

A person may fail to integrate himself when he makes up his mind, of course, since the conflict or hesitancy with which he is contending may continue despite his decision. All a decision does is to create an intention; it does not guarantee that the intention will be carried out. This is not simply because the person can always change his mind. Apart from inconstancy of that sort, it may be that energies tending toward action inconsistent with the intention remain untamed and undispersed, however decisively the person believes his mind has been made up. The conflict the decision was supposed to supersede may continue despite the person's conviction that he has resolved it. In that case the decision, no matter how apparently conscientious and sincere, is not wholehearted: Whether the person is aware of it or not, he has other intentions, intentions incompatible with the one the decision established and to which he is also committed. This may become evident when the chips are down and the person acts in a way ostensibly precluded by the intention upon which he thought he had settled.

VII

But why are we interested in making up our minds at all? It might seem that the point of deciding is to provide for the performance of an action that would otherwise not be performed. Suppose I make up my mind to show anger more openly the next time I am gratuitously insulted by an arrogant functionary. This might be thought of as establishing a connection, which did not previously exist, between insulting behavior of a certain kind and the sort of response upon which I have now decided—a connection such that the response will ensue if the provocation occurs. In fact, however, people often decide to do things which—whether they themselves realize it or not—they would do in any case. The connection between the provocation and the response, which the decision appears to establish, may already exist: I would have shown my anger openly even if I had not previously formed the intention to do so. The point of making up one's mind is not, accordingly, to ensure a certain action.

Nor is it to ensure that one will act well. That is the function of deliberation, which is designed to increase the likelihood that decisions will be good ones. Hobbes suggests that the word "deliberation" connotes an activity in which freedom is lost.[14] It is, after all, *deliberation.*

---

14. *Leviathan*, Part I, Chapter 6: "And it is called *deliberation* because it is a putting an end to the *liberty* we had of doing, or omitting, according to our own appetite, or aversion."

This may seem paradoxical, since we customarily regard deliberation as paradigmatically connected to the exercise of autonomy. The difficulty disappears when we recognize that the liberty with which deliberation interferes is not that of the autonomous agent, but that of someone who blindly follows impulse—in other words, of the wanton. A person who is deliberating about what to do is seeking an alternative to "doing what comes naturally." His aim is to replace the liberty of anarchic impulsive behavior with the autonomy of being under his own control.

One thing a deliberate decision accomplishes, when it creates an intention, is to establish a constraint by which other preferences and decisions are to be guided. A person who decides what to believe provides himself with a criterion for other beliefs: Namely, they must be coherent with the belief upon which he has decided. And a person who makes a decision concerning what to do similarly adopts a rule for coordinating his activities to facilitate his eventual implementation of the decision he has made. It might be said, then, that a function of decision is to integrate the person both dynamically and statically. Dynamically, insofar as it provides—in the way I have just mentioned—for coherence and unity of purpose over time; statically, insofar as it establishes—in the way discussed earlier—a reflexive or hierarchical structure by which the person's identity may be in part constituted.

In both respects, the intent is at least partly to resolve conflict or to avoid it. This is not achieved by eliminating one or more of the conflicting elements so that those remaining are harmonious, but by endorsing or identifying with certain elements which are then authoritative for the self. Of course, this authority may be resisted and even defeated by outlaw forces—desires or motives by which the person does not want to be effectively moved, but which are too strong and insistent to be constrained. It may also turn out that there is conflict within the authority itself—that the person has identified himself inconsistently. This is the issue of *wholeheartedness.*

Wholeheartedness, as I am using the term, does not consist in a feeling of enthusiasm, or of certainty, concerning a commitment. Nor is it likely to be readily apparent whether a decision which a person intends to be wholehearted is actually so. We do not know our hearts well enough to be confident whether our intention that nothing should interfere with a decision we make is one we ourselves will want carried out when—perhaps recognizing that the point of no return has been reached—we come to understand more completely what carrying it out would require us to do or to sacrifice doing.

In making up his mind a person establishes preferences concerning the resolution of conflicts among his desires or beliefs. Someone who makes a decision thereby performs an action, but the performance is not of a simple act that merely implements a first-order desire. It essentially involves reflexivity, including desires and volitions of a higher order. Thus, creatures who are incapable of this volitional reflexivity necessarily lack the capacity to make up their minds. They may desire and think and act, but they cannot decide. Insofar as we construe the making of decisions as the characteristic function of the faculty of volition, we must regard such creatures as lacking this faculty.

In "Freedom of the Will and the Concept of a Person" I asserted that being wanton does not preclude deliberation. My thought then was that although a creature might be wanton with respect to goals, he might nonetheless engage in calculation or reasoning about technical questions concerning how to get what he wantonly desires. But reasoning involves making decisions concerning what to think, which appear no less incompatible with thoroughgoing wantonness than deciding what one wants to do. Making a decision does seem different from figuring out how to implement it, but it is unclear that the latter activity can be accomplished without making up one's mind in ways structurally quite similar to those entailed in the former.

We are accustomed to thinking of our species as distinguished particularly by virtue of the faculty of reason. We tend to suppose that volition or will is a more primitive or a cruder faculty, which we share with creatures of lesser psychic complexity. But this seems dubious not only because of the reflexivity that volition itself requires, but also to the extent that reasoning requires making up one's mind. For to that extent the deliberate use of reason necessarily has a hierarchical structure, requiring higher-order elements that are unavailable to a genuine wanton. In this respect, then, reason depends upon will.

7

What Happens When Someone Acts?

J. DAVID VELLEMAN

I

WHAT happens when someone acts?

A familiar answer goes like this. There is something that the agent wants, and there is an action that he believes conducive to its attainment. His desire for the end, and his belief in the action as a means, justify taking the action, and they jointly cause an intention to take it, which in turn causes the corresponding movements of the agent's body. Provided that these causal processes take their normal course, the agent's movements consummate an action, and his motivating desire and belief constitute his reasons for acting.

This story is widely accepted as a satisfactory account of human action—or at least, as an account that will be satisfactory once it is completed by a definition of what's normal in the relevant causal processes. The story is widely credited to Donald Davidson's *Essays on Actions and Events* (1980), but I do not wish to become embroiled in questions of exegesis.[1] I shall therefore refer to it simply as the standard story of human action.

Reprinted from *Mind* 101 (1992): 461–81 by permission of Oxford University Press.

The material in this paper was originally presented to a seminar in the philosophy of action at the University of Michigan. I am grateful to the participants in that seminar for their comments and questions. A very different paper was presented under a similar title to the philosophy departments of Yale University and the University of Dayton; this paper shows the benefit of comments from those audiences as well. For comments on earlier drafts, I am grateful to Paul Boghossian, Sarah Buss, Daniel Cohen, John Martin Fischer, Harry Frankfurt, Carl Ginet, Brian Leiter, Connie Rosati, and several anonymous reviewers.

1. The story can be traced back at least as far as Hobbes, *Leviathan*, Part I, chapter vi.

I think that the standard story is flawed in several respects. The flaw that will concern me in this paper is that the story fails to include an agent—or, more precisely, fails to cast the agent in his proper role.[2] In this story, reasons cause an intention, and an intention causes bodily movements, but nobody—that is, no person—*does* anything. Psychological and physiological events take place inside a person, but the person serves merely as the arena for these events: he takes no active part.[3]

To be sure, a person often performs an action, in some sense, without taking an active part in it; examples of such actions will be discussed below.[4] But these examples lack that which distinguishes human action from other animal behaviour, in our conception of it if not in reality. I shall argue that the standard story describes an action from which the distinctively human feature is missing, and that it therefore tells us, not what happens when someone acts, but what happens when someone acts halfheartedly, or unwittingly, or in some equally defective way. What it describes is not a human action *par excellence*.

II

Those who believe the story will of course contend that the events recounted in it add up to the agent's participating in his action, as components add up to a composite. The story doesn't mention his participation, they will explain, simply because his participation isn't a component of itself. Complaining that the agent's participation in his action isn't mentioned in the story is, in their view, like complaining that a cake isn't listed in its own recipe.

But this response strikes me as inadequate, because I don't accept the claim that the events recounted in the story add up to a person's activity. Various roles that are actually played by the agent himself in the history of a full-blooded action are not played by anything in the story or are played by psychological elements whose participation is not equivalent to his. In a full-blooded action, an intention is formed by the agent himself, not by his reasons for acting. Reasons affect his intention by influencing him to form it, but they thus affect his intention by affecting him

2. I discuss another problem with the standard story in my (1992).

3. A critique along these lines, with special reference to Hobbes, appears in Dent (1984, Chapter 4). See e.g., p. 99: "a weighty reason does not, like a weighty brick, fall upon one and impart a certain push to one's body".

4. Here I part company with some philosophers of action, who believe that nothing counts as an action unless the agent participates in it. (See, e.g., Bishop 1989, p. 41.) Of course, every action must be someone's doing and must therefore be such that an agent participates in it, in the sense that he does it. But this conception of agential participation doesn't require anything that is obviously missing from the standard story. What's missing from that story is agential participation of a more specific kind, which may indeed be missing from doings that count as cases—albeit defective or borderline cases—of action.

first. And the agent then moves his limbs in execution of his intention; his intention doesn't move his limbs by itself. The agent thus has at least two roles to play: he forms an intention under the influence of reasons for acting, and he produces behaviour pursuant to that intention.

Of course, the agent's performance of these roles probably consists in the occurrence of psychological states and events within him. To insist that the story mention only the agent himself as the object of rational influence, or as the author and executor of intentions, would be to assume a priori that there is no psychological reduction of what happens in rational action. One is surely entitled to hypothesize, on the contrary, that there are mental states and events within an agent whose causal interactions constitute his being influenced by a reason, or his forming and conforming to an intention.

True enough. But the states and events described in a psychological reduction of a fully human action must be such that their interactions amount to the participation of the agent. My objection to the standard story is not that it mentions mental occurrences in the agent instead of the agent himself; my objection is that the occurrences it mentions in the agent are no more than occurrences in him, because their involvement in an action does not add up to the agent's being involved.

How can I tell that the involvement of these mental states and events is not equivalent to the agent's? I can tell because, as I have already suggested, the agent's involvement is defined in terms of his interactions with these very states and events, and the agent's interactions with them are such as they couldn't have with themselves. His role is to intervene between reasons and intention, and between intention and bodily movements, in each case guided by the one to produce the other. And intervening between these items is not something that the items themselves can do. When reasons are described as directly causing an intention, and the intention as directly causing movements, not only has the agent been cut out of the story but so has any psychological item that might play his role.[5]

At this point, defenders of the standard story might wish to respond that it includes the agent implicitly, as the subject of the mental and physiological occurrences that it explicitly describes.[6] The reasons, intention, and movements mentioned in the story are modifications of the agent, and so their causal relations necessarily pass through him. Complaining that the agent takes no part in causal relations posited between reasons and intention, they might claim, is like complaining that the ocean takes no part in causal relations posited between adjacent waves.

5. See Bishop (1989, p. 72); "Intuitively, we think of agents as carrying out their intentions or acting in accordance with their practical reasons, and this seems different from (simply) being caused to behave by those intentions or reasons".
6. See Goldman (1970, pp. 8off).

But reflection on the phenomena of action reveals that being the subject of causally related attitudes and movements does not amount to participation of the sort appropriate to an agent.[7] As Harry Frankfurt has pointed out, an agent's desires and beliefs can cause a corresponding intention despite him, and hence without his participation. When an addict's desire for a drug causes his decision to take it, Frankfurt reminds us, "he may meaningfully make the analytically puzzling [statement] that the force moving him to take the drug is a force other than his own" (1988, p. 18), and so he may be "a helpless bystander to the forces that move him" (p. 21). Similarly, an agent can fail to participate when his intention causes bodily movements. A frequently cited example is the assassin whose decision to fire on his target so unnerves him as to make his trigger-finger twitch, causing the gun to fire.[8] In such a case, the agent's intention has caused corresponding movements of his body, but it has done so without the agent's participation.

III

Proponents of the standard story believe that the agent's participation is lacking from these cases only because the train of causes leading from his motives to his intention, or from his intention to his behaviour, is somehow abnormal.[9] They therefore deny that these cases demonstrate the inadequacy of the standard story. The story is committed only to the claim that the causal sequence from motives to behaviour will involve the agent himself when it proceeds in the normal way.

In my view, however, the discussion of "deviant" causal chains has diverted attention from simpler counterexamples, which omit the agent without lapsing into causal deviance; and it has thereby engendered a false sense of confidence in the requirement of causal normality, as sufficient to protect the standard story from counterexamples. In reality, an agent can fail to participate in his behaviour even when it results from his motives in the normal way. Consequently, no definition of causal normality will fix what ails the standard story.

Suppose that I have a long-anticipated meeting with an old friend for the purpose of resolving some minor difference; but that as we talk, his offhand comments provoke me to raise my voice in progressively sharper replies, until we part in anger. Later reflection leads me to re-

7. See Ginet (1990, pp. 6–7): "For a person S to cause E, it is not enough for S to be the subject of just any sort of event that causes E".
8. The most recent discussion of such "deviant causal chains" appears in Bishop (1989, Chapters 4 and 5). See also Harman (1976, p. 445), Peacocke (1979, p. 124), Taylor (1966, p. 248), Goldman (1970, p. 54), and Davidson (1980, p. 79).
9. See, e.g., Davidson (1980, pp. xiii, 79, 87).

alize that accumulated grievances had crystallized in my mind, during the weeks before our meeting, into a resolution to sever our friendship over the matter at hand, and that this resolution is what gave the hurtful edge to my remarks.[10] In short, I may conclude that desires of mine caused a decision, which in turn caused the corresponding behaviour; and I may acknowledge that these mental states were thereby exerting their normal motivational force, unabetted by any strange perturbation or compulsion. But do I necessarily think that I made the decision or that I executed it? Surely, I can believe that the decision, though genuinely motivated by my desires, was thereby induced in me but not formed by me; and I can believe that it was genuinely executed in my behaviour but executed, again, without my help. Indeed, viewing the decision as directly motivated by my desires, and my behaviour as directly governed by the decision, is precisely what leads to the thought that as my words became more shrill, it was my resentment speaking, not I.[11]

Of course, to say that I was not involved in the formation and execution of my intention is to concede that these processes were abnormal in some sense. My point, however, is that they were not abnormal in respect to the causal operation of the motives and intention involved. When my desires and beliefs engendered an intention to sever the friendship, and when that intention triggered my nasty tone, they were exercising the same causal powers that they exercise in ordinary cases, and yet they were doing so without any contribution from me. Hence what constitutes my contribution, in other cases, cannot be that these attitudes are manifesting their ordinary causal powers. When I participate in an action, I must be adding something to the normal motivational influence

10. We can assume that this causal relation was mediated by any number of subconscious intentions—intentions to sever the friendship by alienating my friend, to alienate my friend by raising my voice, to raise my voice now . . . etc. So long as we assume that these intentions subconsciously crystallized as the conversation progressed (which is not hard to assume) we preserve the intuition that I'm currently trying to evoke—namely, that I did not participate in the resulting action. And surely, this intuition doesn't depend on the assumption that the causal links between these intentions and my behaviour weren't "sensitive" to counterfactual differences in them (in the sense defined by Bishop 1989, Chapter 5). Thus, we can conceive of cases in which reasons cause intentions, intentions cause behaviour in all the "right ways," and yet the agent doesn't participate.

11. I don't mean to suggest that these reflections absolve me of responsibility for my action. I have an obligation to be vigilant against unconsidered intentions and to keep my voice down, no matter what may be causing it to rise. The fact remains, however, that my responsibility for the action in question arises from my having failed to prevent or control it rather than from my having truly initiated it. And I am responsible for having failed to prevent or control the action because it would have yielded to various measures of self-scrutiny and self-restraint that I could have initiated. Thus, my responsibility depends on my capacity to intervene among events in a way in which I failed to intervene among my desires, intentions, and movements in this instance. If my behaviour could come about only in the manner described here—that is, springing directly from intentions that have simply come over me—nothing would owe its occurrence to either my participating or failing to participate in events, and I might bear no responsibility for anything.

of my desires, beliefs, and intentions; and so a definition of when their influence is normal still won't enable the standard story to account for my participation.

IV

In omitting the agent's participation from the history of his action, the standard story falls victim to a fundamental problem in the philosophy of action—namely, that of finding a place for agents in the explanatory order of the world.[12] Our concept of full-blooded human action requires some event or state of affairs that owes its occurrence to an agent and hence has an explanation that traces back to him. As I have already noted, not all actions are full-blooded—witness the aforementioned raising of my voice, which owed its occurrence to my attitudes but not to me. Such an occurrence may still count as the behavioural component of an action, as something that I did; but it lacks those features which seem to set human action apart from the rest of animal behaviour, and which thus provide the philosophy of action with its distinctive subject matter. What makes us agents rather than mere subjects of behaviour—in our conception of ourselves, at least, if not in reality—is our perceived capacity to interpose ourselves into the course of events in such a way that the behavioural outcome is traceable directly to us.

The question whether our practical nature is as we conceive it in this respect—or in any other, for that matter—should be clearly distinguished from the question what we conceive our practical nature to be. Carl Ginet has recently argued (1990, pp. 11–15) that what happens when someone acts is that his behaviour is caused by a mental event whose intrinsic qualities include feeling as if it issues directly from him; but that this feeling corresponds to no actual feature of the event's causal history or structure. Even if Ginet's account correctly describes what actually happens in all or most of the episodes that we describe as actions, the question remains whether it correctly expresses what we mean to say about those episodes in so describing them.

Indeed, Ginet's account strongly suggests that what we mean to say about an event, in calling it an action, is unlikely to be what the account itself says, since it says that an action begins with a mental event that feels as if it were something that, according to this account, it is not—namely, a direct production of the agent. If our actions always begin with mental events that feel as if they are of agential origin, then one might expect the notion of agential origin to crop up in our commonsense concept of action; whereas one wouldn't expect a commonsense

12. I believe that this problem is distinct from the problem of free-will, although the two are often treated together. For my views on the latter problem, see my (1990).

concept to include the philosophical critique of this notion, as having no realization in the history or structure of events. Ginet's account therefore suggests that we are likely to conceive actions as traceable to the agent in a sense in which, according to Ginet, they actually are not.[13]

Of course, if actions can fail to be as we conceive them, then the philosopher of action must specify whether his object of study is the concept or the reality. Does the philosopher seek to explain what we ordinarily mean when we call something an action, or does he seek to explain what something ordinarily is when so called?[14] My aim is to explain the former, at least in the first instance. For I suspect that our practices of deliberation, rationalizing explanation, and moral assessment are designed for action as we conceive it to be, and that any account of a reality substantially different from this conception will not help us to understand the logic of these practices.

In saying that my aim is to explicate our concept of action, as opposed to the reality, I do not mean to imply that I have given up hope of finding that the two are in accord. All I mean is that the concept has an antecedently fixed content that doesn't depend on what actually goes on in all or most or even a privileged few of the cases to which it's applied, and hence that correspondence between concept and reality will count as a cognitive achievement on our part. As for this cognitive achievement, however, I do hope to show that we need not despair of having attained it. For I hope to show that our concept of full-blooded action, as involving behaviour that's ultimately traceable to an agent, can be understood in a way that may well be realized in the world, as we otherwise understand it.[15]

13. Ginet thinks that actions other than simple mental actions do issue from the agent in the sense that they involve the agent's causing something. But he thinks that something can be caused by an agent only insofar as it is caused by one of the agent's actions. And he thinks that the resulting regress, of actions in which things are caused by other actions, must terminate in a simple mental action—usually, the act of willing—which qualifies as an action only because it feels as if it was caused by the agent himself, although it hasn't in fact been caused by him in any sense. Thus, Ginet thinks that complex actions issue from the agent only in the sense that their component behaviour is ultimately caused by a mental event that misleadingly feels as if it issued from the agent. Since the agential ancestry of complex action is thus inherited from a simple mental act whose agential ancestry is itself illusory, the ancestry of all actions would seem to be tainted by illusion.

14. Here, of course, I assume that the term "action" does not function like the Kripkean name of a natural kind, referring to whatever shares the essential nature of all or most or a privileged few of the episodes to which it is applied. I assume that "action" has a *de dicto* meaning in virtue of which it may in fact fail to be a correct description of anything to which it is applied.

15. I therefore think that Ginet dismisses the causal conception of action too quickly. I do agree with Ginet that an agent, as a persisting entity, is the wrong sort of thing to cause particular events. (Ginet cites Broad 1952, p. 215, as the source of this objection.) But this objection militates only against a non-reductive theory of agent-causation. It leaves open the possibility that the causation of events by the right sort of things—that is, by other events—may in some cases amount to, or deserve to be described as, their being caused by the agent himself. It therefore leaves open the possibility of agent-causation that's reduc-

V

The obstacle to reconciling our conception of agency with the possible realities is that our scientific view of the world regards all events and states of affairs as caused, and hence explained, by other events and states, or by nothing at all. And this view would seem to leave no room for agents in the explanatory order. As Thomas Nagel puts it, "Everything I do or that anyone else does is part of a larger course of events that no one 'does', but that happens, with or without explanation. Everything I do is part of something I don't do, because I am a part of the world" (1986, p. 114; cf. Bishop 1989, pp. 39ff.).

I implicitly endorsed this naturalistic conception of explanation when I conceded, earlier, that the standard story of action cannot be faulted merely for alluding to states and events occurring in the agent's mind. Any explanation of human action will speak in terms of some such occurrences, because occurrences are the basic elements of explanation in general.

Some philosophers have not been willing to concede this point. According to Roderick Chisholm (1976), for example, the explanatory order must include not only occurrences but also agents, conceived as additional primitive elements. The causation of occurrences by agents, rather than by other occurrences, is what Chisholm calls "agent-causation".

If the phrase "agent-causation" is understood in Chisholm's sense, then the naturalistic conception of explanation implies that agent-causation doesn't exist. Yet those who endorse the naturalistic conception of explanation, as I do, may still want to reconcile it with our commonsense conception of full-blooded action, in which behaviour is traced to the agent himself rather than to occurrences within him. Such a reconciliation will have to show how the causal role assigned to the agent by common sense reduces to, or supervenes on, causal relations among events and states of affairs. And the agent's being a supervenient

---

ible to, or supervenient on, causation by events. (I discuss this possibility, and its implications, in the next section of the text.) Ginet argues against a conception that characterizes action in terms of event causation (pp. 11–13). But Ginet's argument suffers from two flaws. Ginet's argument is that we can conceive of a simple mental act, such as mentally saying a word, without conceiving of it as comprising a structure of distinct, causally related events. ("I mean that it is not *conceptually required* to have such a structure, under our concept of it as that kind of mental act" (p. 12).) Yet this point doesn't speak to the hypothesis that we conceive of the act in question as comprising behaviour caused by the agent, and that the behaviour's being caused by the agent supervenes on its causal relation to other events. Our concept of action may include agent-causation without including the supervenience base thereof. What's more, the illustrations that Ginet provides for this argument—pairs of mental causes and effects whose structure is clearly different from that of the mental act in question—are all cases in which the imagined cause is itself a mental act. But someone who thinks that a mental act consists in mental behaviour caused by the agent, in a sense that supervenes on its being caused by another event, is not likely to think that the causing event is yet another act.

cause of this sort might also be called agent-causation, in a more relaxed sense of the phrase. If "agent-causation" is understood to encompass this possibility as well as the one envisioned by Chisholm, then naturalists may want a theory of agent-causation, too.

This broader understanding of the phrase "agent-causation" is in fact endorsed by Chisholm himself, in a passage whose obscure provenance justifies extended quotation. Chisholm says:

> [T]he issues about "agent-causation" . . . have been misplaced. The philosophical question is not—or at least it shouldn't be—the question whether or not there is "agent-causation". The philosophical question should be, rather, the question whether "agent-causation" is reducible to "event causation". Thus, for example, if we have good reason for believing that Jones . . . kill[ed] his uncle, then the philosophical question about Jones as cause would be: Can we express the statement "Jones killed his uncle" without loss of meaning into a set of statements in which only events are said to be causes and in which Jones himself is not said to be the source of any activity? And can we do this without being left with any residue of agent-causation—that is, without being left with some such statement as "Jones raised his arm" wherein Jones once again plays the role of cause or partial cause of a certain event? (1978, pp. 622–23)

As the failings of the standard story reveal, we may have difficulty in meeting this challenge even if we help ourselves to a rich inventory of mental events and states. We could of course make the problem even harder, by asking how statements about Jones's action can be reexpressed, not just in terms of occurrences, but in terms of physical occurrences taking place among particles and fields. In that case, we would be worrying, in part, about the mind-body problem. But the problem of agent-causation lingers even if the mind-body problem can be made to disappear. For let there be mental states and events in abundance— motives, reasons, intentions, plans—and let them be connected, both to one another and to external behaviour, by robust causal relations; still, the question will remain how the existence and relations of these items can amount to a person's causing something rather than merely to something's happening in him, albeit something mental.[16] The problem of agency is thus independent of, though indeed parallel to, the mind-body problem. Just as the mind-body problem is that of finding a mind at work amid the workings of the body, so the problem of agency is that of finding an agent at work amid the workings of the mind.[17]

16. Cf. Bishop (1989, p. 43).

17. The standard story of rational action has also illustrated that the problem is more than that of casting the agent in the role of cause. In explaining an action, we trace its history back to the agent who brought the action about; but then we trace back further, to

Now, Chisholm's non-reductionist solution to the problem of agency hasn't been taken seriously by many philosophers, nor do I intend to accord it serious attention here. However, I do sympathize with Chisholm's complaint that those who smirk at his solution do so unjustly, since they haven't taken seriously the problem that it is intended to solve. Chisholm says:

> Now if you can analyze such statements as "Jones killed his uncle" into event-causation statements, then you may have earned the right to make jokes about the agent as [a primitive] cause. But if you haven't done this, and if all the same you do believe such things as that I raised my arm and that Jones killed his uncle, and if moreover you still think it's a joke to talk about the agent as cause, then, I'm afraid, the joke is entirely on you. You are claiming the benefits of honest philosophical toil without even *having* a theory of human action. (*ibid.*)[18]

Here I think that Chisholm has come as close as anyone ever has to speaking frankly about a philosophical disagreement. And I hope that he would recognize it as a token of my respect for this accomplishment if I adopt his locution and declare that the proper goal for the philosophy of action is to earn the right to make jokes about primitive agent-causation, by explaining how an agent's causal role supervenes on the causal network of events and states.[19]

VI

The best sustained attempt at such an explanation, I think, is contained in a series of articles by Harry Frankfurt.[20] These articles begin with the

---

the reasons that persuaded him to do so. And as Donald Davidson has argued (1980), the reasons cited in the explanation of an action must be, not just reasons that were available to the agent, but reasons for which he acted, the difference being precisely that the latter are the reasons that induced him to act. The reasons that explain an action are thus distinguished by their having exerted an influence upon the agent. In the explanation of an action, then, the agent must serve not only as an origin of activity, or cause, but also as an object of rational influence—and hence, in a sense, as an effect.

18. Note the need to insert the word "primitive" in Chisholm's phrase "the agent as cause", which illustrates that Chisholm has reverted to understanding agent-causation in a narrower sense.

19. See Bishop (1989, p. 69): "Of course action differs from other behaviour in that the agent brings it about, but the problem is how to accommodate such bringing about within a naturalist ontology".

20. "Freedom of the Will and the Concept of a Person", "Three Concepts of Free Action", "Identification and Externality", "The Problem of Action", "Identification and Wholeheartedness", all in Frankfurt's (1988). Frankfurt has recently returned to the topic, in his 1991 Presidential Address to the Eastern Division of the APA, entitled "The Faintest Passion". I shall not be discussing the new suggestions contained in this address.

question of what constitutes a person, but the focus quickly narrows to the person as an element in the causal order.[21] What primarily interests Frankfurt, as I have mentioned, is the difference between cases in which a person "participates" in the operation of his will and cases in which he becomes "a helpless bystander to the forces that move him."[22] And this distinction just is that between cases in which the person does and does not contribute to the production of his behaviour.

In attempting to draw this distinction, Frankfurt is working on the same problem as Chisholm, although he is seeking a reductive solution rather than a solution of the non-reductive sort that Chisholm favours. What's odd is that Frankfurt conceives of the problem in a way that initially appears destined to frustrate any reductive solution. In the following sections, I shall first explain why Frankfurt's project can thus appear hopeless; and I shall then suggest a conception of agency that might offer Frankfurt some hope.

VII

Frankfurt's strategy for identifying the elements of agent-causation is to identify what's missing from cases in which human behaviour proceeds without the agent as its cause. Frankfurt figures that if he can find what's missing from instances of less-than-full-blooded action, then he'll know what makes it the case, in other instances, that the agent gets into the act.

The cases of defective action that occupy Frankfurt's attention are cases in which the agent fails to participate because he is "alienated" from the motives that actuate him and which therefore constitute his will, or (as Frankfurt calls it) his "volition". And what's missing when an agent is alienated from his volition, according to Frankfurt, is his "identifying" or "being identified" with it.

Although Frankfurt draws this observation from cases in which the agent consciously dissociates himself from the motives actuating him—cases involving addiction or compulsion—it can equally be drawn from cases of the more familiar sort that I illustrated above. When my latent resentments against a friend yield an intention that causes my voice to rise, for example, I am not consciously alienated from that intention, perhaps, but I do not identify with it, either, since I am simply unaware

21. Frankfurt says that the "essential difference between persons and other creatures" that he wishes to discuss "is to be found in the structure of a person's will" (1988, p. 12). And he later suggests that if someone becomes unable to exercise his will in the relevant way, this inability "destroys him as a person" (p. 21).

22. 1988, p. 21. The same phrase appears on p. 22. In another essay Frankfurt formulates the distinction in terms of a person's "activity or passivity with respect to . . . states of affairs" (p. 54).

of it. Hence Frankfurt might say that I do not participate in raising my voice because, being unaware of my intention, I cannot identify with it.

From this analysis of defective actions, Frankfurt draws the conclusion that what makes the difference between defective and full-blooded actions must be that, in the case of the latter, the agent identifies with the motives that actuate him (pp. 18 ff., 54). Here Frankfurt casts the agent in a role of the general sort that I envisioned in my critique of the standard story. That is, he doesn't think of the agent as entering the causal history of his action by displacing the motivational force of his desires or intentions; rather, he thinks of the agent as adding to the force of these attitudes, by intermediating among them. Specifically, the agent interacts with his motives, in Frankfurt's conception, by throwing his weight behind some of them rather than others, thereby determining which ones govern his behaviour.

VIII

Frankfurt thus arrives at the conclusion that if a causal account of action is to include the agent's contribution to his behaviour, it must include the agent's identifying himself with his operative motives. He therefore looks for mental events or states that might constitute the agent's self-identification.

Frankfurt's first candidate for the role is a second-order motive. The agent's identifying with the motive that actuates him, Frankfurt suggests, consists in his having a second-order desire to be actuated by that motive, whereas his being alienated from the motive consists in his having a desire not to be so actuated. These higher-order desires either reinforce or resist the influence of the agent's operative motive, and they thereby "*constitute* his activity"—that is, his throwing his weight behind, or withholding his weight from, the motive that actuates him, and thereby making or withholding a contribution to the resulting behaviour (p. 54).

As Gary Watson (1982) has pointed out and Frankfurt (pp. 65–6) has conceded, however, the same considerations that show the standard story to be incomplete can be applied to this enhanced version of it. For just as an agent can be alienated from his first-order motives, so he can be alienated from his second-order desires about them; and if his alienation from the former entails that they operate without his participation, then his alienation from the latter must entail similar consequences. Yet if the agent doesn't participate when a second-order desire reinforces his operative motive, then how can its doing so constitute his identifying with that motive and contributing to the resulting behaviour? The occurrence that supposedly constitutes the agent's contributing to his behaviour seems itself to stand in need of some further contribution from him. Hence Frankfurt has failed to identify a mental item that necessarily implicates the agent in producing his behaviour.

Watson and Frankfurt have subsequently sought alternative candidates for the role. Watson argues that Frankfurt's references to second-order desires should be replaced with references to the agent's values. What is distinctive about behaviour in which the agent isn't fully involved, according to Watson, "is that the desires and emotions in question are more or less radically independent of [his] evaluational systems" (1982, p. 110).[23] Watson therefore suggests that the agent's contribution to an action is the contribution made by his system of values.

But this suggestion solves nothing. A person can be alienated from his values, too; and he can be alienated from them even as they continue to grip him and to influence his behaviour—as, for instance, when someone recoils from his own materialism or his own sense of sin.[24] Hence the contribution of values to the production of someone's behaviour cannot by itself be sufficient to constitute his contribution, for the same reason that the contribution of his second-order desires proved insufficient.[25]

Frankfurt has made an attempt of his own to solve the problem, in subsequent papers, but with no more success.[26] Frankfurt now suggests that the agent's involvement in his behaviour can be provided by "decisions" or "decisive commitments" to his operative motives, since these mental items are indivisible from the agent himself. Frankfurt writes, "Decisions, unlike desires or attitudes, do not seem to be susceptible both to internality and to externality"—that is, to identification and alienation—and so "invoking them . . . would appear to avoid . . . the difficulty" (p. 68, n. 3). Yet the example of my unwitting decision to break off a friendship shows that even decisions and commitments can be foreign to the person in whom they arise.[27] How, then, can a deci-

---

23. For a recent discussion of Watson's view, see Wolf (1990, Chapter 2).

24. I owe the latter example to Elizabeth Anderson (MS).

25. Of course, Watson refers not just to values lodged in the agent but to the agent's evaluational system; and he might argue that values are no longer integrated into that system once the agent becomes alienated from them. But in that case, Watson would simply be smuggling the concept of identification or association into his distinction between the agent's evaluational system and his other, unsystematized values. And just as Frankfurt faced the question how a volition becomes truly the agent's, Watson would face the question how a value becomes integrated into the agent's evaluational system. See section X below.

26. Again, the discussion that follows deals only with Frankfurt's published work on the subject, not his 1991 Presidential Address to the Eastern Division of the American Philosophical Association, in which he outlines a somewhat different solution.

27. I can of course imagine defining a phrase "decisive commitments" denoting only those commitments which an agent actively makes. In that case, decisive commitments will indeed be such as cannot fail to have the agent's participation; but in what that participa-

sion's contribution to behaviour guarantee that the agent is involved?

One might wonder, of course, why Frankfurt and Watson assume that the agent's identifying with his operative motives must consist in a mental state or event specifiable in other terms, as a particular kind of desire, value, or decision. Perhaps identifying with one's motives is a mental state or event *sui generis* rather than a species of some other genus.

IX

Tempting though this suggestion may be, it is really just an invitation to beg the question of agent-causation. The question, after all, is how an agent causally contributes to the production of his behaviour; and to observe that he sometimes identifies with the motives producing that behaviour is to answer this question only if identifying with motives entails somehow making a causal contribution to their operation—throwing one's weight behind them, as I put it before. Other kinds of identification may not at all guarantee that the agent gets into the act.

Frankfurt seems to think that an agent cannot fail to get into the act when he identifies with a motive. "It makes no sense", he says, "to ask whether someone identifies himself with his identification of himself, unless this is intended simply as asking whether his identification is wholehearted or complete" (p. 54). What this remark shows, however, is that Frankfurt is using the term "identification" in a specialized sense, since ordinary talk of identifying with something often denotes a mental event or state from which the subject can indeed be alienated. For example, you may find yourself identifying with some character in a trashy novel, even as you recoil from this identification. Identifying with the character may then seem like something that happens to you, or comes over you, without your participation.

One might think that such a case is what Frankfurt has in mind when he says that an agent's identification of himself may not be "wholehearted" or "complete", but I think not. For if it were, then Frankfurt would in effect be conceding that self-identification can sometimes occur without the agent's participation; and in that case, he could no longer claim that self-identification alone is what distinguishes the actions in which the agent participates from those in which he doesn't. An agent who identifies with a motive needn't be implicated in the behaviour that it produces if he can somehow dissociate himself from the identification.

tion consists will remain a mystery, and the claim that the agent participates in his actions by way of decisive commitments will be uninformative. A related criticism of Frankfurt's solution appears in Christman (1991, pp. 8–9). See section X below.

I think that what Frankfurt means, when he refuses to ask whether someone identifies with his self-identification, is that identifying oneself with a motive is unlike identifying with a character in a novel precisely in that it cannot happen at all without one's participation. Identifying with another person is, at most, a matter of imagining oneself in his skin, whereas identifying with a motive entails taking possession of it in fact, not just in imagination. Frankfurt therefore assumes, I think, that identifying with a motive is a mental phenomenon that simply doesn't occur unless one participates, although one may participate halfheartedly or incompletely.

Having put our finger on this assumption, however, we can see that for Frankfurt to posit self-identification as a primitive mental phenomenon would be to beg the question of agent-causation. For if self-identification is something that cannot occur without the agent's contributing to it, then it cannot occur without agent-causation, and we cannot assume that it occurs without assuming that agent-causation occurs—which is what we set out to show, in the first place. The question is whether there is such a thing as a person's participating in the causal order of events and states, and we can't settle this question simply by positing a primitive state or event that requires the person's participation.

Lest the question be begged, then, "self-identification" must not be understood as naming the primitive event or state that provides the needed reduction of agent-causation; it must be understood, instead, as redescribing agent-causation itself, the phenomenon to be reduced. When Frankfurt says that an agent participates in an action by identifying with its motives, he doesn't mean that self-identification is, among mere states and events, the one in virtue of which the agent gets into the act; rather, he is saying that if we want to know which are the mere states and events that constitute the agent's getting into the act, we should look for the ones that constitute his identifying with his motives. Frankfurt and Watson are therefore correct in trying to reduce self-identification to desires, values, or decisions—that is, to mental phenomena whose existence we can assume without presupposing that agent-causation occurs.

X

But how can such a reduction ever succeed? If we pick out mental states and events in terms that do not presuppose any causal contribution from the agent, then we shall have picked out states and events from which the agent can in principle dissociate himself. Since the occurrence of these items will be conceptually possible without any participation from the agent, we shall have no grounds for saying that their occurrence guarantees the agent's participation in the causal order.

The only way to guarantee that a mental state or event will bring the agent into the act is to define it in terms that mandate the agent's being in the act; but then we can't assume the occurrence of that state or event without already assuming the occurrence of agent-causation. Hence we seem to be confronted with a choice between begging the question and not answering it at all.

We may be tempted to slip between the horns of this dilemma, by characterizing some mental items in terms that are sufficiently vague to carry an assumption of agent-causation while keeping that assumption concealed. I suspect that Watson's appeals to "the agent's system of values", and Frankfurt's appeals to "decisive commitments" seem to succeed only insofar as they smuggle such an assumption into the story.[28] But a genuine resolution of the dilemma will require a more radical change of approach.

XI

The main flaw in Frankfurt's approach, I think, is that substituting one instance of agent-causation for another, as the target of reduction, does not advance the reductionist project. Since self-identification won't serve our purpose unless it's conceived as something to which the agent contributes, rather than something that happens to him, reducing self-identification to mere events and states is unlikely to be any easier than reducing action itself.

The way to advance the reductionist project is not to substitute one agent-causal phenomenon for another as the target of reduction, but to get the process of reduction going, by breaking agent-causation into its components. And surely, the principal component of agent-causation is the agent himself. Instead of looking for mental events and states to play the role of the agent's identifying with a motive, then, we should look for events and states to play the role of the agent.

Something to play the role of agent is precisely what I earlier judged to be lacking from the standard story of human action. I pointed out that the agent intermediates in various ways between his reasons and intentions, or between his intentions and bodily movements; and I argued that the standard story omits the agent, not because it fails to mention him by name, but rather because it fails to mention anything that plays his intermediating role.

What plays the agent's role in a reductionist account of agent-causation will of course be events or states—most likely, events or states in the agent's mind. We must therefore look for mental events and states

28. See notes 25 and 27, above.

that are functionally identical to the agent, in the sense that they play the causal role that ordinary parlance attributes to him.

Looking for a mental event or state that's functionally identical to the agent is not as bizarre as it sounds. Of course, the agent is a whole person, who is not strictly identical with any subset of the mental states and events that occur within him. But a complete person qualifies as an agent by virtue of performing some rather specific functions, and he can still lay claim to those functions even if they are performed, strictly speaking, by some proper part of him. When we say that a person digests his dinner or fights an infection, we don't mean to deny that these functions actually belong to some of his parts. A person is a fighter of infections and a digester of food in the sense that his parts include infection-fighting and food-digesting systems. Similarly, a person may be an initiator of actions—and hence an agent—in the sense that there is an action-initiating system within him, a system that performs the functions in virtue of which he qualifies as an agent and which are ordinarily attributed to him in that capacity. A reductionist philosophy of action must therefore locate a system of mental events and states that perform the functional role definitive of an agent.

I sometimes suspect that Frankfurt sees the necessity of this approach and may even think that he's taking it. My suspicion is based on the potential confusions that lurk in Frankfurt's talk of "identifying oneself" with a motive and thereby "making it one's own" (p. 18). The reader, and perhaps the writer, of these phrases may think that when a person identifies himself with motives, they become functionally identical to him, or that when motives become his, they do so by becoming him, in the sense that they occupy his functional role. But the psychological items that are functionally identical to the agent, in the sense that they play the causal role attributed to him in his capacity as agent, cannot be items with which he identifies in Frankfurt's sense, because identifying with something, in that sense, is a relation that one bears to something functionally distinct from oneself. The agent's identifying with an attitude requires, not only something to play the role of the attitude identified with, but also something else to play the role of the agent identifying with it; and the latter item, rather than the former, will be what plays the functional role of the agent and is therefore functionally identical to him.

XII

What, then, is the causal role that mental states and events must play if they are to perform the agent's function? I have already outlined what I take to be the causal role of an agent; but for the remainder of this paper, I want to confine my attention to that aspect of the role which interests Frankfurt, since my approach is simply a modification of his. Frankfurt doesn't think of the agent as having a function to play in implementing his own decisions, nor does he think of the agent as interacting with reasons *per se*. Frankfurt focuses instead on the agent's interactions with the motives in which his reasons for acting are ordinarily thought to consist. The agent's role, according to Frankfurt, is to reflect on the motives competing for governance of his behaviour, and to determine the outcome of the competition, by taking sides with some of his motives rather than others. For the moment, then, I shall adopt Frankfurt's assumption that the agent's role is to adjudicate conflicts of motives (though I shall subsequently argue that such adjudication is best understood as taking place among reasons instead).

Which mental items might play this role? Here, too, I want to begin by following Frankfurt. Frankfurt says that adjudicating the contest among one's motives entails occupying an "identity apart" from them (p. 18); and he says this, I assume, because a contest cannot be adjudicated by the contestants themselves. When an agent reflects on the motives vying to govern his behaviour, he occupies a position of critical detachment from those motives; and when he takes sides with some of those motives, he bolsters them with a force additional to, and hence other than, their own. His role must therefore be played by something other than the motives on which he reflects and with which he takes sides.

Indeed, the agent's role is closed, not only to the actual objects of his critical reflection, but to all potential objects of it as well. Even when the agent's reflections are confined to his first-order motives, for example, his second-order attitudes toward them cannot be what play his role; for he can sustain his role as agent while turning a critical eye on those second-order attitudes, whereas they cannot execute such a critical turn upon themselves. The functional role of agent is that of a single party prepared to reflect on, and take sides with, potential determinants of behaviour at any level in the hierarchy of attitudes; and this party cannot be identical with any of the items on which it must be prepared to reflect or with which it must be prepared to take sides.

Thus, the agent's role cannot be played by any mental states or events whose behavioural influence might come up for review in practical thought at any level. And the reason why it cannot be played by anything that might undergo the process of critical review is precisely that it must be played by whatever directs that process. The agent, in his capacity as agent, is that party who is always behind, and never in front of, the lens of critical reflection, no matter where in the hierarchy of motives it turns.

What mental event or state might play this role of always directing but never undergoing such scrutiny? It can only be a motive that drives practical thought itself. That is, there must be a motive that drives the agent's critical reflection on, and endorsement or rejection of, the potential determinants of his behaviour, always doing so from a position of independence from the objects of review. Only such a motive would occupy the agent's functional role, and only its contribution to his behaviour would constitute his own contribution.

What I'm positing here is an attitude that embodies the concerns of practical thought *per se*, concerns distinct from those embodied in any of the attitudes that practical thought might evaluate as possible springs of action. Frankfurt seems to assume that the concerns animating the agent's critical reflection on his first-order motives are embodied in his second-order desires about whether to be governed by those motives—such as the desire not to act out of anger, for example, or the desire to be actuated by compassion instead. Yet these second-order desires figure in critical reflection only with respect to a particular conflict of motives, and they can themselves become the objects of critical reflection one step further up the attitudinal hierarchy. Hence the concerns that they embody cannot qualify as the concerns directing practical thought as such, concerns that must be distinct from the objects of critical reflection and that must figure in such reflection whenever it occurs. If we want to find the concerns of practical thought *per se*, we must find motives that are at work not only when the agent steps back and asks whether to act out of anger but also when he steps back further and asks whether to restrain himself out of shame about his anger, and so on. Only attitudes that are at work in all such instances of reflection will be eligible to play the role of agent, who himself is at work whenever critical reflection takes place.

One is likely to balk at this proposal if one isn't accustomed to the idea that practical thought is propelled by a distinctive motive of its own. Agency is traditionally conceived as a neutral capacity for appraising and exercising motives—a capacity that's neutral just in the sense that it is not essentially animated by any motive in particular. This traditional conception is not hospitable to the idea that the deliberative processes constitutive of agency require a distinctive motive of their own. My point, however, is that anyone who wants to save our ordinary concept of full-blooded action, as involving behaviour caused by the agent, had better grow accustomed to this idea, because the problem of agent-causation cannot be solved without it. Some motive must be behind the processes of practical thought—from the initial reflection on motives, to the eventual taking of sides; and from second-order reflection to reflection at any higher level—since only something that was always behind such processes would play the causal role that's ordinarily attributed to the agent.

XIII

Is there in fact such a motive? I believe so, though it is not evident in Frankfurt's account. Frankfurt's conception of critical reflection strikes me as omitting a concern that's common to reflection in all instances and at all levels.

The agent's concern in reflecting on his motives, I believe, is not just to see which ones he likes better; it's to see which ones provide stronger reasons for acting, and then to ensure that they prevail over those whose rational force is weaker. What animates practical thought is a concern for acting in accordance with reasons. And I suggest that we think of this concern as embodied in a desire that drives practical thought.

When I speak of a desire to act in accordance with reasons, I don't have a particular desire in mind; any one of several different desires would fill the bill. On the one hand, it could be a desire to act in accordance with reasons so described; that is, the *de dicto* content of the desire might include the concept of reasons.[29] On the other hand, it could be a desire to act in accordance with considerations of some particular kind, which happened to be the kind of consideration that constituted a reason for acting. For example, I have argued elsewhere (1989) that rational agents have a desire to do what makes sense, or what's intelligible to them, in the sense that they could explain it; and I have argued that reasons for a particular action are considerations by which the action could be explained and in light of which it would therefore make sense. Thus, if someone wants to do what makes sense, then in my view he wants to act in accordance with reasons, though not under that description. In any of its forms, the desire to act in accordance with reasons can perform the functions that are attributed to its subject in his capacity as agent. We say that the agent turns his thoughts to the various motives that give him reason to act; but in fact, the agent's thoughts are turned in this direction by the desire to act in accordance with reasons. We say that the agent calculates the relative strengths of the reasons before him; but in fact, these calculations are driven by his desire to act in accordance with reasons. We say that the agent throws his weight behind the motives that provide the strongest reasons; but what is thrown behind those motives, in fact, is the additional motivating force of the desire to act in accordance with reasons. For when a desire appears to provide the strongest reason for acting, then the desire to act in accordance with reasons becomes a motive to act on that desire, and the desire's motivational influence is consequently

29. This possibility may be ruled out by an argument in Bernard Williams' paper "Internal and External Reasons" (1981). In any case, Williams' argument does not rule out the alternative possibility, which is the one that I favour. I discuss Williams' argument in a manuscript tentatively entitled "External Reasons".

reinforced. The agent is moved to his action, not only by his original motive for it, but also by his desire to act on that original motive, because of its superior rational force. This latter contribution to the agent's behaviour is the contribution of an attitude that performs the functions definitive of agency; it is therefore, functionally speaking, the agent's contribution to the causal order.

What really produces the bodily movements that you are said to produce, then, is a part of you that performs the characteristic functions of agency. That part, I claim, is your desire to act in accordance with reasons, a desire that produces behaviour, in your name, by adding its motivational force to that of whichever motives appear to provide the strongest reasons for acting, just as you are said to throw your weight behind them.

Note that the desire to act in accordance with reasons cannot be disowned by an agent, although it can be disowned by the person in whom agency is embodied. A person can perhaps suppress his desire to act in accordance with reasons; but in doing so, he will have to execute a psychic manoeuvre quite different from suppressing his anger or his addiction to drugs or his other substantive motives for acting. In suppressing his anger, the person operates in his capacity as agent, rejecting anger as a reason for acting; whereas in suppressing his desire to act in accordance with reasons, he cannot reject it as a reason for acting, or he will in fact be manifesting his concern for reasons rather than suppressing it, after all. The only way for a person truly to suppress his concern for reasons is to stop making rational assessments of his motives, including this one, thus suspending the processes of practical thought. And in suspending the process of practical thought, he will suspend the functions in virtue of which he qualifies as an agent. Thus, the sense in which an agent cannot disown his desire to act in accordance with reasons is that he cannot disown it while remaining an agent.

Conversely, a person's desire to act in accordance with reasons cannot operate in him without its operations being constitutive of his agency. What it is for this motive to operate is just this: for potential determinants of behaviour to be critically reviewed, to be embraced or rejected, and to be consequently reinforced or suppressed. Whatever intervenes in these ways between motives and behaviour is thereby playing the role of the agent and consequently *is* the agent, functionally speaking. Although the agent must possess an identity apart from the substantive motives competing for influence over his behaviour, he needn't possess an identity apart from the attitude that animates the activity of judging such competitions. If there is such an attitude, then its contribution to the competition's outcome can qualify as his—not because he identifies with it but rather because it is functionally identical to him.

XIV

Note, finally, that this reduction of agent-causation allows us to preserve some aspects of commonsense psychology about which we may have had philosophical qualms. What we would like to think, pre-philosophically, is that a person sometimes intervenes among his motives because the best reason for acting is associated with the intrinsically weaker motive, and he must therefore intervene in order to ensure that the weaker motive prevails. What inhibits us from saying this, however, is the philosophical realization that the weaker motive can never prevail, since an incapacity to prevail over other motives is precisely what constitutes motivational weakness. Every action, we are inclined to say, is the result of the strongest motive or the strongest combination of motives, by definition.

But my reduction of agent-causation enables us to say both that the agent makes the weaker motive prevail and that the contest always goes to the strongest combination of motives. The agent can make the weaker motive prevail, according to my story, in the sense that he can throw his weight behind the weaker of those motives which are vying to animate his behaviour and are therefore objects of his practical thought. But the agent's throwing his weight behind the weaker of these motives actually consists in its being reinforced by another motive, so that the two now form the strongest combination of motives. Thus, the weaker motive can prevail with the help of the agent simply because it can prevail with the help of another motive and because the agent *is* another motive, functionally speaking.

Come to think of it, what else could an agent be?

REFERENCES

Anderson, E. (unpublished manuscript): "The Sources of Norms".
Bishop, J. 1989: *Natural Agency; an Essay on the Causal Theory of Action.* Cambridge: Cambridge University Press.
Broad, C. D. 1952: *Ethics and the History of Philosophy.* London: Routledge and Kegan Paul.
Chisholm, R. 1976: *Person and Object: a Metaphysical Study.* London: Allen and Unwin.
——1978: "Comments and Replies" *Philosophia,* 7, pp. 597–636.
Christman, J. 1991: "Autonomy and Personal History". *Canadian Journal of Philosophy,* 21, 1, pp. 1–24.
Davidson, D. 1980: *Essays on Actions and Events.* Oxford: Clarendon Press.
Dent, N. J. H. 1984: *The Moral Psychology of the Virtues.* Cambridge: Cambridge University Press.
Frankfurt, H. 1988: *The Importance of What We Care About.* Cambridge, Cambridge University Press.

Ginet, C. 1990: *On Action*. Cambridge: Cambridge University Press.
Goldman, A. I. 1970: *A Theory of Human Action*. Princeton: Princeton University Press.
Harman, G. 1976: "Practical Reasoning". *Review of Metaphysics*, 29, 3, pp. 431–63.
Nagel, T. 1986: *The View From Nowhere*. Oxford: Oxford University Press.
Peacocke, C. 1979: "Deviant Causal Chains". *Midwest Studies in Philosophy*, 4, pp. 123–56.
Taylor, R. 1966: *Action and Purpose*. Englewood Cliffs, N.J.: Prentice-Hall.
Velleman, J. D. 1989: *Practical Reflection*. Princeton: Princeton University press.
——1990: "Epistemic Freedom". *Pacific Philosophical Quarterly*, 70, 1, pp. 73–97.
——1992: "The Guise of the Good". *Nous*, 26, 1, pp. 3–26.
Watson, G. 1982: "Free Agency", in his *Free Will*. Oxford: Oxford University Press, pp. 205–20.
Williams, Bernard 1981: "Internal and External Reasons", in his *Moral Luck*. Cambridge: Cambridge University Press, pp. 101–13.
Wolf, S. 1990: *Freedom Within Reason*. Oxford: Oxford University Press.

8

Sanctification, Hardening of the Heart, and Frankfurt's Concept of Free Will

ELEONORE STUMP

IN a much-discussed paper,[1] "Freedom of the Will and the Concept of a Person,"[2] Harry Frankfurt presents an analysis of the self in terms of

1. For good summaries of the literature, see David Shatz, "Free Will and the Structure of Motivation," *Midwest Studies in Philosophy*, vol. X, Peter French, Theodore Uehling, Jr., and Howard Wettstein, eds. (Minneapolis: Minnesota UP, 1986), pp. 451–482; and Gary Watson, "Free Action and Free Will," Mind, XLVI (1987): 145–172. Besides the literature cited in those articles, I also found helpful the following articles (given in no particular order): Lawrence Haworth, *Autonomy: An Essay in Philosophical Psychology and Ethics* (New Haven: Yale, 1986), and "Autonomy and Utility," *Ethics*, XCV (1984): 5–19; William Rowe, "Two Criticisms of the Agency Theory," *Philosophical Studies*, XLII (1982): 363–378; Richard Arneson, "Freedom and Desire," *Canadian Journal of Philosophy*, XV (1985): 425–448; S. I. Benn, "Freedom, Autonomy and the Concept of a Person," *Proceedings of the Aristotelian Society*, LXXVI (1975/6): 109–131; Gerald Dworkin, "The Concept of Autonomy," in *Science and Ethics,* R. Haller, ed. (Amsterdam: Rodopi, 1981), pp. 203–213; Irving Thalberg, "Socialization and Autonomous Behavior," in *Studies in Action Theory*, Robert Whittemore, ed. (New Orleans: Tulane, 1979), pp. 21–37; Marilyn Friedman, "Autonomy and the Split-level Self," *The Southern Journal of Philosophy*, XXIV (1986): 19–35; Susan Wolf, "The Importance of Free Will," this volume.

2. *The Journal of Philosophy*, LXVIII, 1 (January 14, 1971): 5–20. Other papers by Frankfurt which have some bearing on the issues discussed here are the following (given in no particular order): "Necessity and Desire," *Philosophy and Phenomenological Research*, XLV (1984): 1–13; "The Importance of What We Care About," *Synthese*, I.III (1982): 257–272; "The Problem of Action," *American Philosophical Quarterly*, XV (1978): 157–162; "Coercion and Moral Responsibility," in *Essays on Freedom of Action*, Ted Honderich, ed. (London: Routledge & Kegan Paul, 1973), pp. 65–86; "Three Concepts of Free Action II," in *Proceedings of the Aristotelian Society,* supp. vol. XLIX (1975): 113–125; "Alternate Possibilities and Moral Responsibility," *The Journal of Philosophy*, IXVI, 23 (December 4, 1969): 828–839; "Identification and Externality," in *The Identities of Persons*, Amelie Rorty, ed. (Berkeley: California UP, 1976); "The Problem of Action," *American Philosphical Quarterly*, XV (1978): 157–162; and "Identification and Wholeheartedness," this volume (I am grateful to Frankfurt for letting me see this paper in typescript).

hierarchically ordered desires, and he uses his analysis to argue for a certain notion of freedom. His paper has generated considerable debate among philosophers interested in the concept of freedom and the related concept of autonomy. My own interest in Frankfurt's paper is primarily in applying his analysis of the self to problems in the philosophy of religion, especially to puzzles raised by the doctrine of sanctification and the notion of God's hardening hearts, although I think Frankfurt's analysis is remarkably fruitful for understanding a variety of religious claims and practices. In order to apply Frankfurt's views to issues in the philosophy of religion, however, it is important to reconsider his understanding of freedom and to refine his hierarchical analysis of the self. The resulting revised version of Frankfurt's account of freedom and the self is not vulnerable to the sorts of criticisms which have been leveled, quite correctly I think, against Frankfurt's original views. So in what follows I shall first consider Frankfurt's views of freedom and the self and suggest some revisions of them. Then I shall discuss the most important criticisms raised against Frankfurt's original position and argue that the revised Frankfurt account can be successfully defended against them. Finally, I shall show how that account can resolve some long-standing difficulties about sanctification and hardening of the heart.

I. FRANKFURT'S ACCOUNT

It is Frankfurt's view that the essence of a person is to be found in the structure of the will. He takes wants or desires to be the genus of acts of willing, or volitions, and he holds a volition to be an effective desire, which moves an agent all the way to action. According to Frankfurt, agents can have first-order desires and volitions—to do something—and also second-order desires and volitions—to have certain first-order desires. A person, on Frankfurt's view, is someone who has second-order desires and volitions. An agent who has no second-order volitions is "a wanton"; such an individual may be human but is not a person.

This analysis of the notion of a person is the basis for Frankfurt's account of freedom of will. The common conception of freedom as the ability to do what one wants to do, Frankfurt says, is best thought of as applying to freedom of action. Freedom of will can then be construed

Reprinted with permission from *The Journal of Philosophy* 85 (August 1988): 395–420.

I am indebted to the following people for useful suggestions: Don Adams, John Christman, Philip Quinn, Bruce Russell, John Tyson, Peter van Inwagen, and Allen Wood. I owe a special debt to Harry Frankfurt, who corrected some important misunderstandings of his account, and to William Alston, whose objections helped me to think out some essential distinctions. Finally, I am particularly grateful to Norman Kretzmann, who gave me many helpful comments on earlier drafts.

analogously as the ability to will what one wants to will, or the ability to have the sort of will one wants. On Frankfurt's view, in order to have freedom of will, an individual must meet the following conditions: (1) he has second-order volitions, (2) he does not have first-order volitions that are discordant with those second-order volitions, and (3) he has the first-order volitions he has *because of* his second-order volitions (that is, his second-order volitions have, directly or indirectly, produced his first-order volitions; and if his second-order volitions had been different, he would have had different first-order volitions).[3]

This account might appear to imply that only a person who meets these strong criteria for freedom of the will is morally responsible for his actions, but Frankfurt is not committed to such a counter-intuitive view. He distinguishes between acting freely and having freedom of will when one acts. If a person has done what he wanted to do because he wanted to do it and the will by which he was moved when he did it was his own will, then he *acted* freely, even if he did not act with *freedom of will*. Assessments of moral responsibility, according to Frankfurt, should depend primarily on whether or not an agent acted freely, rather than on whether or not he acted with free will.

II. IMPLICATIONS OF FRANKFURT'S ACCOUNT

Following Frankfurt's lead, we can take the basic notion of freedom as the absence of obstacles to what one wants.[4] The expressions 'free from' and 'free to' can then be seen as two branches of the same basic notion. Locutions involving the expression 'free from' specify which obstacles are absent, and locutions involving the expression 'free to' indicate the range of things available to the agent to do without obstacle. What Frankfurt and others call "freedom of action" is the absence of obstacles to doing what one wants to do; freedom of will is the absence of obstacles to willing what one wants to will.

As Frankfurt's work makes clear, obstacles to doing what one wants to do can arise in two ways. They may have their origin in something external to the agent, such as social institutions, or in something internal to the agent, such as psychoses. It is easy to show that there can also be external and internal obstacles to freedom of will by adapting the familiar example of a man who chooses to stay in a room, unaware that the

3. I am grateful to both Frankfurt and Alston for suggestions regarding these conditions.
4. Making precise the rather vague intuition behind this claim would take some doing and is beyond the scope of this paper. Perhaps it is enough for present purposes to say that by 'obstacle' here is surely meant something like "an obstacle which is, for all practical purposes, at the moment, physically insuperable."

door is locked.[5] Suppose that the man's volition to stay in the room is produced in him by means of some device implanted in his brain and controlled by scientists who want him to stay in the room. In this case what the agent wills is not what he himself wants to will; he wills what the scientists want him to will. There is thus an external obstacle to the agent's willing what he wants to will, and so he does not act with free will in staying in the room.

Ordinarily when we ask whether a person acts with free will, what we are asking is in effect whether there is an external constraint of this sort on his will. The issue between compatibilists and libertarians, for example, can be understood at least in part as a dispute over whether the causal influences that compatibilists claim operate on a person constitute an external constraint on his will. Frankfurt's definition of freedom of will is a strong one, because, in order to have free will in his sense of the term, something more is required than the simple absence of external obstacles to willing what one wants. What else is needed can be seen by considering a revised version of the example of the man in the room. This time suppose that the man does want to leave the room—say, in order to get to his classroom to teach—and that the door is not locked, but that there is a black cat asleep on the lintel over the door and he is superstitious about black cats. He struggles with his superstitious fear, but finally his desire not to have to walk past the black cat gets the better of him; he gives up the struggle and wills to stay in the room. As before, he stays willingly, but he does not stay with freedom of will, in Frankfurt's sense of the term. In this case, however, the obstacle to his willing what he wants to will is internal rather than external, because it is his own desires which are the impediments to his freedom of will. Frankfurt's sense of 'freedom of will' is thus different from the ordinary sense of the term which we have in mind when we ask, for example, whether Aquinas believes in free will rather than theological determinism. It seems to me more nearly the sense of 'free' in the theological claim "You shall know the truth and the truth shall make you free." If it were not for the clumsy locution, we might call Frankfurt's sense 'complete freedom of will' since it encompasses and exceeds the ordinary sense of free will as absence of external obstacles to willing what one wants.[6]

5. Discussed in Frankfurt, "Alternate Possibilities and Moral Responsibility," *op. cit.;* cf. John Martin Fischer, "Responsibility and Control," *The Journal of Philosophy,* LXXIX, 1 (January 1982): 24–40.
6. Frankfurt's account is usually employed by those who want to defend compatibilism, but both the revised account and Frankfurt's original views seem to me perfectly consistent also with incompatibilism.

There are, then, four basic sorts of obstacles to what one wants and four corresponding basic senses in which someone can be free in virtue of the absence of one or another of those obstacles:

(1) having no external obstacles to doing what one wants to do,

(2) having no internal obstacles to doing what one wants to do,

(3) having no external obstacles to willing what one wants to will, and

(4) having no internal obstacles to willing what one wants to will.

When an agent lacks freedom in one of the first three senses, we generally do not hold him morally responsible for what he does or fails to do. We would not blame a student for failing to complete his studies if he could not attend the university for lack of funds or if psychosis rendered him incompetent to study. Similarly, we would not hold the man responsible for failing to try to leave the room if his willing to stay in the room were technologically induced by scientists.[7] But most of us would be inclined to blame the faculty member whose failure to meet his class stemmed from a superstitious fear of black cats, and the fact that we would is instructive. The division between freedom in the first three senses and freedom in the fourth sense is similar to Frankfurt's distinction between acting freely and acting with freedom of will. Someone who has freedom in the first three senses, even if he lacks it in the fourth sense, acts freely and so is responsible for his action. Only someone who also has freedom in the fourth sense, however, acts with freedom of will, in Frankfurt's strong sense of free will.

III. The Revised Frankfurt Account

On Frankfurt's analysis, the concept of a person is marked by a single hierarchical distinction, between an agent's first-order desires and volitions and his higher-order desires and volitions. But traditionally philosophers have analyzed a human person into three parts: desires or passions, will, and intellect. If we revise Frankfurt's view to take account of the role of intellect, I think we strengthen it without losing any of its

7. There are, of course, complicated cases in which the agent's lack of freedom in one of these respects is ultimately attributable to the agent himself. The student might be impoverished because he lost all his money gambling, or his psychosis might be one he brought on himself as a result of his use of certain drugs known to cause psychosis. In such cases, the agent's inability to do what he wants is a direct result of something the agent does want. To the extent to which the inability is tied to what the agent wants, the inability does not diminish moral responsibility even if it does diminish the agent's freedom at the time of his inability.

explanatory power. Aquinas held that an agent wills to do some action p (or bring about some state of affairs q) only if the agent's intellect at the time of the action represents p (or q), under some description, as the good to be pursued.[8] Here it is crucial to understand that, in this context, 'an agent's intellect' or 'an agent's reasoning' does not refer to something which is solely rational. By 'an agent's intellect' I mean just the computing faculty of an agent. So understood, an agent's intellect may formulate a reason for an action in a manner that is hasty, thoughtless, ill-informed, invalid, or in any other way irrational.

Furthermore, it is important to understand that an agent's reason for an action may also be only implicit and not an explicit or conscious feature of his thought. Robert Audi[9] has argued cogently that x may count as the reason for an agent's action even when the agent has not consciously formulated some reason x as a reason for his action but would nonetheless give x as the reason for what he did if asked for an explanation. On this view, then, it is possible that an agent's intellect has gone through some process which contributes to a certain action on the agent's part, without the agent's being aware of that process as it is occurring. So to hold, as Aquinas does, that an agent wills to do some action p only if his intellect represents p as the good to be pursued does not entail that an agent does an action willingly only in case he first engages in a conscious process of reasoning about the action.[10] Aquinas's view requires only that some chain of reasoning (even if invalid and irrational reasoning) representing p as the good to be pursued would figure in the agent's own explanation of his action. In what follows, discussions of an agent's reasoning should be understood in light of these caveats: the reasoning in question need not be either rational or conscious.

In the spirit of Aquinas's view of intellect's direction of the will, we can make the following first revision of Frankfurt's account of the self. An agent has a second-order volition V2 to bring about some first-order volition V1 in himself only if the agent's intellect at the time of the willing represents V1, under some description, as the good to be pursued. A second-order volition, then, is a volition formed as a result of some reasoning (even when the reasoning is neither rational nor conscious) about one's first-order desires.

8. Aquinas's understanding of the relation of will to intellect is complicated and cannot be adequately discussed here. Basically, his view is that the intellect moves the will by presenting it with an understanding of the good. In so moving the will, the intellect acts not as an efficient cause but rather as a final cause. The will is a natural inclination or appetite for the good; and the intellect moves the will, without coercion, by showing it what the good to be pursued is in a particular set of circumstances. But the will also moves the intellect directly, as an efficient cause—for example, by directing it to consider certain things and to neglect others. Cf., e.g., ST Ia, q. 82, a.4.

9. "Acting for Reasons," *The Philosophical Review*, XCV (1986); 511–546.

10. I am grateful to Bruce Russell for raising this issue in correspondence.

It will be helpful to make one other revision in Frankfurt's account. His use of the term 'second-order volition' is ambiguous between an agent's second-order desire that is effective in moving him to make the corresponding first-order desire his will and a second-order desire that is not effective in that way. On Frankfurt's account, an unwilling addict who wants not to have the desire for heroin be his will but who nonetheless succumbs to his heroin addiction has a second-order volition for a desire not to take heroin. So, however, does the reformed addict who wants not to have the desire for heroin be his will and who has succeeded in that endeavor. When discussing first-order desires, Frankfurt identifies an agent's first-order volition as a first-order desire which the agent makes his will and on which he acts. Consequently, although an agent may simultaneously have conflicting first-order desires, he cannot simultaneously have conflicting first-order volitions. For the sake of clarity in what follows, I want to make a second revision of Frankfurt's account by disambiguating the sense of 'second-order volition' along the lines of Frankfurt's distinction between first-order desires and first-order volitions.

If an effective desire is one which moves the agent all the way to action, then an effective second-order desire is one which moves the agent all the way to the action of making the corresponding first-order desire his will. So a second-order desire constitutes a second-order volition only if it is an effective desire and the agent has a first-order volition corresponding to it. On this usage, the reformed addict has a second-order volition not to have the desire for heroin be his will, but the unwilling addict who succumbs to his addiction does not. He has a second-order desire not to have the desire for heroin be his will; but because the second-order desire is not an effective desire, it does not constitute a second-order volition. To express Frankfurt's concept of freedom using this revised understanding of second-order desires and volitions, we should say that an individual has freedom of the will just in case he has second-order desires, his first-order volitions are not discordant with his second-order desires, and he has the first-order volitions he has because of his second-order volitions.

As is the case with first-order volitions, it is not possible for an agent to have conflicting second-order volitions, but it is possible for him to have conflicting second-order desires. We might suppose, for example, that Verkhovensky in Dostoyevsky's *The Possessed* has both a second-order desire to have a desire for gambling, because the desire for gambling will make him well-liked by his friends, and a second-order desire not to have a desire to gamble, because stamping out the desire for gambling will win the admiration of Mrs. Stavrogin. It is worth noticing that where second-order desires conflict, it will not be possible for an agent to act on the corresponding first-order desires with freedom of will.

Whether Verkhovensky has a first-order volition to gamble or a first-order volition not to gamble, his will with regard to that volition is not free. In either case his first-order volition is opposed to one of his second-order desires, and so he fails to meet one of the criteria for freedom of will.[11]

IV. Criticisms of Frankfurt and the Revised Frankfurt Account

Of the many criticisms that have been raised against Frankfurt's account, three appear recurrently in the literature and seem especially worth considering. Various critics have charged that (1) on Frankfurt's account, an agent would be free with respect to a certain volition that was in accord with some higher-order volition even if that higher-order volition were directly produced somehow by someone else. But this is surely a counter-intuitive result, because such an agent seems to be just as much the puppet of his manipulator as the agent whose first-order volitions are directly produced by someone else, and no one would want

11. The revised Frankfurt account has some affinities with Wright Neely's account of freedom, which holds that "an agent is free with respect to some action which he performed only if it is true that, if he had been given what he took to be good and sufficient reason for not doing what he did, he would not have done it" [Neely, "Freedom and Desire," *The Philosophical Review*, LXXXIII (1974):48]. On the revised Frankfurt account, an agent may have what he would agree, if asked, is good and sufficient reason for not doing some action *x* and yet still do *x*, because, under the sway of the passions (to take just one example), he interprets doing *x* at this time under some description which makes it mistakenly seem as if the good and sufficient reason does not apply to this particular action. But he would not be free with respect to *x*, even though he might be morally responsible for doing it, since in having what he takes to be good and sufficient reason against doing *x*, he also has a second-order desire not to do *x*. Neely has sometimes been interpreted as holding that what an agent really desires is what he desires when he is thinking rationally, i.e., without epistemic error. If this interpretation were correct (and I think it misses the force of the phrase 'what he took to be' in the preceding quotation from Neely's article), then the revised Frankfurt account would be opposed to Neely's, rather than similar to it, since on the revised Frankfurt account what an agent really desires can be based on a process of reasoning full of epistemic error. The revised Frankfurt account is also in some respects similar to the account of freedom given by Watson in his insightful paper, "Free Agency," *The Journal of Philosophy*, LXXII, 8 (April 24, 1975): 205–220. Watson objects to Frankfurt's account on the grounds that Frankfurt has given us no reason to suppose that second-order desires represent what the agent himself wants just in virtue of being second-order. (I shall defend the revised Frankfurt account against this sort of objection in Section IV below.) Watson substitutes an account based on a distinction between what an agent desires and what he values, and he takes an agent's values to be those principles and ends which the agent desires when he is being rational. Watson is right to introduce intellect into the hierarchical notion of the self, but I think it is a mistake to suppose that the valuings which play a role in free will are just the agent's rational principles and ends. In "Free Action and Free Will" (*op. cit.*), Watson expresses dissatisfaction with his earlier view for the same reason.

to say that the agent in the latter case has free will.[12] Another recurrent complaint is that (2) Frankfurt's account of free will leaves us with an infinite regress of volitions. For an agent to act with free will with respect to some first-order volition V_1 apparently requires that he have a higher-order volition V_2 with which V_1 is in accord. But then it seems that V_2 itself must be freely willed in order for the agent to be acting with free will; for V_2 to be freely willed, however, requires a higher-order volition V_3 with which V_2 is in accord, and V_3 itself will require a higher-order volition V_4, and so on.[13] Finally, some critics have objected to Frankfurt's account on the grounds that (3) it rests on an unwarranted notion of what counts as "the real you" and on a false theory of what counts as external or alien to a person. When we say that freedom is basically a matter of doing what one wants and that what one really wants is determined by considering one's higher-order volitions, we clearly presuppose that the first-order desires not in accord with the second-order volitions are not something the agent himself really wants, that these repudiated first-order desires are not part of the agent's self but somehow external to it. But such an understanding of the real self is at best controversial. Why should we identify an agent's self only with his higher-order volitions? Why should we suppose that these higher-order volitions represent what the agent really wants? Has psychology not made us aware that the darker sides of our nature, the repudiated or repressed first-order desires, are just as much part of our selves as our higher-order desires and the first-order desires we approve of?[14] The revised Frankfurt account is, I think, not vulnerable to any of these criticisms.

On the revised account,[15] an agent forms a second-order desire by reasoning (rationally or otherwise, consciously or not) about his first-order desires; and a second-order desire is a direct result of an agent's intellect representing a certain first-order desire as the good to be pursued. Given this connection between intellect and second-order desires, an agent cannot be a passive bystander to his second-order volitions. To be a second-order volition, a volition must be the result of reasoning on the agent's part. Even if it were coherent to suppose that one agent, say, Verkhovensky, could directly produce some reasoning in the mind of another, such as Stavrogin, that reasoning would not be Stavrogin's but rather Verkhovensky's (or at any rate a product of Verkhovensky's reasoning). If Verkhovensky continuously produced thoughts in Stavrogin, then Stavrogin would have ceased to be a person and would instead be

12. See, e.g., Shatz, *op. cit.*, pp. 468/9.
13. See, e.g., David Zimmerman, "Hierarchical Motivation and Freedom of the Will," *Pacific Philosophical Quarterly*, LXII (1981): 358ff.
14. See, e.g., Thalberg, "Hierarchical Analyses of Unfree Action," *Canadian Journal of Philosophy*, VIII (1978): 211–225.
15. For Frankfurt's own response, see "Three Concepts of Free Action II," pp. 121/2.

something like Verkhovensky's puppet. On the other hand, suppose Verkhovensky produced thoughts in Stavrogin's mind only occasionally, so that Stavrogin remained a person. In the computations leading to an action, Stavrogin's own intellect would take cognizance of the thought Verkhovensky had produced in Stavrogin's mind, and Stavrogin would then either accept or reject Verkhovensky's thought as a result of Stavrogin's own reasoning (however tacit or irrational that reasoning may be). As Stavrogin acts, then, the first-order volition stemming from his reasoning and the accompanying second-order desire will be Stavrogin's, not Verkhovensky's. Either way, Stavrogin would not have any second-order volitions produced by Verkhovensky. So, on the revised Frankfurt account, an agent's second-order volitions cannot be produced by someone else.

As for objection (2), Frankfurt himself believes that there is no theoretical limit to the levels of higher-order desires which a person may have, and that in general only common sense and fatigue keep a person from entertaining ever higher levels of higher-order desires.[16] On the revised Frankfurt account, however, the claim that the levels of higher-order desires may be infinite does not hold. In formulating a second-order volition an agent is bringing reason to bear on a state of his will and either approving or rejecting it. But in forming a third-order volition, the agent is not reiterating the process gone through to formulate a second-order volition. On the model the revised Frankfurt account gives of forming second-order volitions, forming a third-order volition consists in reasoning about and either accepting or rejecting a second-order volition. So an agent has a third-order volition V_3 to bring about some second-order volition V_2 in himself only if his intellect at the time of the willing represents V_2, under some description, as the good to be pursued. But since V_2 is a desire for a first-order volition V_1 generated by reason's representing V_1 (at that time) as the good to be pursued, V_3 will consist just in reaffirming the original reasoning about V_1 which led to V_2. In forming a third-order volition and considering whether he wants to have the relevant second-order volition, the agent will consider whether a desire for a desire for some action p (or state of affairs q) is the good to be pursued. But a desire for a desire for p (or q) will be a good to be pursued just in case the desire for p (or q) is a good to be pursued, and that in turn will depend on whether the agent considers p (or q), under some description, at that time, a good to be pursued. So a third-order volition that supports a currently held second-order volition is in effect just the expression of a reevaluating and affirming of the reason-

16. See "Freedom of the Will and the Concept of a Person," *op. cit.*, p. 16. Frankfurt returns to this problem in "Identification and Wholeheartedness," in this volume where he analyzes the notion of wholeheartedness and uses it as the basis for a response to this problem.

ing that originally led to V1.[17] And, in the same way, a third-order volition that rejects a currently held second-order volition will just be an expression of the reevaluation and rejection of the reasoning that led to the second-order volition. A third-order volition, then, is a result of a recalculation of the reasoning that originally underlay a second-order volition.

I do not mean to suggest that third-order volitions must always collapse into second-order volitions. It is possible for an agent to have third-order desires that are not only distinct from, but even discordant with, his second-order desires. This is so because volitions and desires, like emotions, are not always *immediately* responsive to reasoning. Even after we are quite sure that a danger is entirely past, we may nonetheless continue to feel some fear; and for a while, until the emotion subsides, we may need to remind ourselves recurrently that there is no cause for fear. Similarly, a second-order desire may take time to fade even when the agent has repudiated the reasoning that generated it. Consider someone whose childhood among Southern Baptists has left him with a desire to avoid alcohol and a second-order desire to have such a desire. Suppose that this person subsequently repudiates his childhood religion and, among other things, joins a sailing club where beer is regularly served after races. He will then have a first-order desire to drink beer, in order to fit in and be companionable and perhaps also to indulge a newly acquired taste for beer; but he may also notice in himself, as a surviving trace of childhood inclination, guilt at drinking and a second-order desire to have the sort of will which wills not to drink. Then he will remind himself that he has repudiated his Baptist background and that there is no harm and even some positive good in drinking a few beers. In this case, then, he will have a third-order desire not to have the second-order desire bequeathed him by his upbringing. This third-order desire is thus a temporary measure to bring his second-order desire into line with a change in his reasoning, when he has repudiated his former reasoning and found his second-order desires slow in adjusting to the change.[18]

17. It is, of course, also possible that, in a case of the sort I have been describing, an agent might reevaluate his original reasoning, reject it as unsatisfactory, and yet adopt the same second-order volition as before, although for different reasons. In such a case, the third-order volition is a result of reevaluating the reasoning and reaffirming not the original reasoning but rather just its conclusion.

18. There are also cases in which an agent's reasoning is confused and warrants conflicting second-order desires. An agent who notices such a conflict in his second-order desires and who reflects on it may then sort out the confusion in his reasoning and form a third-order volition in consequence. Nothing in this account entails that the agent's sorting out of his reasoning and accepting only one side of his divided second-order desires will be stable or permanent. In Dostoevsky's novel *The Possessed*, Verkhovensky swings from being contemptuous of Mrs. Stavrogin and rejecting the desires designed to please her to being infatuated with her and yearning to have the desires that will win her admiration. In fact, the revised Frankfurt account and Dostoevsky's portrayal of the vacillating Verkhovensky

Apart from such cases, however, a third-order (or any higher-order) desire or volition will collapse into a second-order desire or volition. Even in the case of the beer-drinking lapsed Baptist, the third-order desire will always be just a reflection of a certain second-order desire. The lapsed Baptist's third-order desire to have a second-order volition that wills to will drinking is just a result of his reasoning that (at the time of the willing, under some description) drinking is a good to be pursued, that a desire for drinking is consequently also a good to be pursued, and that therefore his second-order desire for a will that wills not to drink is a desire to be repudiated. If this Baptist now returns to his childhood convictions and again becomes convinced that drinking is wrong, he will not now form a fourth-order volition not to have his previous third-order volition. Instead, he will have once more reevaluated the reasoning behind the desire to drink and this time rejected it. He will consequently change his second-order volition to accommodate this new alteration in his reasoning, but he will not form a fourth-order volition. The third-order volition stemmed from his efforts to repress the second-order desire habitual from his youth, and his change of beliefs will carry with it the cessation of those efforts. Any attempt, then, to describe his state in terms of a fourth-order (or even higher-order) volition will collapse into the formulation of a second-order volition. So, on the revised Frankfurt account, the number of levels of higher-order desires is not infinite but is rather limited to two or three.

Freedom of the will on the revised Frankfurt account should consequently not be taken as entailing that the will is free only if an act of willing is in accord with some higher-order volition. On this view, the will is free with respect to a volition V just in case V is accepted by the agent because his intellect approves of V (at that time, under some description) as the good to be pursued, and there is no higher-order desire of the agent's with which V is discordant.[19] Second-order desires can fit this definition of freedom without postulating higher-order desires over them. A second-order desire is itself an expression of the agent's reasoning and therefore *eo ipso* accepted by the agent as approved by his

---

give a vivid explanation of the line "a double-minded man is unstable in all his ways." We might add that such a man is also unfree. Because he has conflicting second-order desires, whatever his corresponding first-order volition is, it will be discordant with one of his second-order desires.

19. From this definition of free will together with the description of the relation between intellect and will sketched above, it is easy to see that we can generate the three Frankfurt criteria for freedom of the will. When an agent's reasoning approves a first-order volition V_1 as the good to be pursued at the time of willing, under some description, then the agent's will also forms a second-order desire for that first-order volition; and the intellect's (rational or irrational) approval of V_1, manifested by the second-order desire, is at least part of what makes V_1 a volition rather than an ineffective first-order desire.

reasoning.[20] If an agent's reasoning approves a desire as the good to be pursued, it must also in the very same process approve the desire for that desire. An agent who at one and the same time unambiguously considered a certain desire as a good to be pursued and also rejected the desire for that desire as not good would not be sane. So, on the revised Frankfurt account, a second-order volition may be a free volition without itself being the object of some higher-order volition.

Objection (3) has been given its most forceful presentation by Irving Thalberg.[21] Why, he asks, should we identify ourselves with our higher-order volitions? Have psychologists (and, in particular, Freud) not shown us that the "darker, savage, and nonrational aspects [of ourselves] are equally—if not more—important"? (*ibid.*, p. 224). And if an agent is to be identified with certain of his darker first-order desires, then, in making such desires his will, he would be willing as he himself wants to will. Consequently, Frankfurt is wrong in holding that an agent's freedom depends on his having second-order volitions and governing his first-order desires so that they are not discordant with those second-order volitions. An agent may be doing just what he himself really wants, and so be free, when he acts against his second-order volitions and follows his savage or nonrational desires.

On the revised Frankfurt account, it will not be quite right to say that an agent is to be identified with his second-order volitions. An agent wills what he really wants and is thus free when his first-order volitions are not discordant with his second-order desires, not because the agent is simply declared to be more truly identified with his second-order than with his first-order desires, but rather because the agent's second-order desires are the expressions of his intellect's reflection on his will, and the agent is to be identified with his intellect. It is, of course, possible to recast Thalberg's criticism so that it is directed against the revised version of Frankfurt's account. Why, one could ask, should an agent identify himself with his reasoning faculty rather than with his first-order desires (or his emotions, or subconscious, or any other element of his nature)? But this version of objection (3) is based on a confusion; it depends for its plausibility on a failure to distinguish two different senses of identification.

To see that this is so, consider a fictional variation on the biblical story of Tamar and Amnon (2 Sam. 13:1–20). According to the biblical story, David's son Amnon fell in love with his half-sister Tamar, tried to seduce her, raped her, and then rejected her with hatred. Suppose (contrary to the story in Samuel) that Tamar became pregnant as a result of the rape and bore a son, who quickly grew to look just like his father Amnon, and

---

20. Except for the special sort of case sketched in the example of the beer-drinking lapsed Baptist, where third-order desires fill this role.

21. "Hierarchical Analyses of Unfree Action," *op. cit.*

that no acceptable provisions for the child's care would be available if Tamar rejected him. In such circumstances Tamar would no doubt be torn between conflicting attitudes toward the child. On the one hand, she will recognize that the child is not identical with his father but rather an independent person, who is entirely innocent of the crime that resulted in his conception, and in this spirit she will want to cherish the child and be a good mother to him. On the other hand, when she looks at the child, she will see in him the hated face of the man who raped her; and if she is an ordinary human being, feelings of hatred and revulsion toward the child will rise in her as she recognizes signs of the father in the son. Now, suppose that on one particularly bad day when the child comes running to her, instead of welcoming him she flares up at him for no reason and hits him, because on that occasion the revulsion toward him has gotten the upper hand in her.

As she attempts to sort out her thoughts and feelings after this event, two interpretations of her action are open to her. She could say to herself: "I love my son. How could I treat him in that way? I've lost control of myself." Or she could say: "I can't stand that Amnon-faced child; I hate his father, and the sad truth is that I hate him, too." Tamar has been divided between her first-order desire to cherish the child and her first-order desire to reject the child; and as she reflects on what she had done, she is in effect asking herself with which half of her divided will she identifies herself. We might be inclined to say that she is not to be identified with either side of her conflicting first-order desires; rather, what she is is a person struggling with a divided will. Such an understanding of Tamar may be correct as regards her past state, but it ceases to be viable once she has attacked the child, because she must then decide how to react to what she had done; and which of the two interpretations Tamar places on her action will make a great difference to the way in which life goes on between her and her son. She will, for example, have a very difficult sort of relationship with the child if she identifies herself in her own mind as a hater of the child. In that case she is in effect assenting to her rejection of him, and she will consequently not repent but excuse her action to herself, thinking: "I couldn't help it; I hate him for what his father did to me."

So Thalberg is certainly right in holding that, on some occasions, an agent is in fact to be identified with her darker first-order desires, as in the fictional example of the unrepentant Tamar. Notice, however, that, even in such a case, the reason for postulating such an identification is a second-order volition on the agent's part. In identifying herself with her first-order desire to reject the child, Tamar is evidently assenting to that desire and thereby ceasing to assent to the first-order desire to cherish him. But to say she assents to the first-order desire to reject the child is to say that she has a second-order volition to have a first-order volition to reject the child. On the view of the relation between will and intellect sketched above, what has happened is that her reasoning faculty has (at that time) rationalized her rejecting the child and found it acceptable, and she has consequently formed a second-order volition to make her first-order desire to reject the child her will.

In this sense of identification, then, for an agent to identify herself with some part of herself, such as certain of her first-order desires, is for her to form a second-order volition that accepts or assents to that part of herself. On this sense of identification, it is clear that an agent may identify herself with any of her first-order desires, no matter how savage or irrational they may in fact be; and what an agent identifies herself with is clearly up to her and depends on her reason and will. But it is important to see that, contrary to what Thalberg supposes, this conclusion in no way undermines the hierarchical account of the self. For what distinguishes the Tamar who identifies herself with her darker desires from the Tamar who repents them is not the presence of a first-order desire to reject the child (for that desire is present in both), but rather the presence in the unrepentant Tamar of a second-order volition assenting to those darker first-order desires. This second-order volition the repentant Tamar, who struggles against her desire to reject the child, clearly lacks.[22]

But there is also another sense in which an agent can be identified with some part of her character. However erring and faulty it may be, Tamar's reasoning faculty is essential to her, as no other part of her character is. If she were incapable of emotion, or if she were to become apathetic through depression, it would still be possible to consider Tamar a person.[23] But if her reasoning faculty were destroyed, she could no longer be counted a person; certainly she could not enter into any personal relationships, and the ability to do so seems a hallmark of a person.

There is a second sense of identification, then, in which it is correct to say that any agent is always to be identified with her reasoning faculty (whether it functions well or badly). This is not the same as the sense of identification in which the unrepentant Tamar identifies with her first-order desire to reject the child. An agent does not have a reasoning faculty in virtue of some second-order volition assenting to it;[24] and, in

---

22. The same sort of analysis could be given of an agent who identified herself with her baser first-order desires without the sort of internal struggle I have postulated for Tamar.

23. Even on the revised Frankfurt account, an apathetic Tamar would count as a person if she had second-order desires, since, without first-order desires, there cannot be in her any discord between first- and second-order desires. And even very apathetic or severely depressed people can have the second-order desire not to be depressed any more.

24. Although it is, of course, open to the agent to form a second-order volition regarding a first-order desire to destroy his reasoning faculty. We can imagine a contemporary version of Dostoevsky's Kirilov, wanting to have a first-order volition to lobotomize himself through drugs or surgery in order to put a stop to the torments his reasoning always brings him.

this second sense of identification, it is not up to an agent to decide what she identifies herself with. Rather, in this sense of identification, an agent is to be identified with what is essential to her as a person, namely, her reasoning faculty. So, on the revised Frankfurt account, we are not simply trading Frankfurt's assumption that agents are to be identified with their second-order volitions for the new assumption that agents are to be identified with their intellects. What we have done instead is show that an agent's reasoning faculty is integral to her existence as a person. If we look to know what *she herself* really wants, we must consider what her reasoning faculty (at a certain time, under a certain description) assents to. (And, as the story of Tamar shows, what her reasoning faculty assents to may be something that is, objectively considered, quite irrational.)

Second-order desires represent an agent's reasoning since they stem from the reflection of an agent's intellect on her state of will. Therefore, an agent is to be identified with her second-order desires as much as with her reasoning; her second-order desires represent what her intellect assents to (and so what *she* assents to) among her first-order desires. Consequently, on the revised Frankfurt account, it is correct, contrary to objection (3), to hold that second-order desires represent what an agent really wants. In fact, this second sense of identification is presupposed by the first. We can agree with Thalberg that an agent such as the unrepentant Tamar identifies with her base first-order desires because her identifying with them consists in her forming a second-order volition assenting to them. But the reason why the presence of such a second-order volition suffices for supposing Tamar to be identified with her desire to reject the child is that the second-order volition stems from Tamar's reasoning faculty and, in virtue of that connection, indicates what Tamar herself really wants. So the sorts of considerations Thalberg raises against Frankfurt's account, when they are properly understood, not only do not undermine, but instead actually support, Frankfurt's hierarchical analysis of the self.

V. APPLICATIONS TO ISSUES IN THE PHILOSOPHY OF RELIGION

The revised Frankfurt account of a person and of free will is very fruitful for understanding a variety of religious practices and doctrines, such as the practices of adult baptism, confirmation, asceticism, the doctrine of justification by faith, the nature of heaven and hell, and the point of Romans 7.[25] But in the remainder of this paper I shall concentrate

25. I pursue some of these topics in forthcoming papers.

on the application of that account to just two Christian doctrines, namely, that God sanctifies some people and that he hardens the hearts of others.

The doctrine of sanctification includes as a central component the claim that God intervenes in the minds of some people in order to make them morally better than they would otherwise be. Many Christian theologians, however, also hold that human beings have free will, where 'free will' is to be understood in an incompatibilist sense. From these two views a number of puzzles arise. First, to be morally good one must freely will some moral good. But then it seems that it is not possible even for an omnipotent God to make anyone morally good, since it is not possible for anyone to cause an individual freely to will anything (where freedom of will is understood in an incompatibilist sense). Second, even if it were possible for God to make an agent freely will a good he would not have willed otherwise, it does not seem as if his doing so could count as making that agent morally better. If God causes the agent to will some moral good, then we might attribute some moral goodness to God in consequence, but why would we attribute moral goodness to the agent, who is nothing but a puppet of God's will? Finally, if God could in fact make a person morally good, why would he not do so for all persons? How could a good God fail to impart such a benefit to all human beings, so that there would never be any moral evil on earth and no one would ever be brought to hell?

To see the appropriate resolution of these puzzles it is important to understand that, on the Christian doctrine of sanctification, those whom God sanctifies are Christians who are still struggling with moral evil in themselves. Besides holding the traditional Christian beliefs about God, such a person will also believe both that certain things (such as beating one's wife, for example) are wrong and should not be done and that he himself is engaged in some of these morally wrong practices. Consider, for instance, some Christian Patricius who beats his wife Monica.[26] On the revised Frankfurt account, we will say that, because Patricius believes it is wrong for him to beat Monica, he forms a second-order desire to make the first-order desire not to beat his wife his will. But when the fit of wrath is on him, he acts on his first-order desire to beat her. When the fit has passed, he laments his action and recognizes that by his own lights he should have acted on his general prohibition to himself not to beat her. Patricius does not have control of himself; he does not have the strength of will to make his first-order desires conform

---

26. Of course, the real wife-beating Patricius was pagan, according to the account left us by his son Augustine; and no doubt when the patience of his wife Monica had won his conversion to Christianity, he abandoned his practice of wife-beating along with his paganism.

to his second-order desires, and he is not able to make himself have the will he wants to have.

Suppose that Patricius also recognizes that this is his state and prays to God for help. Patricius has reasoned that his beating Monica is an evil but that he is a failure at his efforts to stop it, and that he needs God's help to be the sort of man he himself can approve of. Patricius's prayer for help expresses a second-order volition for God to alter Patricius's first-order will. What *Patricius* wants is for God to change his will in such a way that he no longer wills to beat his wife. If God were so to alter Patricius's will, Patricius's first-order volitions would be in accord with his second-order desires; and, on the revised Frankfurt account, Patricius's will would consequently be free. In giving Patricius a first-order volition not to beat his wife, then, God would not be destroying Patricius's freedom of the will but actually establishing it, since while Patricius's first-order volitions are discordant with his second-order desires, he does not have free will, however free his action of wife-beating may be.

Of course, the strength of second-order desires may vary. As Augustine tells the story, when he prayed to God to give him a will for sexual continence, he made the mental reservation "But not yet." How exactly to characterize Augustine's second-order desire in this case is not certain; but it is clear that, if God had given Augustine a will for sexual continence on that occasion in response to such a prayer, he would have been acting against Augustine's own second-order desires. The result would have been not to evoke or enhance Augustine's free will but to undermine it, because the consequent first-order volition for sexual continence would have been against Augustine's second-order desire to have continence "but not yet." So, in general, sanctification will be a slow process. In response to such half-hearted prayers for help as Augustine's, God can produce some alteration in an individual's first-order will, by strengthening, to the degree warranted by the prayer for help, those first-order desires which are in accord with that individual's second-order desires. But if he is not to destroy freedom of the will, God will not be able to produce a first-order volition unless the second-order desire in the prayer for help is like the whole-hearted turning of the will experienced by Paul on the road to Damascus. Even with a second-order desire for God to alter his will, then, Patricius may find that his struggle against the habit of wife-beating takes some time to win.

On this understanding of sanctification, it is clear that God is not violating an individual's free will in sanctifying him, even when free will is understood in an incompatibilist sense. What God is doing in sanctification is altering an agent's first-order desires to bring them into accord with that agent's own second-order desires, so that, in sanctifying an agent, God is producing or enhancing the agent's freedom of will. Furthermore, it is also clear that the alteration of will God effects in sanctification really does produce moral goodness on the part of the agent. In being sanctified, the agent does not become God's puppet, a simple adjunct to God's will; on the contrary, in sanctifying him, God is helping that agent to have the will the agent himself wants to have. The consequent moral goodness has its origin in the agent's own volitions, not just in God's as the objection to the doctrine of sanctification had supposed. Finally, on this view of sanctification, it is clear why it is not possible for God simply to sanctify everyone. The process of God's sanctifying a person consists in God's bringing an agent's first-order desires into line with his second-order desires in response to the agent's second-order volition that God do so. Where the requisite second-order desires and volitions are absent, God cannot alter the first-order desires without undermining or destroying freedom of will.[27] And, as the objections to the doctrine of sanctification indicate, it is not possible for an alteration of an agent's will which undermines the will's freedom to result in moral goodness on that agent's part. God cannot make human beings morally better unless they will that he do so.

Someone might think that such an account of sanctification is guilty of Pelagianism. But it does not entail the claim that an agent can achieve sanctification primarily by the exertions of his own will. Instead, this account holds that all the work resulting in moral improvement is done by God in response to the agent's recognition that he needs God's help and his willing to have it. (Of course, a person's willing of God's help is itself a response to God's action in that person's life; but the relation of God's action to such willing is part of the doctrine of justification, and what is at issue here is just the doctrine of sanctification—and not even the whole doctrine of sanctification, since faith, hope, and love are left out of account.) It is true that, on this account of sanctification, an act of free will on the agent's part is necessary for God's work of sanctification, but such a view was also held by Augustine and Aquinas, who are scarcely noted for their adherence to Pelagianism.

As for the doctrine that God sometimes hardens hearts, the classic text is in Exodus 7–14, where God is said to harden Pharaoh's heart so that Pharaoh does not weaken and allow the Israelites to leave Egypt, although the exodus of the Israelites from Egypt is the ultimate object of God's actions in the story, and God punishes Pharaoh for his resistance. That this is not a unique or isolated instance of God's hardening a heart is made explicit in Paul's epistle to the Romans, where Paul generalizes on the story of Pharaoh and concludes that "God hardens whom he

27. If an individual were a wanton, in Frankfurt's sense, it would be possible for God to alter his first-order volitions without undermining any freedom of his, because such an individual by definition has no second-order desires and so fails to meet one of the conditions for freedom of will. If there are any human beings who are wantons, they will then be exceptions to the claim I make here.

will." This doctrine raises two questions concerning God's goodness. First, how could a good God ever intervene in an agent's willing in such a way as to make that agent morally worse? Willing that a human being become morally worse seems the essence of malice, and bringing about a person's moral deterioration is the sort of action typically attributed to Satan. At any rate, it seems utterly incompatible with perfect goodness. Second, even if it were somehow compatible with God's goodness to make an agent morally worse, how could a good God punish that agent for the moral failing God himself has induced in him? On the contrary, since the will that initiated and produced the moral failing is God's, any punishment appropriate for that moral failing seems to be deserved by God, not by the agent manipulated by God. But, on the revised Frankfurt account, there is a way to understand the doctrine that God hardens hearts which satisfactorily answers these questions and which shows this doctrine to be the mirror image of the doctrine of sanctification.

At one point in his diaries, Goebbels pauses to reflect on his own reviewing of German newsreel footage that shows the incredible devastation of Poland wrought by the German armies. Insofar as Goebbels has any morals at all, he seems to hold a primitive sort of divine-command ethics with Hitler fulfilling the role usually assigned to God. So he has no moral compunctions about Poland's devastation; on the contrary, his reason seems to regard it as morally approvable in virtue of having been commanded by Hitler. In addition, Goebbels is determined to further the German war effort in any way he can; and if the war requires inflicting more suffering of the sort visited on Poland, Goebbels is calmly resolute in his willingness to inflict it. In short, Goebbels has first-order desires to wreak the sort of devastation Poland suffered whenever doing so serves Germany's interests, and he also has second-order desires accepting and assenting to those first-order desires.

Nonetheless, as he reviews the newsreel from Poland, those first-order desires begin to slip. It may be that successful efforts at repressing normal human compassion consume a great deal of psychic energy; and since Goebbels's complaint of fatigue is one of the most frequent themes of the diaries, we might suppose that sheer exhaustion is sapping his ability to make his first-order desires conform to his second-order ones. At any rate, Goebbels notices those first-order desires slipping, and he addresses an exhortation to himself: "be hard, my heart, be hard." This exhortation to himself expresses, in effect, a second-order desire. He wants his heart to be hard; that is, he wants to have a first-order will which assents to the sufferings of the Poles and which is consequently in accord with his second-order desires. Patricius's prayer to God for help expresses a second-order volition that God govern Patricius's first-order will for him, and it shows that Patricius despairs of governing his first-order desires himself. Goebbels's exhortation to himself, on the other hand, indicates an attempt on Goebbels's part to reassert his own control over his first-order desires, and it expresses a second-order desire that Goebbels's first-order desires be in conformity with his second-order desires to make his will serve the German war effort.

Now suppose that because of fatigue or some similar reason Goebbels is unable to reassert control over his first-order desires. Then his first-order desires to inflict suffering on the Poles will weaken, and some first-order desires to relieve their suffering may even appear. In his moment of weakness, he might even (for example) order a shipment of food sent to Poland. A first-order volition to relieve the Poles is clearly morally superior to a first-order volition to cause their suffering. So, if Goebbels weakens in this way, we might suppose that he will in consequence become morally better in some sense. And yet this supposed moral improvement will occur by a sort of accident, and it will certainly be against Goebbels's will, since what Goebbels himself really wants is represented by his second-order desires. In fact, insofar as his first-order desires to ravage the Poles weaken and the opposing first-order desires intensify, Goebbels's free will is undermined, because the new first-order desires are an obstacle to Goebbels's willing what he wants to will and thus constitute a hindrance to Goebbels's freedom of will. Suppose that God were to respond to Goebbels's exhortation to himself to be hard as if it were the atheist's analogue to a prayer, and suppose that God hardened Goebbels's heart for him, supplying the strength of will Goebbels in his fatigue was missing. Such an action on God's part would in no way violate Goebbels's free will. Rather, God would in that case be giving Goebbels what Goebbels himself wants. He would, in effect, be preserving Goebbels's free will from being undermined or destroyed, because in strengthening Goebbels's first-order desires for the ravaging of the Poles, God keeps Goebbels's first-order desires from being discordant with his second-order desires and so helps Goebbels to fulfill one of the requirements for freedom of will.

Finally, in hardening Goebbels, God would, I think, not be making Goebbels morally worse than he would have been without God's intervention. One might suppose that, if the sort of strengthening God grants Patricius makes him morally better, then analogously the sort of strengthening given Goebbels must make him morally worse. But the two cases are disanalogous in a way which vitiates this inference. Consider Patricius when he fails to act in accordance with his second-order desire assenting to the first-order desire not to beat his wife. In this case as I have constructed it, Patricius is engaged in a struggle within himself; in beating his wife, he acts against what he himself believes to be good. If it is right that an erring conscience binds (and I think it is), then, even if wife-beating were not in itself a moral evil, Patricius would be made morally worse by beating his wife in virtue of putting into action what *he* believes is morally bad. For the case of Goebbels to be analogous in a way that would warrant saying that God's intervention makes Goebbels morally worse than he would have been without God's intervention, Goebbels's state as he acts to help Poland would have to be a mirror image of Patricius's state as he beats his wife: Goebbels would have to believe that what he was doing in helping Poland was a good thing, and he would thus have to be acting in accordance with his moral beliefs. If this were Goebbels's state, it seems clear that hardening his heart would make him morally worse than he would otherwise have been. It would also violate his free will on the revised Frankfurt account. Given both considerations, a good God would never harden anyone's heart in such a case.

But the actual case of Goebbels under consideration here is different. In fact, Goebbels believes that helping Poland is a bad thing; his intellect and his second-order desires are against doing so. Consequently, his state in helping Poland is not the mirror image of Patricius's but rather just the same: in helping Poland he would be putting into practice what he himself believes morally bad. So he does not become morally better by helping Poland in this frame of mind; and, if an erring conscience binds, then there is even a sense in which he becomes morally worse by doing so when he believes it wrong. At any rate, it is not true that, by hardening Goebbels's heart in these circumstances, God makes him morally worse by preventing an action that would contribute to Goebbels's moral improvement. In such a case, and only in such a case, God can harden a person's heart without making him morally worse than he would have been otherwise.

One might suppose that, even so, Goebbels is made worse just by having his evil first-order desires strengthened. If we suppose that Patricius is made morally better in virtue of having his good first-order desires strengthened even when they are not strengthened enough to constitute an effective desire, a volition on which he acts, then the mere fact that Goebbels's evil first-order desires are strengthened makes him morally worse than he was before. I am willing to concede this claim. The problem with the radical sort of evil in which a moral monster such as Goebbels is sunk is that it blinds and distorts the conscience,[28] and even an erring conscience binds. Consequently, Goebbels is made morally worse than he was before whether he acts to afflict the Poles or refrains. If he refrains from destruction of the Poles, he undermines the German war effort in Poland and so betrays his chosen master, Hitler. He thus knowingly does what he believes to be wicked and is consequently made morally worse. On the other hand, since the destruction of Poland is in reality an objective evil, the desire for contributing to that destruction (apart from mitigating circumstances, absent here) is also evil; and the

28. What makes Goebbels a moral monster is that his intellect and second-order volitions are on the side of a major evil *and* he has no dissenting second-order desires. If he had dissenting second-order desires, then it would not be the case that God enhanced his freedom of will by hardening his heart.

intensification of an evil desire does perhaps imply intensified evil in the desirer. If that is right, then, because Goebbels's conscience is distorted, his moral evil will increase whether God hardens his heart or leaves him alone.

The question, then, is which of the options open to God, hardening Goebbels or leaving him alone, produces the lesser of two evils; and there are several reasons for supposing the answer is hardening Goebbels's heart. As I have been at pains to show, by hardening Goebbels, God preserves a certain freedom of will for Goebbels which would be undermined if Goebbels acted against his moral beliefs. Second, it seems to me arguable that there would be some moral appropriateness in God's fulfilling Goebbels's quasi prayer for hardness of heart. There is something at least morally dubious about a villain such as Goebbels falling into some creditable action simply through fatigue. And, just as it seems right for God to answer Patricius's prayer for help by granting him the strength of will he wants to have, so it seems that Goebbels is getting what he deserves if in answer to his quasi prayer God grants him the strength to persist in the evil he has resolved on. Finally, it may be that in the case of a desperately evil man, such as Goebbels, giving him the strength to have as wicked a will as he wants is hazarding a last shot at reforming him. In hardening him, on my account, God acts only on Goebbels's first-order desires, strengthening them to bring them into conformity with his evil second-order desires; but Goebbels's intellect and second-order desires are in no way cemented in their evil when God hardens Goebbels's heart. In giving Goebbels the first-order desires he wishes, God may be providing Goebbels with a mirror, in his character and its consequences, to show him the evil of his wish; and Goebbels's understanding the evil of his second-order desire is the requisite first step to straightening his distorted conscience, to reforming his reason and second-order desires, and thus to beginning a moral rebirth.

In consequence, I think, we have our answers to the two questions raised above concerning the doctrine of hardening the heart. On this understanding of the doctrine, God hardens a heart when he strengthens evil first-order desires so that a second-order will bent on such evil may maintain its control over those first-order desires when fatigue or some other nonmoral accident might have caused the control to weaken. In doing so, God is not violating the agent's free will, and he is also not causing the agent to become morally worse than he would otherwise have been. And if God were to assign blame and punishment to an agent for what that agent did in consequence of God's hardening his heart, God would in no way be unjust to him, for the agent's own will is the source and origin of the evil the agent does. So, when God is said in Exodus to harden Pharaoh's heart, we should understand the text as claiming that God is doing for Pharaoh just what Pharaoh wants and lacks the strength to do for himself, namely, making Pharaoh's first-order volitions correspond to his evil second-order desire. In fact, this interpretation of the hardening of Pharaoh's heart helps to explain an otherwise perplexing feature of the story, namely, that God's hardening Pharaoh's heart alternates with Pharaoh's own hardening of his heart.

Someone might object to this account that it heartlessly neglects the welfare of the Poles, because whatever we might want to say about the merits of allowing Goebbels to fall into some momentary first-order desires to relieve Poland when we are considering only Goebbels's state of character, it is apparently undeniable that such a moment of weakness would have afforded the Poles relief. Therefore, just for the sake of the Poles, a good God would not harden Goebbels's heart. But this objection rests on the mistaken assumption that the fate of the Poles depends solely on the state of Goebbels's will. On the contrary, it is important to see that, if there is a God, there is *no* sort of inviolable connection between the state of Goebbels's will and the welfare of the Poles; and, from God's point of view, the fate of the Poles and the condition of Goebbels's will constitute two entirely separate issues. If Goebbels failed to have a moment of compassion for Poland's sufferings, it was still open to God to aid the Poles in some other way; and if in consequence of God's hardening Goebbels's heart, Goebbels planned some new suffering for them, it would nonetheless be possible for God to interfere (in any number of ways) to prevent Goebbels from successfully accomplishing what he willed. If God does allow harm to Poland in consequence of some act of will on Goebbels's part, it is because of a separate decision on God's part about the Poles. What sort of decision that might be or how it might be justified are no doubt hard to explain, but no harder than any other instance of the problem of evil; and that problem lies just outside the scope of this paper.

In this way, then, the revised Frankfurt account, which gives a cogent and illuminating analysis of the nature of freedom and the concept of a person, shows divine sanctification and hardening of the heart to be mirror images of each other. In each case, God responds to an agent's desires by giving that agent the first-order volition he wants. When he hardens an agent's heart, he strengthens evil first-order desires in conformity to a second-order desire bent on that evil; and when he sanctifies an agent, he strengthens the first-order desires that the agent's second-order desires want as the good for that agent. In neither case does God's affecting an agent's first-order willing interfere with that agent's free will, on the revised Frankfurt account of freedom of will.

Frankfurt's basic idea of the will as commanding itself seems to me to have great explanatory power in more than one area of philosophy. That it should be particularly fruitful for philosophy of religion is perhaps not surprising given the central role of will in religion.

Part III

MORAL RESPONSIBILITY AND
ALTERNATIVE POSSIBILITIES

cases.[2] A typical Frankfurt-style counterexample to PAP involves an agent, S, a mechanism of coercion, M (hypnosis, manipulation of brain pathways, etc.), and a series of actions, A_1A_n, which S is in the process of deciding among. In the example, S decides on some one of these actions, A_m, and decides in a way which prompts our intuitions to suppose both that his decision is freely made and that he bears responsibility for the action. But, the example continues, if in the process of deciding S had inclined to any action other than A_m, mechanism M would have operated and brought it about that S formed a volition to do A_m. It is consequently not possible for S to do otherwise than A_m, the example implies, and yet in actual fact S is responsible for what he does. PAP is thus false.

As an instance of a Frankfurt-style example, consider the following variation on an incident from Dostoevsky's *The Possessed.* Peter Verkhovensky wants a convict named Fedya to kill the Lebyatkin family, and he offers Fedya a large sum of money to do the murders. But Verkhovensky also has a back-up plan. Verkhovensky recognizes that the bribe may not be enough to make Fedya want to do the murders, and he watches for any sign that Fedya might reject his offer. (Or, we might suppose, he has the technology to monitor Fedya's neural pathways, and he looks for the firing of the first neurons in the neural pathway whose completed firing is necessary for rejection of the bribe.) If he detects in Fedya any movement toward a disinclination to accept the bribe (or if he detects the firing of the first neurons in the pathway necessary for rejection), Verkhovensky will have Fedya anesthetized and surgically fitted with a device that stimulates just those neural pathways necessary to bring about in Fedya an effective desire to murder the Lebyatkins. Because the anesthetizing and surgery put Verkhovensky to more trouble, he prefers to try bribery first; but if it looks as though there is any chance the bribery won't succeed, he will certainly put his alternate plan into effect. As things turn out, however, the alternate plan is unnecessary. Fedya is a

2. See, e.g., "Alternate Possibilities and Moral Responsibility." Frankfurt's case against PAP has been vigorously disputed by Peter Van Inwagen; see his "Ability and Responsibility," *Philosophical Review* 87 (1978), 201–24, reprinted in his book *An Essay on Free Will* (Oxford: Clarendon Press, 1983), pp. 161–82. Van Inwagen's strategy consists of tying responsibility to event particulars, where x and y are identical event particulars just in case they have the same causes. Then an agent is responsible for a particular event only in case he could have prevented that event particular. If successful, this strategy would be effective against certain common kinds of Frankfurt-style examples, including the one involving Fedya given below. It would not be effective, however, against the main cases considered in this paper (cases involving an impeccable deity, the redeemed in heaven, or agents who find inconceivable any alternative to the action they take), because in those cases, even if Van Inwagen's understanding of event particulars is correct and his strategy is successful, an agent who is apparently responsible for a particular event could not have prevented that event. For an interesting argument that Van Inwagen's strategy is in fact not successful, see John Martin Fischer, "Responsibility and Control," *Journal of Philosophy* 79 (1982), 24–40.

hardened criminal and desperate for cash besides; he grasps eagerly at Verkhovensky's offer and commits the murders with relish. It goes counter to the intuitions of most people to suppose that Fedya is not responsible for the murders. Underlying such intuitions is the thought that there is no reason to excuse Fedya in any way just because Verkhovensky had a plan for coercing him which he might have put into effect but in fact did not. It seems that considerations of moral blame or praise should be based on some intrinsic characteristic of Fedya's and not on considerations of what Verkhovensky or anyone else does in some other possible world. Furthermore, Fedya in the example is entirely ready, even eager, to commit the murders, and counterfactual claims about how Fedya might have been made murderous if he hadn't been willing to kill hardly seem to undermine the blameworthiness of the attitude he actually has. But if Fedya is responsible for murdering the Lebyatkins in such circumstances, then we have an apparent violation of PAP, since it was not open to Fedya not to murder the Lebyatkins.

This example also sheds some light on how PAP is to be interpreted. In the first place, PAP is clearly meant to apply to internal actions, such as willing to murder, as well as to external or bodily actions. We can hold a person responsible for what he wills even if he doesn't act on those volitions. A committed Fascist living in occupied France during the last war who willed the death by torture of Jewish men, women, and children but was prevented from acting on his will by his boss, a staunch member of the resistance, would nonetheless be morally blameworthy, and so morally responsible, for what he willed. In the case of Fedya, most of us would find him morally reprehensible for willing to murder an innocent family even if sudden paralysis, say, prevented him from translating his desires into action.[3] And yet in this example it is not open to Fedya not to will to murder the Lebyatkins because Verkhovensky's neurological device would stimulate those neural pathways in Fedya which would produce in him a volition to murder.

Secondly, when we say that it is not open to Fedya to do otherwise, it is clear that we do not mean that it is not possible that Fedya do otherwise. There is a possible world in which Fedya exists and Verkhovensky does not, for example; for that matter, there is a possible world in which Fedya never becomes a criminal and never has any criminal desires. So to say that it is not open to Fedya not to desire to murder the Lebyatkins is not to claim that there is no possible world in which Fedya exists and doesn't kill the Lebyatkins but rather to imply that Fedya's murdering the Lebyatkins is unavoidable for Fedya after a certain time. (And in general in this paper by 'at t it is open to S to do A', I will mean that it

3. An exception to this claim would be cases in which an external agent had implanted this willingness in Fedya when, left to himself, Fedya would have repudiated such willingness.

isn't the case at t that not doing A is unavoidable for S.) Analyses of un-avoidability are, of course, controversial, but for present purposes per-haps this will do:

> (U) An action A is unavoidable for an agent S just in case for any state of affairs x such that S has the power to bring about x, it is nec-essarily the case that, given the laws of nature and the history of the world, if S brings about x, then S does A.[4]

For the sake of clarity, then, we might recast PAP in this way:

> (PAP′) A person is morally responsible for an internal or external ac-tion of his only if that action was not unavoidable for him (where unavoidability is to be understood in the sense given in (U) above).

In subsequent references to PAP in this paper, the principle should be taken in the sense of (PAP′).

Frankfurt is a compatibilist, and attacks on PAP based on Frankfurt-style examples are generally supposed to give aid to compatibilists, who want to deny that causal determination of an agent's actions is incom-patible with the agent's acting freely and being responsible for his ac-tions. But not all incompatibilists can give unqualified adherence to PAP. In particular, Christian philosophers and theologians have traditionally maintained an incompatibilist or libertarian interpretation of free will, and yet there are Christian doctrines which seem to violate PAP. For ex-ample, the good angels (those who did not fall with Satan) and the re-deemed in heaven are said to have free will and to be morally responsible for what they do, but it is not open to them to do evil.[5] So for

---

4. I have based this formulation of unavoidability on one discussed by Thomas Flint, "Compatibilism and the Argument from Unavoidability," *Journal of Philosophy* 84 (1987), 423–40. That definition of unavoidability is couched in terms of a relation between an agent and a proposition; for ease of exposition only, I have rephrased it to substitute ac-tions for propositions. See also Peter Van Inwagen, *An Essay on Free Will*, p. 68. It should be pointed out that as it stands (U) is still too broad. Because we obviously do not want to say that Fedya murders the Lebyatkins in all possible worlds, we need some way of spec-ifying a subset of possible worlds in order to explain our intuition that for Fedya murder-ing the Lebyatkins is inevitable, although it isn't necessary that Fedya commit the murders. But among the worlds picked out by (U) there will be some in which Fedya begins to in-cline not to commit the murders and Verkhovensky dies of a heart attack before he can implant or activate the mechanism causing Fedya to murder, or in which the implanted mechanism is inactivated by some sort of chance event, or in which Fedya dies before the murders can be carried out, and so on. Adding the needed conditions to make (U) pre-cisely right is likely to prove a byzantine process, which would distract from the main focus of this paper; and so for my purposes here I will content myself with this imprecise formulation.

5. See, for example, Anselm, *De libertate arbitrii.*

any set of alternative actions A_1-A_n which a good angel or a redeemed person can imagine doing, if only one action A_m in that set is good, then it is not open to the agent in question to do otherwise. Furthermore, God himself is said to have free will and yet to be impeccable, so that the considerations affecting good angels and redeemed persons in heaven apply to God as well. If we also hold, as is traditional, that God has his attributes essentially, then if only one of the alternative actions God can envisage is good, only that action is possible for him.[6] But it would strike many Christians as odd to say that God is not morally responsible, say, for keeping his promises because it was not open to him, or even possible for him, to do otherwise. One (but, of course, not all) of the reasons generally given for worshipping and praising God is his goodness. If moral responsibility is tied to the ability to do otherwise, however, then it would appear that an essentially impeccable God lacks moral responsibility for at least many of the good actions attributed to him and so shouldn't be praised for moral goodness in connection with them either—a religiously absurd conclusion, which would rule out as confused or mistaken sentiments such as "Praise the Lord, for the Lord is good" (Psalm 135:3). So it seems that PAP is inconsistent with certain traditional Christian views.

It would, of course, take a great deal more work to make a strong argument for the claim that PAP is incompatible with such traditional Christian doctrines; the considerations just adduced are no more than suggestions for how such an argument might go. In this paper, however, it is not my concern to develop or examine such an argument but only to ask what would follow if a sound argument to this effect could be given. In particular, I want to ask two questions. (1) Can we consistently maintain an incompatibilist account of free will, of the sort crucial for formulating an acceptable Christian response to the argument from evil, for example, and still reject PAP? (2) What are the intuitions underlying the common commitment of very many of us to PAP; can those intuitions be accommodated in some other way if PAP is rejected? In considering these questions, I will rely on Harry Frankfurt's hierarchical theory of free will, John Martin Fischer's list of conditions for incompatibilist free will, and Thomas Aquinas's specifically Christian account of the nature of the will and the relation between intellect and will. I will first say something briefly about these positions; then I will argue that, while in most ordinary circumstances PAP applies, on Aquinas's understanding of the will we can reject PAP and still meet not only Fischer's incompatibilist conditions for free will but also Frankfurt's conditions, which are in one respect more stringent. On the account I will defend,

6. In fact, since the laws of nature and the history of the world are either in God's control or irrelevant to considerations of God's ability to do evil, perhaps unavoidability collapses into impossibility in God's case.

Fedya in the example above, the redeemed in heaven, and an essentially impeccable God, all of whom cannot do otherwise (at least at some time or with regard to some actions), nonetheless have free will, both in an incompatibilist sense and in Frankfurt's sense. I will conclude with some considerations designed to show that the intuitions which make many of us feel strongly committed to PAP can be maintained on Aquinas's theory of the will, even when PAP itself is rejected.

FRANKFURT'S HIERARCHICAL THEORY OF THE WILL

Frankfurt considers wanting or desiring to be the genus of acts of willing, or volitions, and he considers a volition to be an effective desire, one that moves an agent all the way to action if unimpeded.[7] According to Frankfurt, agents can have first-order desires, desires to do something, and also second-order desires, desires to have certain first-order desires. Frankfurt uses the term 'second-order desire' ambiguously, and it will be helpful here to make a revision of Frankfurt's account by sorting out that ambiguity. On this revision, when an agent wants to make a certain first-order desire his volition, then he has a second-order desire; and when this second-order desire is effective, that is, when he succeeds in making that first-order desire his volition, then he has a second-order volition.[8] To be a person is to care about one's will, that is, to have second-order desires and volitions. An agent who has no second-order desires or volitions is "a wanton," in Frankfurt's view; such an individual may be human but is not a person.

This notion of a person is the basis for Frankfurt's account of freedom of will. We can take the fundamental notion of freedom as the absence of obstacles to what one wants. Locutions involving the expression 'free from' specify which obstacles are absent, and locutions involving the expression 'free to' indicate the range of things available to the agent to do without obstacle. Freedom of action (as distinct from freedom of will with regard to an action) is the absence of obstacles to doing what one wants to do. Freedom of will is, analogously, the absence of obstacles to willing what one wants to will; an agent has free will, then, just in case

7. Frankfurt's classic paper on the subject is "Freedom of the Will and the Concept of a Person," *Journal of Philosophy* 68 (1971), 5–20; other papers by Frankfurt relevant to the same subject include "The Importance of What We Care About," *Synthese* 63 (1982), 257–72; "Alternate Possibilities and Moral Responsibility," *Journal of Philosophy* 66 (1969), 828–39; and "Identification and Wholeheartedness," in this volume. I have discussed Frankfurt's theory of the will at length in "Sanctification, Hardening of the Heart, and Frankfurt's Concept of Free Will," in this volume; the presentation of Frankfurt's view here is largely taken from that paper.
8. This revision is explained and argued for in "Sanctification, Hardening of the Heart, and Frankfurt's Concept of Free Will."

he has the ability to will what he wants to will. Obstacles to an agent's willing what he wants to will can be external, as when a person wills to stay in a room only because by means of some neurological device a scientist has succeeded in producing in him the volition to stay in the room. They can also be internal, as when a person who wants to leave a room wills to stay in it after all because he cannot conquer his superstitious fear of a black cat asleep on the lintel over the door.

On the revised Frankfurt account, in order to have freedom of will an agent must meet the following conditions: (1) he has second-order desires, (2) he does not have first-order volitions which are discordant with those second-order desires, and (3) he has the first-order volitions he has *because of* his second-order volitions (that is, his second-order volitions have, directly or indirectly, produced his first-order volitions; and if his second-order volitions had been different, he would have had different first-order volitions).[9] On this account, the superstitious man who doesn't succeed in willing to leave the room doesn't have free will because, although he manifests a second-order desire (desiring to have the sort of will which would not be responsive to a fear of black cats), his first-order volition to stay in the room is discordant with that second-order desire; and so he fails to meet the second condition (and possibly also the third, depending on what other second-order volitions he has) of the revised Frankfurt conditions for freedom of will.

Frankfurt's account of freedom of will is thus a strong one, because it requires the absence of both internal and external obstacles to an agent's will if that agent's volitions are to be free. Ordinarily, when we ask whether a person acts with free will, what we are asking is in effect whether there is an external obstacle of this sort acting on his will, and the issue between compatibilists and libertarians can be understood at least in part as a dispute over whether the causal influences which certain compatibilists claim operate on a person constitute an external constraint on his will. If it were not for the clumsy locution, we might call Frankfurt's sense 'complete freedom of will' since it encompasses and exceeds the ordinary sense of free will as absence of external obstacles to willing what one wants.

It is important to add that Frankfurt distinguishes acting freely from acting with freedom of will. If a person has done what he wanted to do because he wanted to do it and the will by which he was moved when he did it was his own will, then he acted freely, whether or not he also acted with freedom of will. On Frankfurt's view, assessments of moral responsibility should depend primarily on whether or not an agent acted freely.

9. I have changed Frankfurt's formulation of these conditions slightly to take account of a distinction between second-order desires and second-order volitions which seems to me useful in this connection; see "Sanctification, Hardening of the Heart, and Frankfurt's Concept of Free Will."

INCOMPATIBILIST FREE WILL

It will be helpful also to say something at the outset about conditions for an agent's having free will in an incompatibilist sense. John Martin Fischer argues[10] that on an incompatibilist understanding of freedom, for any agent S and action A, S's doing A is free just in case A meets the following three conditions.[11]

1. A is not causally determined
2. A is in an appropriate sense S's own act
3. A does not issue from a desire of intensity i, when (i) the desire's having intensity i would explain why A occurs, and (ii) any desire with intensity i is irresistible.

In the subsequent parts of this paper, I will rely on this understanding of incompatibilism, with the following glosses and revisions. (1) To say that S's action A is not causally determined is to deny that A is the result of an unbroken causal sequence which originates in something other than S's beliefs and desires and in virtue of which A is unavoidable for S, in the sense of 'unavoidable' laid out in (U) above. (2) Frankfurt's account of the will has been criticized for relying on unexamined assumptions about what counts as an agent's own desire or act of will.[12] Elsewhere,[13] as part of a revision of Frankfurt's account, I have argued

10. John Martin Fischer, "Responsibility and Control," *Journal of Philosophy* 89 (1982), 24–40. For purposes of this paper, I have slightly altered Fischer's formulation, which is cast in terms of conditions for an action's being unfree.

11. These are clearly necessary conditions for incompatibilist free will, but there is considerable question about whether they are sufficient. Some people suppose that if an agent, S, does an action, A, with free will, there is a possible world like this one in every respect including S's beliefs and desires up to the time of the action, but in which S does the complement of A. If A is refusing an offer to cut up S's daughter into small pieces for the sake of nothing but a dollar, then on this view S does A freely only in case there is a possible world just like this one including S's holding all the same beliefs and desires, but in which S does not refuse the offer. This view seems to me to require too much for freedom of the will. In particular, it isn't clear to me that it is coherent to suppose a person could hold nothing but ordinary beliefs about the value of a dollar and the disvalue of the torture of a small child and yet consent to torture the child for no reason other than gaining a dollar. (In this respect, I am persuaded by an argument of Van Inwagen's; see note 19.) Furthermore, this condition seems to me to embody PAP and build it explicitly into the conditions for freedom of will. The arguments against PAP in this paper are thus also arguments against including such a fourth condition in the list of the Fischer conditions for incompatibilist free will.

12. See, e.g., Irving Thalberg, "Hierarchical Analyses of Unfree Action," *Canadian Journal of Philosophy* 8 (1978), 211–25, and Gary Watson, "Free Agency," *Journal of Philosophy* 72 (1975), 205–20.

13. "Sanctification, Hardening of the Heart, and Frankfurt's Concept of Free Will."

that an agent's volition is his own only if his intellect[14] represents what is willed as the good to be pursued (at that time, under some description), and the agent forms the corresponding volition in consequence of that representation on the part of his intellect. We can add that an agent's action is his own only if it stems from his own volition;[15] and the notion of an agent's own act, employed in Fischer's condition (2), should be understood in this way.

It is worth noticing that Frankfurt's account of acting freely (as distinct from acting with freedom of will) is comprised under condition (2). To act freely, according to Frankfurt, is to do what one wants to do when one wants to do it and when the volition one acts on is one's own. For an agent to act freely, then, in Frankfurt's sense, is for the agent's action to be his own, that is, to stem from his own volition.[16] Frankfurt's conditions for acting freely, and consequently his conditions for being responsible for one's actions, are thus weaker than those an incompatibilist would espouse, since they do not include Fischer's condition (1).

Looked at in another way, all of Frankfurt's conditions for acting with freedom of will can be taken as an additional, stringent gloss on this second condition of Fischer's. To be free, an agent's action must be his own in the sense that it stems from his own volition, and an agent's volition is his own only if his intellect at the time of the volition represents the object of the volition as good under some description. But in cases of conflict, either among second-order desires or between second-order and first-order desires, when the agent acts against some second-order desire, there will always be some part of the agent's intellect which does not represent the object of the volition actually formed as the good to be pursued. And in such cases there is a certain sense in which the volition, and so the subsequent action also, is not the agent's own. Consequently, there is a sense in which it is true to say that for an agent to be fully or completely free, for Fischer's second condition to be met perfectly, all of Frankfurt's conditions for acting with freedom of will need to be met.

(3), Fischer's last condition, seems to me, at best, too broad. The addition of condition (3) is prompted by consideration of heroin addiction or kleptomania or something of that sort, where we feel inclined to attribute to the addicted agent or to the kleptomaniac diminished respon-

14. By 'intellect' here I mean something like the agent's computing faculty and not that part of his mind which is rational as distinct from irrational.

15. An incontinent desire, say, for another helping of lasagna when one means to diet, does not fail to count as the agent's own on this analysis, because a case can be made that at the time of the choice the dieter's intellect represents the second helping, under some description (e.g., necessary means of relaxation or well-earned reward), as the good to be pursued.

16. Frankfurt's analysis of what it is for an agent's volition to be his own is different from mine; see his "Identification and Wholeheartedness."

sibility, because it seems that the agent is moved by irresistible desires which somehow compel him to do what he does, so that he doesn't do it freely. But consider the sort of case suggested by the biblical story of Naomi in Moab with her Moabite daughters-in-law, Ruth and Orpah.

When Naomi's sons die, she anticipates a difficult life for herself and her daughters-in-law. For herself, she can think of nothing better than to return home; but in a spirit of altruism towards Ruth and Orpah, she urges them to return to their families in Moab, who will be much better able to provide for them than she will. After an initial tearful protest, Orpah follows the course that is clearly in her self-interest; she leaves Naomi and goes home. Ruth, on the other hand, is unshakable in her determination not to leave Naomi; and when Naomi repeatedly urges her to do so, Ruth answers her with these well-known lines:

> Entreat me not to leave you or to return from following after you, for where you go, I will go, and where you dwell, I will dwell. Your people shall be my people, and your God my God. Where you die will I die, and there I be buried. The Lord do so to me and more also if anything but death part me and you.

And Naomi, seeing that Ruth is steadfast in her determination to go with her, gives up trying to dissuade her.

We often say of someone that doing a certain action would be inconceivable for her, and we can add to the biblical story here by simply stipulating that, for Ruth, leaving Naomi was unthinkable, that Naomi gave up trying to persuade her just because she saw that what she was urging on Ruth was something which Ruth found inconceivable to do. By saying that Ruth's leaving Naomi was inconceivable to her, I don't mean to suggest that Ruth literally could not conceive the possibility of leaving Naomi. It is clear that she could. She has Orpah's example in front of her and Naomi's urging behind her. Nor do I mean that she has no temptation to leave Naomi, or that she does not contemplate leaving Naomi as a real option. Sometimes she does not contemplate leaving Naomi as a real option. Sometimes we don't know what is inconceivable for us, and we discover it as we perceive the depth of our resistance against yielding to someone else's persuasion or giving in to the temptation of following someone else's example in a course of action we detest. In an example Frankfurt cites from Trollope,[17] a certain British aristocrat doesn't discover that giving in to the temptation he feels to snoop and spy is inconceivable for him until he begins the process and meets with an unconquerable aversion to it in himself.

---

17. "Rationality and the Unthinkable," in Harry Frankfurt, *The Importance of What We Care About* (Cambridge: Cambridge University Press, 1988), pp. 177–90.

What exactly makes an action inconceivable for an agent is hard to spell out and may well vary from person to person;[18] but one way to explain Ruth's speech to Naomi is to suppose that, when all things are considered, her intellect can find no way of presenting the abandonment of Naomi as a good to be pursued. We might imagine Ruth explaining her plan to her Moabite family by saying something like this: "I'm sorry, but it's unthinkable for me to abandon her now. She was always good to me, and it would be heartlessly cruel to repay all her past kindnesses by deserting her just when she needs me most. I know all the prudential arguments in favor of leaving her, and I've thought and thought about them. But in the end it is plain to me that I just couldn't do such a thing, I *must* go with her." We can suppose that Ruth was initially torn between the desire to return to her own family and the desire, arising from love and compassion, or from a sense of duty, to go with Naomi. But on reflection, she can find no way to understand her desire to return home except as base, ignoble, and self-seeking. In short, she can find no way to resist the competing desire to go with Naomi. We can, then speak of this desire as irresistible. It will, of course, not be irresistible in the way that an addict's desire for a drug may be irresistible. The addict's desire stems from an acquired bodily need and is manifested first in urgent physical craving; if it is irresistible, it is so because the addict finds himself powerless to resist this craving. Ruth's desire, on the other hand, originates at least in part in her intellect and has very little if anything to do with physical craving; if it is irresistible, it is so because Ruth's intellect finds it impossible to come to any conclusion other than that going with Naomi is the good to be pursued. Furthermore, if the addict's desire really is irresistible, then if his second-order desire were to be the desire not to take the drug, he would take it nonetheless. But given what was said above about second-order desires as the expression of reasoning, if Ruth's second-order desires were different, she might very well not go with Naomi. If her second-order desires were different, it would be because her intellect did find some way to avoid the conclusion that going with Naomi was the good to be pursued; and in that case, she would be able to resist the desire to go with Naomi, so that that desire would not be irresistible for her then. The irresistibility of the desire in the addict's case is disconnected from his intellect; in Ruth's case, it flows from her intellect and is dependent on it.

Few of us would be inclined to suppose that attributions of praise or blame ought to be withheld in this case because, on reflection, Ruth found it inconceivable to leave Naomi, or that, in deciding to go with Naomi, Ruth acts with diminished responsibility because of the irresist-

18. For an excellent discussion of an action's being inconceivable for a person, see Harry Frankfurt, "Rationality and the Unthinkable."

ibility of her desire. Nor does Ruth's freedom seem diminished in the way that the freedom of a heroin addict or kleptomaniac is, because she finds it impossible to resist her desire to do what she does.[19] But the example of Ruth, as I've explained it here, is apparently an instance cov-

19. In a very interesting paper, "When Is the Will Free?" (*Philosophical Perspectives*, vol. 4: *Action Theory*, ed. James Tomberlin (Atascadero, Ca.: Ridgeview Publishing Co., 1990)), Peter Van Inwagen argues a position in some respects the mirror image of that being defended here. On this view, we rarely have free will, because in cases like that of Ruth in my example as well as in most ordinary cases, it is impossible to conceive coherently of a world in which the agent holds the beliefs and desires that she does in the actual world and in which she yet does something different from what she does in the actual world. Van Inwagen's argument depends on a rule he calls 'Beta-prime': From

$$\text{(i) } p, \text{ and } x \text{ now has no choice about } p,$$

and

$$\text{(ii) } (p{\rightarrow}q), \text{ and } x \text{ has no choice about } (p{\rightarrow}q),$$

deduce

$$\text{(iii) } q, \text{ and } x \text{ now has no choice about } q.$$

His first example of an argument employing Beta-prime includes a conditional he maintains is a necessary truth: If I regard A as indefensible, then I am not going to do A (where A is some action). From that conditional and Beta-prime, he deduces this: I am not going to do A and I now have no choice about whether I am not going to do A. And from this he draws the following further conclusion: "The general lesson is: if I regard a certain act as indefensible, then it follows not only that I *shall not* perform that act but that I *can't* perform it." Because a very tight connection between free will and the ability to do otherwise is a basic assumption for Van Inwagen in this paper, he takes this argument and others like it to show that we very rarely have free will. Now since the tight connection between free will and the ability to do otherwise is what this paper of mine is designed to call in question, it is possible for me to agree with Van Inwagen's arguments and yet not agree with his conclusion that we rarely have free will. But, in fact, I am not entirely persuaded by his arguments either. Even if we have no hesitation about accepting Beta-prime or the necessity of the relevant conditional, it isn't clear to me that Van Inwagen has established the sort of conclusion he wants, namely, that I can't perform A. Beta-prime and the conditional show that I *now* have no choice about whether I am not going to do A; but what we are entitled to deduce from this is only the claim that I can't *now* perform A, and not the broader claim that I can't perform A. One might suppose that Van Inwagen would license the inference from 'S can't now perform A' to 'S can't perform A' in virtue of his theory of event individuation (see note 2). But in discussing responsibility, Van Inwagen grants that a person may be responsible (and so, on his account of responsibility, able to do otherwise) even with respect to actions regarding which he is now unable to do otherwise. Van Inwagen holds that an agent will be responsible in this way if earlier it was in the agent's power whether or not to put himself in the position he is in now, where he is unable to do otherwise; and Van Inwagen accepts the common view that a person's earlier actions contribute to making him the sort of person he is now, with the sorts of beliefs and desires which rule out his now doing otherwise than he does. In that case, however, from the fact that a person's beliefs and desires at t_1 make it very unlikely or even impossible that he do other than he does at t_1, it doesn't follow that he has no choice at all with respect to the actions he performs at t_1, only that he has no choice t_1 simultaneously with the holding of those beliefs and desires; but that he holds those beliefs and desires may itself be the result of choices he has made earlier, and in having those choices he has a choice about the actions he does at t_1. (See also note 24.)

ered by Fischer's condition (3). Given condition (3), we would have to say that Ruth did not act freely, and so condition (3) seems too broad.

What distinguishes the case of Ruth from the case of the heroin addict or kleptomaniac is that we assume the addict or kleptomaniac is moved to do what he does against his will, as it were. A reluctant addict is divided against himself, and the desire for the drug is analogous to an external force coercing him to do what he doesn't want to do. The paradoxical character of these claims is diminished by Frankfurt's hierarchical conception of the will. An unwilling addict has second-order desires not to take heroin, but his effective first-order desires are discordant with those second-order desires and so discordant with what the addict himself really wants.[20] In fact, if the desire for the drug is really irresistible, then it will move the addict to action not only when his second-order desires are against taking the drug but even when (if such a thing is possible) the addict's intellect at the time of taking the drug doesn't represent taking the drug, under any description, as the good to be pursued. (Irresistible desires of this sort are thus distinguished from desires involved in ordinary incontinence, which may move an agent to action against his second-order desires but which do so because at the time the agent's intellect represents the object of that desire, under some description, as the good to be pursued.) In such a case, the desire for taking the drug isn't the addict's own, in the sense of Fischer's condition (2) above. Ruth, on the other hand, is doing precisely what she herself wants to do in acting on the desire which is irresistible for her; there is no discord between her second-order desires and her first-order desire not to leave her mother-in-law, and her intellect clearly does represent going with Naomi as the good to be pursued.

In order not to rule out Ruth's sort of action as unfree, then, condition (3) needs at least to be narrowed to apply only to cases where the irresistible desire moving an agent is in conflict with his own second-order desires, such as the case of an unwilling heroin addict moved by an irresistible desire for the drug. On the other hand, cases of the kind involving heroine addiction seem to be ones in which the irresistible desire isn't really the agent's own. Unlike the case of desires involved in incontinence, irresistible desires of this sort move an agent to action not only against the agent's second-order desires but also (if such a thing is possible) against the representations of the agent's intellect. If this interpretation of the relevant kind of irresistible desire is correct, then condition (3) can simply be dropped, since the sort of irresistible desires it applies to (if in fact there are any of that sort) are all covered by Fischer's condition (2).

20. For an argument that what an agent really wants is what is expressed in his second-order desires, see "Sanctification, Hardening of the Heart, and Frankfurt's Concept of Free Will."

Finally, it is worth pointing out that although Frankfurt is a compatibilist, an agent could meet Frankfurt's conditions for freedom of the will and also meet Fischer's conditions (1) through (3) for incompatibilist free will, as I have glossed them. Frankfurt's conditions neither include nor exclude Fischer's condition (1), but Frankfurt's own explanation of his conditions[21] shows that he means his conditions to include Fischer's condition (2), and perhaps condition (3) also (though not necessarily in the sense in which I have glossed these latter two conditions). What Frankfurt's account of free will adds to Fischer's conditions for incompatibilist free will is the requirement that the agent care about what his will is, and in a way which doesn't produce psychological discord in him. It is thus clearly possible to be an incompatibilist and still adopt Frankfurt's conditions for free will.

AQUINAS ON THE RELATION OF INTELLECT TO WILL

No one can do justice to Aquinas's theory of the will in a few pages. It is rich, complicated and controversial, and a thorough treatment of it would require a book-length study.[22] Furthermore, embedded as it is in medieval psychology, it naturally gives rise to questions about Aquinas's account of the soul and the function of the will in it, which cannot be examined here. In what follows, then, I will simply sketch the basic outlines of Aquinas's theory of the will in order to make us aware of a different conception of will from the one to which we are àccustomed.

Contemporary philosophers tend to operate with a conception of the will founded on a picture of the will as the steering wheel of the mind, neutral in its own right but able to direct other parts of the person. Aquinas's conception of the will is quite different. He takes the will to be not a neutral steering capacity, but a bent or inclination. The will, he says, is a hunger, an appetite, for goodness (*ST* IaIIae, q.10 a.1 and Ia, q.82 a.1). The motivation for this conception of the will is theological. God, who is the ultimate good, has built into human persons the engine by which they can be drawn to him. He has implanted in them a hunger for the good, namely, the will, which (if all goes as it should) will move them with desire and leave them restless and hungry until they find rest and satisfaction in him.

On Aquinas's view, the will is free. It can't be coerced or compelled, and it can move itself (*ST* IaIIae q.6 a.4 ad 1, Ia q.82 a.1, q.83 a.1). Aquinas is sometimes taken for a theological compatibilist (that is, a compatibilist who believes that freedom of the will is compatible with

21. See, e.g., "Freedom of the Will and the Concept of a Person."
22. For a study of Aquinas on this subject, see Jeffrey Hause, *Aquinas on the Will* (Ph.D. dissertation, Cornell University, 1990).

theological determinism), and whether this view of the will's freedom, taken together with his view of divine grace and his general account of God's action in the world as primary cause, constitutes a compatibilist or an incompatibilist account of the will's freedom is a difficult and complicated question which can't be adjudicated in a few paragraphs in passing. But for present purposes, I think we can leave this question to one side. What is at issue here is not whether Aquinas himself is a compatibilist or an incompatibilist, but rather just Aquinas's understanding of the nature of the will and the way it functions. And it is certainly possible to consider Aquinas's understanding of the will without going on to ask what is entailed by combining that understanding with his account of God's grace and operation in the world.

The will is a blind mouth, on Aquinas's theory. It is a hunger for goodness, but by 'goodness' here, Aquinas means goodness in general and not this or that specific good thing; that is, the will wills what is good, where the phrase 'what is good' is used attributively and not referentially. And by itself the will makes no determinations of goodness. Apprehending or judging things with respect to goodness is the business of the intellect. The intellect presents to the will as good certain things under certain descriptions, and the will wills them because the will is an appetite for the good and they are apprehended as good. For this reason the intellect is said to move the will, not as an efficient cause moves but as a final cause does, because what is understood as good moves the will as an end (*ST* Ia q.82 a.4).[23]

The will does will some things by necessity. Because God has created it as a hunger for the good, the will by nature desires the good; and whatever is good to such an extent and in such a way that a person cannot help but see it as good, the will wills by natural necessity. One's own happiness is of this sort, and so a person necessarily wills happiness (*ST* Ia q.82 a.1). But even things which have a necessary connection to happiness aren't willed necessarily unless the willer is cognizant of their necessary connection to happiness (*ST* Ia q.82 a.2). Except for happiness and those things so obviously connected with happiness that their connection is overwhelming and indubitable, however, the will is not determined to one thing, because of its relation to the intellect.

What the intellect determines with respect to goodness is somewhat complicated because the intellect is itself moved by other things. To begin with, the will moves the intellect as an efficient cause, by willing it to attend to some things or to neglect others (cf. *ST* IaIIae q.17 a.1). Of course, the will does so only in case the intellect represents doing so at that time, under some description, as good. Every act of willing is preceded by some apprehension on the part of the intellect, though not

23. My gloss on Fischer's condition (2) above is, of course, based on this part of Aquinas's account of the will's freedom.

every apprehension on the part of the intellect need be preceded by an act of the will (*ST* Ia q.82 a.4). Secondly, the passions—greed, wrath, fear, etc.—can influence the intellect, because in the grip of a passion, such as wrath, something will seem good to a person which wouldn't seem good to him if he were calm (*ST* IaIIae q.9 a.2). The intellect, however, isn't compelled by the passions in any way, but can resist them (cf. *ST* Ia q.81 a.3 and *ST* IaIIae q.10 a.3), for example, by being aware of the passion and correcting for its effects on judgment, as one does when one decides to leave a letter written in anger until the next morning rather than mailing it right away.

The way in which the will is moved is also complicated. A power of the soul, Aquinas says, can be in potentiality in two ways, either with regard to the exercise of its power, as when the sight is not actually seeing, or with regard to the determination of its act, as when the sight sees something white but can see something black (*ST* IaIIae q.9 a.1). The will is similarly moved in two ways. In one way, it is moved to the exercise of its act; that is, it is moved to will rather than not to will. In another way, it is moved to will this particular thing rather than some other. There is no object of the will which can move the will necessarily in the first way, because it is always in a person's power not to think of that object and consequently not to will it actually.[24] In the second way, if the will is presented by the intellect with an object which can be considered good under some descriptions and not good under others, then the will is not necessarily moved by that object either. So, for example, the further acquisition of money can be considered good under some descriptions, for instance, under the description *means of sending the children to school*, and not good under some other descriptions, e.g., *wages from an immoral and*

---

24. For this sort of reason, I think Van Inwagen is wrong to suppose that our beliefs and desires leave us no choice with regard to action even at the time we have those beliefs and desires. Van Inwagen's examples are all cases in which the object of the volition (that is, the thing to be wanted or the state of affairs to be willed) obtrudes itself on the mind of the agent: the telephone rings, for example, and the agent has to decide whether or not to pick it up. In such cases, the beliefs and desires concerning the object of volition are very likely to be occurrent. But, as Aquinas points out, even in those cases in which an agent's beliefs and desires would make his willing something unavoidable for him, he may not will it because his intellect is not attending to the relevant object of volition, either because the object of volition hasn't been called to mind or because the will has directed the intellect not to reflect about that object of volition. Furthermore, unless the case is like that of Ruth, where the agent finds alternative courses of action inconceivable, Aquinas would say that even when the agent attends to the object of volition, the agent's beliefs and desires allow him to choose or to reject that object because the object can be seen under different descriptions, and so can be thought of as good or as not good. Where Aquinas would agree with Van Inwagen is in this, that if an agent sees an object of volition under a certain description as good, that is, if the agent has formed the beliefs and desires that warrant that object of volition as the good to be pursued, and if those beliefs and desires are occurrent, then it isn't at that time open to the agent to will otherwise. (For reasons for thinking that the agent can nonetheless will otherwise, see note 19.)

disgusting job. For these reasons, the will cannot be constrained to move in a particular way by something outside the willer, because, with a salient exception, no matter what object is presented to the intellect, it is open to the intellect to consider it under some description which makes it seem not good. If, however, the will is presented with an object which is good no matter how it is looked at, which is overwhelmingly, obviously good, then the will cannot will the opposite of that object. It is open to the will not to will that object by willing that the intellect not think about it; but if the intellect does see it in all its goodness, then it is not open to the will not to will it. For reasons of this sort, Aquinas says, the will is moved necessarily not only by happiness but also by God's goodness, in the beatific vision in which God's goodness is clearly seen (*ST* IaIIae q.10 a.2; *ST* Ia q.82 a.1).

It is apparent, then, that on Aquinas's account the will is part of a complicated feedback system composed of the will, the intellect, and the passions and set in motion by God's creating the will as a hunger for the good. How this system might be thought to work can be seen by giving a simple example of an interaction between will and intellect. Suppose that Anna has just won some money in a contest and that she plans to use the money to buy a frilly pink canopy bed for her daughter, something she has been coveting but unable to afford. As she sits reading a magazine, she comes across an advertisement urging readers to give money to support children in third-world countries and showing a picture of a ragged, emaciated child. Anna no sooner glances at the ad than she turns the page. Why does she do so? The answer to the question will, of course, involve the will's issuing commands which result in Anna's turning the page; but underlying these commands is something like the will's directive to the intellect not to think about the ad and the needy children it describes. The will makes this directive in virtue of a hasty calculation on the part of the intellect that looking at the ad is not good. That calculation will include some vague or scarcely formed thoughts to this effect, that looking at the ad may stimulate compassion and a desire to help, that helping will involve giving away some or all of the prize money, and that giving away the prize money is not good. Informing or influencing this calculation will be Anna's coveting of the frilly pink canopy bed for her daughter, a passion in Aquinas's sense. Perhaps without the influence of that coveting Anna's calculations about the ad might have been different. Furthermore, that Anna's desire is so strong or is in a position to influence her calculations as it does is itself a result of earlier choices Anna has made. Had she chosen different friends or different reading, for example, she might have developed more altruism and less interest in furniture.

Even now, however, Anna's coveting doesn't compel her to calculate as she does, because it is open to her intellect to recognize the pull of her desire and correct the calculation accordingly. Anna might, for instance, take note of that fact that she has turned the page hastily, reflect on that fact, and conclude that she needs to consider the ad and its request more carefully. She doesn't do so, we might be inclined to say, because she doesn't want to, she doesn't want to risk being moved to give away any of her prize money. But, of course, on Aquinas's theory, if she doesn't want to do so, it is because of a representation by the intellect that at that time, under some description, doing so isn't good. (By talk of the intellect's representations here, it is important to reemphasize, I do not mean to suggest that all acts of will are preceded by explicit, conscious, or self-aware deliberations. The intellect's considerations may be only tacit or implicit, and not in any way conscious, and yet may still count as the reason for a person's willing what she does, if she would give those considerations as the reason for willing as she did, when she is asked to give an explanation.)[25] Any willing of Anna's, then, will be influenced in important ways (but not caused, constrained, or compelled) by previous choices Anna has made; and not only any choice, but even any consent, on Anna's part will involve an often complicated interaction of intellect and will. For that reason, although Aquinas's account of the will assigns a large role to intellect, Aquinas is not committed to seeing immoral actions simply as calculating mistakes. Cases difficult for accounts such as Aquinas's to analyze, cases of incontinence, for example, can also be handled by emphasizing the interaction of intellect and will. In cases where the intellect seems to be representing something as good and yet the will does not will it, the intellect is in fact being moved by opposite motives both to represent that thing as good and not so to represent it, so that the intellect is double-minded or fluctuates between the two representations (cf., e.g., *ST* IaIIae q.17 a.2).

Application of Aquinas's Theory of the Will

In sketching this outline of Aquinas's theory, I don't for a moment suppose I have shown that Aquinas has a coherent, empirically adequate account of the will; it is clear that this brief summary leaves a host of questions unanswered. Aside from questions about whether these views of Aquinas can be reconciled with what he says elsewhere concerning God's action on the will, we might also ask about the large role assigned to the intellect in this theory or about some of the more perplexing features of the relation between intellect and will. On even this brief sketch, however, it is apparent that the part of Aquinas's account laid out here is perfectly consistent with Fischer's conditions for incompatibilist free

25. See Robert Audi, "Acting for Reasons," *Philosophical Review* 95 (1986), 511–46.

will. And while it does not entail Frankfurt's conditions for freedom of the will, it is also not incompatible with them, if we take second-order desires and volitions, as I have argued elsewhere that we ought to do,[26] as resulting naturally from reasoning on the part of the willer's intellect. With Fischer's and Frankfurt's conditions on free will presupposed, what sort of answer does Aquinas's account of the will give to the questions with which this paper began? Can the necessary volitions of God, good angels, and the redeemed in heaven be said to be free? More generally, can we consistently maintain an incompatibilist account of free will and reject PAP? If PAP is rejected, can the intuitions which seem so strongly to support it be accommodated in some other way?

Consider first what Christian doctrine says about the redeemed in heaven. In heaven they are united with God in the beatific vision and they see the goodness of God plainly; in that state they are unable to sin. The reason for their inability to sin is explained by Aquinas's theory of the interaction between intellect and will. Since they see God's goodness plainly, their intellect is no longer in a position to suppose that apparent goods are real goods; by comparison with the overwhelming goodness of God the lack of true goodness in apparent goods is evident. The intellect consequently has no basis on which to represent these apparent goods as real goods, and as a result the will cannot desire them. The inability to sin on the part of the redeemed is thus not a result of an external constraint on the will, imposed from without by some benevolently despotic agent or caused extrinsically by some coercive force. It is a result of the redeemed person's own hunger for goodness; that is, it is a consequence of that person's beliefs and desires, in the interplay of will and intellect brought about by the vision of God's goodness.[27] A redeemed person is thus in a state analogous to that of Ruth in my example above. In my version of the biblical story of Ruth, Ruth cannot bring herself to leave Naomi, even in the face of Orpah's example and Naomi's arguments. The prudential reasons for doing so are clear to her, and she is even tempted to follow Orpah. But in the end it becomes clear to her that she can't bring herself to abandon Naomi—or as we might put it, what becomes clear to her is that her desire not to leave Naomi is irresistible. This irresistible desire of Ruth's is not wrought in her by Naomi or by

26. "Sanctification, Hardening of the Heart, and Frankfurt's Concept of Free Will."

27. Someone might suppose that if the sight of God could keep a person from moral evil, then the fall of Satan is inexplicable and so is the doctrine that a good God doesn't bring it about that everyone comes to heaven, since he can do so readily by giving all persons a vision of his goodness. But on traditional Christian doctrine God keeps all his creatures from full sight of himself until they have had the opportunity to move either toward him or away from him. The reasons for his doing so, in my view, involve at least in part the difficulties of establishing a relationship of love and friendship between an omnipotent, omniscient, perfectly good person and persons limited in knowledge, power, and goodness. For some discussion of these issues, see my paper "Petitionary Prayer," *American Philosophical Quarterly* 16 (1979), 81–91.

any other external agent or force. It stems just from the fact that after all
her reflection and all the temptation to do the prudent thing, Ruth
finds abandoning Naomi unthinkable. And we can explain Ruth's state
in this condition on Aquinas's account of the relation between intellect
and will by saying that in the end for Ruth at that time there is no way
in which, or no description under which, her intellect can represent
abandoning Naomi as a good to be pursued, and therefore there is no
way in which Ruth's will can form the volition to leave Naomi.

I argued above that the case of Ruth is not covered by Fischer's condition (3). Is that case, or the case of the redeemed in heaven, ruled out
as unfree by either of Fischer's first two conditions or by Frankfurt's conditions? The answer seems to me clearly 'no'. An incompatibilist can
plausibly claim that the causal chain responsible for Ruth's going with
Naomi originates in Ruth's beliefs and desires.[28] And it is clear that
Ruth, as well as the redeemed person in heaven, acts on volitions which
are her own, in the sense of stemming from her intellect's representation
of the object of the volition as the good to be pursued. In fact, in both
cases, the willer may be said to have no discord between her second-
order and her first-order desires and volitions. The intellect of Ruth, or
of the redeemed person, represents the object of her will and her willing
of it altogether as good, and so with respect to the volition at issue there
will be no discord between her second-order and her first-order desires
and volitions. Given Aquinas's account of the will, then, both Ruth and
the redeemed person meet all of Fischer's and Frankfurt's conditions for
freedom of will. But on the assumption in my example that Ruth's desire
is irresistible and on Christian doctrine about the redeemed, PAP is vi-
olated with respect to each of them. For both Ruth and the redeemed
person, doing what she does is unavoidable for her. In the case of the
redeemed person, given the laws and the history of the world, there is
no state of affairs she can bring about such that she does an evil action,
because her intellect sees God's goodness so clearly that it cannot represent some object incompatible with that goodness as the good to be
pursued. And something analogous is true of Ruth; because even in the
face of temptation on reflection her intellect finds leaving Naomi, no
matter how it is represented, unthinkably cruel and heartless and thus
inconceivable for her to do, her will cannot form the volition to do so.[29]

28. I put this point in the way I do because the logic of the argument doesn't require,
and it is not part of my purpose here to defend, the claim that incompatibilism is true and
compatibilism is false. The central point at issue in this paper is only whether the assumption of incompatibilism is inconsistent with the rejection of PAP.

29. These cases have some similarity to cases discussed by Susan Wolf in her excellent
paper "Asymmetrical Freedom," *Journal of Philosophy* 77 (1980), 151–66, reprinted in John
Martin Fischer, *Moral Responsibility* (Ithaca, N.Y.: Cornell University Press, 1986), pp. 225–
40. She says of such cases that the character of the agent in question is determined but that
nonetheless "it seems absurd to say that it [the agent's character] is not under his control.

The case of God's impeccability is an extension of the case involving Ruth and the redeemed in heaven. Because God's intellect always sees clearly and plainly what is really good, his intellect never presents apparent goods as real ones, and his will never wills what is not good. God's impeccability, on Aquinas's theory of the will, is thus a consequence of his omniscience; and if God is essentially omniscient, then it will be impossible for God ever to do what is not good. On the other hand, nothing in these conclusions rules out the claim that the causal chain responsible for any action on God's part always originates in God's beliefs and desires,[30] and that the volition on which God acts is appropriately his own. Furthermore, none of the usual reasons for attributing discord between a person's first-order and second-order desires (e.g., intemperance, indecision, etc.) can be applied to God. For these reasons, even with regard to those actions where it is not possible for God to do otherwise, God can always meet both the Fischer and the Frankfurt conditions for freedom of will.

It is worth noting here that attempts to demonstrate an incompatibility between God's omnipotence and his impeccability rely on a different understanding of the cause of divine impeccability, and they tend to assume unreflectively a more contemporary theory of the will.[31] They presuppose a notion of the will as neutral and as sovereign, not subject to anything; and so they see the impossibility of God's doing evil as a restriction, a limitation on his power. Consequently, they conclude that one cannot consistently maintain both omnipotence and impeccability. But, as we have seen, Aquinas would reject such a theory of the will. On his view, there is a sense in which the will is by nature subject to the intellect; and if the intellect has not miscalculated in some way, perhaps as a result of an interaction between intellect and will, the object of the will is invariably a real, rather than an apparent, good. If (as seems reason-

---

His character is determined on the basis of his reasons, and his reasons are determined by what reasons there are" (p. 232). Aquinas's account of intellect and will seems to me to provide the underlying explanation for the truth of this point, although there seems to me something highly misleading, in the context of this discussion, in speaking of a person's character as determined in such cases. In Wolf's sense of 'determined' an agent's character can be both determined and still under his own control, but the sense of 'determination' common in such discussions is usually characterized by opposing it to control on the part of the agent. While much of Wolf's paper seems to me correct and insightful, I don't agree with her analysis of incompatibilism as the view that an agent is free only if there is no causal determination of his *actions* or her general thesis that there is an asymmetry between morally praiseworthy acts and morally blameworthy acts. For helpful discussion showing that Wolf's asymmetry thesis is false, see John Martin Fischer and Mark Ravizza, "Responsibility and Inevitability," *Ethics* 101 (1991), 258–78; I am grateful to the authors for making the paper available to me in typescript.

30. Or the divine analogues to beliefs and desires, if God is simple.

31. See, for example, Nelson Pike, "Omnipotence and God's Ability to Sin," *American Philosophical Quarterly* 6 (1969), 208-16.

able to suppose) intellectual power is a kind of power, then on Aquinas's theory of the will, omnipotence not only is compatible with impeccability but actually entails it, because God will be capable of doing what is not good only in case his intellect is capable of miscalculating and so is deficient in intellectual power.

FISCHER'S REASONS-RESPONSIVE MECHANISM

In "Responsiveness and Moral Responsibility,"[32] Fischer argues for a view which has some resemblance to Aquinas's. Fischer wants to give an outline of a theory of moral responsibility compatible with our basic moral intuitions about responsibility but also consistent with a rejection of PAP. He does so by using what he calls 'an actual-sequence model' of responsibility. In Frankfurt-style examples, Fischer says, "the kind of mechanism which operates is reasons-responsive, although the kind of mechanism that would operate in the alternative scenario is *not*."[33] On Fischer's theory of moral responsibility, "an agent is morally responsible for performing an action insofar as the mechanism that actually issues in the action is reasons-responsive. When an unresponsive mechanism actually operates, it is true that the agent is not free to do otherwise; but an agent who is unable to do otherwise may act from a responsive mechanism and can thus be held morally responsible for what he does."[34] By 'reasons-responsiveness' here Fischer has in mind what he calls 'weak reasons-responsiveness'. For an agent to act on a weak reasons-responsive mechanism, it must be the case that there is some possible world in which there is sufficient reason to do otherwise than the agent does, the agent's actual mechanism operates, and the agent does otherwise. For an agent to be responsible on Fischer's theory, the actual sequence mechanism on which he acts must be weakly reasons-responsive.[35]

Fischer's account of moral responsibility is thus like Aquinas's in emphasizing the role of reason, but it differs from Aquinas's in two respects. In the first place, Fischer doesn't provide a theory explaining the role of reason in ascriptions of responsibility, as Aquinas does. Fischer constructs his account by considering what is common to certain difficult cases where our intuitions are generally inclined to assign moral responsibility to an agent, and he concludes that the crucial common feature in such cases is the operation of a certain mechanism responsive to reasons.

32. In *Responsibility, Character, and the Emotions*, ed. Ferdinand Schoeman (Cambridge: Cambridge University Press, 1987).

33. Ibid., p. 85.

34. Ibid., pp. 85–86.

35. Fischer also adds the qualification that the relevant mechanism must be temporally intrinsic, that is, that its description must not entail the occurrence of the action it is supposed to bring about. For the sake of brevity, I am omitting consideration of this and other details of Fischer's account. (See also note 36.)

But his account does not provide a deeper explanation, as Aquinas's theory does, for why the presence or absence of a "reasons-responsive mechanism" should be crucial to ascriptions of responsibility. This point is, of course, no reason for rejecting Fischer's theory, since it is doubtless possible for Fischer or someone else to construct the missing explanation and add it to Fischer's present account; but it is nonetheless worth noting that, as things stand, Aquinas's theory is broader and deeper than that offered by Fischer.

Secondly, and more importantly, Fischer's way of introducing reason into his account differs from Aquinas's. Aquinas's theory requires that it be the agent's own intellect which represents the object of volition as the good to be pursued if an agent is to be morally responsible for what he does. For Fischer, however, for an agent, S, to be responsible for an action, A, it need be the case only that the following conditions be met:

1. there is some possible world w_1 in which there is sufficient reason for S to do otherwise than A
2. in w_1 S uses the mechanism S used in the actual world in doing A
3. in w_1 S does otherwise than A.

Unlike the role of reason in Aquinas's theory, these conditions of Fischer's are not sufficient for moral responsibility. Consider Raymond, the protagonist of the film *The Manchurian Candidate*, who was programmed by his captors to kill his boss. (Those who find ludicrous the powers the movie attributes to brainwashing can substitute the more fashionable, surgically implanted neurological device, which has the same effect.) Suppose that in some world w_1 Raymond has sufficient reason for not killing his boss; suppose that his boss is his best friend as well as his patron. But suppose also that in w_1 Raymond's captors, too, have sufficient reason for not having Raymond kill his boss, because in that world Raymond's boss is a spy working for Raymond's captors and useful to their organization. In that world Raymond is as much of a robot as he is in the actual world, and yet he does not kill his boss, because in that world Raymond's captors want his boss to live. In this case Raymond meets all of Fischer's conditions for weak reasons-responsiveness: there is some possible world in which there is sufficient reason for Raymond to do otherwise than kill his boss, and in that world Raymond uses the same mechanism he used in the actual world in killing his boss (namely, the mechanism involving brainwashing or a neurological device), but he doesn't kill his boss.[36] And yet, even though Fischer's con-

---

36. Fischer says that he is deliberately leaving vague the notion of 'same mechanism' (p. 95), but in practice he tends to take the relevant mechanism as a type or kind. So, for example, he suggests that the normal faculty of practical reasoning and a procedure involving direct stimulation of an agent's brain are mechanisms of the sort he has in mind

ditions for weak reasons-responsiveness are met, Raymond clearly is not morally responsible for killing his boss in the actual world, in which he is controlled and programmed by his captors.

Fischer's account is thus flawed in a way that Aquinas's is not. Unlike Fischer's account of moral responsibility, Aquinas's theory of the will succeeds in ensuring that the action of the agent in question really is that agent's own. As Fischer's account is constructed, the weak reasons-responsive mechanism whose operation is supposed to guarantee the agent's moral responsibility for what he does could turn out to include the intellect of those who coerce and control the agent. It isn't enough to remedy Fischer's account to add the condition that the mechanism be the agent's own mechanism, because presumably the mechanism Raymond uses when he kills his boss as he is programmed to do is a mechanism which is somehow his; it is his brainwashed mind, or his neurologically altered brain.

To rule out this sort of case involving Raymond, what we need is an account of the sort Aquinas provides, which requires that the mechanism be the agent's own intellect and explains the crucial role of the intellect in volition, thereby denying moral responsibility to an agent whose intellect is programmed or whose will is coerced. On Aquinas's theory, Raymond wouldn't count as morally responsible if he killed his boss while programmed (or in some other way coerced) to do so, because the act Raymond did in such a case wouldn't be appropriately his own. It wouldn't stem from Raymond's own volition, because it wouldn't be Raymond's intellect representing the murder as the good to be pursued, and so Raymond's will would will the murder for some reason other

---

(p. 85); he also speaks of mechanisms as a kind of process, a kind of physical process or a kind of manipulation (p. 97). These passages suggest that Fischer would accept brainwashing or the employment of a neurological device as the kind of mechanism he had in mind. One might suppose that my objection to his account could consequently be undermined simply by adopting a narrower understanding of mechanism. One might suppose, for example, that the mechanism on which Raymond operates in the actual world is the mechanism of being brainwashed to kill his boss. This mechanism is obviously not operative in the possible world in which Raymond does not kill his boss; and so on this understanding of mechanism, my counterexample fails. But Fischer explicitly rules out this understanding of mechanism, and for excellent reasons. On his account of responsibility, if the mechanism is described in such a way that the operation of the mechanism involved in an agent's action includes the occurrence of that action, it would always follow that the agent was not responsible for his action, since on Fischer's account an agent is responsible for an action only in case there is a possible world in which the agent acts on the same mechanism but does a different action. And in general, the problem for Fischer's account in making more precise the notion of 'same mechanism' will be to avoid this sort of dilemma, in which a fine-grained description of the mechanism inappropriately denies responsibility to agents who do seem responsible, and a more coarse-grained description of the mechanism invites counterexamples in which an agent who doesn't seem responsible meets Fischer's conditions for responsibility because the mechanism controlling the agent is in the hands of persons who are themselves acting on reasons-responsive mechanisms.

than that Raymond's intellect represented it as the good to be pursued. Someone might suppose that Raymond's captors could introduce into Raymond's intellect the thought that murdering his boss is good and thereby program Raymond to murder, so that Aquinas's account suffers from the same deficiency as Fischer's: Raymond could meet all the conditions for freedom and still be the puppet of his captors. But this objection will not hold up under scrutiny. If Raymond's captors introduce a thought into his intellect, it is open to Raymond to reflect on that thought and either accept or reject it, so that the resulting judgment will be Raymond's, and there is no embarrassment for Aquinas's account in saying that Raymond is free. On the other hand, if Raymond's captors control all his thoughts, so that he can't exercise his own judgment at all, then it isn't Raymond's intellect which represents the murder as good. In fact, in this case it isn't altogether clear what it means to speak of *Raymond's* intellect, since all the intellectual functioning in Raymond is that of his captors. In this case, then, Raymond isn't free, but that is no problem for Aquinas's account since in this case Raymond's intellect and will aren't functioning as they need to do in order to count as free on Aquinas's account of the will.

Conclusion

Reflection on the differences between Aquinas's account and Fischer's is instructive for the basic question with which this paper began, whether incompatibilists can consistently reject PAP. If we take the root notion of freedom to be doing what one wants, the problem with Raymond's action in the film is that he isn't doing what *he* wants to do in murdering his boss; or if he is, he isn't willing what *he* wants to will in forming the volition to murder. It seems to me arguable that the reason we have strong intuitions supporting PAP is that in most ordinary circumstances there is virtually no chance that we are doing (or willing) what *we* really want to do (or will) unless it is possible for us to do (or will) otherwise. In most ordinary circumstances, if there is no alternate possibility open to us, it is because some external force or agent is constraining us to act as we do, so that what we do isn't what we ourselves really want to do. The theory that PAP is necessary for any acceptable theory of moral responsibility or of free will is consequently something like the Newtonian theory of the will: it holds for the most part, for most situations of the sort encountered in ordinary experience.

But what reflection on queer Frankfurt-style examples or esoteric theological doctrines shows us is that the association between the presence of an alternate possibility and the ability to do what we ourselves really want holds only for the most part. There are certain peculiar cases, cases such as that of Fedya or Ruth or the redeemed in heaven, where (for varying reasons) it isn't open to the agent to do otherwise than she does, and yet it is clear that the agent is doing what she herself really wants to do. How it can be that an agent does what she herself really wants to do when there is no alternate possibility open to her is explained on Aquinas's theory of the will and the Fischer and Frankfurt conditions for free will. Because the will is not a neutral capacity for choosing but a hunger for the good, which takes as good what the intellect represents as good (as a result of a complicated process of interaction between will and intellect), it is possible for a person to will freely and yet have no alternate possibility open to her. The reason for this is that in such a case (as, for example, in the case of Ruth or a redeemed person in heaven) her intellect finds any alternate possibility inconceivable, not possibly representable as good. Furthermore, as the case of Fedya shows, it is possible for a person to will freely when there is no alternate possibility open to him, because while an external force is available to close off alternate possibilities, that force doesn't actually operate. It is Fedya's own intellect which represents his action of murder as good, with the result that it is Fedya's own will which forms a volition for it. In this way, Aquinas's theory of the will, together with the Fischer and Frankfurt conditions on free will, explains why we can consistently maintain an incompatibilist theory of free will and yet reject PAP,[37] and it shows how the intuitions on which PAP is based can be supported while PAP itself is denied.[38]

37. If this result is right, then arguments by incompatibilists against compatibilism need to be restructured. Such arguments often assume PAP, then argue that if determinism is true, no agent has the ability to do otherwise, and conclude that therefore determinism is incompatible with responsibility. But if PAP is not true, or holds only for the most part, then the strategy of such arguments will not be successful. In "Incompatibilism Without the Principle of Alternate Possibilities," *Australasian Journal of Philosophy* 64 (1986), 266–76, Robert Heinaman argues that attacks on PAP based on Frankfurt-style examples leave PAP unscathed because there are two senses of 'could have done otherwise': (1) was not deterministically caused, and (2) had an alternate route open. Agents in Frankfurt-style examples could not have done otherwise only in sense (2), but PAP was intended in sense (1); and therefore, the Frankfurt-style examples in no way undermine PAP. There is some insight in this point of Heinaman's. I don't think it saves PAP, because it isn't clear that there is a distinction of the sort Heinaman wants between two senses of 'could have done otherwise'. But what is right about his point is that the issue between compatibilists and incompatibilists which PAP was supposed to help adjudicate is a controversy about the causal chain eventuating in an action—the actual-sequence chain of events, as Fischer calls it—rather than about the implications of counterfactual mechanisms for coercing actions.

38. I am grateful to William Alston, Thomas Flint, John Martin Fischer, Carl Ginet, William Mann, Philip Quinn, William Rowe, and Peter Van Inwagen for comments on this paper, and I am indebted to Norman Kretzmann for many helpful questions and suggestions on earlier drafts.

10

Responsibility, Agent-Causation, and Freedom: An Eighteenth-Century View

WILLIAM L. ROWE

THERE are logical connections among the three concepts: moral responsibility, agent-causation, and freedom. The logical connections are centered in the concept of a person's actions. If you are morally responsible for your action then you must have played a role in causing your action and the action must have been done freely. I take this claim to be widely accepted, if not self-evident.[1] Disagreement surfaces, however, as soon as we try to bring into focus the concepts of agent-causation and freedom. What is it for an agent to cause her action? And what is it for an action to be done freely? In addition, there is controversy over the implications of the concept of moral responsibility. Is it true that an agent is morally responsible for her action only if she could have avoided performing that action? And if it isn't true, what bearing does this have on the claim that moral responsibility for an action implies that the agent caused the action and did it freely? These are important questions. Some answers to them are well known and respected, others are relatively unknown and neglected. In this article I want to focus on a relatively unknown and neglected answer. Obviously, it is an answer that I believe does not merit this degree of obscurity. Indeed, I think the answer can throw considerable light on the proper connections among our three concepts: respon-

Reprinted by permission of the University of Chicago Press from *Ethics* 101 (January 1991): 237–257.

An earlier version of this article was presented at the fourteenth annual Symposium in Philosophy, April 6–8, 1990, University of North Carolina at Greensboro. I am grateful to Eleonore Stump, my commentator at the conference, for helpful criticism and comments. I also benefited from correspondence with Michael J. Zimmerman.

1. We all agree that this claim is true. What we disagree about is the proper account of what it is for an agent to cause her action or to do it freely.

sibility, agent-causation, and freedom. Of these three concepts, the one that plays the central role in the answer I want to lay before you is agent-causation. Therefore, although it is generally believed to be a concept shrouded in mystery, I will begin with it.

AGENT-CAUSATION

The concept of agent-causation has a long history in philosophy, its demise being a relatively recent affair. In the eighteenth century, for example, the concept was very much alive and played a central role in the work of the Scottish philosopher, Thomas Reid. At the risk of ignoring other important explications of this idea, I will take Reid's account as definitive for purposes of this article. What then did Reid propose as necessary and sufficient for something, X, being the agent-cause of an event e?[2] I suggest the following:

1. X is a substance that had power to bring about e.
2. X exerted its power to bring about e.
3. X had the power to refrain from bringing about e.[3]

Our first point establishes that an agent-cause of an event e is always a substance. Actually, Reid's view is that only intelligent substances possessing will and active power (i.e., agents) can be causes.[4] Inanimate substances, events, motives, laws of nature, etc., therefore, cannot be causes for the simple reason that they are not intelligent beings with will and active power. To forestall misunderstanding, however, we must note that Reid thought that the words 'cause', 'power', and 'agent' are ambiguous, used both in the sense we are engaged in explicating, the "original, strict and proper" sense (as he called it), and in what he calls the "lax and pop-

2. Several editions of Reid's works are available. Unless stated otherwise, references in this article are to the 1983 printing by Georg Olms Verlag of *The Works of Thomas Reid, D.D.*, 8th ed., ed. Sir William Hamilton (Edinburgh, 1895). When Reid is quoted or there is a reference to his works in the text of this article, the numbers immediately following the quotation or reference refer to the pages of this volume.

3. In his June 14, 1785, letter to Dr. James Gregory, Reid remarks, "In the strict and proper sense, I take an efficient cause to be a being who had power to produce the effect, and exerted that power for that purpose" (p. 65). He also says, "Power to produce an effect supposes power not to produce it; otherwise it is not power but necessity, which is incompatible with power taken in the strict sense" (p. 65). In light of this last remark we should note that the sense of 'power' at work in condition 1 renders condition 3 redundant. However, since 'power' has a sense in which 3 would *not* be redundant, I state it as a separate condition, even though this could be misleading.

4. "I am not able to form a conception how power, in the strict sense, can be exerted without will; nor can there be will without some degree of understanding. Therefore, nothing can be an efficient cause, in the proper sense, but an intelligent being" (p. 65).

ular" sense.[5] In the lax and popular sense of 'cause', 'power', and 'agent', substances lacking intelligence, events, laws of nature, and even motives may be causes.

As I have noted, it is Reid's conviction that only beings endowed with will and understanding are causes in the primary sense of 'cause', only they are agent-causes. But aren't there inanimate substances that in this primary sense have power to cause events? Doesn't a brick, as opposed to a feather, have the power to shatter a window? And doesn't acid, as opposed to water, have the power to dissolve zinc? Whatever we say about these questions, it is clear that neither the brick nor the acid meets Reid's conditions for being causes of the events mentioned. For neither a brick nor acid meets Reid's third condition, and it is questionable whether either meets the second. When a brick is thrown against a window, is it right to say that the brick then exerts its power to shatter the window? Perhaps we can say, somewhat anthropomorphically, that when a piece of zinc is placed in a vat of acid, the acid then exerts its power to dissolve the zinc. But clearly the acid has no power to refrain from dissolving zinc. When the conditions are right, the acid must dissolve the zinc. It isn't up to the acid whether or not it dissolves the zinc. But to be a cause in the strict and proper sense entails having the power to refrain from bringing about *e*. So, the brick does not cause the shattering of the window nor does the acid cause the dissolving of the zinc.

Suppose I invite you to write down the word 'cause'. Let's suppose that you have the power to do so and that you exert that power with the result that a change in the world occurs, the word 'cause' is written on a piece of paper. Here, when we look at Reid's third condition, we believe that it does obtain. We believe that you had the power to refrain from initiating your action of writing down the word 'cause'. The acid had no such power of refraining from dissolving the zinc, but you had the power not to bring about your action of writing down the word 'cause'. If these things are so, then in this instance you are a true agent-cause of a certain change in the world, for you had the power to bring about that change, you exerted that power by acting, and finally, you had the power not to bring about that change.

This conclusion has been criticized for leaving the physical world devoid of active causes, for reducing all physical particulars to the level of passive things.[6] Surely, the sea has the power to crush a submarine that goes too deep, and a stick of dynamite the power to explode when detonated. To deny power and causation to these physical entities, so the

---

5. See his letters to Dr. James Gregory, September 23, 1785 (p. 67), July 30, 1789 (pp. 73–74), and one with no date (pp. 77–78).

6. E. H. Madden, "Commonsense and Agency Theory," *Review of Metaphysics* 36 (1982): 319–41.

criticism goes, is to violate our commonsense view of the world, and, therefore, on Reid's own grounds, to commit an egregious error.[7]

This criticism is right in concluding that on Reid's view of what it is to be a cause in the "strict and proper" sense, the sea and the dynamite are not causes at all. For, on Reid's view, the sea has active power to crush a submarine that ventures too deep only if the sea has power not to crush a submarine that ventures too deep, only if, that is, it is "up to the sea" whether to exercise its power.[8] But why should this be at all paradoxical? Why should this be against common sense? Wouldn't it be more paradoxical to attribute active power and agency to physical particulars when we know that part of what it is to have active power and agency is for it to be "up to the agent" whether or not to exercise its power? Given what Reid means by the "strict and proper" sense of 'cause', 'power', and 'agency', isn't the conclusion he reaches exactly right? Physical particulars are one and all passive, lacking power, agency, and causality.

Of course, if Reid insists that there is *no sense* of 'cause', 'power', and 'agency' in terms of which we can properly describe the sea and a stick of dynamite as possessing causal power, as being agents of change, then the criticism is surely right in arguing that his view conflicts with commonsense beliefs. But, as we noted above, Reid does recognize a sense of these terms—what he calls the "lax and popular" sense—in virtue of which certain inanimate things can be described as causes, as agents possessed of power. In correspondence, he remarks:

> A cause, in the proper and strict sense (which, I think, we may call the metaphysical sense) signifies a being or mind that has power and will to produce the effect. But there is another meaning of the word cause, which is so well authorized by custom, that we cannot always avoid using it, and I think we may call it the physical sense; as when we say that heat is the cause that turns water into vapour, and cold the cause that freezes it into ice. A cause, in this sense, means only something which, by the laws of nature, the effect always follows. I think natural philosophers, when they pretend to shew the *causes* of natural phenomena, always use the word in this last sense; and the vulgar in common discourse very often do the same. [P. 67][9]

7. Ibid., pp. 329–30.
8. Similarly for the stick of dynamite. Once it is detonated, the dynamite has no power not to explode. It is not up to the dynamite whether to exercise its power of exploding.
9. Reid even notes that Hume is right in holding constant conjunction as important to physical causes. (He elsewhere argues that constant conjunction is not sufficient for physical causes.) "Between a physical cause and its effect, the conjunction must be constant, unless in the case of a miracle or suspension of the laws of nature. What D. Hume says of causes, in general, is very just when applied to physical causes, that a constant conjunction with the effect is essential to such causes, and implied in the very conception of them" (p. 67).

So, far from denying that the sea or a stick of dynamite has causal power to produce certain effects, it is clear that Reid affirms that they are physical causes and agents.[10] It is a mistake, then, to charge Reid with denying our commonsense claims that some physical particulars have causal powers and can be described as agents in bringing about changes in other things. It remains true, however, that physical particulars are not agent-causes; they are not causes in the "strict and proper" sense.

What I think is doubtful in Reid's view of causation is not his denial that physical particulars are causes in the primary sense of 'cause', but his claim that every event in the universe has an agent-cause (p. 627). For what this implies is that whenever some event or inanimate substance causes (in the "lax and popular" sense) some change there must be an agent-cause somewhere in the background that acted in such a way as to assure that the inanimate substance or event is the physical cause of that change. It is one thing to accept Reid's claim that we view ourselves as agent-causes of many of our actions. For this is nothing more than to believe that it was in our power to cause these actions, that we exerted this power, and that it was in our power not to cause them. But it is another thing to accept his claim that every event in the universe is the immediate or ultimate result of the action of an intelligent being. Whether he was right about this is not a question we need pursue here. For the Reidian view that moral responsibility and free action require that we be agent-causes is logically separable from his metaphysical thesis that every event has an agent-cause. And it is his view that we are the agent-causes of some of our actions that is our concern here.

Reid, Samuel Clarke, and other free will advocates used the expression 'efficient cause' for a cause that satisfies Reid's three conditions. Reid used the expression 'physical cause' mainly for events (or things) that are connected to their effects by a law of nature. (To simplify matters, I will take Reid's physical causes to be events connected to their effects by a law of nature.) From his remarks it is clear that Reid believes that efficient causes and physical causes are not two species of a common genus. An efficient cause is a substance that exercises its power to produce an effect, having the power not to produce that effect. A physical cause is an event whose effect follows by virtue of a law of nature. In deference to contemporary usage, I will henceforth use the expression 'agent-cause' for any cause that satisfies Reid's three conditions, and will

10. He also notes that in physics the law of nature according to which something is produced is itself often called the cause of that thing. "When a phenomenon is produced according to a certain law of nature, we call the law of nature the cause of that phenomenon; and to the laws of nature we accordingly ascribe power, agency, efficiency. The whole business of physics is to discover, by observation and experiment, the laws of nature, and apply them to the solution of the phenomena: this we call discovering the causes of things. But this, however common, is an improper sense of the word *cause*" (p. 66).

use 'event-cause' for (our simplification of) Reid's physical causes. An agent-cause is a cause in what Reid calls the "strict and proper" sense; an event-cause is a cause in what Reid calls the "lax and popular" sense.[11]

Although the concept of agent-causation is expressible in a set of three conditions, it is clear that these conditions do not constitute a proper definition of agent-causation, for each condition embodies the causal notion of 'bringing about'. Whether these conditions can be stated without using such obvious synonyms for 'cause' as 'produce' or 'bring about' is not a question we need pursue here. What is important to note is that Reid's concept of agent-causation is fundamentally dependent on the notion of active power, the power an agent has to bring about or not bring about a certain event.

Following Locke, Reid argues that our idea of active power is acquired not from changes observed in external things but from our consciousness of changes within ourselves. Reflecting on certain changes in our thoughts, in the motions of our bodies and, Reid would add, in the determinations of our will (volitions), we are irresistibly led to attribute to ourselves the power to bring about these changes. The changes in thought and bodily motion over which we attribute such power to ourselves are occasioned by our willing them. But in order to will some change one must understand what is being willed. So, power with respect to bringing about changes in our thoughts and the motions of our body is exerted by our willings, and will implies some degree of understanding. "From this, I think, it follows, that, if we had not will, and that degree of understanding which will necessarily implies, we could exert no active power, and consequently could have none; for power that cannot be exerted is no power. It follows also, that the active power, of which only we can have any distinct conception, can be only in beings that have understanding and will" (p. 523).

Reid proposes no definition of 'active power'. His view is that this notion, like a good many others, is indefinable. He does, however, make a number of observations and remarks about active power, some of which it will be helpful to have before us.

11. It is remarkable that in two hundred years our view of causation has so shifted that what for Reid was rather mysterious (event-causation) now seems commonplace, and what for Reid was so commonplace (agent-causation) is viewed by many as obscure, if not unintelligible. After reviewing some objections of present-day philosophers to agent-causation, Alan Donagan remarks, "These objections uncannily reverse the objections Reid made in the eighteenth century against event-causation. Reid pointed out that the necessity possessed by the laws of Newtonian physics was so mysterious that Newton himself indignantly denied that he thought it causal, whereas for centuries the model of causality had been that of the relation of an agent to his actions, and above all, that of the divine agent to his creative actions. . . . In terms of this, the original notion of cause, Reid complained that the post-Newtonian concept of event-causation was improper and obscure" ("Chisholm's Theory of Agency," in *Essays on the Philosophy of Roderick M. Chisholm*, ed. Ernest Sosa [Amsterdam: Rodopi, 1979], p. 218).

1. Unlike the operations or activities of the mind (exertions of power), power itself is not something of which we are directly conscious. [P. 512]
2. "We cannot conclude the want of power from its not being exerted; nor from the exertion of a less degree of power, can we conclude that there is no greater degree in the subject." [P. 514]
3. Power is a quality and cannot exist without a subject to which it belongs. [P. 514]
4. Every change is brought about by some exertion of power or by the cessation of some exertion of power. [P. 515]
5. The being that produces a change by the exertion of its power is the *cause* of that change. [P. 515]
6. "Power to produce any effect implies power not to produce it." [P. 523]

Reid insists that we all share a belief that we possess active power with respect to some of our actions and willings. As he puts it: "All our volitions and efforts to act, all our deliberations, our purposes and promises, imply a belief of active power in ourselves; our counsels, exhortations, and commands, imply a belief of active power in those to whom they are addressed" (p. 517). If I deliberate about whether to mow the lawn today, I must believe that mowing the lawn is in my power, that it is up to me whether or not I mow the lawn. It could be that I am mistaken in this belief. Someone may have stolen my lawn mower; while sitting and deliberating, without my knowledge I may have suffered a nervous disorder that has rendered my legs useless, etc. So genuine deliberation can occur even though mowing the lawn today is not within my power. But unless I believe that it is in my power, I cannot deliberate.[12] Since it is an obvious fact that we deliberate, make promises, etc., then, whether we have active power or not, we are constantly in the position of believing that many actions are within our power.

FREEDOM

We've had a look at the concept of agent-causation. It is now time to link up this notion of causation with the concept of freedom. And this task can best be approached by first considering the question of what it is for a person to perform some action freely.

As is well known, Locke took a free action to be one that a person does as a result of willing to do it, provided that the person could have done

---

12. Compare Richard Taylor, *Action and Purpose* (Englewood Cliffs, N.J.: Prentice-Hall, 1966), p. 171: "One can only deliberate about what he believes to be within his own power. Thus, 'I am deliberating whether Smith shall be reprieved' entails 'I believe it to be within my power alone to reprieve Smith.'" This position, like Reid's, may be too strong. Perhaps all that is entailed by my deliberation about whether to mow the lawn today is that I *not* believe that mowing the lawn is not in my power.

otherwise had he so willed. If the person could not have done otherwise had he so willed, the action may be voluntary, but it is not done freely. In one form or another, this conditional account of what constitutes a free action has dominated the debate about freedom from Locke's day to the present. It has two appealing features. First, it has an initial claim to being all we could want with respect to freedom. As Locke put it, "For how can we think any one freer than to have the power to do what we will."[13] And second, it does not conflict with causal determinism, since it may be true both that a person's action is causally necessitated by his circumstances and act of will, and that the person could have done otherwise had he willed differently. So there is nothing in Locke's account of a free action that would preclude the act of will being causally necessitated by earlier events over which the person had no control. But it is precisely at this point that many have found Locke's concept of freedom inadequate. For although it may be true that you have the power to do something *if* you will to do that thing, what if you have no power over your will? To see the problem here, suppose you are sitting down, someone asks you to get up and walk over to the window to see what is happening outside, but you are quite satisfied where you are and choose to remain sitting. Now had I injected you with a powerful drug so that you can't move your legs, Locke would say that you don't continue sitting freely since it was not in your power to do otherwise if you had willed otherwise—say, to get up and walk to the window. But let's now suppose that instead of paralyzing your legs I had hooked up a machine to your brain so that I can and do bring about your decision to remain sitting and thus deprive you of the capacity to will to do otherwise. It's still true that you have the power to get up and walk if you should will to do so—I haven't taken away your physical capacity to walk, as I did when I paralyzed your legs. Here the problem is that you have no power over your will. In this case, it seems clear that you sit of necessity, not freely. On Locke's account of freedom, however, it remains true that you sit freely and not of necessity. And this being so, we must conclude that Locke's account of freedom is simply inadequate. Freedom that is worth the name, it seems, must include power to will or not will, not simply power to do if we will.

In contrast to Lockean freedom I want to advance a conception of free action that recognizes the importance of power over the will. Moreover, as we shall see, this conception of freedom rests on the conception of agent-causation with which we began. In presenting this conception, which I will call "Reidian freedom," I will suppose, along with Locke and Reid, that actions for which we are morally responsible are among those which we do as a result of willing (deciding, choosing) to do them.

13. John Locke, *An Essay concerning Human Understanding*, ed. Peter H. Nidditch (Oxford: Oxford University Press, 1975), bk. 2, chap. 21, sec. 21.

Suppose that a person wills to do a certain action and does it as a result of willing to do it. What is it for that action to be one that is freely done? Here is Reid's answer: "If the person was the cause of that determination of his own will, he was free in that action, and it is justly imputed to him, whether it be good or bad" (p. 602).[14] There is something wonderfully simple, some would say naive, in this account of a free action. For the entire matter is made to rest on one simple question, Who caused the act of will (the volition) that resulted in the action? This question implies two distinct points. First, it implies that an act of will (a determination of the will) is an event occurring in the agent and, as such, requires a cause. Second, the question implies that the act of will must have an agent-cause, some intelligent being who had the power to bring about that act of will and exerted that power. Reid clearly held both points. If you are hesitant, as I am, about his metaphysical thesis that every event has an agent-cause, we might take the question as, Who or what caused the act of will that resulted in the action? Be this as it may, Reid's point is that the action is free just in case the person whose action it is was the agent-cause of the volition resulting in the action.

Now that we have linked freedom to agent-causation, I want to consider several objections that come to mind when one reflects on this agent-causation account of freedom of action.

Objection 1

What if some event over which the agent has no control event-causes the agent's causing of that act of will?[15] That is, what if the person agent-causes her volition but her doing so is causally necessitated by some event or circumstances over which she has no control? Clearly, if this were so the agent would not enjoy power over her will and we should not, on Reid's own theory, regard the action resulting from that act of will as a free action. So, contrary to Reid, it seems that the fact that the person agent-causes the act of will is insufficient to ensure that her action is free.[16] The answer to this objection is that what it asks about is impossible. We sometimes speak of causing someone to cause something else. But if we fully understand the notion of agent-causation, we can

14. I must warn the reader that my account of Reidian freedom is not the standard account. For a discussion of the standard account and a defense of my account, see my essay "Two Concepts of Freedom," *Proceedings of the American Philosophical Association* 61, suppl. (1987): 43–64.

15. Another supposition might be that some person has agent-caused our agent's causing of that act of will.

16. This point is nicely put by William Hamilton as a critical note to the very sentence in Reid that we are discussing. "Only if he were not determined to that determination. But is the person an *original undetermined cause* of the determination of his will? If he be not, then is he not a *free* agent, and the scheme of Necessity is admitted" (p. 602).

see, I think, that no event or agent can cause someone to agent-cause some change. And this, again, is because of Reid's third condition of agent causation, the condition that requires that you have the power to refrain from bringing about the change.[17] Since having the power not to cause a change is required for you to be the agent-cause of some change, and since being caused to cause some change implies that you cannot refrain from causing that change, it follows that no one can be caused to agent-cause a change. If you are the agent-cause of some change, you were not caused to agent-cause that change.

Objection 2

A more difficult objection emerges when we try to reconcile agent-causation with Reid's metaphysical claim that every event has an agent-cause. An indeterminist about free will is likely to hold that the act of will is an event without a cause, thus encountering the apparent difficulty that the agent's volition is an event without explanation, something that simply occurs "out of the blue." Reid's view appears to be immune to this difficulty because the act of will is an event and, as such, requires a cause. If the act of will is free, its cause is not some event; it is the agent whose act of will it is. Being the cause of the act of will, the agent must satisfy Reid's three conditions of agent-causation. Thus the agent must have had the power to bring about the act of will, the power to refrain from bringing about the act of will, and must have exerted her power to bring about the act of will. The last of these conditions, however, appears to generate an infinite regress of events that an agent must cause if she is to cause her act of will. For what it tells us is that to produce the act of will the agent must exert her power to bring about the act of will. Now an exertion of power is itself an event. As such, it too must have a cause. On Reid's view the cause must again be the agent herself. But to have caused this exertion the agent must have had the power to bring it about and must have exerted that power. Each exertion of power is itself an event which the agent can cause only by having the power to cause it and by exerting that power. As Reid reminds us, "In order to the production of *any effect,* there must be in the cause, not only power, but the exertion of that power: for power that is not exerted produces no effect" (p. 603, emphasis mine). The result is that in order to produce any act of will whatever, the agent must cause an infinite number of exertions.

My answer to the infinite regress objection is this.[18] I think Reid takes an event to be either the coming into existence of a substance or a

---

17. Put somewhat differently, it is because the concept of active power requires that you as agent have the power *to cause or not to cause* that change.

18. I warn the reader that what I now present is not based on direct evidence from Reid's writings. It is my speculation as to what he could (should) say were he confronted with this objection.

change that a substance undergoes. An act of will occurring in a person is an event, a change that person undergoes. Any change a being undergoes must have a cause. Either that being itself is the efficient cause of the change it undergoes, in which case it has active power and acts in producing that change, or some other being is the efficient cause of the change, in which case the being undergoing the change is merely passive with respect to the causing of that change, the exertion of active power being only in that being that produced the change. What is it for a being to act in producing some change which it undergoes? It is nothing more than for that being to exert the power it has to produce that change. "All that is necessary to the production of any effect, is power in an efficient cause to produce the effect, and the exertion of that power" (p. 603). Now my speculation is that apart from a thing's coming into existence, Reid believes that it is only the *changes things undergo* that require causes. A volition occurring in a person is a change that person undergoes. And if the person herself is the efficient cause of that change then she acted in producing it. Her acting to produce that volition is simply her exerting her power to produce that change (the occurrence of the volition) within herself. Now the exertion of power, unlike the volition, is not a change she undergoes; for it is her own activity, her own exercise of active power. As such, it does not require a cause. The exertion of our active power by which we produce some change in us is not itself a change in us that we undergo. Therefore, it is not the sort of thing for which Reid's causal principles would require a cause.

To support this line of reasoning, I offer what I regard as a compelling argument for the view that the exertion of power by which an agent produces an effect cannot itself be an effect produced by an efficient cause. For suppose it were. Suppose, following Reid's remarks about volitions, I say, "I consider the exertion of active power as an effect." If so, then like my volition that could be produced in me by God or some other efficient cause, my exertion of active power in bringing about something could be caused by God or some other efficient cause distinct from me. But it is a conceptual impossibility within Reid's theory for God or any other efficient cause to produce in me an exertion of my active power. For my exertion of active power in producing something is identical with my agent-causing that thing. And, as we saw earlier, it is impossible that I should be caused to agent-cause anything. If x causes y to cause something then y does not have the power not to cause that thing.[19] And an agent has power to cause only if he has power not to cause. For Reid this is a conceptual truth. "Power to produce any effect, implies power not to produce it" (p. 523).

The conclusion just reached, however, ignores (*a*) that an exertion of active power certainly appears to be an event and (*b*) that Reid declares

19. I take this to be a truth on Reid's theory even when $x = y$.

that every event has an efficient cause. How then can we accept the arguments just given to show that Reid's true view is that an exertion of active power is the activity of an agent and, as such, has no efficient cause? My suggestion (speculation) is that Reid is using 'event' to denote just what his more elaborate principles specify: the coming into existence of a substance; any change that a substance undergoes. This suggestion is, of course, ad hoc.[20] But the result is that a solution is possible for the infinite regress objection that leaves the fundamental themes of Reid's agency theory intact. No major surgery on his system is required.

For those of us who would hold that an exertion of power, no less than an act of will, is a change in an agent and, therefore, an event, the only conclusion the above arguments will permit is that Reid is, after all, an indeterminist. Not all events have efficient causes. In particular, any event that consists in an exertion of active power will lack an efficient cause. The deeper point that has emerged, however, is that Reid's theory precludes an efficient cause of an exertion of active power by an agent. And this point provides the solution to the infinite regress of causes objection. Of less importance is the matter of whether or not an exertion of active power qualifies as an event. If it does, Reid is an indeterminist. If it does not, Reid is not an indeterminist, for every event has an efficient cause.[21]

Objection 3

According to some recent advocates of agent-causation, there is an irreducible causal relation binding a substance (the agent) to an event (the act of will).[22] One apparent trouble with the notion of such an irreducible causal relation is that the act of will takes place at a particular time, whereas the agent that causes it is an enduring substance. As Baruch Brody puts it, "After all, the agent presumably existed for a long time

---

20. In one of his letters to Dr. Gregory there is some slight indication that Reid may have taken an event to be nothing more than a change a thing undergoes. But at best this is only one reading of the following remark: "I apprehend that there is one original notion of *cause* grounded in human nature, and that this is the notion on which the maxim is grounded—that every change or event must have a cause" (p. 75).

21. Where S is an agent and *e* is an event that S agent-causes, does "S's agent-causing *e*" depict an event? If so, there is no escape from the conclusion that Reid is an indeterminist. For such events can have neither an agent-cause nor a physical cause. But it would still be instructive to note that Reid is a peculiar sort of indeterminist. For his position would then best be construed as holding that every event that logically can have a cause does have a cause.

22. See, e.g., Roderick Chisholm, "Freedom and Action," in *Freedom and Determinism*, ed. Keith Lehrer (New York: Random House, 1966), pp. 16–23. Also see Taylor, pp. 99–138.

before that particular act of willing, so it is not the mere existence of the agent that produces the act of willing. What then causes the act of willing to take place when it does? The answer to this question is the missing link in Reid's theory of human liberty."[23] I believe this is a confusion in an otherwise excellent introduction to Reid's *Essays*. When Reid says that the agent is the cause of the act of will, he does not mean that we are left with nothing more than an enduring substance that mysteriously brings about an event (an act of will) without doing anything to bring it about. A person agent-causes her act of will by exercising her active power to bring about the act of will. The exercise of her active power is an event.[24] It is incorrect, therefore, to suppose that when a person agent-causes her act of will the only event to be found in the neighborhood of the agent is the act of will. Without the exercise of active power there can be no occurrence of the act of will (assuming that the agent is truly the cause of the volition). Indeed, Reid says as much: "So every change must be caused by some exertion, or by the cessation of some exertion of power. That which produces a change by the exertion of its power, we call the *cause* of that change; and the change produced, the *effect* of that cause" (p. 515).

Although Brody is incorrect in his representation of Reid's theory, it would be a mistake to take the correction I have made as implying that the agent causes her act of will by first causing some other event—an exertion of active power. Often enough, the agent does cause an event by causing some other event that event-causes the event in question. I cause my action of breaking the window by causing my action of throwing the brick against the window. The latter action causes the former.[25] But if agent-causation is correct, there must be some event the agent directly causes in the sense that there is nothing else the agent causes that brings about that event.[26] On Reid's theory the event the agent directly

23. Baruch Brody, introduction, in *Essays on the Active Powers of the Human Mind*, by Thomas Reid (Cambridge, Mass.: MIT Press, 1969), p. xix. The same criticism and others are advanced by Irving Thalberg, *Misconceptions of Mind and Freedom* (New York: University Press of America, 1983), pp. 153–84.

24. I am here expressing my own view. Earlier, in discussing the infinite regress objection, I proposed that Reid would not have viewed the exertion of power (resulting in an act of will) as an event.

25. Actually, this is something of an oversimplification. The event that event-causes another event will be rather complex since it must be physically necessary that given it the second event occurs. Also, following Goldman, we should perhaps say that the second action "causally generates" the first. Alvin Goldman, *A Theory of Human Action* (Englewood Cliffs, N.J.: Prentice-Hall, 1970), pp. 20–25.

26. Compare Chisholm's view of an agent's undertaking as something the agent brings about directly; Roderick Chisholm, *Person and Object* (La Salle, Ill.: Open Court, 1976), pp. 84–85.

causes is the act of will. He directly causes it by exercising his active power to bring it about.

Objection 4

When we compare Reidian freedom with Lockean freedom we note that in Reid's account there is no mention at all of a power to do or will otherwise. In view of this, suppose we conjure up a Frankfurt-type example wherein a mad scientist has gained access to your volitional capacity and not only can tell what act of will you are about to bring about but, worse yet, can send electrical currents into your brain that will cause a particular act of will to occur even though it is not the act of will that you would have brought about if left to your own devices. We will suppose that you are deliberating on a matter of great concern: killing Jones. Our mad scientist happens to be interested in Jones's going on to his reward, but he wants Jones to die by your hand. And rather than activate the machine to cause your act of will to kill Jones, he would prefer that you bring about the act of will and the subsequent action of killing Jones. As it turns out, you do conclude your deliberations by agent-causing your act of will to kill Jones. The mad scientist could and would have caused that act of will in you had you been going to will not to kill Jones. But no such action was necessary on his part. There is a process in place (the mad scientist's machine, etc.) that assures that you shall will to kill Jones. But the process is activated if, but only if, you are not going to cause your volition to kill Jones. Given the machine, your willing to kill Jones was inevitable; it was not in your power to avoid willing to kill Jones. Are we to say in such circumstances that your action of killing Jones is free? And if Reid's account of free action requires such a conclusion, shouldn't we reject it?

In answering this objection, the first point to note is that Reid's account does imply that in these circumstances you acted freely in killing Jones. Initially, just the opposite point of view would recommend itself. For in this first and frequently quoted statement of what it is for an action to be free he says, "If, in any action, he had power to will what he did, or not to will it, in that action he is free" (p. 599). And in our mad scientist case it is clear that you do not have the power not to will to kill Jones. (Should you be about to will to do something else or to refrain from willing to kill Jones, the machine is programmed to cause in you the volition to kill Jones.) So initially the mad scientist case seems to be one in which you do not have power over the volition to kill Jones. (This in fact might be what Reid would have said had he been confronted with our mad scientist case.)

But I think the concept of agent-causation requires a different answer. For there is nothing in our mad scientist case that conflicts with the view that you are the agent-cause of the act of will to kill Jones. Indeed, you are the cause; the scientist's machine monitors your brain but does nothing in the way of causing your volition. What this means is that we must distinguish between

1. It was in your power not to will to kill Jones.

and

2. It was in your power not to cause your volition to kill Jones.

In our mad scientist case, 1 is false. But 2 is not false. You do have the power not to cause your volition to kill Jones. The mad scientist has so arranged matters that the machine automatically causes the volition to kill Jones in you if, but only if, you are about to not will to kill Jones. This being so, 1 is clearly false. You cannot prevent your willing to kill Jones; for if you do not cause your willing to kill Jones the machine will cause it. But 2 is not false. You do have the power not to cause your volition to kill Jones. The mad scientist has so arranged matters that the machine automatically causes that volition in you if, but only if, you are about to not will to kill Jones. But it still may be up to you whether you shall be the cause of your volition to kill Jones. This power, Reid would argue, depends on a number of factors: the will of God, the continued existence of the agent, the absence of prior internal events and circumstances determining the occurrence of the volition to kill Jones, etc. It also depends on the mad scientist's decision to activate the machine only if you are about to not will to kill Jones. The scientist can cause you to will to kill Jones. He does this by causing that act of will in you.[27] But if he does so, you do not agent-cause your volition to kill Jones. The real agent-cause is the scientist. So if you have the power to cause your volition to kill Jones, you also have the power not to cause that volition. It is impossible to have the one power without having the other.

In saying that Reid's account of a free action requires that you act freely in the mad scientist case I am interpreting Reid's "power to will or not will" as the power to cause or not cause the act of will. Under this interpretation, as I have argued, you do have power over your will in the mad scientist case.[28] Since this is all Reid requires for your act to be free, it seems that his view requires that you kill Jones freely in the mad sci-

27. I take Reid to hold (rightly) that causing a volition to do A in an agent is to cause the agent's willing to do A. Thus when an agent wills to do A we can raise the question of whether the cause of his so willing is the agent himself or something else.

28. The mad scientist case is an example of *fail-safe causation*. It should not be confused with cases of *causal overdetermination* where there are two independent causal processes causally responsible for the same event.

entist case. My own intuitions suggest that you do act freely in this case and are prima facie responsible for what you have done. So my answer to the objection is (1) that Reid's theory does imply that you kill Jones freely (in the mad scientist case) and (2) that this conclusion is no reason to reject his theory.

RESPONSIBILITY

Many philosophers have held that an agent is morally responsible for her action only if she could have done otherwise. This position has come under attack.[29] From our earlier discussion, it is clear that on the agent-causation view of freedom—at least as I see it—the power to do or will otherwise is not required for a person's action or act of will to be freely done. Thus, it is reasonable to side with those who oppose the principle that moral responsibility for an action implies the power (at the time) to have done otherwise. But surely there must be some connection between moral responsibility and active power. What then is that connection?

In the course of arguing from the fact that we are sometimes morally accountable for what we do to the conclusion that we possess libertarian freedom, Reid says the following: "Another thing implied in the notion of a moral and accountable being, is *power to do what he is accountable for.* That no man can be under a moral obligation to do what it is impossible for him to do, or to forbear what it is impossible for him to forbear, is an axiom as self-evident as any in mathematics. It cannot be contradicted, without overturning all notion of moral obligation; nor can there be an exception to it, when it is rightly understood" (p. 621).

Reid's argument, I believe, proceeds as follows. We are morally accountable beings. To be a morally accountable being is to be such that sometimes one has a moral obligation to do (forbear doing) an action. This is the first premise of his argument. The second premise is an appeal to the principle that ought implies can. If a person has a moral obligation to do (forbear doing) an action then that person has it in his power to do (forbear doing) that action. Therefore, a person sometimes has it in his power to do an action and sometimes has it in his power to forbear doing an action.[30]

Reid thinks that the basic claim (that we are morally accountable beings) on which this argument is based "affords an invincible argument

29. Harry Frankfurt, "Alternate Possibilities and Moral Responsibility," *Journal of Philosophy* 16 (1969): 828–39.

30. As we have seen, on Reid's account of human freedom, once it is established that it is in our power to do a certain action (or in our power to forbear doing an action), it is thereby established that we are sometimes at liberty to do an action and sometimes at liberty to forbear doing an action.

that man is endowed with Moral Liberty" (p. 620). For he thinks that the second premise of his argument is a necessary truth. "*Active power*, therefore, is necessarily implied in the very notion of a morally accountable being" (p. 622). Moreover, although he notes an objection to his second premise, it is clear that he believes that premise to be not only necessary, but fairly obviously so. In examining his argument it will be helpful to consider the most common response of those who accept Lockean freedom but believe our volitions to be causally determined by events beyond our control, to examine the objection Reid notes to his second premise, along with his reply, and, finally, to see what modification of his second premise is, or may be, required by our earlier account of Reid's conception of human freedom.

Let's call those who hold both that we have Lockean freedom and that our volitions are necessitated by earlier events beyond our control "necessitarians." The most common necessitarian reply to Reid's argument is to reject Reid's second premise (or to give it an interpretation from which the conclusion of the argument will not follow). According to this view, being morally obligated to do an action requires only that we have power to do the action if we should will to do it. But since the necessitarian does not extend to the agent power over the determinations of his will, he cannot agree with Reid that at the time in question the agent must have it in his power to will to do the action. For on the necessitarian account the volition to do A is rendered either causally necessary or causally impossible by factors over which the agent had no control.[31] He can allow that agent has the capacity to have a volition and the capacity not to have a volition. But it is one thing to have the capacity to have or not have a volition, as opposed to something like a stone that has no such capacity, and quite another thing to have the active power at the time in question to determine which capacity is to be realized. On Reid's view, if I am morally obligated to do A then, even though I did not will to do A, it must have been in my power to will to do A. On the necessitarian view, if I did not will to do A then, given the causes, my willing to do A was causally impossible—in which case, it was not in my power at the time to will to do A.

In denying Reid's second premise, the necessitarian claims that power over the determinations of the will is not necessary for being morally

31. Actually, necessitarians such as Hobbes and Anthony Collins appear to have held that the necessary connection between a cause and its effect is logical. That is, if A causes B it is logically impossible that A should exist and B not exist or not be produced by A; see Thomas Hobbes, *The English Works of Thomas Hobbes* (London, 1841), vol. 5, p. 385. Concerning the death of Caesar, Collins remarks: "Whereas let them suppose all the same circumstances to come to pass that did precede his death; and then it will be as impossible to conceive (if they think justly) his death could have come to pass anywhere else, as they conceive it impossible for two and two to make six" (*A Philosophical Inquiry concerning Human Liberty* [London, 1717], pp. 105–6).

accountable for doing (failing to do) an action. All that is necessary in the way of power—if an agent was morally obligated to perform some action—is that the agent could have done the action if she had willed to do it. But I think this isn't right. For suppose that by stimulating various parts of your brain I can effectively control your volitions. And suppose I thus brought it about that you actively willed to forbear doing that action. Suppose further that, given the circumstances, your willing to forbear doing that action necessitated your not doing that action. Of course, it may still have been true that had you willed to do the action you could have done the action. You were not driven not to do the action regardless of what your will might be. But given my activity you could not will other than to not do the action. Once all this is made clear, isn't it obvious that it is a mistake to suppose that your moral duty was to perform the action in question? For in the circumstances there was nothing you could will that would have resulted in your voluntarily performing that action. Since ought implies can, and since you could not do other than will to forbear, and thus not do the action in question, you cannot really have had an obligation to do that action on that occasion. Therefore, you are not morally accountable for that particular failure to act. And since on the system of necessity we never have power over our wills, we will never be morally accountable for doing (forbearing to do) an action. As Reid notes, "accountableness can no more agree with necessity than light with darkness" (p. 616).[32]

Reid notes an objection that has been raised against the axiom that no one can be under a moral obligation to do what is not within his power. The objection is this: "When a man, by his own fault, has disabled himself from doing his duty, his obligation, they say, remains, though he is now unable to discharge it" (p. 621). The objector proposes that we distinguish between the case where some other agent (against your will or knowledge) deprives you of your ability to fulfill your obligation and the case where you willingly and knowingly deprive yourself of your ability to fulfill your obligation. In the former case you would not be morally accountable for failing to do what, without the loss of your ability, you would be obligated to do. But in the latter case, so the objection goes, you continue to be obligated to do what you no longer are able to do. For in the latter case your inability to fulfill your duty is your own fault. Thus, to take one of Reid's examples, if a sailor's duty is to climb aloft at his captain's order, and if someone should cut off the sailor's fingers, the sailor would cease to be obligated to climb aloft, for it is no longer in his power to do so. But, so the objection goes, if out of desire for the ease of hospital life the sailor cuts off his own fingers, he does not cease to have

---

32. The basic point here is that the necessitarian's conception of what it is for an agent to have had the power to do A (could have done A if she had so willed) is inadequate to satisfy the sense of 'can' in *ought implies can*.

the obligation to climb aloft at his captain's command—even though it is no longer in his power to fulfill his command. Reid disagrees: "He is guilty of a great crime; but after he has been punished according to the demerit of his crime, will his captain insist that he shall still do the duty of a sailor? Will he command him to go aloft when it is impossible for him to do it, and punish him as guilty of disobedience? Surely, if there be any such thing as justice and injustice, this would be unjust and wanton cruelty" (p. 621).

Reid's point is that we must distinguish the sailor's duty not to render himself unable to climb aloft from his duty to climb aloft at his captain's command. Once we make this distinction we will see that the sailor's fault and just punishment is connected solely with his violation of his first duty—a violation he, presumably, could have avoided. But, once he has cut off his fingers, it is a mistake for us to think that the sailor remains obligated to climb aloft. We may take into account his motive to avoid his duty when we assess his blameworthiness for having cut off his fingers. But once they have been cut off, there can be no obligation any longer for the sailor to climb aloft at his captain's command.[33]

On the interpretation I gave of a Reidian free action, an action is free if (*a*) it results from the agent's act of will to perform that action and (*b*) the agent caused that act of will (having the power not to cause it). Suppose I am deliberating about killing Jones and conclude my deliberations by agent-causing the volition to kill Jones, with the result that I kill him. On Reid's theory, since it was in my power not to produce that volition ("Power to produce implies power not to produce"), my action was free; I had active power with respect to that action. Suppose, however, that a mechanism exists (a fail-safe cause) that would produce in me the act of will to kill Jones if but only if I do not produce it myself. We shall suppose that the volition, regardless of its causal origin (whether me or the mechanism), results in my action of killing Jones. It turns out, then, that my action of killing Jones is unavoidable. For although it is in my power not to cause the act of will to kill Jones, I cannot prevent the occurrence of that volition and the action that flows from it. Moreover, regardless of causal origin, the volition will be my act of willing. For it is conceptually impossible for a volition to kill Jones to occur in me without it being true that *I* will to kill Jones.[34] So even if I do not cause the volition to kill Jones, I, nevertheless, will to kill Jones and perform the action of killing him.

Now killing Jones is an action that, if freely done, is a fit subject for moral evaluation. Since my action was freely done I am morally respon-

33. For some criticisms of Reid's view that ought implies can, see Keith Lehrer, *Thomas Reid* (London and New York: Routledge, 1989), pp. 257–58, 273–76.

34. Willing (like thinking, imagining, and believing) cannot occur in a person without it being true that *the person* wills (thinks, imagines, believes).

sible for it. Thus, given Reid's account of a free action, it turns out that a person may be morally responsible for an action even though the agent could not have done otherwise, could not have avoided doing the action. And the question before us is whether this conclusion is consistent with the principle of ought implies can that constitutes a key premise in Reid's second argument for the reality of human freedom.

My answer is that there is no inconsistency. For an inconsistency arises only if Reid's principle:

1. An agent is morally obligated to do A (forbear doing A) only if it is in the agent's power to do A (forbear doing A).

is conjoined with a second principle that he does not assert:

2. If it is morally wrong for an agent to do A (forbear doing A) then the agent is morally obligated to forbear doing A (do A).

For given that it was morally wrong for me to kill Jones, it follows from 2 that I was morally obligated to forbear killing Jones. And given Reid's principle, it then follows that it was in my power to forbear killing Jones, to avoid killing Jones.

What we've seen is that on my interpretation of Reid's account of a free action, if we follow Reid in holding an agent morally responsible for what he does freely then an agent may be morally responsible for an action even though it was not in his power to avoid doing that action, was not in his power to forbear doing it or to do otherwise. What we've also seen is that this result leads to a contradiction if both principles 1 and 2 are adopted. For it will turn out that it both was and was not in my power to avoid killing Jones.[35] Since Reid clearly embraces principle 1, we need either to modify my interpretation of Reid's account of a free action or to abandon principle 2. Since I think the interpretation has good textual support and since, given principle 1, I think we have independent grounds for doubting principle 2, I propose that we reject principle 2.[36] For quite apart from Reid's theory of freedom, I think our intuitions support the view that I freely kill Jones and am responsible for doing so, even though the existence of the fail-safe cause renders me unable to do otherwise. Therefore, if we stick with our intuitions about such cases and accept the fundamental principle that ought implies can, we really have

35. Since Reid would allow that we are morally accountable for our free acts of will (those we cause, having the power not to cause), a similar inconsistency would arise when we reformulate principles 1 and 2 with respect to volitions.

36. In place of principle 2 I suggest the following principle: If it is morally wrong for an agent to do A (forbear doing A) then the agent is morally obligated to forbear doing A (do A) *if* forbearing doing A (doing A) is in his power.

no alternative but to reject principle 2 along with the principle of alternate possibilities (if an agent is morally responsible for an action then he could have done otherwise). This does not mean, however, that the person who does what is morally wrong has no moral obligation not to cause his act of will to do that thing.

Because of the fail-safe cause (something that causes my volition if and only if I do not), my volition and action may be unavoidable. Suppose, however, that instead of a fail-safe cause there is another being or causal process that simultaneously with me produces my volition and resulting action. If this is possible, my volition to kill Jones could be overdetermined and again unavoidable. Is this possible on Reid's theory of what it is to act freely? Could my volition and action be free (in Reid's sense) and also the inevitable causal product of another causal process or agent over which I have no control?

A familiar example of overdetermination is when two light switches turn on the same light. Flipping either switch is causally sufficient for the light going on. If both switches are flipped simultaneously, the event of the light going on is causally overdetermined. The question before us is whether an act of will (and its resulting action) can be overdetermined in the following manner. You as agent cause the occurrence of a particular volition. We will suppose that the volition occurs at t. Perhaps unknown to you some actual causal process, independent of your causal activity, also causes that very same volition to occur at t. If so, then your act of will is causally overdetermined; its occurrence is assured both by the exercise of your power as agent to cause it and by the independent causal process that brings it about at t. Moreover, it appears that we have a further example in which you may be morally accountable for an act of will (and resulting action) that is unavoidable for you. For we will suppose that you exercise no control over the independent causal process that results in the occurrence of your volition at t.

Harry Frankfurt treats the case of overdetermination in the same way that I have treated the case of fail-safe causation. He views it as a genuine counterinstance to the principle of alternate possibilities, the principle that holds that one is morally responsible for an action only if one could have avoided performing it (could have done otherwise). Thus, Frankfurt considers the case of the drug addict who wills to take the drug because that is the desire that he wants to move him all the way to action. On Frankfurt's account, such a person acts freely and of his own free will.[37] But his desire to take the drug is also efficacious because of

37. Harry G. Frankfurt, "Freedom of the Will and the Concept of a Person," *Journal of Philosophy* 68 (1971): 5–20. Although on Frankfurt's view the addict acts freely and of his own free will in taking the drug, he does not have freedom of will because he is not free to make the first-order desire not to take the drug *his will*. Given his addiction, he is bound to will to take the drug.

his physical addiction. The efficaciousness of his first-order desire to take the drug is therefore overdetermined. That desire moves him to action because he wants it to and also because of the force of his physical addiction, either being sufficient to make that desire his will. Suppose, however, that the addiction plays no role in his deliberations. Suppose that had the addiction not been present the addict would still have wanted his first-order desire for the drug to be his will, with the result that that desire would have moved him all the way to action. Given the addiction, the addict could not avoid taking the drug. But, so Frankfurt argues, the fact that he could not do otherwise is here irrelevant to assessing his moral responsibility.

My own view is that the drug addict does not act freely in taking the drug and, accordingly, is not morally responsible for his action. He does not will or act freely because his act of will occurs of necessity. We may say that a volition occurs of necessity when it is the product of an actual causal process over which the agent has no control. Undoubtedly, this would be Reid's own view as well. "If . . . the determination of his will be the necessary consequence of something involuntary in the state of his mind, or of something in his external circumstances, he is not free; he has not what I call the Liberty of a Moral Agent, but is subject to Necessity" (p. 599).[38] Perhaps, then, we should amend Reid's account of what it is to act freely. We can say that an agent acts freely just in case the act of will involved in the action is caused by the agent and is not the causal result of an actual causal process outside the agent's control. In the case of the fail-safe cause, the act of will, when produced by the agent, does not occur of necessity, for there is no actual causal process outside the agent's control that results in the volition.[39]

In this article I have tried to explicate Reid's theory of agent-causation, defend it against several objections, extend it in certain directions that are not clearly justified by his own writings, and draw out some of its connections with human freedom and moral responsibility. I have done so in the belief that the theory both is coherent and can help us in understanding the relations among agency, freedom, and responsibility. Even if I have been successful to some extent in this task, very serious questions remain to be answered by the theory. For example, since the exertion of active power by which the agent brings about his act of will is an event that has no cause whatever, it would seem that its occurrence is fortuitous, "out of the blue," and not something for which the agent has any responsibility or over which he can have any control.

38. What is less clear is how Reid's theory of agent-causation can preclude the kind of overdetermination envisaged in the drug addict case.

39. In the fail-safe case it is not up to the agent whether his volition will or will not occur, but it is up to the agent whether it will occur freely or not. For more on this matter see my essay, "Causing and Being Responsible for What Is Inevitable," this volume.

But if this should be so, Reid's entire theory is a rope of sand. And what explanation (causal or otherwise) can be given for an agent's exertion of power at a certain time? What role is to be assigned to the agent's motives when she acts with libertarian freedom? These are hard questions. It remains to be seen whether the theory has the resources to answer them and others that lie in its path.[40]

40. I address these questions in *Thomas Reid on Freedom and Morality* (Ithaca, N.Y.: Cornell University Press, 1991).

11

What We Are Morally Responsible For

HARRY FRANKFURT

It might have been expected that the freedom of a person's *will* would most naturally be construed as a matter of whether it is up to him what he wills. In fact, it is generally understood as having to do with whether it is up to the person what he *does*. Someone's will is regarded as being free at a given time, in other words, only if at that time it is up to him whether he does one thing or does another instead. When this conception of free will is joined to the supposition that free will is a necessary condition for moral responsibility, the result is the Principle of Alternate Possibilities (PAP): a person is morally responsible for what he has done only if he could have done otherwise.

For those who accept PAP, it is an important question whether people ever *can* do anything other than what they actually do. Incompatibilists maintain that if determinism is true, this is not possible. On the other hand, compatibilists insist that even in a deterministic world a person may have genuine alternatives in the sense PAP requires. In my view, PAP is false.[1] The fact that a person lacks alternatives does preclude his being morally responsible when it alone accounts for his behavior. But a lack of alternatives is not inconsistent with moral responsibility when someone acts as he does for reasons of his own, rather than simply because no other alternative is open to him. It is therefore of no particular significance, so far as ascriptions of moral responsibility are concerned,

Reprinted by permission of the author and editors from *How Many Questions? Essays in Honor of Sidney Morgenbesser*, ed. Leigh S. Cauman, Isaac Levi, Charles Parsons, and Robert Schwartz (Indianapolis: Hackett, 1982).

1. I argue for this in "Alternate Possibilities and Moral Responsibility," *Journal of Philosophy*, LXVI (1969): 829–39.

whether determinism is true or false, or whether it is compatible or in-compatible with free will as PAP construes it.

I

The appeal of PAP may owe something to a presumption that it is a cor-ollary of the Kantian thesis that "ought" implies "can."[2] In fact, however, the relation between Kant's doctrine and PAP is not as close as it may seem to be. With respect to any action, Kant's doctrine has to do with the agent's ability to perform *that* action. PAP, on the other hand, concerns his ability to do *something else.* Moreover, the Kantian view leaves open the possibility that a person for whom only one course of action is avail-able fulfills an obligation when he pursues that course of action and is morally praiseworthy for doing so. On the other hand, PAP implies that such a person cannot earn any moral credit for what he does. This makes it clear that renouncing PAP does not require denying that "ought" im-plies "can" and that PAP is not entailed by the Kantian view.

Constructing counterexamples to PAP is not difficult. It is necessary only to conceive circumstances which make it inevitable that a person will perform some action but which do not bring it about that he per-forms it. Thus let us say that a person decides to take and does take a certain drug, just in order to enjoy the euphoria he expects it to induce. Now suppose further that his taking the drug would have been made to happen in any case, by forces which were in fact inactive but which would have come into play if he had not on his own decided and acted as he did. Let us say that, unknown to himself, the person is addicted to the drug and would therefore have been driven irresistibly to take it if he had not freely gone about doing so. His dormant addiction guarantees that he could have avoided neither deciding to take nor taking the drug, but it plays no role in bringing about his decision or his act. As the actual sequence of events develops, everything happens as if he were not ad-dicted at all. The addiction is clearly irrelevant in this case to the ques-tion of whether the person is morally responsible for taking the drug.

The distinctively potent element in this sort of counterexample to PAP is a certain kind of overdetermination, which involves a sequential fail-safe arrangement such that one causally sufficient factor functions exclusively as backup for another. The arrangement ensures that a cer-tain effect will be brought about by one or the other of the two causal factors, but not by both together. Thus the backup factor may contrib-ute nothing whatever to bringing about the effect whose occurrence it guarantees.

2. Cf. Robert Cummins, "Could Have Done Otherwise," *The Personalist,* LX,4 (October 1979): 411-414.

II

Peter van Inwagen has argued forcefully that even if counterexamples of this kind—adapting his usage I shall refer to them as "F-style counter-examples"—do require that PAP be abandoned, the compatibilism-incompatibilism dispute retains its significance.[3] In his view the supposition that PAP is false does not, as I have claimed, entail the ir-relevance to questions concerning moral responsibility of the relation-ship between determinism and free will. "Even if PAP is false," he says,

> it is *nonetheless* true that unless free will and determinism are compat-ible, determinism and moral responsibility are incompatible. Thus, Frankfurt's arguments do not, even if they are sound, rob the compatibilist-incompatibilist debate of its central place in the old con-troversy about determinism and moral responsibility. (223)

To support this position van Inwagen formulates three principles, which he regards as "very similar to PAP" but which he believes are unlike it in being immune to objections of the sort by which PAP is undermined (203). He contends that demonstrating this immunity serves to reestab-lish the relevance of alternate possibilities and, hence, of the compati-bilism issue, to the theory of moral responsibility.

Van Inwagen calls his first principle "the Principle of Possible Action":

> PPA A person is morally responsible for failing to perform a given act only if he could have performed that act. (204)

This principle concerns "unperformed acts (things we have left un-done)" (203). The second and third principles, which van Inwagen calls "Principles of Possible Prevention," have to do with "the consequences of what we have done (or left undone)" (203):

> PPP$_1$ A person is morally responsible for a certain event (particular) only if he could have prevented it. (206)

and

> PPP$_2$ A person is morally responsible for a state of affairs only if (that state of affairs obtains and) he could have prevented it from ob-taining. (210)

3. Peter van Inwagen, "Ability and Responsibility," *Philosophical Review*, LXXXVII, 2 (April 1978): 201–24. Hereafter in my text, numbers within parentheses refer to this essay.

PAP is concerned only with a person's moral responsibility for *what he has done*. Thus the supposition that PAP is false leaves it open that there may be things *other* than items of his own behavior—viz., unperformed acts or events or states of affairs that are consequences of what he has done or left undone—for which a person cannot be morally responsible unless his will is or was free.

Corresponding to each of his three principles van Inwagen provides a version of incompatibilism. According to the first of these, determinism entails that anyone who has failed to perform a given act could not have performed it. The second and third add up to the claim that determinism entails that there are no events or states of affairs—and hence no consequences of what someone has done—such that anyone could have prevented them from occurring or from obtaining. Now van Inwagen is convinced that PPA, PPP_1, and PPP_2 are true. So his position is that if the versions of incompatibilism that correspond to those principles are also true, then "determinism entails that no one has ever been or could be responsible for any event, state of affairs, or unperformed act" (222).

I believe that, despite van Inwagen's denial, his first principle actually is vulnerable to F-style counterexamples. On the other hand, it may well be that the same strategy does not also work against his other two principles. But if this is so, it is only because PPP_1 and PPP_2 are irrelevant to the relation between free will and determinism. Their immunity to F-style counterexamples therefore provides no support for the conclusions van Inwagen proposes to draw concerning how the theory of moral responsibility is affected by considerations pertaining to determinism and to free will.

III

In his discussion of PPA van Inwagen does not consider the rather natural suspicion that the principle is simply equivalent to PAP. Instead he proceeds directly to examine a putative counterexample. Since he regards the construction of the example as adapting to the case of unperformed acts the general strategy that makes trouble for PAP, he supposes that the example provides a critical test of whether this strategy is effective against PPA.

In the example, van Inwagen witnesses a crime and considers telephoning the police to report it. Because he does not want to get involved, he decides against calling the police and does nothing. However, unknown to him, the telephone system has in fact collapsed, and every relevant telephone is out of order. Concerning this situation, he poses the following question: "Am I responsible for failing to call the police?"

His response is unequivocal and emphatic: "Of course not. I couldn't have called them." Given the circumstances, he says,

> I may be responsible for failing to *try* to call the police (that much I *could* have done), or for refraining from calling the police, or for . . . being selfish and cowardly. But I am simply not responsible for failing to call the police. (205)

In van Inwagen's opinion, then, the example leaves PPA altogether un-scathed. His conclusion is that "Frankfurt's style of argument cannot be used to refute PPA" (205).

Now being responsible for something may mean, in a certain strong sense of the notion, being *fully* responsible for it, i.e., providing for it *both* a sufficient *and* a necessary condition. A person is fully responsible, then, for all and only those events or states of affairs which come about because of what he does and which would not come about if he did oth-erwise. The person in van Inwagen's example (hereafter, "*P*") is not in this sense responsible for his failure to call the police. The fact that he behaved as he did was a sufficient condition for his having failed, but it was not a necessary condition: given the collapse of the telephone sys-tem, he would have failed no matter what he had done. Perhaps the rea-son van Inwagen finds it so obvious that *P*'s inability to do what he failed to do entails that *P* is not morally responsible for his failure is that he construes moral responsibility as presupposing responsibility in this strong sense.

In my opinion, full responsibility is not a necessary condition for moral responsibility. Thus I believe that *P* may be morally responsible for failing to call the police even though he could not have avoided the failure. But I do not propose to defend this position here. Instead I shall attempt to establish two other points, which I think are more germane to van Inwagen's ultimate conclusions. The first is that the question of whether moral responsibility presupposes full responsibility has no *moral* interest. The second is that even if moral responsibility does pre-suppose full responsibility, van Inwagen's putative counterexample to PPA cannot serve his purpose.

IV

Suppose that, as it happens, we do not know whether the telephones were working when *P* made and acted upon his decision against calling the police. The fact that we lack this information would not stand in the way of our making a competent moral appraisal of *P* for what he did. At the very most it would make us uncertain just how to *describe* *P*'s failure to act—i.e., just how to *identify* what it is that we are evaluating him *for*. If the telephones were working, it might be more appropriate to refer to his failure to *call* the police; if they were out of order, it might be more appropriate to refer to his failure *to try to call the police*. But both the quality of the moral judgment and its degree—whether *P* is blameworthy or praiseworthy, and to what extent—will be exactly the same in both cases.

Which of the two failures his moral responsibility is construed as being *for* depends entirely, after all, upon the condition of the telephone system. In no way does it depend upon any act or omission or psychological state or property, whether faulty or meritorious, of his own. The difference between evaluating *P* for failing to call and evaluating him for failing to try to call can therefore have no *moral* significance. It is pertinent only to a decision concerning whether it would be more suitable to couch in one set of terms or in another what, in either case, remains the same moral estimate.

The point is not that a person's behavior is relevant to moral judgments concerning him only as evidence of his character or of his mental state. To be sure, *P*'s intentions and his other psychological characteristics do remain identical regardless of whether circumstances dictate that he be judged for failing to call the police or for failing to try to call them. But the reason why the moral evaluation of *P* will be the same in either case is not that he is subject to moral praise or blame exclusively for his psychological characteristics. What a person does is not relevant to moral evaluations of him merely because it is an indicator of his mental state. People merit praise and blame *for* what they do, and not just *on the basis of* what they do.

Notice that *P*'s intentions and the like are not the only things that remain the same whether the telephones are working or out of order. It is also clear that, whatever the condition of the telephone system, *P* makes or does not make the same bodily movements. Now *this* is what *P* is morally responsible for: it is for making these movements. He is morally responsible for making them, of course, only under certain conditions—only, for instance, when he makes them with certain intentions or expectations. But if those conditions are satisfied, then what he is morally responsible for is just making the movements themselves.

There are various ways in which a person's movements can be identified or described. Whether it will be more appropriate to describe what *P* does as calling the police or only as trying to call them will depend heavily upon what consequences his movements have. And the consequences of his movements will in turn depend upon whether the telephones are working. But it is precisely because *P* is judged simply for the making of his movements that the quality and the degree of his moral responsibility for what he does remain the same in either case. It goes without saying that his movements are unaffected by the consequences to which they lead, however decisively those consequences may affect the terms in which it is appropriate for the movements to be described.[4]

V

Since P would have failed to call the police no matter what he had done, he is not *fully* responsible for failing to call them. This provides van Inwagen with a reason for his claim that P is not *morally* responsible for the failure. But even if we suppose that moral responsibility requires responsibility in the strong sense, the judgment that PPA is immune to counterexamples would still be unwarranted. This is because the ineffectiveness of van Inwagen's counterexample is due to the particular characteristics of P's failure rather than to the characteristics of all failures as such. Therefore the counterexample does not provide a decisive test of PPA.

Why is P not fully responsible for his failure to call the police? It is because it is not within his power to bring it about that the police telephone rings: regardless of what bodily movements he makes, his movements will not have consequences of the kind that must occur if P is to be correctly describable as having called the police. But there are also failures which, unlike P's, do not depend at all upon the consequences of what a person does. They are failures for which the person's movements themselves, considered wholly apart from their consequences, are both a sufficient and a necessary condition. For example, suppose that as Q is driving he fails to keep his eyes straight ahead because he prefers to examine the interesting scenery to his left; and suppose further that if the scenery had not distracted him something else would have brought it about that he was looking to his left at that time. In these circumstances, Q cannot keep his eyes straight ahead. Is he morally responsible for failing to do so? Of course he is! The fact that he cannot avoid failing has no bearing upon his moral responsibility for the failure, since it plays no role in leading him to fail.

Notice that Q is *fully* responsible for his failure. Failing to keep one's eyes straight ahead is exclusively a matter of what movements a person makes; it is *constituted* by what the person himself does, and what the person does is therefore both a sufficient and a necessary condition for it. It

---

4. I am here invoking Donald Davidson's well-known view—developed with compelling lucidity in his essay entitled "Agency" (in Brinkley, Bronaugh, and Marras [eds.], *Agent, Action and Reason* [New York: Oxford, 1971], pp. 3–25)—according to which "we never do more than move our bodies; the rest is up to nature" (23). Adapting and paraphrasing his account (cf. 21) to the case of P, it might be said that after P has moved his hands in the ways one must move them in order to make a telephone call, he has done his work; it only remains for the telephone company to do its.

cannot be said, then, that Q's failure would have occurred no matter what he had done—i.e., regardless of what bodily movements he made. If he had not moved his eyes to the left at all he would not have failed. Thus there is not the same reason for denying that Q is morally responsible for his failure as there is for denying that P is morally responsible for having failed to call the police. Even if the assumption that moral responsibility presupposes full responsibility is granted, accordingly, it is possible to find counterexamples that are effective against PPA.

Evaluating PAP and the three principles van Inwagen adduces is a matter of deciding whether a person may be morally responsible for performing or failing to perform an action, or for consequences of what he has done, despite the fact that the action or the failure or the consequences could not have been avoided. Now there are two ways in which a person's action, or his failure to act, or a consequence of what he has done, may be unavoidable. It may be unavoidable in virtue of certain movements which the person makes and which he cannot avoid making; or it may be unavoidable because of events or states of affairs that are bound to occur or to obtain no matter what the person himself does. For want of better terminology, I shall refer to the first type of unavoidability as "personal" and to the second as "impersonal."

personal

impersonal

Apparently van Inwagen supposes that a person cannot be fully responsible for a failure which he is unable to avoid. This supposition would be correct if unavoidable failures were all like P's failure—i.e., if their unavoidability were always *impersonal*. In fact, however, the unavoidability of some failures is *personal*. Of these it is not true that they will occur no matter what the person in question does. They are unavoidable just because the person, like Q, cannot avoid making the bodily movements by which they are constituted.

VI

It seems to me that there is no inherent difference between performances and failures, in virtue of which PPA might be true even though PAP is false. Nor is PPA immune to counterexamples of the sort to which PAP succumbs. On the other hand, there is a variant of PPA which *does* enjoy immunity to F-style counterexamples. This restricted version of PPA, which I shall call "PPA'," refers exclusively to failures whose unavoidability is impersonal. It concerns a person's moral responsibility for failing to bring about some event or state of affairs, when the fact that he does not bring it about is independent of what he himself does—i.e., of the movements he makes. Thus PPA' closely resembles PPP_1 and PPP_2, since these also concern a person's moral responsibility for events or states of affairs that can occur or obtain regardless of what movements the person himself makes.[5]

Now it is true by definition that a person cannot be *fully* responsible for something that happens or comes about regardless of his own bodily movements. Whether he can be *morally* responsible for such things depends upon the relationship between moral and full responsibility. Let us suppose that the former presupposes the latter. In that case PPA', PPP_1, and PPP_2 are immune to F-style counterexamples. But this does not imply, as van Inwagen evidently believes, that there are things for which a person can be morally responsible only if his will is free. Unlike PAP and PPA, the three principles in question have nothing at all to do with free will.

The fact that there are events or states of affairs which a person cannot bring about plainly does not in itself mean that the person lacks free will. Given that the freedom of a person's will is essentially a matter of whether it is up to him what he does, it is more a matter of whether it is up to him what bodily movements he makes than of what consequences he can bring by his movements. Imagine that the equipment malfunction that makes it impossible for P to call the police, despite his freedom to move his body in any way he likes, is due to negligence on the part of the telephone company; and imagine that because of this negligence large numbers of people are unable to do various things. These people may quite properly be resentful. But they will be carrying their resentment too far, and attributing too portentous a role in their lives to the telephone company, if they complain that the company has through its negligence diminished the freedom of their wills.

Just as PPA', PPP_1, and PPP_2 have nothing to do with the relationship between moral responsibility and free will, neither have they anything to do with the relationship between free will and determinism. Suppose that it is causally undetermined whether the telephones are working. Then it is also undetermined whether P can call the police. But this implies nothing whatever concerning the freedom of P's will.

It has a significant bearing, of course, on the extent of his *power*—i.e., on the effectiveness of what he does. However, in no way does it affect

---

5. As I have already pointed out, van Inwagen says that PPP_1 and PPP_2 have to do with "the consequences of what we have done (or left undone)" (203). This is not explicit in his formulations of the principles. On a rather natural reading of them, in fact, they are vulnerable to any counterexample that is effective against PAP. For, assuming that doing something entails the occurrence of an event and the obtaining of a state of affairs, anything that shows that a person may be morally responsible for what he has done even though he could not have done otherwise also shows that he may be morally responsible for an event or a state of affairs which he could not have prevented. However, in view of van Inwagen's assurances that PPP_1 and PPP_2 concern the *consequences* of what people do, I shall construe them as *not* referring to the bodily movements people make or to what those movements necessarily entail.

his freedom to move as he likes; nor is it pertinent to the question of whether his movements themselves are undetermined. It is altogether irrelevant, in other words, to the sorts of interests and anxieties by which people have been driven to resist the doctrine that human life is wholly and ineluctably subject to causal determination.

12

Incompatibilism without the Principle of Alternative Possibilities

ROBERT HEINAMAN

THE incompatibilist argues in the following way for his conclusion that moral responsibility is incompatible with determinism:

(PAP) The Principle of Alternative Possibilities: An agent is morally responsible for an action only if he could have done otherwise.

(1) If determinism is true, then whenever an agent performs an action he could not have done otherwise.

Hence, the incompatibilist concludes, no agent is responsible for any of his actions if determinism is true.

Many compatibilists have rejected (1), but Harry Frankfurt thinks he can avoid the incompatibilist's conclusion by rejecting PAP.[1] Suppose that, unknown to Jones, Black has inserted certain devices into Jones' brain that enable him to monitor and control Jones' thoughts, deliberations, decision and actions. Jones is considering whether or not to vote for Reagan. Black wants Jones to vote for Reagan. If it appears that Jones will vote for Reagan on his own, Black will not intervene. But if Jones gives signs of not voting for Reagan, Black will intervene and ensure that he does vote for Reagan.—Jones deliberates, decides to vote for Reagan and does so. Then, according to Frankfurt, Jones is respon-

Reprinted with permission from *Australasian Journal of Philosophy* 64 (September 1986): 266–276.

1. 'Alternate Possibilities and Moral Responsibility', *Journal of Philosophy* 66 (1969), pp. 829–839.

sible for voting for Reagan even though he could not have done otherwise. Hence, PAP is false, and the incompatibilist's argument fails.

Peter van Inwagen has argued that the incompatibilist conclusion can be demonstrated independently of PAP.[2] He argues that the following three principles are immune to Frankfurt-style counterexamples:

> PPA A person is morally responsible for failing to perform a given act only if he could have performed that act.
>
> PPP1 A person is morally responsible for a certain event only if he could have prevented it.
>
> PPP2 A person is morally responsible for a certain state of affairs only if he could have prevented it.

PPP1 and PPP2 concern consequences of actions. PPP1 concerns individual events, and PPP2 concerns *types* of states of affairs.[3]

Suppose further that the following three propositions are true

> (2) If determinism is true, then if a given person failed to perform a given act, that person could not have performed that act.
>
> (3) If determinism is true, then no event is such that any person could have prevented it.
>
> (4) If determinism is true, then no state of affairs is such that anyone could have prevented it.

PPA and (2) entail

> (A) If determinism is true, then nobody is morally responsible for failing to perform any action.

PPP1 and (3) entail

> (B) If determinism is true, then nobody is morally responsible for any event.
>
> PPP2 and (4) entail
>
> (C) If determinism is true, then nobody is responsible for any state of affairs.
>
> Assume further that, where øing is any action and S any agent

2. 'Ability and Responsibility', *Philosophical Review* 87 (1978), pp. 201–224.

3. Although PPP1 does not refer to individual states of affairs and PPP2 does not refer to types of event, van Inwagen says that there would only be verbal differences between his arguments and arguments involving individual states of affairs and types of event (p. 206).

R If (i) S is responsible for øing, then (ii) there is some event or state
of affairs for which S is responsible.

R together with (B) and (C) entail that if determinism is true, then nobody is responsible for any action. For the assumption of determinism
together with (B) and (C) entail that

(ii) there is some event or state of affairs for which S is responsible

is always false. Hence, by modus tollens, if determinism is true,

(i) S is responsible for øing

is always false, i.e. nobody is ever responsible for any action. Thus, we
demonstrate the incompatibilist conclusion independently of PAP.
Hence, even if Frankfurt's argument against PAP is sound, incompatibilism can be maintained.—So argues van Inwagen.

PPP1 and PPP2 are misleadingly stated since they are not supposed to
deal with *any* event or *any* state of affairs, but only with those that are
consequences of actions. If they covered actions themselves, then they
would be versions of PAP and hence van Inwagen could not claim to establish incompatibilism independently of PAP. Let us restate PPP1 and
PPP2 more clearly:

PPP1′ A person is morally responsible for a certain event that is a consequence of his action only if he could have prevented it.

PPP2′ A person is morally responsible for a certain state of affairs that
is a consequence of his action only if he could have prevented it.

PPP1′ and (3) yield, not (B), but

(B′) If determinism is true, then nobody is responsible for any event
that is a consequence of his action.

Likewise, PPP2′ and (4) yield, not (C), but

(C′) If determinism is true, then nobody is responsible for any state of
affairs that is a consequence of his action.

(B′) leaves open the possibility that, even if determinism is true, then the
event which is not a consequence of an agent's action but *is* the agent's
action is an event for which he is responsible. Likewise, (C′) leaves open
the possibility that even if determinism is true, then the state of affairs

which is not a consequence of an agent's action but is the state of affairs that he performs the action is a state of affairs for which he is responsible.

So (B') and (C') allow that a person may be responsible for the particular event that is his action and may be responsible for the state of affairs that he performs that action, even if determinism is true. Hence, we cannot use R together with (B') and (C') to derive the conclusion that determinism is incompatible with responsibility for our actions. For the assumption of determinism together with (B') and (C') does not yield the negation of

(ii) there is some event or state of affairs for which S is responsible,

and hence does not yield the negation of

(i) S is responsible for øing.

Van Inwagen will hastily reply that I am misconstruing R: its consequent was intended to refer only to the consequences of actions, not to actions themselves.[4] To make this explicit, replace R with

R' If S is responsible for øing, then there is some event or state of affairs which is a consequence of the øing for which S is responsible.

And R' in conjunction with (B') and (C') does yield the conclusion that no agent is ever responsible for his action.

But why should we believe R'? Van Inwagen says: 'I cannot conceive of a case in which an agent is responsible for having performed some act but is responsible for *none* of the results or consequences (either universal or particular) of this act.'[5]

I think I can. Suppose A is standing in pitch dark and moves his hand and is responsible for doing so. This event has many consequences, for example the motion of air molecules. But A may not be morally responsible for the motion of the air molecules because, through no fault of his own, he is completely unaware of the existence of such things as air molecules. Likewise, for all the other consequences of A's action it may be that he is ignorant of them and is not morally responsible in any way for his ignorance. Then he will escape moral responsibility for all the consequences of his action.

It might be said that A must be responsible for the event which is his hand's moving. But it is implausible to suppose that this event is a con-

4. 'Ability and Responsibility', p. 223.
5. *Ibid.*

sequence of the action rather than a part of the action or identical with the action. If it is at least a part of A's moving his hand, then it cannot be a consequence of the action for which A is responsible.

It might be said that A must be responsible for the state of affairs *that A's hand moved,* which is a consequence of A's action. But suppose that A is in the grips of some mad philosopher who has brought it about that A believes that there are no states of affairs, and in particular has induced in A the belief that when he moves his hand there results no such thing as the state of affairs *that A's hand moved.* Presumably, there is at least one method M by which a human being could be made to believe certain claims where we would agree that the person is not responsible for holding those beliefs because he was made to acquire them by method M. Suppose our mad philosopher used method M to make A believe the previously stated views concerning states of affairs. Then A is not responsible for holding those beliefs. Likewise, he is not responsible for the state of affairs *that A's hand moved* because, through no fault of his own, he believes there is no such thing. (Similarly for the state of affairs that A moved his hand).

I conclude that R' is false and hence van Inwagen has failed to demonstrate that determinism is incompatible with responsibility for our actions independently of PAP. At best, he has established with (A), (B') and (C') that determinism is incompatible with our responsibility for failing to perform actions, and with our responsibility for the consequences of our actions.

However, van Inwagen may reply that all I have shown, at best, is that R' is not a *necessary* truth. R' still holds for ordinary agents who are not ignorant of all their actions' consequences through no fault of their own. Hence, as far as ordinary agents go, the argument still stands.

But van Inwagen's argument faces more serious objections, for it rests on the three principles PPA, PPP1' and PPP2', the defence of which constitutes the bulk of his paper. And I believe it can be shown that *if* Frankfurt-style counterexamples refute the Principle of Alternative Possibilities, then they also refute PPA, PPP1' and PPP2'.

First, consider

> PPA A person is responsible for failing to perform a given act only if he could have performed that act.

Van Inwagen defends PPA by describing a purported Frankfurt-style counterexample and claiming that the agent is *not* responsible for the action he could not perform; whereas we would have a counterinstance to PPA only if we were to produce a case where the agent is responsible for failing to do what he could not do.—Suppose Jones sees a crime being committed and considers whether he should call the police. He decides not to do so and does not call the police. But suppose that, unknown to Jones, there was a catastrophe at the telephone exchange, all the phones are out of order, and hence he could not have called the police even if he had tried. Then Jones is *not* responsible for failing to call the police when he could not call the police. So we do not get a counterexample to PPA.

But of course, the fact that this case fails to provide a counterexample to PPA does not show that there are not other examples which do. For example, in our earlier case with Black and Jones, simply replace *voting for Reagan* with *not voting for Reagan:* Suppose Jones is considering whether or not to vote for Reagan. Unknown to Jones there is a mad scientist named Black who is able to control Jones in the manner explained before. But Black now wants Jones not to vote for Reagan. If Jones looks like he is not going to vote for Reagan on his own he will let Jones alone. But if Jones shows any signs of voting for Reagan, Black will intervene and ensure that Jones fails to vote for Reagan.—Jones considers, decides not to vote for Reagan and does not do so. Then, Frankfurt would say, Jones is responsible for failing to vote for Reagan although he could not have voted for Reagan. For it might be argued that Jones is responsible for *refraining from voting for Reagan,* which in this instance is the same "act" as *failing to vote for Reagan.* Hence, if the original example where Jones votes for Reagan refutes PAP, then the present example refutes PPA. If I am wrong about this it will still not affect my main concern, viz. van Inwagen's defence of PAP, which relies solely on PPP1′ and PPP2′.

Next consider

> PPP1′ A person is morally responsible for a certain event that is a consequence of his action only if he could have prevented it.

There is no need to examine this principle in detail since van Inwagen's defence of it has already been effectively criticised by others: he assumes the incredible premise that the causes of an event are essential to it.[6]

So consider

> PPP2′ A person is morally responsible for a certain state of affairs that is a consequence of his action only if he could have prevented it.

A purported Frankfurt-style counterexample to PPP2′ would go like this: Suppose Gunnar deliberately shoots Ridley and this action is sufficient to make it true that the following state of affairs obtains—*that*

6. W. R. Carter, 'On Transworld Event Identity', *Philosophical Review* 88 (1979), pp. 443–451.

Ridley dies. There is present some factor F which would have caused someone else to kill Ridley if Gunnar had not done so. If this constitutes a counterexample to PPP2', then it must be a case where Gunnar is responsible for the obtaining of the state of affairs *that Ridley dies* although he could not prevent it. But in fact, van Inwagen argues, although Gunnar could not prevent that state of affairs from obtaining, neither is he responsible for it.

It might be urged that Gunnar is responsible for that state of affairs because he did something—shoot Ridley—that was sufficient for the obtaining of it. But van Inwagen claims that this argument is invalid. For when Gunnar shot Ridley he also did something that was sufficient for the obtaining of the following state of affairs—*that Ridley is mortal.* Gunnar is not responsible for the latter state of affairs although he did something sufficient for its existence. Hence, the fact that in shooting Ridley he did something sufficient for the state of affairs *that Ridley dies* fails to show Gunnar's responsibility for it.

It might rather be suggested that Gunnar is responsible for the state of affairs *that Ridley is killed,* where this could not have been prevented by Gunnar. But, van Inwagen argues, consider the following state of affairs

K Ridley is killed by someone who is caused to kill him by F or Ridley is killed by someone who is not caused to kill him by F.

Gunnar is not responsible for K. But this is the same state of affairs as *that Ridley is killed.* Hence, Gunnar avoids responsibility for the latter.[7]

It is not clear what van Inwagen has in mind with his first argument that the fact that Gunnar did something sufficient for the existence of the state of affairs *that Ridley dies* fails to show that Gunnar is responsible for it. His argument rests on the claim that Gunnar did something sufficient for the state of affairs *that Ridley is mortal* but is not responsible for it. But in what sense did Gunnar do something sufficient for the state of affairs *that Ridley is mortal?* In shooting Ridley Gunnar did something sufficient in the circumstances to cause Ridley's death. The event of Ridley's death could only have occurred if it was a fact that Ridley was mortal. But Gunnar's shooting Ridley in no sense made it the case that Ridley is mortal. No more than my striking a glass with a hammer and shattering it made it the case that the glass was brittle.[8]

---

7. Van Inwagen says that his argument need not rest on the assumption that 'Gunnar is responsible for *x*' is an extensional context (p. 214, n. 18). But I will assume that it is extensional to simplify the exposition. Nothing turns on our using this assumption rather than the other principle appealed to by van Inwagen in his n. 18.

8. Van Inwagen appears to think the following states of affairs are identical: *that Ridley dies* and *that Ridley is mortal* (p. 213). But to be mortal is to be subject to death. This might be true of Ridley for his first sixty years which, by luck, he survives. But then he might take

Whatever van Inwagen means by 'sufficient', we can replace it by the notion of 'causal sufficiency', where 'X is causally sufficient for Y' entails that X at least partially explains the existence of Y. Then we can argue: In shooting Ridley Gunnar knowingly and intentionally did something which, in the circumstances, was causally sufficient for the obtaining of the state of affairs *that Ridley dies*. Whenever an agent knowingly and intentionally does something which is in the circumstances causally sufficient for a state of affairs S, then the agent is responsible for S.[9] Hence, Gunnar is responsible for the state of affairs *that Ridley dies*.

This argument is immune to van Inwagen's example with the state of affairs *that Ridley is mortal*, for in shooting Ridley Gunnar did not do anything causally sufficient for the state of affairs *that Ridley is mortal*. Gunnar's shooting Ridley does nothing to explain why it is the case that Ridley is mortal; no more than my hitting the glass with a hammer plays a part in explaining why it is the case that the glass is brittle.

Van Inwagen might reply that there must be something wrong with my argument because the sort of argument which he used to show that Gunnar is not responsible for the state of affairs *that Ridley is killed* could also be used to show that he is not responsible for the state of affairs *that Ridley dies*. But van Inwagen's argument fails to show that Gunnar is not responsible for the state of affairs *that Ridley is killed*.

He said that this last state of affairs is the same state of affairs as

K Ridley is killed by someone who is caused to kill him by F or Ridley is killed by someone who is not caused to kill him by F.

and since Gunnar is not responsible for K, neither is he responsible for the state of affairs *that Ridley is killed*, for these are the same state of affairs. But we can use a similar argument which is as plausible as van Inwagen's to establish the contrary conclusion.

---

a miracle drug that makes him deathless. Then he would *no longer* be mortal. In these circumstances the state of affairs *that Ridley is mortal* was exemplified, but *that Ridley dies* does not obtain at any time. So they cannot be the same state of affairs.

9. Since I reject compatibilism, I am not presenting this as a claim which I myself believe. The last two pages have been arguing only for a limited claim that *if* Frankfurt-style counterexamples refute PAP, corresponding examples also refute PPA, PPP1', and PPP2'. Van Inwagen concedes that Frankfurt's examples refute PAP. So he must also concede to Frankfurt that there is some principle stating a sufficient condition for responsibility for one's individual acts which may be satisfied even if determinism is true. Likewise in the case of one's actions, van Inwagen cannot object to the compatibilist's appeal to a principle purporting to state a sufficient condition for responsibility on the grounds that it may be satisfied even if determinism is true. The principle used in the text is merely a simple example of the sort of principle which the compatibilist out to refute PPP2' must appeal to. But a priori it seems that any such principle acceptable to the compatibilist can be used to construct a counterexample to PPP2' similar to the one that I give.

Suppose that if Gunnar does not kill Ridley, factor F will, as before, ensure that Ridley is killed anyway. In fact, Gunnar shoots Ridley and kills him. Then Gunnar is responsible for the state of affairs *that Ridley is killed by Gunnar.* Van Inwagen has nothing to disprove Gunnar's responsibility for this state of affairs, since, given the circumstances, he cannot construct a K-style argument for the conclusion that Gunnar is not responsible for it. Nor can he say that I am illegitimately assuming that Gunnar is responsible for a state of affairs he could not have prevented, for it is not true that Gunnar could not have prevented it. (Or so we are assuming.) He would have prevented it if he had not shot Ridley: Now, it seems that we can assume

> (I) If S is responsible for a state of affairs A, then if 'F' is any false statement (other than '~A')[10] then S is responsible for the state of affairs that A or F.

Then, since Gunnar is responsible for the state of affairs *that Ridley is killed by Gunnar,* we can infer that Gunnar is responsible for

> L Ridley is killed by Gunnar or Ridley is killed by someone other than Gunnar.

But, à la van Inwagen, we can claim that L is the same state of affairs as the state of affairs *that Ridley is killed.* Hence, since Gunnar is responsible for L, he is also responsible for the state of affairs *that Ridley is killed.*

We now have van Inwagen's argument for the conclusion that Gunnar is not responsible for the state of affairs *that Ridley is killed* and the present argument that he *is* responsible for that state of affairs. But the sort of argument that I just gave can also be used to undermine van Inwagen's argument. For just as Gunnar is responsible for the state of affairs *that Ridley is killed by Gunnar,* so he is responsible for the state of affairs *that Ridley is killed by someone who is not caused to kill him by F.* This state of affairs could have been prevented by Gunnar and van Inwagen will have no reason to deny Gunnar's responsibility for it. Further, it is false that Ridley is killed by someone who is caused to kill him by F. Then by (I) we can conclude that Gunnar is responsible for

> K Ridley is killed by someone who is caused to kill him by F or Ridley is killed by someone who is not caused to kill him by F.

But if Gunnar is responsible for K, then van Inwagen cannot argue that since Gunnar is not responsible for K, and K is identical with the state of

10. I expect other exceptions would need to be added in an accurate statement of such a principle, and my argument assumes that they would not exclude my example.

affairs *that Ridley is killed,* Gunnar is not responsible for the state of affairs *that Ridley is killed.* On the contrary, we can now appeal to that identity to derive the conclusion that Gunnar is responsible for the state of affairs *that Ridley is killed.*

What grounds did van Inwagen have to support his contention that Gunnar is not responsible for K? His argument is the same as the argument he gives for saying that Gunnar is not responsible for

D Ridley is killed by Gunnar or Ridley is killed by Pistol

where, if Gunnar had not killed Ridley, Pistol would have. He argues as follows: Gunnar could not prevent D, just as he could not prevent

E Ridley is killed by Gunnar or $2 + 2 = 4$

or

F Ridley is killed by Gunnar or grass is green.

Gunnar is not responsible for E or for F. There is no relevant difference between D, E and F. Therefore Gunnar is not responsible for D.[11]

The argument seems to be circular: van Inwagen's reason for claiming that Gunnar is not responsible for E or for F is that Gunnar could not prevent them. But the fact that Gunnar could not prevent them shows that he is not responsible for them only if the fact that one cannot prevent a state of affairs entails that one is not responsible for it. Part of what this last claim asserts is that one is not responsible for states of affairs one cannot prevent that are consequences of one's actions. But this is the claim van Inwagen is supposed to be arguing for: PPP2'. The argument for PPP2' presupposes PPP2'.

Perhaps van Inwagen would reply that he has no argument for his assertion that Gunnar is not responsible for E or F. Rather, the argument is: it is just obvious that Gunnar is not responsible for E, or for F. There is no 'relevant difference' between E, F and D. Therefore Gunnar is not responsible for D.

But there does seem to be a relevant difference between E, F and D: in D the second disjunct is false, whereas in E and F the second disjunct is true. Hence, principle (I) allows us to conclude that Gunnar is responsible for D, while it does not allow us to conclude that Gunnar is responsible for E or for F.

Why is Gunnar not responsible for E or for F? On the present interpretation of van Inwagen's argument, he does not say why he considers

11. 'Ability and Responsibility', pp. 213–214.

this obvious, but a plausible answer is this: Gunnar is not responsible for the fact that $2 + 2 = 4$ and he is not responsible for the fact that grass is green. In general, where A is an existing state of affairs

> (II) If S is not responsible for A, then for any proposition P, S is not responsible for the state of affairs that A or P.

Hence, Gunnar is not responsible for E, or for F. But (II) does not allow us to conclude that Gunnar is not responsible for D. For Gunnar *is* responsible for the state of affairs *that Ridley is killed by Gunnar* and the state of affairs *that Ridley is killed by Pistol* does not obtain. This is a relevant difference between D on the one hand and E and F on the other.

I conclude that van Inwagen's argument that Gunnar is not responsible for D fails. Hence, there is so far no reason to accept his claim that Gunnar is not responsible for K. And therewith falls his argument that Gunnar is not responsible for the state of affairs *that Ridley is killed* and his defence of PPP2'.

Perhaps van Inwagen would complain about my appeal to

> (I) If S is responsible for a state of affairs A, then if 'F' is any false statement (other than '~A') then S is responsible for the state of affairs that A or F.

in some of my arguments. He might claim that Frankfurt-style examples provide clear counterexamples to it. In the Gunnar-Ridley case, Gunnar is not responsible for the circumstances which make it inevitable that Ridley will be killed by Gunnar on his own or by someone who is caused to kill him by F. So he is not responsible for the state of affairs

> L Ridley is killed by Gunnar or Ridley is killed by someone other than Gunnar.

But Gunnar is responsible for the first disjunct and the second disjunct is false. Hence (I) is false.

However, consider a slightly different case. Gunnar deliberately shoots and kills Ridley as before, but now there is nobody waiting in the wings who would have killed Ridley if Gunnar had not done so. Here Gunnar is responsible for the fact that L obtains. But why is Gunnar responsible? It seems that the answer to this question must appeal to (I): Gunnar is responsible for the state of affairs *that Ridley is killed by Gunnar* and hence he is responsible for the state of affairs *that Ridley is killed by Gunnar or F* for any false statement 'F'. I am responsible for the disjunctive state of affairs because I am responsible for the first disjunct and because (I) is true.—Call this *Case* 2 and call the original example with Gunnar and Ridley *Case* 1.

Van Inwagen might reject my appeal to (I). But now, notice that L obtains in *both* Case 1 and Case 2, and that what makes L true in both cases is the same: the truth of the first disjunct of L. Therefore *what it is for L to obtain* cannot involve anything in Case 1 that is not present in Case 2. In Case 2 it is false to say that

> J If Ridley had not been killed by Gunnar then he would have been killed by somebody else.

And therefore it is no part of what it is for L to obtain in Case 1 that if Ridley had not been killed by Gunnar then he would have been killed by somebody else, i.e. that J. In Case 2 it is also false to say

> H It was unavoidable that one or the other of the disjuncts in L would obtain.

Hence it is not any part of what it is for L to obtain in Case 1 that it was unavoidable that one or the other of the disjuncts in L would obtain, i.e. that H.

For the same reason L does not entail J: L but not J obtains in Case 2. Nor does L entail H: L but not H obtains in Case 2.

It is, I submit, only because we are inclined to confuse the obtaining of L with the obtaining of J or of H (or of something similar) that we are initially attracted by the suggestion that Gunnar is not responsible for L in Case 1. Obviously, in Case 1 Gunnar is not responsible for the fact that J obtains or for the fact that H obtains. But once J and H are clearly distinguished from L, Gunnar's lack of responsibility for J or for H can be seen to provide no support for the claim that Gunnar is not responsible for L.

Van Inwagen might defend the claim that Gunnar is not responsible for L by appealing to the following principle:

> (III) If S is not responsible for a state of affairs A, and 'A' entails 'B' (where B is some state of affairs) then S is not responsible for B.

Gunnar is not responsible for H, and H entails L. Hence, by (III), Gunnar is not responsible for L.

But (III) is false. Suppose I hire Smith to kill Brown but let Smith decide what means he will use to dispose of Brown. Suppose Smith kills Brown with a gun. Then I am responsible for the fact that

> N Smith killed Brown

although I am not responsible for the fact that

M Smith killed Brown with a gun

and M entails N. Hence (III) is unacceptable.

So, although (I) may not be obviously true, the impression that Frankfurt-style examples provide counterexamples to it is, I think, mistaken.

In any case, (II) seems secure and we have seen that (II) can be used to undermine van Inwagen's only argument for the claim that Gunnar is not responsible for K and hence is not responsible for the state of affairs *that Ridley is killed*. Further, we seem to have a sound argument that Gunnar is responsible for the state of affairs *that Ridley is killed* because he did something causally sufficient for the obtaining of that state of affairs.

In conclusion: van Inwagen has not succeeded in showing that the incompatibility of determinism and responsibility for actions can be established independently of the Principle of Alternative Possibilities. And his defence of PPA, PPP1′ and PPP2′ fails to undermine the view that, if Frankfurt-style counterexamples refute the Principle of Alternative Possibilities, then they also refute PPA, PPP1′ and PPP2′, and hence refute the incompatibilist's arguments for the claim that determinism is incompatible with responsibility for failures to act and the consequences of actions.

I do not believe it follows that the incompatibilist has any cause for worry. For I do not believe—as I have hitherto assumed—that Frankfurt-style examples provide counterexamples to the Principle of Alternative Possibilities. When the principle asserts that an agent is responsible for his action only if *he could have done otherwise*, the emphasized statement is true only if prior conditions together with the laws of nature do not (physically or naturally) necessitate the action. If prior conditions together with the laws of nature do necessitate the action, then the agent could not have done otherwise in the sense of 'could not have done otherwise' relevant to the Principle of Alternative Possibilities. Call this sense 1.

This is not the sense in which Jones cannot do otherwise in the original example. For in Frankfurt's use of that expression Jones cannot do otherwise even if determinism is false and it is not the case that prior conditions together with the laws of nature necessitate the act. Suppose Jones is indeterministically caused to vote for Reagan on his own. Then, in the sense of the phrase relevant to PAP—sense 1—Jones *could* have done otherwise. But if all the alternative routes that, in this sense, Jones could have taken, would have ended in his voting for Reagan, then in Frankfurt's sense Jones *could not* have done otherwise.

The incompatibilist can readily agree that an agent may, in Frankfurt's sense, be unable to do otherwise and still be responsible for his action. But that will do nothing to upset the Principle of Alternative Possibilities. In Frankfurt's example with Black and Jones, determinism either holds or it does not. If it does not, then in sense 1 Jones could have done otherwise if his act was indeterministically caused while in Frankfurt's sense he could not then have done otherwise. So the incompatibilist will agree that here Jones may be responsible for his action even though he could not have done otherwise in Frankfurt's sense. But of course this will not upset PAP for we have a counterexample to it only when we have a case where the agent is responsible even though he could not have done otherwise in sense 1. But here, although the agent is responsible, he *could* have done otherwise in sense 1.

If, on the other hand, we suppose determinism to hold in the Jones-Black case, then Jones could not have done otherwise in sense 1. Now we will get a counterexample to PAP if Jones is responsible for his action. But since Frankfurt has no grounds to support his view that, here too, Jones is responsible for his action, beyond the bare assertion that he is responsible, there is no reason why the incompatibilist should accept that Jones is responsible for his act, even though he could not have done otherwise in sense 1.[12]

Briefly, then, in response to Frankfurt's example the incompatibilist should say this: If we suppose determinism not to hold in the example, then Jones may be responsible for his act, but also he could have done otherwise. Hence there is no counterexample to PAP. If we suppose determinism to hold, then Jones could not have done otherwise but there is no reason to accept that Jones is responsible. Here too, then, PAP emerges unscathed.[13]

12. Frankfurt might appeal to his account of moral responsibility developed in his papers 'Freedom of the Will and the Concept of a Person', *Journal of Philosophy* 68 (1971), pp. 5–20; 'Three Concepts of Free Action', *Proceedings of the Aristotelian Society*, suppl. Vol. XLIX (1975), pp. 113–125; 'Coercion and Moral Responsibility', in T. Honderich (ed.) *Essays on Freedom of Action* (London: Routledge and Kegan Paul, 1973), pp. 75–84. For some relevant difficulties with this account, see G. Watson, "Free Action and Free Will," *Mind* 96 (1987), pp. 145–172.

13. I thank an anonymous referee for his comments on an earlier draft of this paper.

13

Causing and Being Responsible for What Is Inevitable

WILLIAM L. ROWE

WHEN a person does something that results in a state of affairs obtaining that would not have obtained had he not done what he did, it is clear that the person *causes* (or causally contributes to) the obtaining of that state of affairs. Moreover, if the person could have avoided doing what he did, thus preventing the state of affairs from obtaining, the person is *responsible* for the state of affairs provided he foresaw (or ought to have foreseen) that it would result from his action. But what if he does something that, although sufficient (in the circumstances) for that state of affairs obtaining, is not necessary for its obtaining? What if the state of affairs would have obtained *regardless* of what he did? Can he then properly be said to have *caused* that state of affairs to obtain? And, if he did what he did, intending to bring about that state of affairs, can he be held *responsible* for that state of affairs, given that it was inevitable and would have obtained regardless of what he did? In this paper I will defend an affirmative answer to both questions with respect to a certain class of cases. I also will suggest that an affirmative answer should not be taken as positive support for the compatibilist's thesis that causal determinism is consistent with human freedom.

I

Suppose there is a speeding train approaching a fork in the track controlled by a switch. The left fork (No. 1) leads on to where a dog has been

Reprinted with permission from *American Philosophical Quarterly* 26 (April 1989): 153–59.

tied to the track. If the train proceeds on 1 it will hit the dog. Track No. 2, however, leads to a safe stopping point for the train. The switch is set for 2. You have it in your power to throw the switch to 1 or to leave it as is. You throw the switch with the result that the train proceeds on 1, hitting the dog. Your throwing the switch is sufficient, in the circumstances, for the train's proceeding on track 1 and for the train's hitting the dog. We will suppose that in the circumstances your throwing the switch was also necessary for both of these consequences: had you not thrown the switch, the train would not have proceeded on 1 and would not have hit the dog. This is case *A*.

In the above case we have no reluctance in concluding that you caused the train to proceed on 1 and caused the train to hit the dog. We are also entitled, *prima facie*, to hold you responsible for these consequences.[1] After all, neither of these consequences of your act was inevitable. Had you not thrown the switch, neither would have occurred. And, as we noted, it was in your power not to throw the switch.

Let us again suppose that there is a speeding train approaching a fork in the track controlled by a switch. As in case *A*, the switch is set for track 2. It is again in your power to switch the train to track 1 by throwing the switch. It is also in your power not to throw the switch. Unfortunately, unlike case *A*, both tracks 1 and 2 converge later at the point where the dog is tied to the track. It is inevitable, therefore, that the train will hit the dog. Nevertheless, you throw the switch so that the train proceeds on track 1. This is case *B*.

In case *B*, what did you cause or bring about? As in case *A*, we can distinguish (1) the train's hitting the dog, and (2) the train's proceeding on track 1. We might also want to consider (3) the train's hitting the dog *via* track 1 (as opposed to *via* track 2). In the circumstances, what you do (throw the switch) is both *sufficient* and *necessary* for (2), the train's proceeding on track 1, and for (3), the train's hitting the dog via track 1. But what about (1)? Do you cause or bring about the train's hitting the dog? Well, it is true that you do something that in the circumstances is sufficient for the train's hitting the dog. But what you do is not necessary for that consequence. Had you not thrown the switch, the train would still have hit the dog. In the circumstances, the train's hitting the dog is inevitable, regardless of what you do. Although you may be the cause of the train's hitting the dig via track 1, you are not the cause of the train's hitting the dog.[2] Nor would we hold you responsible for the fact that the

---

1. We are entitled only *prima facie* because there are a variety of factors that might obtain that would absolve you from responsibility. Elsewhere in this paper ascriptions of responsibility are to be taken as *prima facie* only.

2. I am supposing here that between the switch and the place where the dog is tied tracks 1 and 2 are of equal length. What if the length of track 2 between the switch and the place where the dog is tied is twice the length of track 1? If so, then if you throw the switch

train hits the dog. If something is inevitable, will happen regardless of what you do, then you do not cause it to happen and you are not responsible for it. We must now challenge this principle by considering a third case.

In case *C*, we find a curious mixture of features in one or the other of our first two cases. As in Case *A*, track 2 does not converge with track 1. Instead, it leads to a safe stopping point for the train. Only track 1 leads to the spot where the dog is tied to the track. Unlike case *A*, however, some other person, Peter, is so situated that he most certainly will throw the switch if, but only if, you do not. If you throw the switch, the train will be routed to track 1 and hit the dog. If you do not throw the switch, Peter will, with the result that the train will be routed to track 1 and hit the dog. Moreover, it is not in your power to prevent Peter's throwing the switch, should you not throw it yourself. As in our other two cases, you throw the switch, the train is routed to track 1 and hits the dog.

Let's focus here on just two of our earlier consequences: (1) the train's hitting the dog, (2) the train's proceeding on track 1. My intuitions pull very strongly toward the view that you cause or bring about the train's proceeding on track 1 and the train's hitting the dog. I would also feel entitled to hold you responsible for each of these. The problem is that these intuitions collide with the principle that you neither cause nor are responsible for what is inevitable. To justify these intuitions we need to uncover some relevant differences between case *C* and case *B*, between ways in which something may be inevitable.

Perhaps the relevant difference between cases *B* and *C* is this. In case *B* it is *causally inevitable* that the train will hit the dog. Given that both tracks lead to where the dog is tied, that the train is speeding toward a switch that only has two settings—one for track 1 and one for track 2— the unfortunate outcome is causally inevitable *prior to your act*. In case *C*, however, the inevitability of the train's hitting the dog seems to rest on Peter's determination to throw the switch if you do not. Perhaps at the last second Peter could change his mind and elect not to throw the switch. To forestall such considerations, we will suppose that a mechanism has been implanted in Peter's brain so that he is programed to throw the switch if you do not; it is not in his power not to throw the switch should you fail to throw it. In both cases, then, prior to your act it is causally inevitable that the train will hit the dog.

---

the train's hitting the dog will occur *earlier* than it would occur were you not to throw the switch. Moreover, although the train's hitting the dog is inevitable, its hitting the dog at *t* (the time at which it hits the dog if you throw the switch) is not inevitable. In this case, therefore, we may hold that although you do not cause the train's hitting the dog (that being inevitable) you do cause it to obtain at *t* (that not being inevitable). This suggests a need to distinguish "*S* causes *E* by doing *X*" and "*S* causes *E* at *t* by doing *X*." I think this distinction is important. However, for sake of simplicity I will ignore the refinement "at *t*."

A second possible difference between cases *C* and *B* is this. In case *C*, although *your* throwing the switch is not necessary for the train's hitting the dog, *someone's throwing the switch* is necessary for this unfortunate result. In case *B*, however, what you do—throw the switch—is an action that in the circumstances need not be done by anyone if the train is to hit the dog.

The above difference between *B* and *C* suggests the following: *S* causes *E* by doing *X* if and only if

(1) *S* does *X* prior to or at the same time as *E*'s occurrence.

(2) *S*'s doing *X* is part of a sufficient causal condition of *E*.[3]

(3) Either *S*'s doing *X* is a necessary condition of *E*'s occurrence or someone's doing *X* is a necessary condition of *E*'s occurrence.[4]

Condition (3), however, is inadequate. We can see this by considering a modification of case *C*. Suppose things are such that if you do not throw the switch to the track 1 position some very powerful being will *bend* track 2 so that it leads to where the dog is tied. Again, you cause the train's hitting the dog by throwing the switch to track 1, but it is not true that either you or someone else (or some mechanism) must move the switch if the train is to hit the dog. Clearly, then, condition (3) is far too narrow. How shall we revise it?

Among the circumstances that obtain in case *C*, the following seem particularly relevant:

(a) Track 1 leads to where the dog is tied.

(b) Track 2 does not lead to where the dog is tied.

(c) The switch is set for track 2.

(d) The train is speeding toward the switch.

In these circumstances

(e) You throw the switch to track 1 (at the appropriate time).

3. The notion I'm endeavoring to explicate is that of an agent *causing* (or causally contributing to) some event *E* by doing something *X*, when what the agent does is a part of *sufficient causal condition* of *E*. I don't mean to imply, however, that the only important causal relation between an agent and an event *E* is of this sort. Following Chisholm, I would argue that agents may *causally contribute to* events by doing things even though what the agent does is not part of a sufficient causal condition of that event. Thus, if I give you a ticket to the football game and you then *freely* choose to go, I may have causally contributed to your choosing to go to the game, even though your so choosing has no sufficient causal condition.

4. To deal with certain difficulties it would be important to replace "*E*" and "*E*'s occurrence" by "*E* at *t*" and "*E*'s occurrence at *t*" (see note 3).

is sufficient for the train's hitting the dog. But (e) is not necessary for this result, for

> (f) Peter is programed to throw the switch if, but only if, you do not.

is, given (a)-(d), also sufficient for the train's hitting the dog.[5] It was our consideration of this fact that led to our condition (3). What we've now seen, however, is that other modifications of case *C* will yield additional *sufficient conditions,* given (a)-(d), conditions that are not countenanced by our condition (3). In light of this, how can we give an account that will leave you the cause in case *C* without making you the cause in case *B?* The answer, I believe, will be discovered if we focus attention on the *relation* these sufficient conditions (in case *C*) bear to your throwing (or not throwing) the switch.

Suppose that in addition to (f) we have

> (g) A very powerful being is programed to bend track 2 to the place where the dog is tied if, but only if, you do not throw the switch.

What relation is there between both (f) and (g) and your throwing the switch? Both (f) and (g) have a part that is *actualized* only if you do not throw the switch. For if you throw the switch, this part is not actualized at all. (In (f), the part in question is *Peter throwing the switch.* In (g), the part in question is *A very powerful being bends track 2 to the place where the dog is tied.*) This suggests the following version of our third condition:

> (3') Either *S*'s doing *X* is necessary for *E*'s occurrence or any other condition that is sufficient (in the circumstances) for *E* has a part that is actualized only if *S* does not do *X*.[6]

Granted that each of (f) and (g) contains a part that is actualized only if you do not throw the switch, how does that support or explain our intuition that by throwing the switch (in case *C*) you cause the train's hit-

5. In asserting (f) to be *sufficient,* given (a)-(d), for the train's hitting the dog, I don't mean that (f) is *causally sufficient* for the train's hitting the dog. A causally sufficient condition of *E* is, roughly, a complex, conjunctive condition such that given it and the laws of nature it *follows* that *E* occurs. To say that a condition like (f) or (e) is *sufficient* for some event *E* is to say (roughly) that the conjunction of it with other events and/or conditions that obtain constitutes a causally sufficient condition of *E*.

6. David Widerker has pointed out that on a fine-grained account of "action" there may be several distinct actions of *S* that are sufficient in the circumstances for *E*, and that a problem for condition (3') is created when one of these actions of *S* constitutes *S*'s doing *X* and another is taken as one of the *other conditions* sufficient (in the circumstances) for *E*. To avoid this difficulty I propose that "any other condition" in (3') be taken to refer to sufficient conditions that neither causally generate *S*'s doing *X* nor are causally generated by *S*'s doing *X*.

ting the dog? The answer, I believe, is as follows. In case C examples the sufficient conditions, (f) and (g), present us with two *potential generators* of the train's hitting the dog. Condition (g), for example, presents *your throwing the switch* and *A powerful person's bending track 2 to the place where the dog is tied* as potential generators of the train's hitting the dog. For each is such that given just (a)–(d), it, *if actualized,* is sufficient for the train's hitting the dog. Now, as we've seen, things are such that the second potential generator can be actualized only if the first is not. In condition (g) the powerful being bends the track only if you do not throw the switch. This means that your throwing the switch *prevents* the actualization of other potential generators of the train's hitting the dog. And my suggestion is that if you do something that is sufficient in the circumstances for *E,* and your doing it *prevents the actualization of other potential generators of E,* then you cause *E* by doing that thing.[7]

What if the causal process is such that, where possible, the second potential generator occurs regardless of what you do? Suppose, for example, that a very powerful being is programed in advance to bend track 2 to the place where the dog is tied *whether or not you throw the switch.* We will suppose that the time at which you throw the switch (or do not throw it) is t-2, the time at which the powerful being has been programed to bend track 2 to the place where the dog is tied is a moment later, t-1, and the time at which the train passes over the switch is t, a moment later than t-1. With these suppositions in mind, we need to compare our condition.

(g) A very powerful being is programed to bend track 2 to the place where the dog is tied, *if, but only if, you do not throw the switch.*

with

(g′) A very powerful being is programed to bend track 2 to the place where the dog is tied *whether or not you throw the switch.*

When (g) obtains, by throwing the switch you effectively prevent the *actualization* of the other potential generator of the train's hitting the dog. But if it is (g′) that obtains, your act of throwing the switch does not prevent the actualization of the other potential generator. Indeed, that potential generator will be actualized whether you throw the switch or not. I've argued that although prior to your throwing the switch condition (g) is sufficient in (a)-(d) for the train's hitting the dog, it is true, nevertheless, that by throwing the switch you cause the train's hitting the

7. The potential generators in question are those that would be actualized if you did not do that thing.

dog. Suppose, however, it is (g'), and not (g), that obtains. Given (a)-(d), (g') is also sufficient for the train's hitting the dog. If you throw the switch when (g') obtains, do you thereby cause the train's hitting the dog? This is a difficult question. But on the view I'm presenting you do *not* cause the train's hitting the dog. For your throwing the switch does not prevent the *actualization* of the other potential generator—the powerful being bending track 2 to the place where the dog is tied. Against my view, it should be noted that your throwing the switch, although not preventing the actualization of the other potential generator, does prevent *it* from playing any causal role in bringing about the train's hitting the dog. For by the time (*t*-1) the powerful being starts to bend track 2, the switch already has been set (at *t*-2) to send the train along track 1. What he does, therefore, is in no way needed for the train to hit the dog. We might say that although your throwing the switch does not prevent the *actualization* of the potential generator, it does prevent it from being *efficacious*, from playing any causal role in the train's hitting the dog. And if this be so, why not conclude that by throwing the switch when (g') obtains you do cause the train's hitting the dog?

When either (g) or (g') obtains the following is true.

> (X) Prior to your throwing the switch it is causally determined that some event will occur that is sufficient (in the circumstances) for the train's hitting the dog.

But if (g') obtains it is also true that

> (Y) Prior to your throwing the switch it is causally determined that some event sufficient for the train's hitting the dog (*other than your throwing the switch*) will occur.

For if (g') obtains the very powerful being bends track 2 so that it leads to where the dog is tied. And this event, given the other conditions (a)-(d) that obtain, is sufficient for the train's hitting the dog. But if it is (g) that obtains, *Y* is not true. For when (g) obtains, it is not causally determined that some event sufficient for the train's hitting the dog (other than your throwing the switch) will occur. Although in (g) it is causally determined that some event will occur that is sufficient for the train's hitting the dog, it is *up to you* whether that event is an action of yours or the action of the powerful being. In (g'), however, it is causally determined that the powerful being will bend the track (a condition sufficient in (a)-(d) for the train's hitting the dog) *regardless of what you do*. And this difference between (g) and (g') renders the (g') case more like case *B* than *C*. This being so, what do you then cause by throwing the switch in (g')? You cause just what you cause in case *B*; you cause the train's hitting the dog *via* track 1. You do not cause the train's hitting the dog.

The general point emerging from these reflections on (g) and (g') is this. When there already exists a causal process that assures that E will occur, and the way in which the causal process is actualized is *independent* of your doing or not doing X, then by doing X you do not cause E to occur. You may, however, cause E to occur at a particular time, *via* a certain path, or at a particular place. But when there already exists a causal process that assures that E will occur, and the way in which the causal process is actualized is *dependent* on your doing or not doing X, then by doing X you may cause E to occur.

Our revision of condition (3) leaves our intuitions concerning cases C and B intact. In case B, your throwing the switch is sufficient (in the circumstances) for the train's hitting the dog. But there is another sufficient condition of the train's hitting the dog, a condition that does not satisfy our revised condition (3'). For, among the circumstances that obtain in case B, we may list the following as particularly relevant.

(i) Track 1 leads to where the dog is tied.

(j) Track 2 leads to where the dog is tied.

(k) The switch has no setting other than for 1 or 2.

In these circumstances,

(l) The train is speeding toward the switch.

is sufficient for the train's hitting the dog. But (l) has no part that is actualized only if you do not throw the switch. Thus, by throwing the switch in case B you do not cause the train's hitting the dog.[8]

II

In an important article, Peter van Inwagen has endeavored to prove that our intuitions are thoroughly wrong in case C.[9] His main interest in the article is to defend a form of the principle Harry Frankfurt calls "the Principle of Alternate Possibilities."[10] The form of the principle van Inwagen defends that is of particular interest here is:

8. A full account of causing E by doing X would need to accommodate cases of simultaneous overdetermination. Such cases, however, need not be considered in order to establish that one may cause and be responsible for what is inevitable.

9. Peter van Inwagen, "Ability and Responsibility," *The Philosophical Review*, vol. 87 (1987), pp. 201–24.

10. Harry Frankfurt, "Alternate Possibilities and Moral Responsibility," *The Journal of Philosophy*, vol. 66 (1969), pp. 828–39.

A person is morally responsible for a certain state of affairs only if (that state of affairs obtains and) he could have prevented it from obtaining.[11]

In case C our intuitions tell us that you bring about and are responsible for the state of affairs; it being the case that the train hits the dog. But, as we've seen, the obtaining of this state of affairs is something you are powerless to prevent. It will be helpful, therefore, to consider van Inwagen's argument.

Suppose, to use van Inwagen's example, Gunnar shoots Ridley, thus doing something sufficient for its being the case that Ridley dies.[12] Let's also suppose that Pistol is so situated that he will shoot Ridley if Gunnar does not. Pistol's shooting Ridley also would be sufficient for its being the case that Ridley dies. Moreover, if Gunnar does not himself shoot Ridley, he cannot prevent Pistol's doing so.

Thus far, van Inwagen's example parallels case C. But, as it turns out, it does not parallel only case C. For van Inwagen claims that the state of affairs *Ridley dies* is identical with *Ridley does not live forever*. Each of these, he holds, is identical with *Ridley is mortal*. Now surely, reasons van Inwagen, Gunnar neither causes nor is responsible for its being the case that Ridley is mortal. After all, the obtaining of this state of affairs is already guaranteed by the aging process and the laws of nature. So God, Adam and Eve perhaps, but surely not Gunnar, is/are responsible for its being the case that Ridley dies.

I am persuaded by this argument that Gunnar neither causes nor is responsible for its being the case that Ridley dies. It is important, however, to note that van Inwagen's example is not simply an example that parallels case C; it also parallels case B. Indeed, van Inwagen's entire argument to show that in this example Gunnar is not responsible for Ridley's death has nothing whatever to do with the parallel to case C. Pistol's readiness to shoot if Gunnar does not is not mentioned in the considerations van Inwagen advances to show that Gunnar is not responsible for Ridley's death. It is the fact that the aging process and the laws of nature already make certain Ridley's death that precludes Gunnar from bringing about or being responsible for his death. At most, Gunnar brings about Ridley's death *via* his shooting him, just as, in case B, the most that you bring about and are responsible for is the train's hitting the dog *via* track 1. The parallel between van Inwagen's example and case B is this. In each, there already exists a causal process that assures the obtaining of the state of affairs in question (Ridley dies, the train's hitting the dog), and the way in which the process is actualized is *independent* of what

11. Van Inwagen, *op cit.*, p. 210.
12. To avoid confusion, we should note that van Inwagen understands the state of affairs *Ridley dies* as identical to the state of affairs *Ridley dies at some time or other*.

Gunnar or you do (shooting Ridley, throwing the switch). Small wonder then, that the proper conclusion is that Gunnar neither causes nor is responsible for its being the case that Ridley dies. In terms of our formulation of what it is for an agent to cause E (or the obtaining of a state of affairs) by doing X, condition (3′) is not satisfied. For condition (3′), in its second part, requires that the actualizing of a part of the causally sufficient condition be dependent on your not doing X.

Having made his case that Gunnar is not responsible for its being the case that Ridley dies, van Inwagen next considers a more *specific* state of affairs; *Ridley's being killed*. Again we are to suppose that Pistol will shoot Ridley if Gunnar does not, thus doing something sufficient for its being the case that Ridley is killed. This time, however, there is no independent causal process (like the aging process) that is in place and will bring it about that Ridley is killed, regardless of what Gunnar or Pistol might do. Thus, van Inwagen now presents an example that parallels case C, but not case B. Again, van Inwagen argues that Gunnar neither brings it about nor is responsible for Ridley's being killed.[13] How does the argument go? First, van Inwagen notes (correctly) that we cannot show that Gunnar is responsible for Ridley's being killed simply by pointing out that he does something (shooting Ridley) that (in the circumstances) is sufficient for Ridley's being killed. For he also did something (shooting Ridley) that is sufficient for Ridley dies. So far, so good. We are then asked to consider the state of affairs: its being the case that Pistol kills Ridley or Gunnar kills Ridley. This state of affairs, no less than its being the case that Ridley does not live forever or its being the case that grass is green or Gunnar kills Ridley, "would have obtained no matter what Gunnar had done."[14] What then, asks van Inwagen, is the difference between

Pistol kills Ridley or Gunnar kills Ridley

on the one hand, and

Ridley does not live forever

and

Grass is green or Gunnar kills Ridley

on the other? There is only one non-trivial difference that van Inwagen can see. And that difference is that some worlds in which Gunnar is re-

13. Van Inwagen, *op cit.*, pp. 213–14.
14. *Ibid.*

sponsible for *Pistol kills Ridley or Gunnar kills Ridley* are "closer" to actuality than any of the worlds in which he is responsible for either *Ridley does not live forever* or *Grass is green or Gunnar kills Ridley.*

Now we can certainly agree with van Inwagen that if this is the only non-trivial difference, then it is incorrect to affirm that Gunnar brings it about or is responsible for Ridley's being killed.[15] But this is not the only non-trivial difference. There is a crucial difference between *Pistol kills Ridley or Gunnar kills Ridley* and both *Ridley does not live forever* and *Grass is green or Gunnar kills Ridley.* The difference is this. In the latter two cases there are causal processes in effect that are *completely independent* of Gunnar's action of shooting Ridley, a causal process that determines grass to be green, and a causal process that determines Ridley to be mortal. But since Pistol shoots Ridley if, but only if, Gunnar does not, there is no such independent causal process in the case of *Pistol kills Ridley or Gunnar kills Ridley.*[16] For, although Pistol may have been programed to shoot Ridley if, and only if, Gunnar does not, this sufficient condition of Ridley's being killed has a part (Pistol's shooting Ridley) that depends for its actualization on Gunnar's not shooting Ridley. It is inevitable that Ridley be killed. But it is up to Gunnar to determine whether he or Pistol is the cause of Ridley's being killed. It is not up to Gunnar to determine whether he or the process that makes grass green brings it about that *Grass is green or Gunnar kills Ridley.* The causal process that makes grass green obtains whether or not Gunnar shoots Ridley. It seems that van Inwagen has failed to see this non-trivial difference.[17]

The above, I believe, is sufficient to refute van Inwagen's argument for the conclusion that Gunnar neither causes nor is responsible for its being the case that Ridley is killed. For that example parallels exactly our case *C*. Since it does parallel it, I believe that our intuitions are on the side of the view that Gunnar causes and is responsible for Ridley being killed. And this is so even though it is inevitable (in the circumstances) that Ridley is killed. The argument van Inwagen gives against our intuitions depends on the premise that there is no *non-trivial difference* between case *B* and case *C* that is *relevant* to the question of deter-

15. The argument here is that if Gunnar is not responsible for *Pistol kills Ridley or Gunnar kills Ridley* then he is not responsible for *Pistol kills Ridley or Gunnar kills Ridley or someone else kills Ridley.* But this last state of affairs is identical with *Ridley is killed.* See van Inwagen, *ibid.*

16. If Pistol is programed to shoot Ridley whether or not Gunnar does, van Inwagen's example will closely resemble case *B*. But since his argument is intended to work against *any situation* in which Gunnar is claimed to cause and be responsible for what is inevitable, we are free to take it that Pistol is programed to shoot Ridley if, and only if, Gunnar does not.

17. Or perhaps van Inwagen has seen this difference but concluded that it is a *trivial* difference. It is difficult, however, to see how this judgment of triviality could be defended without simply falling back on the principle that one neither causes nor is responsible for what is inevitable.

mining whether (in case *C*) you cause and are responsible for the train's hitting the dog. What we've seen, however, is that there is a non-trivial difference, a difference that does seem relevant to the issues of causation and responsibility. Until this difference is shown to be trivial or irrelevant, I believe we should stick with our intuitions.

If what I have argued is correct, the principle van Inwagen defends is false. It is not true that a person causes and is responsible for a certain state of affairs only if it obtains and he could have prevented it from obtaining. This principle has figured in the controversy over whether causal determinism is consistent with genuine human freedom and responsibility. Compatibilists see this principle as an obstacle to their attempts to establish consistency. I think they are right to see it so. But the defeat of this principle should not be viewed as settling the question in favor of compatibilism. On at least one historically prominent version of the agency theory, an agent acts freely (and is responsible) provided he caused the act of will that resulted in his action *and had the power not to cause it*. Perhaps a mad scientist had access to his brain and would have caused that act of will in him (and the resulting action) if, but only if, he had not caused it. If so, the agent's volition and action were inevitable. Nevertheless, if the agent caused his volition, having the power not to cause it, he may be both free and responsible. And if the agent caused his volition, having the power not to cause it, his volition and action cannot have been causally necessitated by events and circumstances that antedated the exercise of his causal power.[18]

18. For an account of such a theory see my "Two Concepts of Freedom," *Proceedings and Addresses of the American Philosophical Association*, vol. 61 (1987), pp. 43–64. I have benefited from discussions with Rod Bertolet, Larry May, Lilly Russow and Ted Ulrich. I have also been greatly helped by discussions and correspondence with David Widerker.

14

Responsibility for Consequences

JOHN MARTIN FISCHER
and MARK RAVIZZA

I

In his essay "The Interest in Liberty on the Scales," Joel Feinberg says:

> We can think of life as a kind of maze of railroad tracks connected
> and disjoined, here and there, by switches. Wherever there is an un-
> locked switch which can be pulled one way or the other, there is an
> 'open option'; wherever the switch is locked in one position the option
> is 'closed.' As we chug along our various tracks in the maze, other per-
> sons are busily locking and unlocking, opening and closing switches,
> thereby enlarging and restricting our various possibilities of move-
> ment. Some of these switchmen are part of a team of legislators, po-
> licemen, and judges; they claim *authority* for their switch positionings.
> Other switchmen operate illicitly at night, often undoing what was au-
> thoritatively arranged in the daylight. This model, of course, is simpler
> than the real world where the 'tracks' and 'switches' are not so clearly
> marked; but it does give us a sense for how some closed options can be
> more restrictive of liberty than others. When a switchman closes and
> locks a switch, he forces us to continue straight on, or stop, or back up.
> What we cannot do is move on to a different track heading off in a
> different direction from the one we are on.
> ... The 'open option' theory of liberty is to be preferred, I think, to
> its main rival, the theory of liberty as the absence of barriers to one's
> actual desires, whatever they should happen to be. Suppose that Mar-

"Responsibility for Consequences," will appear in Jules Coleman and Allen Buchanan, eds., *In Harm's Way: Essays in Honor of Joel Feinberg*, © 1994 by Cambridge University Press, and is printed here by permission of Cambridge University Press.

tin Chuzzlewit finds himself on a trunk line with all of its switches closed and locked, and with other 'trains' moving in the same direction on the same track at his rear, so that he has no choice at all but to continue moving straight ahead to destination *D*. On the 'open option' theory of liberty, this is the clearest example of a total lack of liberty: all of his options are closed, there are no alternative possibilities, he is forced to move to D. But now let us suppose that getting to *D* is Chuzzlewit's highest ambition in life and his most intensely felt desire. In that case, he is sure to get the thing in life he wants most. Does that affect the way the situation should be described in respect to liberty? According to the theory that one is at liberty to the extent that one can do what one wants, a theory held by the ancient Stoics and Epicureans and many modern writers too, Chuzzlewit enjoys perfect liberty in this situation because he can do what he wants, even though he can do nothing else. But since this theory blurs the distinction between liberty and compulsion, and in this one extreme hypothetical case actually identifies the two, it does not recommend itself to common sense. . . . If Chuzzlewit is allowed no alternative to *D*, it follows that he is forced willy-nilly to go to *D*.

. . . What then is the basis of our interest in liberty? Why should it matter that we have few 'open options' if we have everything else we want and our other interests are flourishing? Our welfare interest in having a tolerable bare minimum of liberty is perhaps the easiest to account for of the various kinds of interests persons have in liberty. If human beings had no alternative possibilities at all, if all their actions at all times were the *only* actions permitted them, they might yet be contented provided their desires for alternative possibilities were all thoroughly repressed or extinguished, and they might even achieve things of value, provided that they were wisely programmed to do so. But they could take no credit or blame for any of their achievements, and they could no more be responsible for their lives, in prospect or retrospect, than are robots, or the trains in our fertile metaphor that must run on 'predestined grooves.' They could have dignity neither in their own eyes nor in the eyes of their fellows, and both esteem for others and self-esteem would dwindle. . . . The self-monitoring and self-critical capacities, so essential to human nature, might as well dry up and wither; they would no longer have any function. The contentment with which all of this might still be consistent would not be a recognizably human happiness.[1]

In this extended passage, Feinberg gives voice to what might be called the "traditional" picture of the relationship between such notions as moral responsibility, accountability, and dignity, on the one hand, and

---

1. Joel Feinberg, "The Interest in Liberty on the Scales," in *Rights, Justice, and the Bounds of Liberty* (Princeton: Princeton University Press, 1980), 30–44, esp. 36–40.

liberty in the sense of the existence of alternative possibilities, on the other. Simply put, the traditional view is that moral responsibility and the related notions *require* liberty in the sense of the existence of genuine alternative possibilities. Without such freedom, it is alleged, there is no responsibility.

We disagree with the traditional picture; there are cases in which a person is morally responsible for an action, although he could not have done otherwise. Here is a rather graphic case of this sort.[2] Sam confides to his friend Jack that he plans to murder the mayor of the town in which they live. Sam is disturbed about the mayor's liberal policies, especially his progressive taxation scheme. Whereas Sam's reasons for proposing to kill the mayor are bad ones, they are *his* reasons: he has not been hypnotized, brainwashed, duped, coerced, and so forth. He has deliberated coolly, and he has settled on his murderous course of action.

Sam is bad, and Jack is no better. Jack is pleased with Sam's plan, but Jack is a rather anxious person. Because he worries that Sam might waver, Jack has secretly installed a device in Sam's brain that allows him to monitor all of Sam's brain activity and to intervene in it, if he desires; the device works by electronic stimulation of the brain. Jack can employ the device to ensure that Sam decides to kill the mayor and that he acts on this decision. Let us imagine that Jack is absolutely committed to activating the device to ensure that Sam kills the mayor, should Sam show any sign of not carrying out his original plan. Also, we can imagine that Sam can do nothing to prevent the device from being fully effective, if Jack employs it to cause him to kill the mayor.

Sam and Jack both go to a meeting at the town hall, and Sam methodically carries out his plan to kill the mayor. He does not waver in any way, and he shoots the mayor as a result of his original deliberations. Jack thus plays absolutely no role in Sam's decision and action; the electronic device monitors Sam's brain activity, but it does not have any causal influence on what actually happens. Sam acts exactly as he would have acted, had no device been implanted in his brain.

Evidently, Sam is morally responsible for what he has done. Indeed, he is blameworthy for deciding to kill the mayor and for killing the mayor. But whereas he is morally responsible for his action, he could not have done otherwise because of the existence of a "counterfactual intervener" (Jack), who would have caused him (in a certain manner) to behave as he actually did, had Sam been inclined to do otherwise. Sam acts freely and is morally responsible for what he does because no "responsibility-undermining factor" operates in the actual sequence leading to his action. Rather, such a factor—Jack's use of the electronic

2. We introduce this (and some of the other examples presented below) in John Martin Fischer and Mark Ravizza, "Responsibility and Inevitability," *Ethics* 101 (January 1991): 258–78.

device to stimulate Sam's brain—operates in the *alternative* sequence. When a responsibility-undermining factor operates in the alternative sequence but not in the actual sequence, an agent can be held morally responsible for an action, although he could not have done otherwise. The case of Sam and Jack is such a case; let us call it "Assassin." "Assassin" is a "Frankfurt-type" case.[3]

In "Assassin," Sam is morally responsible for a bad action, although he could not have done otherwise. Here is a case—let's call it "Hero"—in which an agent is morally responsible for a good action, although he could not have done otherwise. Matthew is walking along a beach, looking at the water. He sees a child struggling in the water, and he quickly jumps into the water and rescues the child. Matthew doesn't even consider not trying to rescue the child, but we can imagine that if he had considered refraining, he would have been overwhelmed by literally irresistible guilt feelings, which would have caused him to jump into the water and save the child anyway. We simply stipulate that in the alternative sequence the urge to save the child would be genuinely irresistible.

Apparently, Matthew is morally responsible—indeed, praiseworthy—for his action, although he could not have done otherwise. Matthew acts freely in saving the child; he acts exactly as he would have acted if he had lacked the propensity toward strong feelings of guilt. In this case no responsibility-undermining factor operates in the actual sequence, and thus Matthew is morally responsible for what he does. Whether a responsibility-undermining factor operates in the alternative sequence is controversial, but at least it seems clear that the nature of the alternative sequence renders it true that Matthew could not have done otherwise.[4]

The cases just presented appear to show that moral responsibility and dignity do not require the sort of liberty that involves alternative possibilities. Consider, again, a few sentences from Feinberg:

> All of [Chuzzlewit's] options are closed, there are no alternative possibilities, he is forced to move to *D*. But now let us suppose that getting to *D* is Chuzzlewit's highest ambition in life and his most intensely felt desire. . . . According to the theory that one is at liberty to the extent that one can do what one wants, . . . Chuzzlewit enjoys perfect liberty. . . . But . . . this theory blurs the distinction between liberty and compulsion. . . . If Chuzzlewit is allowed no alternative to *D*, it follows that he is forced willy-nilly to go to *D*.

3. Harry G. Frankfurt, "Alternate Possibilities and Moral Responsibility," *Journal of Philosophy* 66 (1969): 828–39, and "Freedom of the Will and the Concept of a Person," *Journal of Philosophy* 68 (1971): 5–20.

4. Of course, the case could be altered so that there would be a "counterfactual intervener" associated with Matthew. The case would then be precisely parallel to "Assassin."

Now we can see why these sentences are problematic. From the lack of alternative possibilities, is does *not* follow that the agent in question does what he does as a result of *force* or *compulsion*. The lack of the existence of alternative possibilities is a fact about the set of alternative scenarios, whereas being forced or compelled to perform an action is a fact about the actual sequence that issues in an action. As "Assassin" and "Hero" show, one can freely perform an action (without being forced or compelled to do so) even though one has no option but to perform it. In other examples it may well be the case that some factor that actually operates ensures both that the agent has no genuine alternative possibilities and that the agent does not act freely. But the examples adduced above show that certain factors can ensure that the agent has no alternative possibilities without playing any role in the actual sequence and thus without making it the case that the agent does what he does as a result of force or compulsion.

So we deny the claim that moral responsibility for action requires alternative possibilities. But rejecting this traditional view does *not* require one to accept the simple-minded Stoic and Epicurean theory according to which an agent acts freely insofar as he does what he wants to do. The dichotomy between the "open-options" theory and the Stoic/Epicurean theory is not exhaustive. Elsewhere, we have sketched a theory of moral responsibility for action that is more refined than the Stoic/Epicurean theory but still rejects the traditional association of moral responsibility for action with the existence of genuine alternative possibilities.[5] This theory is an "actual-sequence" theory of responsibility for actions: it fixes on the properties of the actual sequence of events issuing in the action, and it does not require the existence of genuine alternative possibilities. We limn the outlines of such a theory below.

II

We have been focusing on moral responsibility for *actions*. Now we turn to the issue of moral responsibility for *consequences*. The events and states of affairs that are consequences of what we do can be construed as either particulars or universals. For our purposes, the distinction between consequence-particulars and consequence-universals will be made in terms of criteria of individuation. We stipulate that a consequence-particular is individuated more finely than a consequence-universal. Specifically, the actual causal pathway to a consequence-particular is an

5. John Martin Fischer, "Responsiveness and Moral Responsibility," in *Responsibility, Character, and the Emotions*, ed. Ferdinand Schoeman (Cambridge: Cambridge University Press, 1987), 81–106; and Fischer and Ravizza, "Responsibility and Inevitability."

essential feature of it, so that if a different causal pathway were to occur, then a different consequence-particular would occur. In contrast, the same consequence-universal can be brought about via different causal antecedents.

For example, in "Assassin" one can distinguish between the consequence-particular, *the mayor's being shot,* and the consequence-universal, *that the mayor is shot.* Had Sam shown some indication that he would not shoot the mayor, and had Jack's device played a causal role in producing the outcome, a different consequence-particular would have occurred. (A different consequence-particular would have been denoted by "the mayor's being shot.") In contrast, even if Jack's device had played a causal role, then the same consequence-universal, *that the mayor is shot,* would have occurred. (Note that what is important in the distinction between consequence-particulars and consequence-universals is the issue of individuation, not the sort of phrase used to refer to the different sorts of consequences. Here we generally follow the convention of referring to consequence-universals with such phrases as "that the mayor is shot.")

In the case of "Assassin," Sam shoots the mayor without the intervention of Jack's electronic device. In this case, the state of affairs *that the mayor is shot* obtains. But this same state of affairs could have been caused to obtain in different ways; in particular, it would have obtained even if Jack had caused Sam to shoot the mayor. Now the question arises as to whether an agent can be morally responsible for a consequence-universal if he could not have prevented it from obtaining. Are there cases in which an agent is morally responsible for the occurrence of a consequence that is inevitable (for him)? (In what follows, we are primarily concerned with consequence-universals.)

It appears as if there are such cases. Take, for example, "Assassin." It is plausible to say that Sam is morally responsible not only for shooting the mayor but also for the consequence-universal, *that the mayor is shot.* And note that Sam cannot prevent the mayor from being shot in one way or another.

Consider a similar case, "Missile 1." In "Missile 1" an evil woman, Elizabeth, has obtained a missile and missile launcher, and she has decided (for her own rather perverse reasons) to launch the missile toward Washington, D.C. Suppose that Elizabeth's situation is like that of Sam; she has not been manipulated, brainwashed, and so forth. Further, imagine that she has had exactly the same sort of device implanted in her brain as had been put into Sam's and that there is a counterfactual intervener associated with her who would ensure that Elizabeth would launch the missile, if she were to show any sign of wavering. We also suppose that, once the missile is launched toward the city, Elizabeth cannot prevent it from hitting Washington.

Now when Elizabeth launches the missile toward Washington, she does so freely, and we believe that she is morally responsible for the occurrence of the consequence-universal *that Washington, D.C., is bombed.* She is morally accountable for this state of affairs, even though it is inevitable for her; there is nothing she can do to prevent the obtaining of the state of affairs *that Washington, D.C., is bombed.*

"Missile 2" is exactly like "Missile 1," except that there is no counterfactual intervener poised to manipulate Elizabeth's brain. Rather, there is another woman, Carla, who would launch the missile if Elizabeth were to refrain. Further, there is nothing that Elizabeth could to do prevent Carla from launching the missile or to prevent the missile from hitting Washington, once launched. In "Missile 2" Elizabeth can also be held morally responsible for the fact that Washington is bombed, although she cannot prevent this fact from obtaining.

"Missile 1" and "Missile 2" are cases in which an agent *is* morally responsible for a consequence of what she does, although she cannot prevent that state of affairs from occurring. But there are other cases in which an agent *is not* morally responsible for a consequence of what she does, and this judgment seems based precisely on the fact that she *cannot* prevent that state of affairs. Consider, for example, "Missile 3."

In "Missile 3" Joan knows that Elizabeth has already launched a missile toward Washington. But Joan has a weapon that she could use to deflect the missile in such a way that it would hit a less populous area of the city. Unfortunately, Joan is located very close to Washington, and because of this fact as well as the bomb's trajectory and the nature of her weapon, she knows that, whereas she can deflect the bomb onto a different part of the city, she cannot prevent the bomb from hitting the city at all.

Imagine that Joan uses her weapon to deflect the bomb. In doing so she may well be morally responsible for the fact that one section of Washington (rather than another) is bombed. But is Joan morally responsible for the consequence-universal, *that Washington, D.C., is bombed?* It seems that she is not. And there is a strong tendency to say that she is not morally responsible for the state of affairs *that Washington, D.C., is bombed* exactly because she cannot prevent this state of affairs from obtaining.

Here is a similar case, called "Train." Ralph is the driver of a train whose brakes have failed. The train is hurtling toward a fork in the tracks. Ralph knows that although he can cause the train to take the right fork or the left fork, he cannot stop the train. He also knows that both forks lead to Syracuse. When he turns the train onto the left fork, he can be held morally responsible for the consequence-universal *that the train takes the left fork* (rather than the right fork). But it just seems obvious that Ralph is not morally responsible for the consequence-universal *that the train ends up in Syracuse,* given that Ralph is not morally responsible for the fact that he is on this stretch of track in the first place. (Notice that even if Ralph did not know that both tracks lead to Syracuse, we would not hold him morally responsible for the consequence-universal *that the train ends up in Syracuse.*) And what could explain Ralph's lack of moral responsibility for the consequence *that the train ends up in Syracuse,* other than the fact that he cannot prevent the train from going to Syracuse in one way or another?[6]

Consideration of the above examples leaves us in the following situation. First, there are cases in which an agent is morally responsible for performing an action, although he cannot avoid performing that action. Further, there are cases in which it appears that an agent is morally responsible for a consequence of what she has done that she cannot prevent from occurring. But there are also cases in which an agent is not morally responsible for a consequence-universal and in which it is very tempting to say that it is precisely the fact that the agent cannot prevent the state of affairs from obtaining that makes it false that he is morally responsible for it. An adequate theory of moral responsibility for consequences should fit naturally with the theory of responsibility for actions. Further, it should explain the fact that, whereas in some cases in which an agent could not prevent a consequence from obtaining he is morally responsible for the consequence, in other such cases he is not morally responsible for the consequence.

III

The theories presented (or suggested) by other philosophers fail, we believe, to generate an acceptable account of moral responsibility for consequences. Here we examine several such theories.

Van Inwagen/Feinberg

The analogue of the traditional approach to moral responsibility for actions would claim that moral responsibility for a consequence-universal requires the freedom to prevent the consequence from obtaining. To the

---

6. The "Train" case is related in an interesting way to Feinberg's railroad metaphor. In Feinberg's example of Martin Chuzzlewit, all the switches leading onto alternative tracks are locked. Thus, Chuzzlewit has no open options with regard to the particular tracks along which he proceeds. In contrast, in "Train" there are such alternatives, but all of the tracks lead to the same place. Thus, whereas Ralph has options with regard to the tracks along which he proceeds, he has no option but to end up in Syracuse.

extent that Feinberg's claims can be applied to consequences, he can be associated with this view. And Peter van Inwagen explicitly argues for this approach.[7]

A very serious problem for this view is that it does not allow one to say what we take to be the plausible and natural thing about "Assassin": that Sam is morally responsible for the consequence *that the mayor is shot.* This result in itself seems to be a decisive refutation of the view. Another (obviously related) problem for this approach is that it forces one to say that "Missile 1," "Missile 2," "Missile 3," and "Train" are on a par. But we believe that, whereas in "Missile 3" Joan is not morally responsible for the consequence-universal *that Washington, D.C., is bombed,* in "Missile 1" and "Missile 2" Elizabeth *is* morally responsible for it. (Also, whereas in the first two missile cases Elizabeth is morally responsible for the consequence-universal, in "Train" Ralph is *not* morally responsible for the consequence-universal *that the train ends up in Syracuse.*) We believe, then, that the van Inwagen/Feinberg approach—the "traditional approach"—implies an implausible assimilation of cases. We need a subtler theory of moral responsible for consequences.

Heinaman

Next consider an account of moral responsibility for consequence-universals suggested by Robert Heinaman.[8] Heinaman's suggestion is that an agent is morally responsible for a consequence-universal insofar as he knowingly and intentionally performs some action that is causally sufficient for the occurrence of the consequence-universal.

There are various problems with this formulation of Heinaman's suggestion. First, one can do something "knowingly and intentionally" without doing it freely. If one is acting as a result of the irresistibility of some urge, one can, nevertheless, be acting "knowingly and intentionally." But if one does not act freely in bringing about a consequence-universal, one might not be morally responsible for it. So let us revise Heinaman's criterion: a person is morally responsible for a consequence-universal insofar as she freely performs some action that is causally sufficient for the occurrence of the consequence-universal.[9]

7. Peter van Inwagen, *An Essay on Free Will* (Oxford: Clarendon, 1983), esp. 171–80.

8. Robert Heinaman, "Incompatibilism without the Principle of Alternative Possibilities," this volume. In Heinaman's note 9, which was added after the publication of the original version of the paper, Heinaman claims he does not wish to endorse the principle he suggests. Thus, by "Heinaman's suggestion" and "Heinaman's criterion," we mean to refer to the principle commended for consideration by Heinaman.

9. In the discussion of responsibility for consequence-universals, we assume that an agent can act freely, although she lacks the freedom to do otherwise. Further, in reformulating Heinaman's view, we assume (for simplicity's sake) that when an agent acts freely, he acts knowingly and intentionally.

But the notion of "causal sufficiency" employed here is rather vague. Heinaman appears to think that, when an agent does something that is causally sufficient for the occurrence of a consequence-universal, he does something that at least in part explains why the consequence-universal occurs. So one way of formulating Heinaman's suggestion is as follows: an agent is morally responsible for the occurrence of a consequence-universal insofar as he freely does something that at least in part explains why the consequence-universal obtains.

Heinaman points out that one can do something that entails that a state of affairs obtains without doing something that at least in part explains *why* the state of affairs obtains. So, for example, when one drops a vase and breaks it, one has done something that entails that the vase is breakable, but one has not done something that in any way explains *why* the vase is breakable. Thus, on Heinaman's suggestion, one will not be morally responsible for the consequence-universal *that the vase is breakable*, although one might be morally responsible for the consequence-universal *that the vase is broken*.

Yet even with such revisions and qualifications, problems remain for Heinaman's account. One wants to say that in "Assassin" Sam is morally responsible for the consequence-universal *that the mayor is killed*, and in "Missile 1" and "Missile 2" Elizabeth is morally responsible for the fact that Washington, D.C., is bombed. But it is unclear that Heinaman's criterion yields these results. For instance, it is at best unclear that in "Assassin" Sam's free action in any way explains the occurrence of the state of affairs *that the mayor is killed*. Given the presence of Jack and the existence of the electronic device, it appears that we *already* have a full explanation of the fact that the mayor will be killed in some way or another. Given that Jack and his device are *sufficient* for the occurrence of the consequence-universal *that the mayor is killed*, it is dubious whether Sam's free action constitutes part of an explanation of the occurrence of the consequence-universal. Heinaman is relying on a notion of "explanatory factor" according to which such a factor need not be a necessary condition of the *explanandum*, and this idea is, at best, obscure.[10]

Perhaps Heinaman's suggestion can be defended against this criticism by making an important (although admittedly delicate) distinction: between a "modalized" consequence-universal and a "purely descriptive" consequence-universal. The modalized consequence-universal is something like the fact that it *has to occur* that the mayor is killed, or perhaps that if the mayor were not killed in one way, he would certainly be killed in another way. In contrast, the purely descriptive consequence-universal is simply the fact that the mayor is killed in one way or another.

Now it might be argued that the apparent plausibility of the above response to Heinaman's criterion issues from a conflation of the modal-

10. For this point we are indebted to correspondence with Carl Ginet.

ized and purely descriptive consequence-universals. That is, it is admittedly implausible to suppose that Sam's free action of pulling the trigger in any way explains the *modalized* consequence-universal. But this is irrelevant, because what is at issue is the appropriate explanation of the obtaining of the purely descriptive consequence-universal. And it *is* plausible to think that Sam's free action in part explains the obtaining of this consequence.

Even if this statement is correct, however, Heinaman's criterion now faces the following problem. Heinaman must say that in "Missile 3" Joan is morally responsible for the (purely descriptive) state of affairs *that Washington, D.C., is bombed (somewhere or another)*. That is to say, *if* it is plausible to suppose that Sam's free act of pulling the trigger at least in part explains why the purely descriptive state of affairs *that the mayor is killed (in some way or another)* obtains, then it is equally plausible to suppose that Joan's free act of deflecting the bomb at least in part explains why the purely descriptive state of affairs *that Washington, D.C., is bombed (somewhere or another)* obtains. But it is an implausible result that Joan must be deemed responsible for this consequence-universal—even the purely descriptive one. Whereas it is plausible to think that Joan is morally responsible for the fact that Washington is bombed *in one area rather than another*, it is implausible to say that she is morally responsible for the fact that Washington is bombed somewhere or another.[11] (A similar analysis applies to "Train.")

There is a way of supplementing Heinaman's criterion that might seem to allow him to avoid the implausible result in "Missile 3" and "Train." In both of these cases, there is "already in motion" a causal sequence that would lead to the occurrence of the consequence-universal, no matter what action the agent performs (among those she can perform). So one might refine Heinaman's criterion further: an agent is morally responsible for a consequence-universal insofar as (1) she freely

11. In response, one might begin with the (indisputable) claim that in "Missile 3" Joan *is* morally responsible for the fact that the bomb hits the particular area it actually hits in Washington, D.C. Allegedly, then, it would follow that Joan is responsible for the purely descriptive consequence-universal *that Washington, D.C., is hit somewhere or another*. But notice that whereas the first consequence-universal entails the second, it is *not* the case that the second entails the first. (The second is a disjunctive state of affairs of which the first is a component disjunct.) And notice further that the general principle (apparently required in order to underwrite the response to the criticism of Heinaman) that whenever an agent is morally responsible for P and P entails Q the agent is morally responsible for Q is invalid.

We conclude also that "Missile 3" provides the material for a criticism of Heinaman's Principle (I) presented on p. 306: "(I) If S is responsible for a state of affairs, A, and if 'F' is any false statement (other than 'not-A'), then S is responsible for the state of affairs that A or F." Joan is responsible for the fact that the missile hits a particular part of Washington, D.C. Now form the disjunction of the true statement about where the missile hit and all the false statements about where the missile hit the city of Washington. Joan is *not* responsible for this state of affairs. After all, this disjunction is equivalent to the fact *Washington, D.C., is bombed in some place or other*, and Joan is not morally responsible for this fact.

performs an action that at least in part explains why the universal is brought about in one way rather than another, and (2) there is no causal sequence already in motion that would lead to the occurrence of the consequence-universal, no matter what the agent does (among the set of things she *can* do).

Regrettably (for Heinaman), this will not do either. For suppose that in "Missile 1" a timing device has already been set. This device would cause the missile to be launched if Elizabeth were to refrain from launching it herself. The revised Heinaman criterion implausibly entails that Elizabeth would *not* be morally responsible for Washington's being bombed in this version of "Missile 1," called "Timer." But Elizabeth freely launches the bomb in "Timer," and it seems as if she *should* be considered morally responsible for the consequence-universal *that Washington, D.C., is bombed;* certainly, she should be held morally responsible for it in "Timer," if she is in "Missile 1." Thus, the refined Heinaman approach would lead to an implausible result: the differentiation of "Timer" and "Missile 1." Finally, we do not see any way of further refining the suggestion of Heinaman so that it would yield adequate results.

A Frankfurt-Type Strategy

Harry Frankfurt has proposed the following principle regarding moral responsibility for actions: if a person acts only because he could not have done otherwise, then he is not morally responsible for his action.[12] This principle applies to actions, rather than consequences, and it specifies only a necessary and not a sufficient condition for moral responsibility. We shall very briefly explain the possibility of extending Frankfurt's suggestion to apply to consequences; we should emphasize that Frankfurt himself is not committed to this sort of extension.

Suppose that an agent freely performs some action that has a certain consequence that she cannot prevent. Imagine, further, that the agent's inability to prevent this consequence plays no role in her decision and action. Under such circumstances, the agent still might be morally responsible for the consequence. This scenario suggests a principle of responsibility for consequence-universals that is similar to Frankfurt's approach to responsibility for actions: if (1) an agent freely performs some action that has a consequence (which she foresees) and (2) the fact that this consequence is unavoidable plays no role in the agent's decision so to act, then the agent can be held morally responsible for the consequence-universal.

To see the problem with this approach, consider again "Missile 3." Joan knows that she cannot prevent the missile from hitting Washing-

12. Harry Frankfurt, "Alternate Possibilities," 838.

ton, D.C. Intuitively, she is not morally responsible for the fact that Washington is bombed in one place or another. And it seems to us that she would not be morally responsible for this fact, even if she mistakenly believed that she could prevent Washington from being bombed. So, in the latter case—"Missile 4"—the situation is exactly as it is in "Missile 3," except that Joan falsely believes that she can deflect the missile so that it will not hit Washington. Still, we claim that, in "Missile 4," Joan is not morally responsible for the consequence-universal *that Washington, D.C., is bombed.* But the two conditions of the extended Frankfurt approach are met: Joan freely does something (deflects the bomb in a certain way) that she foresees will result in Washington's being bombed, and the fact that she cannot avoid this result plays no role in her decision and action. It plays no role in part because she (falsely) believes that she *can* avoid this result. (Similarly, in "Train" Ralph would not be morally responsible for the fact that the train goes to Syracuse, even if he did not know that all tracks go to Syracuse.) Thus, although the Frankfurt-type strategy would say the correct thing about "Missile 1," "Missile 2," and "Missile 3," it would not say the correct thing about such cases as "Missile 4."

Berofsky

A case very similar to "Missile 4" shows the theory of moral responsibility for consequence-universals proposed by Bernard Berofsky to be inadequate. Berofsky says:

> Let us describe conditions in which an agent Walters is derivatively responsible for a state of affairs [S] he cannot help producing in virtue of a prior, free act A.
> (1) Walters performed A in order to bring [S] about.
> (2) Walters believed that the probability that A would lead to [S] is very high.
> (3) [S] is not causally remote from A.
> (4) Walters freely undertook as part of his responsibilities the avoidance of states of affairs of which [S] is an instance.
> (5) Walters believed that he would be unable to prevent [S] once he did A.
> (6) [S] is morally significant.[13]

Note that, in "Missile 4," it is not the case that Joan deflects the bomb in order to bring it about that Washington is bombed. Thus, Berofsky's condition (1) is not satisfied, and Berofsky can say the correct thing

13. Bernard Berofsky, *Freedom from Necessity* (New York: Routledge and Kegan Paul, 1987), 35.

about "Missile 4." But imagine that in "Missile 5" Walters has freely undertaken to protect Washington from attack. Unhappily, Walters is a secret agent working for the Soviet Union. When he sees that a Soviet missile is proceeding toward the east coast of the United States, he falsely believes that it will miss its intended target, Washington. In order to cause the missile to hit Washington, Walters deflects it with his deflecting weapon. The bomb hits Washington, but, unbeknownst to Walters, it would have hit Washington no matter what he did (including not employing his deflecting weapon at all). That is, the missile was proceeding in such a way that, given Walter's weapon and his location very close to Washington, the missile would have hit the city no matter what Walters did. Just as in "Missile 4," we believe that Walters is not morally responsible for the fact that Washington is bombed (in one area or another). He might well be morally responsible for his action of employing his deflecting gun and also for the fact that Washington is bombed in one area rather than another. But it really is implausible to say that Walters is morally responsible for the consequence-universal *that Washington, D.C., is bombed.* Berofsky's account is problematic insofar as it appears to yield this unsettling result. Thus, although Berofsky's theory adequately handles all the other "Missile" cases, it does not say the correct thing about "Missile 5."[14]

Rowe

William Rowe has discussed a number of examples that are related in interesting ways to the ones we have developed above.[15] Further, he has suggested a theory of responsibility for consequence-universals. Here we lay out some of the examples and the theory that was developed to systematize them. But the theory cannot be adequately generalized to apply to examples similar to the "Missile" cases above.

Here is Rowe's Case A:

> There is a train approaching a fork in the track controlled by a switch. The left fork (#1) leads on to where a dog has been tied to the track. If the train proceeds on #1 it will hit the dog. Track #2, however, leads to a safe stopping point for the train. The switch is set for #2. . . . You throw the switch to #1 with the result that the train proceeds on #1, hitting the dog.[16]

14. For a different approach to such issues, see Berofsky's interesting discussion in ibid., 28–30.

15. William L. Rowe, "Causing and Being Responsible for What Is Inevitable," this volume.

16. Ibid., 310–311.

In Case A, Rowe says that you can be held (at least *prima facie*) morally responsible for the consequence-universal *that the dog is hit.* We agree.

Now here is Rowe's Case B:

> Let us again suppose that there is a speeding train approaching a fork in the track controlled by a switch. As in Case A, the switch is set for track #2. It is again in your power to switch the train to track #1 by throwing the switch. It is also in your power not to throw the switch. Unfortunately, unlike Case A, both tracks (#1 and #2) converge later at the point where the dog is tied to the track. It is inevitable, therefore, that the train will hit the dog. Nevertheless, you throw the switch so that the train proceeds on track #1.[17]

In Case B Rowe believes that you are not morally responsible for the fact that the dog is hit. Again, we agree. Rowe's Case B is relevantly similar to our "Train" and "Missile 3."

Next here is Rowe's Case C:

> In Case C we find a curious mixture of features in one or the other of the first two cases. As in Case A, track #2 does not converge with #1. Instead, it leads to a safe stopping point for the train. Only track #1 leads to the spot where the dog is tied to the track. Unlike Case A, however, some other person, Peter, is so situated that he most certainly will throw the switch if, but only if, you do not. If you throw the switch, the train will be routed to track #1 and hit the dog. If you do not throw the switch, Peter will, with the result that the train will be routed to track #1 and hit the dog. Moreover, it is not in your power to prevent Peter's throwing the switch, should you not throw it yourself. As in our other two cases, you throw the switch, the train is routed to track #1 and hits the dog.[18]

In Case C, Rowe thinks that you can be held (at least *prima facie*) morally responsible for the consequence-universal *that the dog is hit.* And, again, we agree. Rowe's Case C is relevantly similar to our "Missile 2."

Let us now consider a case that is exactly like A except that a powerful being is poised to bend track #2 around to the place where the dog is tied if, but only if, you do not switch the train to track #1. (Call this Case D.) In D—as in Case A—you actually switch the train to track #1. Whereas in Case B you are intuitively *not* morally responsible for the fact that the dog is hit, in Case D you are so responsible. Thus, a difference in conditions that are actualized can make a difference to moral responsibility, even if the difference is not causally efficacious. Rowe wishes to

17. Ibid.
18. Ibid., 312.

distinguish D from another case E, which is the same as D except that the powerful being is programmed to bend track #2 to the place where the dog is tied *whether or not you throw the switch.* Rowe claims that in Case E you are not morally responsible for the fact that the dog is hit. He explains the difference in our intuitions concerning Cases D and E by pointing to the fact that in D your action prevents the relevant "ensuring condition" from being actualized, whereas in E your action does not prevent this condition from being actualized—it just prevents it from being efficacious.[19]

According to Rowe, the above examples suggest the following theory: S is responsible for E by doing X if and only if

1) S does X prior to or at the same time as E's occurrence.
2) S's doing X is a part of a sufficient causal condition of E, and
3') Either S's doing X is necessary for E's occurrence or any other condition that is sufficient (in the circumstances) for E has a part that is actualized only if S does not do X.[20]

To see the problem with Rowe's proposal, start with "Missile 3." This is the case presented above in which Elizabeth has launched a missile toward Washington, D.C. Joan has a deflecting ray that can turn the missile away from the center of the city and toward a less populated area, but unfortunately the ray is not strong enough to deflect the missile away from the city entirely. In order to save the most people, Joan deflects the missile. Our intuition here is that Joan is *not* morally responsible for the consequence-universal *that Washington, D.C., is bombed.* (Of course, she may well be responsible for the fact that D.C. is bombed in one place rather than another.)

Consider now "Missile 6." This is like "Missile 3" except for the fact that Elizabeth's missile has misfired and is now heading away from Washington. Elizabeth realizes the situation and prepares to use her own deflecting ray to redirect the missile toward the center of the city. Joan learns of this plan but fortunately realizes that she can redirect the missile to a less populated area of Washington before Elizabeth can fire her ray. In this case, Joan deflects the missile to a less populated area only because she knows that if she does not do so, Elizabeth will use her ray to deflect it to the most populated part of the city.

Clearly, if Joan is not morally responsible for the consequence-universal *that Washington, D.C., is bombed* in "Missile 3," then she is not

19. Ibid., 316.
20. Ibid., 313–314. Rowe means to be giving an account of causal responsibility that, together with certain epistemic conditions, would give us the account of moral responsibility. Here we can assume that the epistemic conditions are met, and we can scrutinize the theory as a theory of moral responsibility for consequence-universals.

morally responsible for it in "Missile 6." Rowe, however, must say that Joan *is* morally responsible for the relevant consequence-universal in "Missile 6." He must say this because "Missile 6" is analogous to Case D. Just as Rowe claims that you are morally responsible for the fact that the dog is hit in D because your action prevents the relevant ensuring condition from being actualized (i.e., your act prevents the powerful being from bending the track), so he should claim that in "Missile 6" Joan is responsible for the fact that Washington is bombed because her action prevents Elizabeth from "bending" the missile back to the city. (This is analogous to bending the track in Case D, since one can imagine that the "smart" missile is being guided on a "laser track.") Thus, Rowe's theory is not suitably generalizable.

IV

Responsibility for Actions

Here we present just the barest sketch of a theory of moral responsibility for actions. This theory has been elaborated elsewhere in greater detail, and it must be further refined and developed in future work.[21] But it is useful here to see how our theory of moral responsibility for consequences builds on and fits together with the theory of responsibility for actions.

The basic idea is that (given that the relevant epistemic conditions are met[22]) an agent is morally responsible for performing an action insofar as (1) it is not the case that the agent does what he does solely because he could not have done otherwise, and (2) the bodily movement identical to the action issues from a weakly reasons-responsive mechanism. To say whether an action issues from a weakly reasons-responsive mechanism, we first need to identify the kind of mechanism that actually issues in action. It is important to see that, in some cases, intuitively different kinds of mechanisms operate in the actual sequence and the alternative sequence. So, for instance, in "Assassin" the ordinary process of practical reasoning issues in Sam's act of squeezing the trigger,

21. Fischer, "Responsiveness and Moral Responsibility." See, also, Mark Ravizza, "Is Responsiveness Sufficient for Responsibility?" (typescript, University of California, Riverside).

22. Following Aristotle, *Nicomachean Ethics* 1109b30–1111b5, one might distinguish between an epistemic and a freedom-relevant component of a theory of responsibility. Aristotle held that one acts voluntarily insofar as one is not in a relevant sense ignorant of what one is doing and one is not compelled to do what one does. We focus here primarily on the freedom-relevant component. For a useful discussion of issues pertinent to the epistemic component, see Joel Feinberg, *Harm to Self* (Oxford: Oxford University Press, 1986), 269–315.

but a different type of mechanism (involving direct electronic stimulation of Sam's brain) would have operated, had Sam shown any sign of wavering. We cannot here develop an explicit account of mechanism-individuation. It suffices, for our purposes, to note that Sam's actual-sequence mechanism is intuitively of a different sort from the alternative-sequence mechanism. Similarly, we would want to say that in "Hero," Matthew's actual-sequence mechanism is of a different sort from his alternative-sequence mechanism; in the actual sequence, he quickly deliberates and decides to save the struggling child, and his reasoning is uninfluenced by any overwhelming urge. In the alternative sequence, however, his deliberations are influenced by an overwhelming and irresistible urge to save the swimmer.

In order to determine whether an actual-sequence mechanism of a certain type is weakly reasons-responsive, one asks whether there exists some possible scenario (with the same natural laws as the actual world) in which that type of mechanism operates, the agent has reason to do otherwise, and the agent does otherwise (for that reason). That is, we hold fixed the actual type of mechanism, and we ask whether the agent would respond to *some* possible incentive to do otherwise. If so, then the actually operative mechanism is weakly reasons-responsive. In contrast, strong reasons-responsiveness obtains when a certain kind K of mechanism actually issues in an action and if there were sufficient reason to do otherwise and K were to operate, the agent would recognize the sufficient reason and thus choose to do otherwise and do otherwise.

Under the requirement of strong reasons-responsiveness, we ask what would happen if there were a sufficient reason to do otherwise (holding fixed the actual kind of mechanism). Strong reasons-responsiveness points us to the alternative scenario in which there is a sufficient reason for the agent to do otherwise (and the actual mechanism operates) which is *most similar* to the actual situation. In contrast, under weak reasons-responsiveness, there must simply exist *some* possible scenario in which there is a sufficient reason to do otherwise, the agent's actual mechanism operates, and the agent does otherwise. This possible scenario need *not* be the one in which the agent has a sufficient reason to do otherwise (and the actual mechanism operates) which is *most similar* to the actual situation.

Responsibility for Consequences

The account of moral responsibility for consequences is in certain respects parallel to (and also an extension of) the account of moral responsibility for actions. The leading idea is that (given that certain epistemic constraints are satisfied) an agent is morally responsible for a consequence insofar as (1) it is not the case that the agent brings about the consequence solely because she believes that she cannot prevent it from occurring (in some way or another), and (2) the consequence emanates from a responsive *sequence*. It is necessary to distinguish two components of the sequence leading to a consequence. The first component is the mechanism leading to action (bodily movement), and the second component is the process leading from the action to the event in the external world. We shall say that, in order for the sequence leading to a consequence to be responsive, the mechanism leading to the action must be weakly reasons-responsive and the process leading from the action to the consequence must be "sensitive to action."

It is important to note that the counterfactual intervener in a Frankfurt-type case need not be another agent (whose action in the alternative sequence would bring about the consequence in question). As Frankfurt points out, the role of counterfactual intervener may be played "by natural forces involving no will or design at all."[23] Thus, in "Missile 2" we could eliminate Carla and suppose instead that had Elizabeth not freely launched the missile, natural forces would have caused the missile's triggering mechanism to malfunction and fire the rocket at Washington, D.C. (Perhaps a stray bird would have flown into the missile's launching apparatus and triggered the firing.) Given these types of examples, it seems that in evaluating the sensitivity of a process one wants to hold fixed not only the actions of other agents in the actual sequence, but also any natural events that play no role in the actual sequence but would, in the alternative sequence, *trigger* causal chains leading to the consequence in question. For convenience we can group *both* other actions that would trigger causal chains leading to the consequence (e.g., Carla's firing the missile in the alternative sequence) *and* natural events that would do so (e.g., the bird triggering the missile's firing in the alternative sequence) under the heading "triggering events."

Let us think of a triggering event (relative to some consequence *C*) as an event that would *initiate* a causal sequence leading to *C*, if it were to occur. Such events as Carla's firing the missile and the bird's flying into the missile's launching apparatus are triggering events (relative to the relevant consequences) in the examples above.

Suppose that in the actual world an agent *S* performs some action *A* via a type of mechanism *M*, and *S*'s *A*-ing causes some consequence *C* via a type of process P.[24] We shall say that the sequence leading to the con-

23. Frankfurt, "Alternate Possibilities," note 4.
24. We shall here assume that there is just one causal sequence leading to the consequence. We believe that our theory can be generalized so as to apply to cases in which more than one causal chain leads to a consequence. We shall not discuss such cases in this essay; here we are concerned with cases of "preemptive overdetermination" rather than "simultaneous overdetermination." Further, the focus here is on what might be called

sequence C is responsive if and only if there exists some action A^* (other than A) such that: (1) there exists some possible scenario in which an M-type mechanism operates, the agent has reason to do A^*, and the agent does A^*; and (2) if S were to do A^*, all triggering events that do not actually occur were not to occur, and a P-type process were to occur, then C would not occur.[25]

Before proceeding to show how this principle can be applied to explain our intuitive judgments about the cases discussed above, we need to discuss a few points that should help both to clarify and to illustrate our principle. (1) In formulating the definition of a responsive sequence, we make use of the intuitive notion of a "type of process" leading from the action to the event in the external world. This "type of process" is parallel to the notion of a "kind of mechanism" issuing in action. As above, we concede both that process-individuation might be problematic and that we do not have an explicit theory of process-individuation. But, as above, we believe that there is a relatively clear intuitive distinction between different types of processes.

We do not deny that there will be difficult questions about process-individuation. Nevertheless, all that is required for our purposes is that there be agreement about some fairly clear cases. If we are unsure about an agent's moral responsibility for a consequence in precisely those cases in which we are unsure about process-individuation, then at least the vagueness in our theory will match the vagueness of the phenomena it purports to analyze.

(2) In ascertaining the responsiveness of a particular sequence involving a mechanism issuing in action, an action, and a process leading from the action to a consequence, we "hold fixed" the type of mechanism and the type of process. If it is the case that a different mechanism or process would have taken place if things had been different (i.e., if the case is a "Frankfurt-type" case), this is irrelevant to the responsiveness of the *actual* sequence. Further, imagine that we are testing the sensitivity of a

---

"action-triggered" consequences. There might also be "omission-triggered" consequences for which an agent might be morally responsible. For example, in "Assassin" it seems as if the counterfactual intervener, Jack, might also be (fully) morally responsible for the fact that the mayor is assassinated, insofar as it is assumed that Jack could have prevented this consequence. We believe that omission-triggered consequences can be handled in a way parallel to the way suggested in the text for handling action-triggered consequences.

25. It should be noted that the analysis of a responsive sequence given above is for cases of individual responsibility; it is not intended to address cases of simultaneous overdetermination in which several agents may be jointly responsive for the consequence produced. We believe that a similar analysis may work in these cases, but in evaluating the responsibility of any one agent it might be necessary to "bracket" the other triggering events that simultaneously produce the consequence, in order to ascertain if the agent's action was part of a responsive sequence that was sufficient to produce the consequence. The issues involved in such cases of joint responsibility are complex and we cannot fully pursue them here.

particular process leading from an action to a consequence. Suppose that the agent actually performs a certain action, thus causing some consequence, and that no one else actually performs that type of action. Under these conditions, we "hold fixed" others' behavior when we test for the sensitivity of the process leading from action to consequence. The point is that, when we are interested in the sensitivity of the process to action, we are interested in whether there would have been a different outcome if the agent had not performed a certain sort of action *and all non-occurring triggering events were not to occur.*

The theory claims that the sequence leading to a consequence includes more than just the mechanism issuing in action. Thus, it is not surprising that both components—the mechanism leading to the action and the process leading from the action to the event—are relevant to responsibility for a consequence, where only the first component is relevant to responsibility for an action. Thus, the theory of responsibility for a consequence involves two stages. It will be seen below that this two-stage approach helps us appropriately to distinguish different cases of responsibility for consequences that are inevitable. Further, it is important to note that when considering responsibility for consequences the second component should not be considered in isolation from the first. Our definition of the responsiveness of the sequence leading to a consequence requires a certain sort of *linkage* of the two components of the sequence.

(3) The notion of a "triggering event" is—like the notions of "mechanism" and "process"—fuzzy around the edges. But, again, we believe that it is tolerably clear for the present purposes. Note that a triggering event is one that would "initiate" a causal chain leading to a certain consequence. Although the concept of "initiation" is difficult to articulate crisply, we rely on the fact that there are some fairly uncontroversial instances of it. For example, if a lightning bolt hits a house and there is a resulting fire, the event of the lightning's hitting the house could be said to initiate the sequence leading to the destruction of the house. And this is so even if there were certain atmospheric events that antedated the lightning bolt and led to it. Of course, the notion of "initiation" is highly context-dependent, and the truth of claims about purported initiations will depend on the purposes and goals of the individuals making (and considering) the claims. But we believe that the notion of initiation issues in tolerably clear intuitive judgments about the cases relevant to our purposes. So, for example, such events as Sam's (or Carla's) pulling the trigger, the bird's flying into the launching mechanism, and the timing device activating the bomb (in "Timer") are all intuitively events that initiate the sequences leading to the relevant consequences. In contrast, consider the event of the train's proceeding in a certain direction in the example "Train." Given the set-up of the example, if this event were to

occur, the train would (still) end up in Syracuse. But note that this event is not plausibly thought to *initiate* the sequence leading to the consequence in question. (The initiating event here would be Ralph's turning the train one way or another—or perhaps his choice to do so.)[26]

With the principle of moral responsibility for consequences in hand, we can explain the intuitive judgments about cases described above. In "Assassin" Sam is morally responsible for the consequence-universal *that the mayor is killed*. In this case, the actual-sequence mechanism (ordinary practical deliberation) is weakly reasons-responsive, and the process leading from action to consequence (ordinary physical laws, no "abnormal circumstances") is sensitive to action: had Sam not squeezed the trigger (either as a result of his own deliberation or because of Jack's intervention) and others' relevant behavior were held fixed, the mayor would not have been killed. Thus, the two components necessary for responsiveness are present, and Sam can be held morally responsible for the fact that the mayor is killed, although he could not have prevented it.

Exactly the same considerations apply to "Missile 1." Elizabeth is morally responsible for the consequence-universal *that Washington, D.C., is bombed:* both components of the actual sequence issuing in the consequence-universal are suitably responsive and thus the total sequence is responsive. (Further, the same analysis applies to Rowe's Case A.)

Above we claimed that if Elizabeth is morally responsible for the consequence-universal *that Washington, D.C., is bombed* in "Missile 1," she should also be considered morally responsible for it in "Timer." ("Timer" is just like "Missile 1" except that a timing mechanism has been set that would activate the bomb, if Elizabeth were to refrain from doing so.) The timing mechanism operates in the actual sequence, but it does not actually activate the bomb. Thus the triggering event of the timing mechanism's activating the bomb (relative to the consequence-universal *that Washington, D.C., is bombed*) is a non-occurring triggering mechanism. As such, its non-occurrence is held fixed, on our approach to ascertaining responsiveness: on our theory, the actual sequence issuing in the consequence-universal is responsive, and thus Elizabeth is deemed morally responsible for it.

Note that Elizabeth is also deemed morally responsible for the consequence-universal *that Washington, D.C., is bombed* in "Missile 2." Again, the actual sequence issuing in the consequence is responsive. When ascertaining whether the actual sequence leading to the bomb's

26. The notions of initiation and "triggering" need more discussion in future work. We believe that the lightning bolt could be said to "initiate" the sequence leading to the destruction of the house in the example in the text, even in a causally deterministic world. But the discussion of this point must await another occasion.

hitting Washington is responsive, we hold fixed the inaction of Carla. (The same analysis applies to Rowe's Case C.)

But in "Missile 3" Joan is not morally responsible for the consequence-universal *that Washington, D.C., is bombed* because the sequence including Joan's action and the process leading from her action to the event of Washington's being bombed is not responsive. Of course, the first component *is* weakly reasons-responsive (and thus Joan can be held morally responsible for her *action* of deflecting the bomb). But the sequence is not responsive, because the second component—the process leading from action to event in the world—is *not* sensitive to action. That is, the world is such that, no matter how Joan acts, the bomb will hit Washington (Exactly parallel remarks apply to "Train.")

Our principle of moral responsibility for consequences, then, explains the intuitive judgments about various examples presented above. (We do not here explicitly apply the theory to all the cases, but our claim is that our theory handles all the cases in a felicitous manner.) Further, the theory explains why there is an important difference between such cases as "Missile 1" and "Missile 2," on the one hand, and "Missile 3" and "Train," on the other. The agent could have prevented the relevant consequence-universal in *none* of these cases. But, whereas in the first two cases the relevant consequence-universal issues from a responsive sequence, in the last two cases it does not.

Once it becomes evident that responsiveness of a sequence leading to a consequence requires the second component—sensitivity to action— as well as the first, it becomes clear that the latter two states of affairs are interestingly different from the former two. In "Missile 1" and "Missile 2" the responsibility-undermining factor occurs in the *alternative* to the first component of the actual sequence. In "Missile 3" and "Train," the factor that rules out responsibility for the consequence-universal is part of the second component of the *actual* sequence. If one did not recognize that the actual sequence leading to a consequence contains two components, one could mistakenly think that the only way to explain the agents' lack of responsibility in "Missile 3" and "Train" is to say that the agent could not have prevented the consequence-universal from obtaining. But our theory allows us to avoid using this sort of explanation, which in any case would lead to the wrong result in such cases as "Missile 1" and "Missile 2."

The difference between Rowe's Cases A and B illustrates an important feature of our theory of moral responsibility. The only difference between Cases A and B consists in facts about the world that play no role in what actually happens: whether or not track #2 "bends around" so as to converge with track #1 is irrelevant to what actually transpires in both cases. But it is relevant to the responsiveness of the sequences issuing in the consequences, and, thus, to your moral responsibility for them.

What is relevant here is that certain conditions in the world are *actualized,* not that they are efficacious. Thus, there is a distinction between Case B and Case D presented above (Case D is exactly like A except that a powerful being is poised to bend track #2 around if, but only if, you do not switch the train to track #1). In Case D—as in Case A—you actually switch the train to track #1. Whereas in Case B you are *not* morally responsible for the fact that the dog is hit, in D you are so responsible. Thus, a difference in conditions that are actualized can make a difference to moral responsibility, even if the difference is not causally efficacious.

Note that there seems to be a difference between the first component of the sequence issuing in the consequence (the mechanism leading to action) and the second component (the process leading from the action to the consequence), as regards the relevance of inefficacious factors. If an agent actually has an irresistible desire to do something, but the irresistibility of the desire plays no role in his actual decision or action, then it seems that he can be morally responsible for *his action.* Further, under such conditions, it would seem that the agent could be morally responsible for a consequence-universal. Consider, for instance, Frankfurt's "willing addict." When he takes the drug, he might not even know that he has an irresistible desire to take it. He can be held morally responsible for his taking the drug and also, seemingly, for the fact that the drug is taken. Because the irresistibility of the desire is inefficacious, it is not relevant to the actual-sequence mechanism issuing in the action, and thus it is not relevant to the responsiveness of the sequence issuing in the consequence.[27] But in a case such as B, the fact that track #2 actually bends around is relevant to the sensitivity to action of the process leading from the action to the consequence, and hence it is relevant to the responsiveness of the sequence issuing in the consequence. Thus, there is a difference between action-producing mechanisms and the processes that go from actions to consequences: inefficacious factors are irrelevant to the responsiveness of the former, but relevant to the sensitivity of the latter.

Having sketched out our approach to moral responsibility for consequences, we are in a position to address an argument van Inwagen

27. Harry Frankfurt discusses the willing addict in "Freedom of the Will," 19–20. The willing addict is supposed to act on a desire that is in fact irresistible, but whose irresistibility plays no role in the outcome. Thus, there are scenarios in which the *same mechanism* (involving a desire for the drug with the intensity level *that is actually manifested*) issues in the agent's not taking the drug. Although the actual desire for the drug is irresistible, the level of intensity in virtue of which it is irresistible plays no role in the actual sequence; thus, this level of intensity is not preserved across the relevant possible worlds. This case is precisely parallel to one in which a counterfactual intervener's presence ensures that an agent cannot choose or do otherwise, and yet the counterfactual intervener plays no role in what actually happens.

employs to defend his approach to moral responsibility for consequence-universals.[28] Consider again "Assassin." We have said that it is plausible to consider Sam morally responsible for the consequence-universal *that the mayor is killed*. Van Inwagen would deny this, because Sam cannot prevent the mayor from being killed in some way or another. And van Inwagen might argue for his position as follows. If Sam is morally responsible for the state of affairs *that the mayor is killed*, then Sam is morally responsible for the state of affairs *Sam kills the mayor on his own or Sam kills the mayor as a result of the intervention of Jack's device*. But there is no difference between being morally responsible for this disjunctive state of affairs and such states of affairs as *Sam kills the mayor on his own or grass is green* and *Sam kills the mayor on his own or two plus two equals four*. But for the latter two states of affairs Sam is clearly *not* morally responsible. Thus, Sam should not be considered morally responsible for the state of affairs *that the mayor is killed*.

But we claim that there is a relevant difference between *Sam kills the mayor on his own or Sam kills the mayor as a result of the intervention of Jack's device* and such states of affairs as *Sam kills the mayor on his own or grass is green*. The latter state of affairs contains a disjunct that would obtain even if the first disjunct obtains and that does not result from a responsive sequence: *grass is green*. In contrast, the former state of affairs does *not* contain a disjunct of this kind. In killing the mayor on his own, Sam can make it false that he kills the mayor as a result of Jack's device, and because Sam's killing the mayor on his own issues from a responsive sequence, the state of affairs *Sam kills the mayor on his own or Sam kills the mayor as a result of Jack's device* issues from a responsive sequence. Thus, on our approach Sam can be held morally responsible for the fact that the mayor is killed, but we need not say that Sam is morally responsible for the states of affairs *Sam kills the mayor on his own or grass is green* and *Sam kills the mayor on his own or two plus two equals four*.

V

Return to Chuzzlewit. He finds himself with but one open option. But his lack of open alternatives need not imply that he acts as a result of force or compulsion. Martin Chuzzlewit may be like Sam (in "Assassin") and Matthew (in "Hero") and Elizabeth (in "Missile 1" and "Missile 2"). He may act freely, even though he cannot do otherwise. And his acting freely is not explained simply in virtue of his acting in conformity with his desire (as in the simple-minded Stoic/Epicurean theory). Martin Chuzzlewit acts freely insofar as he acts as the result of a certain sort of

28. Van Inwagen, *An Essay on Free Will,* 171–80.

weakly reasons-responsive mechanism.[29] Thus, we believe that it is *false* that, in Feinberg's words,

> if human beings had no alternative possibilities at all, if all their actions at all times were the *only* actions permitted them, they . . . could take no credit or blame for any of their achievements, and they could no more be responsible for their lives, in prospect or retrospect, than are robots, or the trains in our fertile metaphor that must run on 'predestined grooves.' They could have dignity neither in their own eyes nor in the eyes of their fellows, and both esteem for others and self-esteem would dwindle.[30]

Further, in certain cases in which an agent cannot prevent a consequence-universal from occurring, the agent can nevertheless be responsible for it. Within the class of consequences that are inevitable for an agent, there is a proper subclass that emanate from certain sorts of responsive sequences. An agent may be morally responsible for the members of this subclass. The partitioning of the larger class into the two pertinent subclasses issues from a theory that builds on the theory of responsibility for actions.

It is natural to think of the future as a "garden of forking paths," in Borges's phrase. Similarly, we might think of life as the "maze of railroad tracks" with at least some unlocked switches, as envisaged by Feinberg. But if it turned out that there were just one path into the future, it would *not* follow that we could not sometimes be morally accountable and that we could not have pride, indignation, or dignity. We could take pride in the way in which we take the path into the future.

29. We wish to assimilate Chuzzlewit to the other agents in regard to his *actions*. But of course we do not wish to suggest that he is in a similar situation in regard to the *consequences* of his actions, since the sequences issuing in certain of these consequences are not responsive.

30. Feinberg, *Harm to Self*, 36.

Bibliography

Adams, Robert Merrihew. 1985. "Involuntary Sins." *Philosophical Review,* 94: 3–31.

Albritton, Rogers. 1985. "Freedom of Will and Freedom of Action." *Proceedings of the Fifty-ninth Annual Pacific Division Meeting of the American Philosophical Association,* 239–51.

Alston, William. 1977. "Self-Intervention and the Structure of Motivation." In Mischel 1977.

Andre, Judith. 1983. "Nagel, Williams, and Moral Luck." *Analysis,* 43: 202–7.

Antony, Louise, 1979. "Why We Excuse." *Tulane Studies in Philosophy,* 28: 63–70.

Arenella, Peter. 1990. "Character, Choice, and Moral Agency: The Relevance of Character to Our Moral Culpability Judgments." *Social Philosophy & Policy,* 7: 59–83.

Arneson, Richard. 1985. "Freedom and Desire." *Canadian Journal of Philosophy,* 15: 425–48.

Audi, Robert. 1974. "Moral Responsibility, Freedom, and Compulsion." *American Philosophical Quarterly,* 11: 1–14.

——. 1986. "Acting for Reasons." *Philosophical Review,* 95: 511–46.

——. 1991. "Responsible Action and Virtuous Character." *Ethics,* 101: 304–21.

Austin, J. L. 1956–57. "A Plea for Excuses." In *Responsibility,* ed. Joel Feinberg and Hyman Gross. Encino, Calif.: Dickenson, 1975.

Baier, Kurt. 1970. "Responsibility and Action." In *The Nature of Human Action,* ed. Myles Brand. Glenview, Ill.: Scott, Foresman.

——. 1975. "Rationality, Reason, and the Good." In *Morality, Reason, and Truth,* ed. David Copp and David Zimmerman. Totowa, N.J.: Rowman & Allanheld.

——. 1984. "The Concepts of Punishment and Responsibility." In *Morality in Practice,* ed. James Sterba. Belmont, Calif.: Wadsworth, 1988.

Bennett, Jonathan. 1980. "Accountablity." In van Straaten 1980.

Benson, Paul. 1987a. "Ordinary Ability and Free Action." *Canadian Journal of Philosophy,* 17: 307–335.

——. 1987b. "Freedom and Value." *Journal of Philosophy,* 84: 467–86.

Bernheim, Hippolyte. 1888. *Hypnosis and Suggestion in Psychotherapy.* 2d rev. ed. Trans. Christian Herter. New Hyde Park, N.Y.: University Books, 1965.

Bernstein, Mark. 1989. Review of Kane's *Free Will and Values. Nous,* 23: 557–59.

——. 1992. *Fatalism.* Lincoln: University of Nebraska Press.

Berofsky, Bernard, ed. 1966. *Free Will and Determinism.* New York: Harper & Row.

——. 1980. "The Irrelevance of Morality to Freedom." In Bradie and Brand 1980.

——. 1987. *Freedom from Necessity: The Metaphysical Basis of Responsibility.* New York: Routledge and Kegan Paul.

Blumenfeld, David, and Gerald Dworkin. 1965. "Necessity, Contingency, and Punishment." *Philosophical Studies,* 16: 91–94.

——. 1971. "The Principle of Alternate Possibilities." *Journal of Philosophy,* 68: 339–45.

——. 1972. "Free Action and Uncommon Motivation." *Monist,* 56:426–43.

Bradie, Michael, and Myles Brand, eds. 1980. *Action and Responsibility.* Bowling Green, Ohio: Bowling Green State University Press.

Brandt, Richard B. 1958. "Blameworthiness and Obligation." In Melden 1958.

——. 1970. "Traits of Character: A Conceptual Analysis." *American Philosophical Quarterly,* 7: 23–37.

Caplan, Lincoln. 1984. *The Insanity Defense and the Trial of John W. Hinckley, Jr.* Boston: Godine.

Cauman, Leigh, Isaac Levi, Charles D. Parsons, and Robert Schwartz, eds. 1983. *How Many Questions? Questions in Honor of Sidney Morgenbesser.* Indianapolis: Hackett.

Chisholm, Roderick M. 1958. "Responsibility and Avoidability." In *Determinism and Freedom in the Age of Modern Science,* ed. Sidney Hook, 2d ed. New York: New York University Press.

——. 1976. *Person and Object.* La Salle, Ill.: Open Court.

Christman, John. 1987. "Autonomy: A Defense of the Split-level Self." *Southern Journal of Philosophy,* 25: 281–93.

——. 1988. "Constructing the Inner Citadel: Recent Work on Autonomy." *Ethics,* 99: 109–24.

——, ed. 1989. *The Inner Citadel.* New York: Oxford University Press.

——. 1991. "Autonomy and Personal History." *Canadian Journal of Philosophy,* 20: 1–24.

Collins, Steven. 1982. *Selfless Persons.* Cambridge: Cambridge University Press.

Cooper, D. E. 1968. "Collective Responsibility." *Philosophy,* 43: 258–68.

——. 1969. "Collective Responsibility—Again." *Philosophy,* 44: 153–55.

Cummins, Robert. 1979. "Could Have Done Otherwise." *Personalist,* 60: 411–14.

——. 1980. "Culpability and Mental Disorder." *Canadian Journal of Philosophy,* 10: 207–32.

Dennett, Daniel, 1971. "Intentional Systems." *Journal of Philosophy,* 68: 87–106.

——. 1973. "Mechanism and Responsibility." In Honderich 1973.

——. 1976. "Conditions of Personhood." In Rorty 1976.

——. 1981. *Brainstorms.* Cambridge: MIT Press.

——. 1984a. *Elbow Room: The Varieties of Free Will Worth Wanting.* Cambridge: MIT Press.

——. 1984b. "I Could Not Have Done Otherwise—So What?" *Journal of Philosophy,* 81: 553–65.

Double, Richard. 1989. "Puppeteers, Hypnotists, and Neurosurgeons." *Philosophical Studies,* 56: 163–73.

——. 1991. *The Non-Reality of Free Will.* New York: Oxford University Press.

Downie, R. S. 1969. "Collective Responsibility." *Philosophy,* 44: 66–69.

Duff, Antony. 1977. "Psychopathy and Moral Understanding." *American Philosophical Quarterly*, 14: 189–200.

Duggan, Timothy J., and Bernard Gert. 1967. "Voluntary Abilities." *American Philosophical Quarterly*, 4: 127–35.

——. 1986. "Free Will as the Ability to Will." *Nous*, 13: 197–217; reprinted in Fischer 1986.

Dworkin, Gerald. 1970a. "Acting Freely." *Noûs*, 4: 367–83.

——, ed. 1970b. *Determinism, Free Will, and Moral Responsibility*. Englewood Cliffs, N.J.: Prentice-Hall.

——. 1976. "Autonomy and Behavior Control." *Hastings Center Report*, 6: 23–28.

——. 1988. *The Theory and Practice of Autonomy*. New York: Cambridge University Press.

Dworkin, Gerald, and David Blumenfeld. 1966. "Punishment for Intentions." *Mind*, 75: 396–404.

Feinberg, Joel. 1968. "Collective Responsibility." *Journal of Philosophy*, 65: 674–88.

——, ed. 1969. *Moral Concepts*. London: Oxford University Press.

——, ed. 1970. *Doing and Deserving*. Princeton: Princeton University Press.

——. 1980a. "The Interest in Liberty on the Scales." In Feinberg 1980b.

——. 1980b. *Rights, Justice, and the Bounds of Liberty*. Princeton: Princeton University Press.

Fingarette, Herbert. 1967. *On Responsibility*. New York: Basic Books.

——. 1972. *The Meaning of Criminal Insanity*. Berkeley: University of California Press.

Fischer, John Martin. 1982. "Responsibility and Control." *Journal of Philosophy*, 89: 24–40; reprinted in Fischer 1986.

——. 1985. "Responsibility and Failure." *Proceedings of the Aristotelian Society*, 86: 251–70; reprinted in French 1991.

——, ed. 1986. *Moral Responsibility*. Ithaca: Cornell University Press.

——. 1987. "Responsiveness and Moral Responsibility." In Schoeman 1987.

Fischer, John Martin, and Mark Ravizza. 1991. "Responsibility and Inevitability." *Ethics*, 101: 258–78.

——. 1992. "The Inevitable." *Australasian Journal of Philosophy*, 70: 388–404.

Frankfurt, Harry G. 1969. "Alternate Possibilities and Moral Responsibility." *Journal of Philosophy*, 45:829–39; reprinted in Fischer 1986 and French 1991.

——. 1971. "Freedom of the Will and the Concept of a Person." *Journal of Philosophy*, 68: 5–20; reprinted in Fischer 1986.

——. 1973. "Coercion and Moral Responsibility." In Honderich 1973.

——. 1975. "Three Concepts of Free Action II." *Proceedings of the Aristotelian Society*, 44, supp. 113–25; reprinted in Fischer 1986.

——. 1976. "Identification and Externality." In Rorty 1976.

——. 1978. "The Problem of Action." *American Philosophical Quarterly*, 15: 157–62.

——. 1988. *The Importance of What We Care About*. Cambridge: Cambridge University Press.

French, Peter A., ed. 1972. *Individual and Collective Responsibility*. Cambridge, Mass.: Schenkman.

——. 1984. *Collective and Corporate Responsibility*. New York: Columbia University Press.

——, ed. 1991. *The Spectrum of Responsibility*. New York: St. Martin's.

——. 1992. *Responsibility Matters*. Lawrence: University Press of Kansas.

Friedman, Marilyn. 1986. "Autonomy and the Split-level Self." *Southern Journal of Philosophy*, 24: 19–35.

Ginet, Carl. 1990. *On Action*. New York: Cambridge University Press.

Glover, Jonathan. 1970. *Responsibility.* London: Routledge & Kegan Paul.
Green, O. H. 1979. "Refraining and Responsibility." *Tulane Studies in Philosophy,* 28: 103–13.
Greenspan, Patricia. 1978. "Behavior Control and Freedom of Action." *Philosophical Review,* 87: 225–40; reprinted in Fischer 1986.
———. 1987. "Unfreedom and Responsibility." In Schoeman 1987.
Haksar, Vinit. 1964. "Aristotle and the Punishment of Psychopaths." *Philosophy,* 39: 323–40.
———. 1965. "The Responsibility of Psychopaths." *Philosophical Quarterly,* 15: 135–45.
Hampshire, Stuart. 1983. *Morality and Conflict.* Cambridge: Harvard University Press.
Hampton, Jean. 1990. *"Mens Rea." Social Philosophy & Policy,* 7: 1–28.
Hart, H. L. A. 1968a. "Responsibility and Retribution." In Hart 1968b.
———. 1968b. *Punishment and Responsibility.* New York: Oxford University Press.
Haworth, Lawrence. 1984. "Autonomy and Utility." *Ethics,* 95: 5–19.
———. 1986. *Autonomy: An Essay in Philosophical Psychology and Ethics.* New Haven: Yale University Press.
Henberg, Marvin. 1990. *Retribution: Evil for Evil in Ethics, Law, and Literature.* Philadelphia: Temple University Press.
Hill, Christopher. 1984. "Watsonian Freedom and Freedom of the Will." *Australasian Journal of Philosophy,* 62: 294–98.
Hill, Thomas, Jr. 1991. *Autonomy and Self-Respect.* Cambridge: Cambridge University Press.
Honderich, Ted. ed. 1973. *Essays on Freedom of Action.* London: Routledge & Kegan Paul.
Houlgate, Laurence D. 1968. "Knowledge and Responsibility." *American Philosophical Quarterly,* 5: 109–16.
Husak, Douglas N. 1980. "Omission, Causation, and Liability." *Philosophical Quarterly,* 30: 318–26.
Irwin, Terence. 1980. "Reason and Responsibility in Aristotle." In Rorty 1980.
Jeffrey, C. R. 1967. *Criminal Responsibility and Mental Disease.* Springfield, Ill.: Thomas.
Jeffrey, Richard. 1974. "Preferences among Preferences." *Journal of Philosophy,* 71: 377–91.
Jensen, Henning. 1984. "Morality and Luck." *Philosophy,* 59: 323–30.
Kane, Robert. 1985. *Free Will and Values.* Albany: State University of New York Press.
Kenny, A. J. P. 1978. *Freewill and Responsibility: Four Lectures.* London: Routledge & Kegan Paul.
Levin, Micheal. 1979. *Metaphysics and the Mind-Body Problem.* Oxford: Clarendon.
Locke, Don. 1975. "Three Concepts of Free Action I." *Proceedings of the Aristotelian Society,* 44: supp., 95–112; reprinted in Fischer 1986.
May, Larry. 1992. *Sharing Responsibility.* Chicago: University of Chicago Press.
Meldon, A. I., ed. 1958. *Essays in Moral Philosophy.* Seattle: University of Washington Press.
Mellema, Gregory. 1984. "On Being Fully Responsible." *American Philosophical Quarterly,* 21: 189–93.
Mischel Theodore, ed. 1977. *The Self: Philosophical and Psychological Issues.* Oxford: B. Blackwell.
Morris Herbert, ed. 1961. *Freedom and Responsibility.* Stanford: Stanford University Press.

——. 1968. "Persons and Punishment." *The Monist,* 4: 475–501.

——. 1976. *On Guilt and Innocence: Essays in Legal Philosophy and Moral Psychology.* Berkeley: University of California Press.

Murphy, Jeffrie G. 1969. "Criminal Punishment and Psychiatric Fallacies." In *Punishment and Rehabilitation,* ed. Jeffrie Murphy. 2d ed. Belmont, Calif: Wadsworth, 1985.

——. 1972. "Moral Death: A Kantian Essay on Psychopathy." *Ethics,* 82: 284–98.

Murphy, Jeffrie G., and Jean Hampton. 1988. *Forgiveness and Mercy.* Cambridge: Cambridge University Press.

Nagel, Thomas. 1979. *Moral Questions.* Cambridge: Cambridge University Press.

——. 1986. *The View from Nowhere.* New York: Oxford University Press.

Naylor, Margery Bedford. 1984. "Frankfurt on the Principle of Alternate Possibilities." *Philosophical Studies,* 46: 249–58.

Neely, Wright. 1974. "Freedom and Desire." *Philosophical Review,* 83: 32–54.

Nozick, Robert. 1969. "Coercion." In *Philosophy, Science, and Method,* ed. S. Morgenbesser, P. Suppes, and M. White. New York: St. Martin's.

——. 1981. *Philosophical Explanations.* Cambridge: Harvard University Press.

O'Shaughnessy, Brian. 1980. *The Will.* Vols. 1 and 2. Cambridge: Cambridge University Press.

Parfit, Derek. 1984. *Reasons and Persons.* Oxford: Clarendon.

Parker, Richard. 1984. "Blame, Punishment, and the Role of Desert." *American Philosophical Quarterly,* 21: 269–76.

Pears, Davis. 1984. *Motivated Irrationality.* New York: Oxford University Press.

Pincoffs, Edmund L. 1966. "Classical Retributivism." In *Morality in Practice,* ed. James Sterba. 3d ed. Belmont, Calif.: Wadsworth, 1991.

Pritchard, Michael L. 1974. "Responsibility, Understanding, and Psychopathology." *Monist,* 58: 630–45.

Radden, Jennifer. 1982. "Diseases as Excuses: Durham and the Insanity Plea." *Philosophical Studies,* 42: 349–62.

——. 1985. *Madness and Reason.* London: G. Allen & Unwin.

Raz, Joseph. 1986. *The Morality of Freedom.* Oxford: Clarendon.

Richards, Norvin. 1986. "Luck and Desert." *Mind,* 95: 198–205.

Rorty, Amelie Oksenberg, ed. 1976. *Identities of Persons.* Berkeley: University of California Press.

——, ed. 1980. *Essays on Aristotle's Ethics.* Berkeley: University of California Press.

Rowe, William L. 1987. "Reid's Conception of Human Freedom." *Monist,* 70: 430–41.

——. 1991. *Thomas Reid on Freedom and Morality.* Ithaca: Cornell University Press.

Russell, Paul. 1992. "Strawson's Way of Naturalizing Responsibility." *Ethics,* 102: 287–302.

Sabini, John, and Maury Silver. 1987. "Emotions, Responsibility, and Character." In Schoeman 1987.

Sankowski, Edward. 1977. "Responsibility of Persons for Their Emotions." *Canadian Journal of Philosophy,* 7: 829–40.

Schlick, Moritz. 1939. "When Is a Man Responsible?" In Berofsky 1966.

Schlossberger, Eugene. 1986. "Why We Are Responsible for Our Emotions." *Mind,* 95: 37–56.

——. 1992. *Moral Responsibility and Persons.* Philadelphia: Temple University Press.

Schoeman, Ferdinand. 1978. "Responsibility and the Problem of Induced Desires." *Philosophical Studies,* 34: 293–301.

———, ed. 1987. *Responsibility, Character, and the Emotions.* Cambridge: Cambridge University Press.

Shatz, David. 1985. "Free Will and the Structure of Motivation." In *Midwest Studies in Philosophy,* vol. 10, ed. Peter A. French, Theodore E. Uehling, Jr., and Howard K. Wettstein. Minneapolis.

———. 1988. "Compatibilism, Values, and 'Could Have Done Otherwise.' " *Philosophical Topics,* 14: 151–200.

Slote, Michael, 1980. "Understanding Free Will." *Journal of Philosophy,* 77: 136–51; reprinted in Fischer 1986.

Smith, Holly M. 1983. "Culpable Ignorance." *Philosophical Review,* 92: 543–71.

———. 1991. "Varieties of Moral Worth and Moral Credit." *Ethics,* 101:279–303.

Sorabji, Richard. 1983. *Necessity, Cause, and Blame: Perspectives on Aristotle's Theory.* Ithaca: Cornell University Press.

Sprigge, T. L. S. 1974. "Punishment and Moral Responsibility." In *Punishment and Human Rights,* ed. Milton Goldinger. Cambridge, Mass.: Schenkman.

Stern, Lawrence, 1974. "Freedom, Blame, and Moral Community." *Journal of Philosophy,* 71: 72–84.

Strawson, Galen, 1986. *Freedom and Belief.* Oxford: Clarendon.

Strawson, P. F. 1968. *Studies in the Philosophy of Thought and Action.* London: Oxford University Press.

Swanton, Christine, 1992. *Freedom: A Coherence Theory.* Indianapolis: Hackett.

Swinburne, Richard. 1989. *Responsibility and Atonement.* Oxford: Clarendon.

Szasz, Thomas S. 1970. *Ideology and Insanity.* Garden City, N.Y. Anchor Books.

Taurek, John. 1972. "Determination and Moral Responsibility." Ph.D. thesis, University of California, Los Angeles.

Taylor, Charles. 1976. "Responsibility for Self." In Rorty, 1976; reprinted in French, 1991.

Taylor, Richard. 1966. *Action and Purpose.* Englewood Cliffs, N.J.: Prentice-Hall.

———. 1976. "Action and Responsibility." In *Action Theory* ed. Myles Brand and Douglas Walton. Dordrecht: D. Reidel.

———. 1983. *Metaphysics.* Englewood Cliffs, N.J.: Prentice-Hall.

Thalberg, Irving. 1963. "Remorse." *Mind,* 72: 545–55.

———. 1978. "Hierarchical Analyses of Unfree Action." *Canadian Journal of Philosophy,* 8: 211–26.

Thomson, Judith Jarvis. 1984. "Remarks on Causation and Liability." *Philosophy and Public Affairs,* 13: 101–33.

———. 1989. "Morality and Bad Luck." *Metaphilosophy,* 20: 203–21.

Thorp, John. 1980. *Free Will: A Defense against Neurophysiological Determinism.* London: Routledge & Kegan Paul.

Trusted, Jennifer. 1984. *Free Will and Responsibility.* Oxford: Oxford University Press.

van Inwagen, Peter. 1978. "Ability and Responsibility." *Philosophical Review,* 87: 201–24; reprinted in Fischer 1986.

———. 1980. "The Incompatibility of Responsibility and Determinism." In Bradie and Brand 1980; reprinted in Fischer 1986.

———. 1983. *An Essay on Free Will.* Oxford: Clarendon.

———. 1984. "Comments on Dennett's 'I Could Not Have Done Otherwise—So What?' " Presented at the Eastern Division meeting of the American Philosophical Association, December 30.

———. 1989. "When Is the Will Free?" In *Philosophical Perspectives,* vol. 3, ed. James Tomberlin. Atascadero, Calif: Ridgeview.

van Straaten, Zak. ed. 1980. *Philosophical Subjects.* Oxford: Clarendon.

Velleman, J. David. 1989. *Practical Reflection.* Princeton: Princeton University Press.

Vuoso, George. 1987. "Background, Responsibility, and Excuse." *Yale Law Journal,* 96: 1661–86.

Watson, Gary. 1975. "Free Agency." *Journal of Philosophy,* 72: 205–20; reprinted in Fischer 1986.

——, ed. 1982. *Free Will.* Oxford: Oxford University Press.

——. 1986. "Review of *An Essay on Free Will,* by Peter van Inwagen." *Philosophy and Phenomenological Research,* 46:507–22.

——. 1987. "Free Action and Free Will." *Mind,* 96: 145–72.

Weinryb, Elazar. 1980. "Omissions and Responsibility." *Philosophical Quarterly,* 30: 118–30.

Williams, Bernard. 1981. *Moral Luck.* Cambridge: Cambridge University Press.

Wolf, Susan. 1980. "Asymmetrical Freedom." *Journal of Philosophy,* 77: 151–60; reprinted in Fischer 1986.

——. 1987. "Sanity and the Metaphysics of Responsibility." In Schoeman 1987.

——. 1990. *Freedom within Reason.* New York: Oxford University Press.

Wootton, Barbara. 1963. "Eliminating Responsibility." In *Responsibility,* ed. Joel Feinberg and Hyman Gross. Encino, Calif.: Dickenson, 1975.

Young, Robert. 1979. "Compatibilism and Conditioning." *Noûs,* 13: 361–78.

——. 1980a. "Autonomy and the 'Inner Self.'" *American Philosophical Quarterly,* 27: 35–43.

——. 1980b. "Autonomy and Socialization." *Mind,* 89: 565–76.

——. 1986. *Personal Autonomy: Beyond Negative and Positive Liberty.* London: Croom Helm.

Zimmerman, David. 1981. "Hierarchical Motivation and Freedom of the Will." *Pacific Philosophical Quarterly,* 62: 354–68.

Zimmerman, Michael J. 1982. "Moral Responsibility, Freedom, and Alternate Possibilities." *Pacific Philosophical Quarterly,* 63: 243–54.

——. 1984. *An Essay on Human Action.* New York: P. Lang.

——. 1985a. "Intervening Agents and Moral Responsibility." *Philosophical Quarterly,* 35: 347–58.

——. 1985b. "Sharing Responsibility." *American Philosophical Quarterly,* 22: 115–22.

——. 1986a. "Negligence and Moral Responsibility." *Noûs,* 20: 199–218.

——. 1986b. "Subsidiary Obligation." *Philosophical Studies,* 50: 65–75.

——. 1987a. "Luck and Moral Responsibility." *Ethics,* 97: 374–86.

——. 1987b. "Remote Obligation." *American Philosophical Quarterly,* 24: 199–205.

——. 1988. *An Essay on Moral Responsibility.* Totowa, N.J.: Rowman & Littlefield.

Contributors

JOHN MARTIN FISCHER is Professor, Department of Philosophy, University of California, Riverside.

HARRY FRANKFURT is Professor, Department of Philosophy, Princeton University.

ROBERT HEINAMAN is Lecturer, Department of Philosophy, University College, University of London.

MARK RAVIZZA is Assistant Professor, Department of Philosophy, University of California, Riverside.

WILLIAM L. ROWE is Professor, Department of Philosophy, Purdue University.

GALEN STRAWSON is a Fellow at Jesus College, University of Oxford (Sub-Faculty of Philosophy).

PETER STRAWSON is Professor Emeritus of Philosophy, University of Oxford.

ELEONORE STUMP occupies the Robert J. Henle Chair of Philosophy, Department of Philosophy, Saint Louis University.

J. DAVID VELLEMAN is Associate Professor, Department of Philosophy, University of Michigan, Ann Arbor.

GARY WATSON is Associate Professor, Department of Philosophy, University of California, Irvine.

SUSAN WOLF is Professor, Department of Philosophy, The Johns Hopkins University.

Index

Abélard, Peter, 142

Abelson, Raziel, 27n.62

Action, 195–98, 297–98; actual-sequence theory of responsibility for, 324–26, 338–39; and agent's alienation from own mental states, 198–201; agent's failure to participate in, 189–93, 198–99, 201–3; vs. choice, 96; concept vs. reality of, 193–94; vs. consequences, 291–92, 294, 298–300, 341–42, 345; and decision, 185–87; freedom of, vs. freedom of will, 212–13, 215, 242–43, 245, 286; impossibility of, 82–84; and mental states identical with agent, 203–9; standard story of, 188–89, 195

Active power, 268–69, 275–76, 278–83; efficient cause for exercise of, 272–74; as event without cause, 284–85

Actual-sequence theory, 30, 34, 38–39, 258–61, 326–27; responsibility for actions in, 324–26, 338–39; responsibility for consequence-universals in, 327–29, 342–47; responsive sequence defined in, 339–42

Adams, Robert, 125n.10

Addiction, 108–9, 112, 191, 198, 217, 245–46; and actual-sequence mechanism, 345; and intellect, 247–49; and overdetermination, 283–84, 287

Agent: action of, as own, 245; as adjudicator among conflicting motives, 205, 206; alienated from own mental states, 155–57, 198–201; as cause of own powerlessness, 280–81; and concept vs. re-ality of action, 193–94; faculties of, 215–16; identified with intellect, 223, 225–26; incapacitated, 20–21, 51–52, 53–55, 58–59. 60–61, 123–24, 137; as independent of desires, 89; intention-forming role of, 189–90, 191, 192; as irreducible cause of act of will, 274–76; mental states identical with, 203–9; power to cause act of will of, 276–78; reasons of, as own, 259–61; role in action, 189–93, 198–99, 201–3; self-awareness of, 162. *See also* Agent-causation; Excuse; Real self; Responsible agent; Self

Agent-based theory. *See* Reasons-responsiveness

Agent-causation, 10–11, 36–37, 194n.15, 195–97, 268–69, 276–81; and active power as event without cause, 284–85; as adjudication among conflicting motives, 205; and agent's alienation from own mental states, 198–201; components of, 203–4; event-cause as cause of, 271–72; and identification as action, 201–2; as irreducible cause of act of will, 274–76; and motive for practical thought, 206–9; and overdetermina-tion, 281–84, 287; and physical causa-tion contrasted, 264–68; as requirement for every event, 267, 272–74

Alcohol, 156. *See also* Addiction

Allen, Woody, 110n.8

Alternative possibilities. *See* Principle of alternative possibilities

RECEIVED
JAN 1996
Mission College
Learning Resource
Services

Library of Congress Cataloging-in-Publication Data

Perspectives on moral responsibility / John Martin Fischer and Mark
Ravizza, editors.
    p. cm.
  Includes bibliographical references and index.
    ISBN 0-8014-2943-9 (cloth : alk. paper)—ISBN 0-8014-8159-7 (pbk.: alk. paper)
    1. Responsibility.   2. Free will and determinism.   I. Fischer,
John Martin, 1952– .   II. Ravizza, Mark, 1958– .
BJ1451.P47   1993
  170—dc20   93-25712